Study Guide & Selected Solutions Manual

Marcia Gillette

Indiana University, Kokomo

Richard Jones

Sinclair Community College

Chemistry

FOR CHANGING TIMES

Thirteenth Edition

John W. Hill

Terry W. McCreary

Doris K. Kolb

PEARSON

Boston   Columbus   Indianapolis   New York   San Francisco   Upper Saddle River
Amsterdam   Cape Town   Dubai   London   Madrid   Milan   Munich   Paris   Montréal   Toronto
Delhi   Mexico City   São Paulo   Sydney   Hong Kong   Seoul   Singapore   Taipei   Tokyo

Editor in Chief: Adam Jaworksi
Senior Marketing Manager: Jonathan Cottrell
Senior Project Editor: Jennifer Hart
Assistant Editor: Coleen McDonald
Managing Editor, Chemistry and Geosciences: Gina M. Cheselka
Senior Project Manager: Beth Sweeten
Operations Specialist: Jeffrey Sargent
Supplement Cover Designer: Seventeenth Street Studios
Cover Photo Credit: Nicky Linzey/Dreamstime

1 2 3 4 5 6 7 8 9 10—BRR— 15 14 13 12

www.pearsonhighered.com   ISBN-10: 0-321-76781-0; ISBN-13: 978-0-321-76781-3

Contents

How to Survive in Chemistry

With a Satisfactory Grade

Handling any challenging and unfamiliar task requires a thoughtful and purposeful strategy. Because chemistry classes often fall in the category of "challenging" and "unfamiliar," it is very important that you adopt a strategy that will allow you to be successful. The first tool you have at your fingertips is your chemistry textbook. Read the appropriate chapter material *before* you attend class so that you'll have a general idea about what the instructor will be covering. After class, review your notes and reread the sections of the textbook that help explain any parts of your notes you don't understand. Fill in your notes with text material to make them more meaningful. Try to relate one topic to another. The different topics should seem integrated to you. Go over the practice problems in the chapter and complete the problems at the end of the chapter. There's a slogan: "CHEMISTRY IS NOT A SPECTATOR SPORT." This means that you have to get off the sidelines and be able to apply yourself to chemistry. Success in chemistry, like success in sports or music, requires practice. If you need help completing the problems, ask for it. Your teacher will be able to help you.

In addition, take good advantage of this study guide. It provides a summary (in outline form) of each chapter, a list of learning objectives, and a self-test, as well as the answers to the odd-numbered end-of-chapter problems. Where appropriate, a discussion of the material in the chapter is also provided. Please note that there isn't a self-test item for every objective or an objective for every test item, but the self-test questions should provide you with an indication of how well you understand the material. For some chapters, additional worked-out examples are provided and additional problems are included. You should work those problems when they, or similar ones from the textbook, are assigned.

Your instructor and the textbook can be of considerable help as you learn chemistry, but your success in the course will depend mainly on the way in which *you* approach the challenge. Be sure, before each test, that you have completed all assignments and used the self-test to be sure that you understand the material in each chapter.

We hope that you find this study guide helpful. Please send us any criticisms and suggestions for improvement. A notation of any errors that you find would be especially helpful.

John W. Hill
Department of Chemistry
University of Wisconsin
River Falls, WI 54022

Richard F. Jones
Sinclair Community College
Dayton, OH 45402-1460

Marcia L. Gillette
Indiana University Kokomo
Kokomo, IN 46904-9003

Study Strategy Suggestions

There are many effective ways to study, but most of them incorporate one or more of the following methods:

1. Preview the material in the text to be covered in the lecture.

   Just 10 minutes of leafing through the appropriate text pages can make the lecture more meaningful and your note-taking easier.

2. Quickly read through the notes from the last lecture within two hours of that lecture.

   You forget most of what you hear within two hours. Ten minutes of refreshing your memory shortly after the lecture is a very effective way to retain information.

3. Spend a minimum of three hours of study for each hour of lecture.

4. Move quickly to the problems at the end of the chapter and the self-tests in the study guide after reading the text and studying the lecture notes,

5. Be aware that four ½-hour study periods are better than two 1-hour study periods, which are better than one 2-hour study period.

6. Study with a friend and/or a study group if possible.

   Each member of an effective study group should prepare individually for the study session. The strengths of each person will help eliminate the weaknesses of the others.

7. Prepare for the exams well in advance. Arrive early and have all materials needed for the test.

CHAPTER

1

Chemistry

A Science for All Seasons

CHAPTER SUMMARY

1.1 Science and Technology: The Roots of Knowledge
  A. Knowledge may be technological (factual) or philosophical (theoretical).
  B. The ancient Greeks formulated theories about nature.
  C. Alchemists tried unsuccessfully to turn various metals into gold.
      1. Alchemists perfected some chemical techniques such as distillation and extraction.
  D. Science developed out of natural philosophy but had its true beginnings when people began to rely on experiments.

Answers to Self-Assessment Questions

  1. c Alchemists learned from practice but had little theoretical knowledge to back up their results.
  2. d Philosophers convinced others through intellectual argument.
  3. b Science began as a combination of all the known ways of thinking about observations.
  4. a The "usefulness" of science is manifest in its real-life applications.

1.2 Changing Perceptions and Changing Practices
  A. Francis Bacon envisioned that science would bring new inventions and prosperity.
  B. Galileo advanced the science of astronomy and was called the father of modern science.
  C. Rachel Carson predicted disaster from the use of chemicals to control insects.
  D. In response to public concern, scientists developed green chemistry and extended it to include the idea of sustainability.

Answers to Self-Assessment Questions

  1. b Francis Bacon is the first person who argued that experimentation is required and that new inventions would enrich people's lives.
  2. d Rachel Carson described the effect of long-lasting pesticides on the earth.
  3. b Galileo is called the father of modern science because of his insistence that hypotheses must be tested by experiment.

4.   c   The focus of green chemistry is to select materials and processes that will prevent or reduce pollution at its source.

5.   b   Hardwood trees are renewable resources. In each of the other cases, nonrenewable resources are required.

1.3   Science: Reproducible, Testable, Tentative, Predictive, and Explanatory
A. Data must be reproducible.
B. Scientists formulate testable hypotheses.
C. Scientific facts are verified by testing.
D. Scientific laws summarize large amounts of data.
     1. Scientific laws can often be stated mathematically.
E. Correlation between data does not necessarily prove cause and effect.
F. Scientific theories are used to predict and explain the behavior of matter.
G. Scientific models help us to visualize invisible processes.
H. Science is testable, explanatory, and tentative to the establishment of cause and effect.
I. Scientists try to control variables in an experiment.
J. It is difficult to control variables in social experiments.
     1. Social scientists use some of the methods of scientists.

Answers to Self-Assessment Questions

1.   a   Hypotheses are tested by experiment.
2.   c   A law is a summary of experimental data.
3.   a   In order to be useful, a theory must be able to be tested.
4.   c   This statement cannot be tested.
5.   d   A theory is the result of a hypothesis surviving experimental testing.
6.   a   Experimental results are difficult to interpret if all variables cannot be effectively controlled.

1.4   Science and Technology: Risks and Benefits
A. Technology is the sum of the processes by which we modify materials to better serve us.
B. Risk–benefit analysis involves the calculation of a desirability quotient: $DQ = benefits/risks$
C. Benefits and risks often are difficult to quantify, and lead to uncertain DQs.

Answers to Self-Assessment Questions

1.   d   Risk assessment is often based on a social judgment.
2.   c   Risk can be evaluated using statistical data.

1.5   Chemistry: Its Central Role
A. Chemistry is important to the other sciences and to social goals.
B. Chemistry is important to the economy.
     1. Chemical trade helps lower the United States trade deficit.

Answers to Self-Assessment Questions

1.   c   All scientific disciplines focus on matter of one kind or another; the properties and behavior of matter make up the study of chemistry.
2.   c   Technological developments are an example of applied chemistry.

1.6   Solving Society's Problems: Scientific Research
    A.   Many chemists are involved in applied research.
    B.   Applied research is directed toward the solution of a particular problem in industry or in the
          environment.
    C.   Many chemists are engaged in basic research.
    D.   Basic research is the pursuit of knowledge for its own sake.

Answers to Self-Assessment Questions

    1.   b   Drug development is done for the benefit of society.
    2.   b   Genetic engineering is done to improve the nutritional intake of consumers.
    3.   a   Identification of naturally occurring biologically active compounds provides the basis for
               inquiry into the relationship of structure and function of substances.
    4.   a   Biochemists seek to understand the relationship between the structure of a compound and
               its biological function.

1.7   Chemistry: A Study of Matter and Its Changes
    A.   Chemistry deals with matter and the changes it undergoes.
    B.   Matter occupies space and has mass.
          1. Mass measures a quantity of matter that is independent of its relative location.
          2. Weight measures a force, such as the gravitational force or attraction between an object and
             the earth.
    C.   Matter is characterized by its properties.
          1. Physical properties can be observed and specified without reference to any other substance.
          2. Physical changes do not change the composition or chemical nature of a substance.
          3. Chemical properties describe and determine how substances combine with other
             substances.
          4. Chemical changes result in a change in chemical properties.

Answers to Self-Assessment Questions

    1.   d   All but a sentiment (e.g., love) have mass and occupy space.
    2.   a   Air has mass and occupies space.
    3.   c   The identical items will have the same mass but different weight because of differences in
               gravitational forces on Earth and Mars.
    4.   b   The identity of a material depends upon its chemical composition.
    5.   d   There is no change in composition, so this is a physical change.
    6.   d   This is a physical change as there is no change in the composition.
    7.   b   Copper tarnishes as the result of a chemical reaction.
    8.   c   There is no change in the composition of wool.
    9.   c   There is a change in composition of the tree as it absorbs nutrients and grows.

1.8   Classification of Matter
    A.   The states of matter.
          1. Solids maintain their shape and their volume.
          2. Liquids maintain their volume but not their shape.
          3. Gases maintain neither their volume nor their shape.
    B.   Matter: pure substances and mixtures.
          1. Pure substances have a fixed composition.

    2. A mixture is a collection of two or more substances that can be mixed in any proportion because they are not chemically bonded.
  C. Elements and compounds.
    1. An element is a pure substance that is defined by a single type of atom.
      a. At present there are more than 100 known elements.
      b. Each element is represented by a chemical symbol.
    2. A compound is made up of two or more elements and has a fixed composition.
    3. Elemental symbols are made up of one or two letters derived from the English (or Latin) name of the element.
      a. Only the first letter of a chemical symbol is capitalized.
    4. Atoms and molecules.
      a. Atoms are the smallest characteristic part of an element.
      b. Molecules are the smallest characteristic part of a compound.

Answers to Self-Assessment Questions

1. a Only gases have indefinite volume and shape. Liquids have definite volume and indefinite shape while solids have definite volume and definite shape. Aqueous refers to solutions.
2. d Carbon, copper, and silver are elements – carbonated water is water with carbon dioxide dissolved in it.
3. b Brass is an alloy of copper and tin.
4. a Only a chemical method of separation can separate a compound.
5. a An element has the atom as the smallest unit and a compound has a molecule as the smallest unit.
6. a K is the symbol for potassium.
7. d Br is the symbol for bromine. (B is the symbol for boron, Be is the symbol for beryllium, and brass is a mixture not an element).

1.9 The Measurement of Matter
  A. SI is a modernized version of the metric system.
  B. Length: meter (m)—slightly more than a yard.
  C. Mass: kilogram (kg)—(2.2 lb).
  D. Time: second (s).
  E. Temperature: kelvin (K)—0 K is the lowest temperature possible.
  F. Amount of a substance: mole (mol)—6.022×10^{23} units.
  G. Electric current: ampere (A).
  H. Luminous intensity: candela (cd).
  I. The commonly used metric prefixes
    1. kilo- (k) x 1000. (10^3)
    2. deci- (d) x 0.1 (10^{-1})
    3. centi- (c) x 0.01 (10^{-2})
    4. milli- (m) x 0.001 (10^{-3})
    5. micro- (μ) x 0.000001 (10^{-6})

Answers to Self-Assessment Questions

1. d The meter is the SI unit for length.
2. d The kilogram is the SI unit for mass.
3. c 10^{-6} is the prefix for micro.

4. d   The meter is about 39 inches, or a little longer than a yard.
5. d   1 cm^3 = 1 mL.
6. c   One quart is 0.946 liters.
7. d   5.775 cm = 57.75 mm.
8. c   This textbook is around 4 kg, an orange is around 125 g, an ant is far less than a gram. A peanut is around a gram.
9. b   An inch is 2.54 cm.
10. a   An 8-ounce cup is about 250 mL.

1.10 Density is mass per unit volume.
   A. D = m/v.
   B. For liquids and solids, density is usually expressed in units of grams per milliliter (g/mL) or grams per cubic centimeter (g/cm^3).
   C. At 4 °C the density of water is 1.0 g/mL.

Answers to Self-Assessment Questions

   1. b   In order to float, wood must be less dense than water.
   2. b   Because they sank, both a pebble and a lead sinker must have densities higher than water.
   3. a   Because it floats on water, the density of ice must be less than that of water.
   4. b   Shaking a pan of mud, gravel, and gold allows the higher-density gold to sink to the bottom of the pan.
   5. d   Of the choices, only uranium has a density higher than that of mercury, allowing it to sink.
   6. c   D = m/V; 160.0 g/80.0 cm^3 = 2.00 g/cm^3.

1.11 Energy: Heat and Temperature
   A. Energy is the ability to do work; to change matter, either physically or chemically.
   B. Definition of heat and temperature.
      1. Heat: energy on the move; measure of how much energy a sample contains.
      2. Temperature: measure of the average energy of a particle in a given sample; how hot or cold an object is.
      3. Heat flows from more energetic (higher-temperature) to less energetic (lower-temperature) atoms or molecules.
   C. Temperature and heat.
      1. The Celsius scale unit is (°C). Water freezes at 0 °C and boils at 100 °C.
      2. The Kelvin scale unit is (K): absolute scale. 0 K = –273.15 °C.
      3. Conversion between Celsius and Kelvin scales: K = °C + 273.15.
   D. Energy: joule (J) or calorie (cal).
      1.0 cal = 4.18 J; 1 Kcal = 1 Calorie (foods) = 1000 cal = 4.18 kJ.

Answers to Self-Assessment Questions

   1. b   Heat is energy in motion (heat flowing from a hotter body to a colder one).
   2. c   Kelvin is the SI temperature unit.
   3. a   Water freezes at 0 °C (273 K).
   4. d   The size of the Celsius degree is the same as the Kelvin degree but higher by 273.
   5. b   The joule is the SI energy unit.

1.12 Critical Thinking: FLaReS
      1. Falsifiability: Can you prove something wrong?

2. Logic: Does conclusion follow from premises; are premises true?
3. Replicability or Reproducibility: If experiment is cited, can experiment be repeated to produce the same evidence?
4. Sufficiency: Evidence provided must be adequate.
    a. The burden of proof is on the claimant.
    b. Extraordinary claims require extraordinary evidence.
    c. Evidence based on authority and/or testimony is not adequate.

LEARNING OBJECTIVES

These objectives are a minimal list. In addition to knowing the material specifically indicated here, you should do the assigned problems in the text. Your instructor may provide additional (or alternative) objectives for any chapter.

You should be able to...

1. Distinguish science from technology. (1.1)

2. Define *alchemy* and *natural philosophy*. (1.1)

3. Briefly describe the contributions of Bacon, Galileo, and Carson to the perceptions of science.(1.2)

4. Define *green chemistry* and *sustainable chemistry*. (1.2)

5. Define *hypothesis*, *scientific law*, *scientific theory*, and *scientific model*, and explain their relationships in science. (1.3)

6. Explain what a variable is, and describe how variables introduce uncertainty. (1.3)

7. Define *risk* and *benefit*, and give an example of each. (1.4)

8. Estimate a desirability quotient from benefit and risk data. (1.4)

9. Give an example of a use of chemistry in your daily life and in society at large. (1.5)

10. Distinguish basic research from applied research. (1.6)

11. Differentiate: mass and weight; physical and chemical change; physical and chemical properties. (1.7)

12. Classify matter according to state and as mixture, substance, compound, and/or element. (1.8)

13. Assign proper units of measurement to observations, and manipulate units in conversions. (1.9)

14. Calculate the density, mass, or volume of an object given the other two quantities. (1.10)

15. Distinguish between heat and temperature. (1.11)

16. Explain how the temperature scales are related. (1.11)

17. Use critical thinking to evaluate claims and statements.   (1.12)

18. Define green chemistry.

19. Describe how green chemistry reduces risk and prevents environmental problems.

DISCUSSION

Much of Chapter 1 of the textbook is intended to place chemistry in both historical and contemporary perspective—to give you a feel for chemistry as it affects society. If, after reading the chapter, you recognize chemistry as something more than just a course that meets certain requirements, you have indeed understood what we were trying to say. In addition to this overview, Chapter 1 introduces several concepts important to our further study of chemistry. These include the international system of measurement, the meaning of terms such as matter and energy, different temperature scales, chemical symbols, and density. Green chemistry represents the recognition of the impacts modern technology has on the environment and on the sustainability of the planet for future generations. The problems at the end of the chapter are meant to check your understanding of this material. The following questions offer another opportunity for you to test yourself on Chapter 1.

Note: Many of these problems are more than tests of your memory. A number of them require preliminary calculations before an answer can be selected. You are expected to know the metric prefixes and units of measure, but consult **Appendix A** in the text if you need help with the metric conversion factors.

EXAMPLE PROBLEM

Challenge: Name something that is not a chemical.

Answer: Everything is a chemical. Energy and matter are equivalent. A vacuum is the absence of matter: It is nothing. Also a complete vacuum does not exist even in space. Some other possible responses: An idea (Can a thought exist without a brain with neurons and electrons?) Time (Can time exist without something around to mark its passing?) Basically, chemistry is the study of just about everything.

ADDITIONAL PROBLEMS

1. An ad on TV invites you to call for a free "psychic reading." As proof of their legitimacy the psychics offer several testimonials by people claiming that the psychic they called knew facts about the caller that were known by only themselves. Which part of the "FLaReS" test does the ad fail?

      a. Falsifiability   b. Logic
      c. Replicability   d. Sufficiency
      e. All of the above

e. It fails all parts of the test:

    *a.   Falsifiability—can't ask testimonial givers questions
    *b.   Logic—not applicable
    *c.   Replicability—can't reproduce results
    *d.   Sufficiency—no evidence given

2. A horoscope printed in the newspaper (*Dayton Daily News*; Joyce Jillson, UPS 1997 ®) for a Leo states: "Creative energy is limitless, so set aside plenty of time for projects. A romantic involvement with a Libra moves to a deeper level of commitment. Make sure that a relative knows how much you are willing to help with a family project."

Which part of the "FLaReS" test does the horoscope fail?

a.	Falsifiability	b.	Logic
c.	Replicability	d.	Sufficiency
e.	All of the above		

It fails all parts of the test:

    *a.   Falsifiability—claims are too vague to be evaluated
    *b.   Logic—not everyone with birthdays July 23–August 22 has the same circumstances
    *c.   Replicability—can't reproduce experiment
    *d.   Sufficiency—no evidence provided

ANSWERS TO ODD-NUMBERED REVIEW QUESTIONS AND SOLUTIONS FOR ODD-NUMBERED END OF CHAPTER PROBLEMS

Review Questions

1. Science is testable, reproducible, explanatory, predictive, and tentative. Testability best distinguishes science.

3. These problems usually have too many variables to be treated by the scientific method.

5. Risk–benefit analysis compares benefits of an action to risks of that action.

7. DQ, the Desirability Quotient, is benefits divided by risks. A large DQ means that risks are minimal compared to benefits. Often it is hard to quantify risks and benefits.

9. The SI-derived unit for volume is liter (L). Because one liter represents a relatively large quantity, volumes measured in milliliters (mL) and, sometimes, in microliters (µL) are often used in the laboratory.

11. a. applied: This is an example of the application of a technology to a problem with economic consequences.
    b. applied: The Purdue engineer is developing a method for improving operation of automobiles so their operation will be more environmentally safe. If the method can be applied, automobiles will not require large amounts of fossil fuels and their exhaust will not include greenhouse gases.

c. basic: Studying atoms under different conditions helps us understand general atomic behavior but does not have a specific application.

Problems

13. The benefits to society are very high. The risk to selected individuals is high but is managed by restricting access to penicillin by prescription and requiring the care of a physician. The DQ (Desirability Quotient) is high.

15. The use of isocyanates can cause allergic reactions in some individuals.
    a. When proper safety precautions are taken (proper ventilation and, when necessary, individual masks for workers), the risk of an automotive factory worker being exposed to isocyanates is low and the benefit is high. The DQ is high. The DQ can be increased by ensuring that all safety precautions are observed.
    b. While exposure time is likely to be relatively short, the hobbyist restoring a 1965 Mustang is less likely to be able to work under ideal safety conditions but should know to wear breathing protection and to work in a well-ventilated garage or other area. The DQ is high (but lower than in scenario a) and can be increased by ensuring that all safety precautions are observed.

17. The manufacturers, wholesalers, and retailers benefit most from the use of food colors. The greatest risk is assumed by the consumer.

19. Cellular phones are light, but not as light as 100 mg; 100 g is a more likely weight for a cell phone. Laptop computers vary in weight but are likely to weigh several pounds (2.12 pounds = 1 Kg). The choice of 100 g, 2 kg is the best.

21. Yes. Since the lab has a constant gravitational field, the weight would be proportional to mass. Sample B has twice the mass of Sample A.

23. An 8-ounce tea cup holds about 250 mL.

25. The volume in $mile^3$ is 3.50×10^8 $mile^3$. One mile = 1.6 km. Since we are working with a volume with the length cubed, the conversion factor is one $mile^3$ = 4.10 km^3. (You cube the conversion factor.) 3.50×10^8 $mile^3$ times 4.10 km^3/1 $mile^3$ = 1.44×10^9 km^3.

27. One inch = 2.54 cm. Without doing a detailed calculation, we know that 0.998" is nearly 1" or 2.54 cm (to be precise, it is 0.998 in times (2.54 cm/1 in) or 2.53 cm). The other tube with an inside diameter of 26.3 mm is equivalent to 2.63 cm. Therefore, the 0.998" tube will fit inside the 26.3 mm tube.

29. a. No change in composition: a physical property.
    b. The chemical composition of black silver sulfide is different than the chemical composition of the silver metal, so it is a chemical property of silver that it can undergo this change.
    c. The chemical composition of sodium does not change when it is cut, so its softness is a physical property.
    d. When a substance melts, its chemical composition does not change, so the melting point of a substance is a physical property.

31. a. A physical change, assuming that the plastic was just melted and reformed into a new shape.

9

b. A chemical change: a chemical reaction is required to transform used cooking oil into biodiesel fuel.

c. There is no change in the composition: the concentrated orange juice was diluted, which represents a physical change.

33. a. Helium gas is a substance.
    b. Orange juice is a mixture of a variety of substances, including vitamin C, pulp, and water.
    c. Distilled water is water from which all impurities have been removed. It is a substance.
    d. Carbon dioxide is a compound, and thus a substance.

35. a. The composition of the copper water pipe is consistent throughout its length and, therefore, a homogeneous mixture of components.
    b. Distilled water is a substance that is homogeneous throughout.
    c. Liquid oxygen is a substance that is homogeneous throughout.
    d. The composition of one spoonful of chicken noodle soup likely differs from the composition of another spoonful. The soup is a heterogeneous mixture.

37. Since glucose has a consistent composition, it is a substance.

39. a. H is an element.
    b. He is an element.
    c. HF is a compound (two elements combined).
    d. Hf is an element (Hafnium, atomic number 72).

41. a. aluminum
    b. calcium
    c. chlorine
    d. silver

43. Observations a–e could apply to an element or a compound. Observation f indicates that baryte is the chemical combination of the particular element that burned and oxygen, making it a compound rather than an element.

45. a. $8.01 \times 10^{-6}\,g = 8.01\,\mu g$
    b. $7.9 \times 10^{-3}\,L = 7.9\,mL$
    c. $1.05 \times 10^{3}\,m = 1.05\,km$

47. a. $(37.4\ mL)(1\ L/1000\ mL) = 0.0374\ L$
    b. $(1.55 \times 10^{2}\,km)(1000m/1\ km) = 1.55 \times 10^{5}\,m$
    c. $(0.198\ g)(1000\ mg/1\ g) = 198\ mg$
    d. $1.19\ m^{2} \times 100\ cm/m \times 100\ cm/m = 1.19 \times 10^{4}\ cm^{2}$
    e. $(78\ \mu s)(1\ millisecond/1000\ \mu s) = 0.078\ ms$

49. a. 1 cm is larger than 1 mm (1 cm = 0.01 m; 1 mm = 0.001 m)
    b. 1 kg is larger than 1 g (1 kilogram = 1000 g)
    c. 1 dL is larger than μL (1 dL = 0.1 L; 1 μL = 0.000001L)

51. 1 cm = 10 mm. (1.83 m)(100 cm/m)(10 mm/cm) = 1830 mm.

53. a. $d = m/V = 43.75\ g/37.5\ mL = 1.17\ g/mL$

10

b. $d = m/V$ 2.75 L = 2750 mL
    d = 3465 g/2750 mL
    d = 1.26 g/mL

55. a. $d = m/V$ so $m = dV$
        m = 0.962 g/mL x 125 mL
        m = 120. g or 1.20×10^2 g
    b. $d = m/V$ so $m = dV$
        m = 1.027 g/mL x 477 mL
        m = 490. g or 4.90×10^2 g

57. a. $d = m/V$ so $V = m/d$
       V = 227 g/0.660 g/mL
       V = 344 mL
    b. $d = m/V$ so $V = m/d$
       V = 454 g/0.917 g/cm^3
       V = 495 cm^3

59. Mercury will be on the bottom, water in the middle, and hexane will be on top.

61. $d = m/V$ 37.9 L = 37,900 mL or 37,900 cm^3
    $m = dV = (1.03$ g/cm$^3)(37,900$ cm$^3)$
    m = 39,037 g
    Convert to pounds: (39,037 g)(1 lb/454 g) = 85.98 lb or 86.0 lb
    Aquarium plus seawater = 59.5 lb + 86.0 or 145.5 lb
    Yes, the stand will hold the filled aquarium.

63. $d = m/V$ Change mass to g and calculate before 10% loss: 2.72 kg = 2.72×10^3 g
    $V = m/d = 2.72 \times 10^3$ g/1.60 g/cm^3 = 1700 cm^3
    $V = 4\pi r^3/3 = 1700$ cm^3
    $r^3 = [(1700$ cm$^3)(3)]/[(4)(3.14)] = 406$ cm^3
    r = cube root of 406 cm^3 = 7.41 cm
    diameter = radius x 2 = (2)(7.41 cm) = 14.8 cm

65. K = °C + 273.15 or rearranging the equation to solve for °C, °C = K – 273.15
    °C = 195 K – 273 = –78 °C

67. 1 food Calorie = 1 kilocalorie which equals 4184 Joules
    (161,000 Joules)(1 kilocalorie/4184 Joules) =38.5 kilocalories

69. time, min = (1 x 10^{-6} cen)(100 yr/cen)(365 day/yr)(24 hr/day)(60 min/hr)
                   = 52.6 min

71. The answer is b. The relationship describes a law. Henry's collected data could be expressed in the
    form of a mathematical equation which predicts the relationship between concentration of
    dissolved gas and the partial pressure of that gas in the atmosphere over the liquid.

73. years = (200 kw)(1000 w/kw)(15 min/w)(1 hr/60 min)(1 day/24 hr)(1 yr/365 day) = 5.7 yr

75. (1) d, repeated observations.

11

(2) e, a theory that explains the rising power of potassium bromate.
(3) b, a hypothesis or suggested explanation for the observed behavior.
(4) a, an experiment designed to produce some sort of effect.
(5) d, an observation made when the experiment was performed.

77. $d = m/V$ $V = (7.6 \text{ cm})(7.6 \text{ cm})(94 \text{ cm}) = 5430 \text{ cm}^3$
     $= dV = (0.11 \text{ g/cm}^3)(5430 \text{ cm}^3) = 597 \text{ g} = 6.0 \times 10^2 \text{ g}$

79. Convert all to a common unit, kg.
Potatoes: 5 pounds of potatoes to kg: $(5 \text{ lb})(0.454 \text{ kg/1 lb}) = 2.3 \text{ kg}$
Cabbage: 1.65 kg of cabbage
Sugar: 2500 g of sugar is 2.5 kg
Cabbage (lightest) < potatoes < sugar (heaviest)

81. $d = m/V$.
Mass of the metal (mass of metal + paper) - mass of paper = 18.43 g - 1.21 g = 17.22 g
$d = 17.22 \text{ g}/3.29 \text{ cm}^3 = 5.23 \text{ g/cm}^3$

83. 5.79 mg = 0.00579 g
Density of gold = 19.3 g/cm^3 (from Table 1.7)
$V = m/d = 0.00579 \text{ g}/19.3 \text{ g/cm}^3 = 0.000300 \text{ cm}^3$
V = area x thickness
Thickness = V/area
Thickness = 0.000300 cm^3/44.6 cm^2
Thickness = 6.73×10^{-6} cm

85. $V = 36.1 \text{ cm} \times 36.1 \text{ cm} \times 36.1 = 47,046 \text{ cm}^3$
$d = m/V$ so $m = dV$
$m = 19.3 \text{ g/cm}^3 \times 47,046 \text{ cm}^3$
$m = 907989 \text{ g}$ or 907.989 kg
908 kg x (1 metric ton/1000 g) = 0.908 metric tons

87. a. $7.0 \times 10^4 \text{ km} = 7.0 \times 10^9 \text{ cm}$
Volume of Jupiter $= [4 \times 3.14 \times (7.0 \times 10^9 \text{ cm}) \times (7.0 \times 10^9 \text{ cm}) (7.0 \times 10^9 \text{ cm})]/3$
     $= 1.44 \times 10^{30} \text{cm}^3$
Mass of Jupiter = 1.9×10^{30} g
     $d = m/V = 1.9 \times 10^{30} \text{ g}/ 1.44 \times 10^{30} \text{ cm}$
     $d = 1.3 \text{ g/cm}^3$
b. $6.4 \times 10^3 \text{ km} = 6.4 \times 10^8 \text{ cm}$
Volume of Earth $= [4 \times 3.14 \times (6.4 \times 10^8 \text{ cm}) \times (6.4 \times 10^8 \text{ cm}) \times (6.4 \times 10^8 \text{ cm})]/3$
     $= 1.10 \times 10^{27} \text{ cm}^3$
Mass of Earth = 5.98×10^{24} kg
     $d = m/V = 5.98 \times 10^{27} \text{ g}/1.10 \times 10^{27} \text{ cm}^3$
     $d = 5.44 \text{ g/cm}^3$
c. $5.82 \times 10^4 \text{ km} = 5.82 \times 10^9 \text{ cm}$
Volume of Saturn $= [4 \times 3.14 \times (5.82 \times 10^9 \text{ cm}) \times (5.82 \times 10^9 \text{ cm}) \times (5.82 \times 10^9 \text{ cm})]/3$
     $= 8.25 \times 10^{29} \text{ cm}^3$
Mass of Saturn = 5.68×10^{29} g
     $d = m/V$
     $d = 5.68 \times 10^{29} \text{ g}/ 8.25 \times 10^{29} \text{ cm}$

$d = 0.688 \text{ g/cm}^3$

The density of water is 1 g/cm^3. Saturn would float on water.

89. Green chemistry is the design of chemical products and processes that reduce or eliminate the generation and use of hazardous substances from the beginning to the end of the process.

91. The answer is a. Through the use of less hazardous materials and designing more effective production processes, workers and the environment both benefit.

Atoms

Are They for Real?

CHAPTER SUMMARY

2.1 Atoms: Ideas from the Ancient Greeks
   A. The prevailing view of matter held by Greek philosophers in the fifth century B.C. was that it was endlessly divisible.
   B. Democritus, a student of Leucippus, believed that there must be a limit to the divisibility of matter and called his ultimate particles *atomos*, meaning "cannot be cut" or "indivisible."
   C. The Greeks believed that there were only four elements: earth, air, fire, and water.

Answers to Self-Assessment Questions

   1. a   Apple juice, like the water Democritus was considering, cannot be separated into individual particles or units. The cherries, paper, and chocolate chips can easily be separated.
   2. c   It took centuries before an experiment was designed to disprove the continuity of matter.

2.2 Scientific Laws: Conservation of Mass and Definite Proportions
   A. Lavoisier (1780s) helped establish chemistry as a quantitative science.
      1. The law of conservation of mass states that matter is neither created nor destroyed during a chemical change. It is conserved.
         a. We make new materials by changing the way atoms are combined.
      2. Lavoisier was the first to use systematic names for elements.
      3. Lavoisier is often called the father of modern chemistry.
   B. Boyle (1661) proposed that substances capable of being broken down into simpler substances were compounds, not elements.
   C. Proust (1799) concluded from analyses that elements combine in definite proportions to form compounds, and formulated the law of definite proportions (also called the law of constant composition).
   D. J. J. Berzelius, Henry Cavendish, William Nicholson, and Anthony Carlisle further proved this law.
   E. The law of definite proportions is the basis for chemical formulas.

F.   The law of definite proportions also means that compounds have constant properties in addition to constant composition.

Answers to Self-Assessment Questions

1.   a   The law of conservation of mass tells us that the mass of the reactants must equal the mass of the products of any chemical transformation.
2.   c   According to the law of conservation of mass, the sum of the masses of the hydrogen and oxygen gases produced must be equal to the mass of the water that was decomposed to produce the gases.
3.   d   The decomposition of water into hydrogen and oxygen indicates that the formula for water contains H and O so water must be a compound, not an element.
4.   c   Sodium chloride, from whatever source, always contains the same percentage by mass of the constituent elements.
5.   c   Ammonia, in whatever quantity, always contains the same percentage by mass of the constituent elements.
6.   c   The mass proportions of carbon and oxygen in carbon dioxide are constant; once the carbon was consumed, no additional carbon dioxide could form.

2.3   John Dalton and the Atomic Theory of Matter
   A.   Dalton extended the ideas of Lavoisier and Proust with the law of multiple proportions.
       1.   Elements may combine in more than one set of proportions, with each proportion corresponding to a different compound.
   B.   Dalton proposed his atomic theory (model) to explain the laws of chemistry.
       1.   A chemical law is a statement that summarizes data obtained from experiments.
       2.   A theory is a model that consistently explains observations.
   C.   Dalton's atomic theory.
       1.   All matter is composed of small, indestructible, and indivisible atoms.
       2.   All atoms of a given element are identical, but different elements have different atoms.
       3.   Compounds are formed by combining elements in fixed proportions.
       4.   A chemical reaction involves a rearrangement of atoms. No atoms are destroyed or broken apart in the process.
   D.   Modern modifications of items listed under C above.
       1.   Atoms can be divided, as we shall see in the next chapter.
       2.   Atoms can have different masses, as we shall see in the next chapter.
       3.   Unmodified for chemical reactions, but atoms are broken apart in nuclear reactions.
       4.   Unmodified for chemical reactions (but not for nuclear reactions).
   E.   Explanations using atomic theory.
       1.   Elements are composed of one kind of atom.
       2.   Compounds are composed of two or more kinds of atoms chemically combined in definite proportions.
       3.   Matter must be atomic to account for the law of definite proportions.
       4.   The rearrangement of atoms explains the law of conservation of mass.
       5.   The existence of atoms explains how multiple proportions can exist.
   F.   Isotopes
       1.   Atoms of an element can have different masses. Such atoms are called isotopes.

Answers to Self-Assessment Questions

1.   d   The mass ratio of C to H in acetylene is 92.26 g C to 7.74 g H or 11.9 while the mass ratio in ethylene is 46.13 g C to 7.74 g O or 5.96. Ethylene has twice the amount of hydrogen as acetylene, so the formula of ethylene must be C_2H_4.
2.   d   Dalton based his theory on the atomic weights of atoms.
3.   c   Conservation of mass was the key factor for Dalton to propose his theory.
4.   c   Dalton thought that atoms were conserved and only rearranged to make new materials.
5.   a   Compounds are composed of two or more elements.
6.   d   The 4.0:12.0 ratio represents four atoms of H and one of C so each H atom must be 1/12 the mass of one C atom.
7.   b   Only one kind of species is shown and each is composed of one kind of atom.
8.   a   Only one kind of species is shown and each is composed of two kinds of atoms.
9.   c   There are two different types of species shown.

2.4   Mendeleev and the Periodic Table
   A.   By the mid-1800s 55 elements were known, but no successful way existed to classify them.
     1.   Only relative atomic weights could be determined.
   B.   Mendeleev's periodic table (1869) grouped 63 elements by increasing atomic weight.
     1.   In some instances, heavier elements were placed before lighter elements in order to group similar properties in the same column.
     2.   Blank spots, or gaps, were left in the table for elements that were not yet discovered.
     3.   Mendeleev predicted the properties of some of the undiscovered elements with remarkable success.

Answers to Self-Assessment Questions

1.   a   Mendeleev did not announce the discovery of any new elements although he predicted properties of unknown elements.
2.   a   The carbon-12 isotope is the basis for all relative masses in the periodic table.
3.   b   There are a few more than 100 elements known.

2.5   Atoms and Molecules: Real and Relevant
   A.   "Atom" is a concept that is very useful in explaining chemical behavior.
   B.   Atoms are not destroyed in chemical reactions and thus can be recycled.
   C.   Materials can be "lost" by scattering their constituent atoms too widely and making it impractical to recover them.
   D.   A molecule (formula unit) is the smallest constituent particle of a compound that still retains the properties of that compound.
   E.   Molecules (formula units) can be divided into atoms.

Answers to Self-Assessment Questions

1.   b   Matter cannot be created or destroyed, only transferred from one place to another.
2.   c   Molecules are atoms of elements combined together chemically.

LEARNING OBJECTIVES

You should be able to...

1. Explain the Greeks' ideas about the characteristics of matter. (2.1)

2. Describe the significance of the laws of conservation of mass and definite proportions. (2.2)

3. Calculate the amounts of elements from the composition of a compound. (2.2)

4. Explain why the idea that matter is made of atoms is a theory. (2.3)

5. Understand how atomic theory explains the law of conservation of mass. (2.3)

6. Describe how the elements are arranged in the periodic table and why the arrangement is important. (2.4)

7. Distinguish atoms from molecules. (2.5)

8. Identify elements that can be classified as hazardous or rare.

9. Describe how green chemistry is applicable to technologies that rely on hazardous or rare elements.

DISCUSSION

Chapter 2 is a survey of the history of the atomic theory. The Greek philosopher Democritus, who thought that matter was discontinuous, gave us the word atom. Dalton proposed the first successful attempt to explain the chemical laws of conservation of matter and definite proportion. We use the atomic theory because it is useful for explaining chemical behavior. You should focus on practicing identifying the interplay between experimenting and theorizing.

The green chemistry emphasis in this chapter relates to the potential impacts of certain elements on human health and on the environment. The green chemistry essay emphasizes issues related to lead and mercury, two particularly hazardous elements, as well as some of the rarer elements. Finding ways to recycle elements is critical to the well-being and sustainability of life on our planet.

EXAMPLE PROBLEMS

1. When 60 g of carbon is burned in air, 220 g of carbon dioxide is formed. How much carbon dioxide is formed when 90 g of carbon is burned?

Using unit conversions (Appendix C of the textbook), we can multiply the 90 g of carbon by a conversion factor that preserves the original relationship between 60 g of C and 220 g of CO_2 and then apply it to the current question of increasing the amount of carbon to 90 g.

$$60 \text{ g carbon} = 220 \text{ g carbon dioxide}$$

Multiply both sides by 1.5

90 g carbon = 330 g carbon dioxide

2. When burned in limited air, 6.0 g of carbon forms 14 g of carbon monoxide. How much carbon monoxide is formed when 360 g of carbon is burned?

6.0 g carbon = 14 g carbon monoxide

360 g carbon = 840 g carbon monoxide

ADDITIONAL PROBLEMS

1. When 12 g of carbon is burned in air, 44 g of carbon dioxide is formed. How much carbon dioxide is formed when 0.060 g of carbon is burned?

2. When burned in air, 8.0 g of sulfur forms 16 g of sulfur dioxide. How much sulfur dioxide is formed when 400 g of sulfur is burned?

3. When electricity is passed through water, it decomposes into hydrogen and oxygen. When 9.0 g of water is electrolyzed, 1.0 g of hydrogen is formed. How much hydrogen is formed when 36 g of water is electrolyzed?

ANSWERS TO ODD-NUMBERED REVIEW QUESTIONS AND SOLUTIONS FOR ODD-NUMBERED END OF CHAPTER PROBLEMS

Review Questions

1. a. The atomic view states that matter is discontinuous.

    b. The modern definition of an element is based upon experimentation, while the ancient Greek definition was a philosophical concept based on four elements: earth, air, fire, and water.

3. People, calculators, and M&M candies are discrete at the macroscopic level. Cloth and milk chocolate are continuous, giving the impression that they can be infinitely divided.

5. Boyle said that an element must be tested to see if it could not be broken down into simpler substances.

7. The law of multiple proportions states that elements can combine in more than one set of proportions, with each set corresponding to a different compound.

    a. ClO_2 has one atom of Cl and two atoms of O. That could be 35.5 g of Cl and 32 g of O. ClO has one atom of Cl and one atom of O. That could be 35.5 g of Cl and 16 g of O. The ratio of oxygen atoms is 32 to 16 or 2 to 1.

18

b. ClF_3 has one atom of Cl and 3 atoms of F. That could be 35.5 g of Cl and 57 g of F. ClF has one atom of Cl and one atom of F. That could be 35.5 g of Cl and 19 g of F. The ratio of fluorine atoms is 57 to 19 or 3 to 1.

c. P_4O_6 has 4 atoms of P and 6 atoms of O. That could be 124 g of P and 96 g of O. P_4O_{10} has 4 atoms of P and 10 atoms of O. That could be 124 g of P and 160 g of O. The ratio of O atoms is 96 to 160 or 3 to 5.

9. Rectangle (c) has 15 oxygen atoms and cannot be representative of the reaction product because there are only 14 reactant oxygen atoms.

11. $C + O_2 \rightarrow CO_2$

a. Atoms are not created or destroyed. 12 g of carbon combine with 32 g of oxygen to give 44 g of carbon dioxide each and every time.

b. Only whole atoms combine. Carbon dioxide always contains 12 g of carbon for every 32 g of oxygen.

c. Carbon and oxygen combine to form CO_2. They also combine to make carbon monoxide, CO.

13. These compounds illustrate the law of multiple proportions.

Problems

15. No, the law of conservation of mass has not been violated. The gases that escaped from the reaction vessel account for the missing mass.

17. No. The vessel would contain water only if the hydrogen and oxygen reacted with each other to form water.

19. Acetylene contains 2.02 g of H for every 24.02 g of C. The number of g of H that would combine with 78.5 g of C to form acetylene = (78.5 g C)(2.02 g H/24.02 g C) = 6.60 g H.

21. The total mass of the reactants is 37.7 g + 20.1 g = 57.8 g. According to the student, these reactants can form 59.8 g of product, which is a violation of the law of conservation of mass.

23. b. The mass of the reactants is 1.00 g + 0.80 g = 1.80 g. The mass of the product, which contains 1.00 g Zn is 1.50 g. Therefore, 0.30 g of the S did not react.

25. a. The ratio of hydrogen to water is 2.02 g to 18.02 g or 0.112. The same ratio applies to 775 g of water or 0.112 x 775 g = 86.8 g of hydrogen.

b. The ratio of oxygen to water is 16.00 g to 18.02 g or 0.888. The same ratio applies to 775 g of water or 0.888 x 775 g = 688 g of oxygen.

27. 3 parts of carbon/11 parts of carbon dioxide = x parts of carbon/14 kg of carbon dioxide or 3.82 kg. (3 parts of carbon plus 8 parts of oxygen gives 11 parts of carbon dioxide.)

29. Divide the percentage of C and O by the percentage of C to get a mass ratio of C = 1.000 and oxygen = 0.888. 2.664/0.888 = 3.00; 1.332/0.888 = 1.50; 0.888/0.888 = 1.00.

31. The ratio of the first compound is 0.742 g Sn/0.100 g O = 7.42 Sn to O. The ratio of the second compound is 0.555 g Sn/0.150 g O = 3.70 Sn to O or half the amount of Sn. If the first compound is SnO, then the second compound must be SnO_2.

33. Compound T has a ratio of S to F of 0.447/1.06 = 0.422 while compound U has a ratio of S to F of 0.438/1.56 = 0.281. Comparing the ratios: 0.422/0.281 = 1.50.

35. a. Dalton assumed that different atoms had different masses. This is consistent with Dalton's theory.

    b. Dalton assumed that different atoms had different masses. This is inconsistent with Dalton's theory.

37. Dalton thought that atoms were indivisible; this violates his theory.

39. If there are two hydrogen atoms for every one oxygen atom, then the ratio must be answer (d) 16 times.

41. Yes; the ratio of the carbon to hydrogen in the three samples is 14.90, 14.97, and 14.92. These ratios are in agreement within the limits of experimental error.

Answers and Solutions to Additional Problems

43. The total mass of reactants is 0.7581. If the product weighs 0.3114, then the unreacted magnesium weighs 0.7581 – 0.3114 or 0.4467 g.

45. A uranium atom weighs 12.5 times as much as a fluorine atom (238/19 = 12.5). In order for the mass ratio of U to F in the compound to be 2.09 then the number of F atoms must be 12.5/2.09 or 5.99. Therefore, there must be 6 F atoms for every U atom in the compound.

49. mass of mercuric oxide = 100.0 g mercury (100.00 g mercuric oxide/92.61 g mercury) = 108.0 g.

51. Divide 0.5836 g by 0.4375 to get 1.334. This gives a ratio of N to O of 1.334 to 1. Multiply both by 3 to get a ratio of 4.002 to 3 or 4 to 3.

53. (1) Lead compounds, previously used in paints, have been replaced with titanium dioxide, a much safer material. (2) Metal salts with lower toxicity now substitute for the lead stabilizers in plastics.

Atomic Structure

Images of the Invisible

CHAPTER SUMMARY

3.1 Electricity and the Atom
   A. Volta invented an electrochemical cell (1800) much like a modern battery.
   B. Electrolysis.
      1. Davy produced elements from compounds by passing electricity through them (electrolysis).
      2. Faraday continued to work in this field.
      3. Electrolytes are compounds that conduct electricity when melted or dissolved in water.
      4. Electrodes are carbon rods or metal strips that carry electric current when inserted into a molten compound or solution.
      5. The anode is the positively charged electrode. The cathode is the negatively charged electrode.
      6. The anion is a negatively charged ion attracted to the anode. A cation is a positively charged ion attracted to the cathode.
   C. Crookes (1875) discovered cathode rays by passing electricity through a partially evacuated gas discharge tube.
      1. Cathode rays (beams of current) travel from the cathode to the anode.
   D. Thomson (1897) found that cathode rays were deflected in an electric field and thus must contain charged particles.
      1. These negatively charged particles were called electrons and were found to be the same for all gases used to produce them.
      2. Cathode rays travel in straight lines in the absence of an applied field.
      3. Thomson calculated the ratio of the electron's mass to its charge.
   E. Goldstein (1886) used an apparatus similar to Crookes's tube to study positive atomic particles.
      1. The positively charged particles were found to be more massive than electrons, and to vary with the type of gas used in the experiment.
      2. The lightest positive particle obtained was derived from hydrogen and had a mass 1837 times heavier than that of an electron.
   F. Millikan (1909) determined the charge of the electron.

1. The charge on an electron is –1.
2. The mass of the electron is 9.1×10^{-28} g.

Answers to Self-Assessment Questions

1. c   Electrolysis is the process of producing a chemical reaction by means of electricity.
2. b   Negatively charged ions move toward the positively charged electrode (anode).
3. b   Cathode rays are the same as electrons: –1 charge and very little mass.
4. a   Thomson deflected cathode rays in an electrostatic field.
5. d   Thomson could only obtain the charge-to-mass ratio as neither the mass nor the charge was known independently.
6. b   Millikan observed the amount of deflection that occurred when he manipulated the charges on two plates.

3.2   Serendipity in Science: X-Rays and Radioactivity
  A.   Roentgen (1895) discovered X-rays.
  B.   Becquerel discovered radioactivity while studying fluorescence.
  C.   Marie and Pierre Curie studied radioactivity.
     1.   They discovered the radioactive elements radium and polonium.

Answers to Self-Assessment Questions

1.   a   X-rays are absorbed more by hard, fairly dense materials than by soft, less dense tissues.
2.   b   Unstable elements become more stable after emitting radiation.

3.3   Three Types of Radioactivity
  A.   Rutherford classified three types of radioactivity.

Name	Symbol	Mass	Charge
1. Alpha rays	α particles	4 amu	2+
2. Beta rays	β particles	1/1837 amu	1-
3. Gamma rays	γ rays	0	0

Answers to Self-Assessment Questions

1.   a   An alpha particle is the same as a helium nucleus which has four times the mass of a hydrogen atom.
2.   d   An alpha particle with 2 protons would have a 2+ charge.
3.   b   The properties of a beta particle and an electron are the same.
4.   b   Experiments show that a gamma ray is pure energy with neither mass nor charge.

3.4   Rutherford's Experiment: The Nuclear Model of the Atom
  A.   Rutherford's experiment showed that the positive charge and nearly all the mass are concentrated in the tiny core called the nucleus.
  B.   Rutherford proposed that negatively charged electrons have almost no mass but occupy nearly all the volume of the atom.

Answers to Self-Assessment Questions

1.   b   Gold is very dense and it was surprising how "empty" it seemed to be.
2.   c   Since only a few alpha particles were deflected, the nucleus had to be a very small positive target.

3.   b   Most alpha particles missed any obstruction; most of the atom was empty space.

4.   b   Positive alpha particles had to be repelled by positive nuclei.

3.5   The Atomic Nucleus

    A.   Rutherford (1914) proposed that protons constitute the positively charged matter of all atoms, not just that of hydrogen.

    B.   Chadwick (1932) discovered a nuclear particle, called a neutron, which has about the same mass as a proton but has no charge.

        1.   The number of protons in the nucleus (atomic number, Z) determines the identity of the atom.

    C.   Isotopes have the same number of protons (that is, the same atomic number) but a different number of neutrons (different atomic mass).

    D.   The mass number (A), or nucleon number, is the number of nucleons, or nuclear particles (protons and neutrons).

        1.   Atomic symbols are written with the atomic number as a subscript and the mass number as a superscript to the left of the atomic symbol.

Answers to Self-Assessment Questions

1.   c   Experimental evidence has shown that the atom consists of protons, neutrons, and electrons.

2.   d   The number of protons, which is given by the atomic number, determines the element's identity.

3.   c   Experiments deflecting proton beams and electron beams show that electrons are approximately 1800 times lighter than protons.

4.   d   Experiments have shown that protons and neutrons have about the same mass.

5.   b   Because the number of protons determines the identity of an element, a change in this number would change the element's identity.

6.   d   The nucleon number, or mass number, is the sum of the number of protons and neutrons.

7.   b   The atomic number (subscript) is 7, indicating 7 protons; the nucleon number (superscript) is 15, indicating a total of 15 protons and neutrons. Subtracting the atomic number from the nucleon number gives 8 neutrons.

8.   b   In order for an atom to be neutral, it must have the same number of protons (positively charged particles) as electrons (negatively charged particles): atomic number = 5.

9.   c   Potassium has atomic number 19; the mass number of this isotope is 40.

3.6   Electron Arrangement: The Bohr Model

    A.   Flame tests rely on the color of flames to identify elements.

        1.   A prism separates the light of the flame into specific colored lines.

        2.   These different colored lines represent different wavelengths or energies.

    B.   A line spectrum is a pattern of lines, with each line corresponding to a different wavelength or energy emitted by an element. A continuous spectrum contains all colors of the spectrum (and all wavelengths and all energies).

        1.   Some lines are in the infrared or ultraviolet regions and cannot be seen by the unaided eye.

    C.   Bohr's explanation of line spectra stated that discrete spectra arise because the energy of the electrons in an atom is quantized, meaning electrons can absorb only discrete values of energy.

        1.   Quantum: A tiny unit of energy whose magnitude depends on the frequency of the radiation.

        2.   Energy level: Specified energy value for an electron.

        3.   Ground state: Electrons in the lowest possible energy levels.

        4.   Excited state: Due to added energy, an electron jumps to a higher energy level.

5. The maximum number of electrons in any given energy level is given by the formula $2n^2$.
6. Various energy levels are called shells.
D. Atoms in the ground state and excited state.
   1. Ground state: All electrons are in lowest possible energy levels (this is stable).
   2. Excited state: One (or more) electrons is elevated to a higher energy level, leaving an empty lower energy level open below it (this is unstable).
F. Building atoms: Main shells.
   1. Add electrons to energy levels closest to nucleus.
   2. Once an energy level is filled, the electrons start filling the next higher level.
   3. An electron configuration (e.g., 2, 6) lists number of electrons in each shell or level.

Answers to Self-Assessment Questions

1. a Each element is unique in its electron configuration and unique in its spectrum.
2. d Electrons release (lose) energy in going from a higher energy level to a lower energy level.
3. a Excited electrons are electrons that are higher in energy than normal.
4. a Experiments have shown that only two electrons can be in the first shell.
5. c Experiments have shown that no more than 18 electrons can populate the third shell.
6. b The atomic number of Al is 13 and thus it has 13 electrons, two in the first shell, eight in the second shell, and three in the third shell.
7. b The atomic number of sulfur is 16 and thus has 16 electrons, two in the first shell, eight in the second shell, and six in the third shell.

3.7 Electron Arrangement: The Quantum Model
   A. de Broglie suggested the wavelike properties of electrons.
   B. Schrödinger developed equations to describe the behavior of electrons in atoms.
   C. Electrons move in specifically shaped volumes of space, called orbitals.
      1. These different shapes are indicated by the letters s, p, d, and f.
      2. The s sublevel has one orbital.
         The p sublevel has three orbitals.
         The d sublevel has five orbitals.
         The f sublevel has seven orbitals.
      3. An orbital can hold a maximum of two electrons.
   D. Electron configurations are expressed by numbers that indicate the main energy level (shell) and letters that indicate the sublevel(s). For example, the notation $2p^5$ indicates that there are 5 electrons in the p orbitals of the second energy level.
   E. Valence electrons are the electrons in the outermost main shell.
   F. An order-of-filling chart is extremely useful for determining the electron configuration of an atom.

Answers to Self-Assessment Questions

1. c Very complex mathematical calculations show that the $1s$ orbital has a spherical shape.
2. c Very complex mathematical calculations show that an orbital can hold 2 electrons.
3. c The $3p$ orbital is higher than the $3s$ orbital (see the order-of-filling chart).
4. c The third main shell is the first one that is large enough to accommodate d orbitals.
5. c Nitrogen with 7 electrons has 3 p electrons, which means that the p subshell is half-filled.
6. c The p subshell can accommodate a total of 6 electrons in 3 orbitals.
7. b For a $3d$ subshell the number 3 indicates the shell number.
8. c All p subshells can hold a maximum of 6 electrons.

3.8 Electron Configurations and the Periodic Table
  A. The modern periodic table is arranged in order of increasing atomic number, and grouped according to electronic structure.
    1. Vertical columns are called groups or families.
    2. Horizontal rows are called periods, and indicate how many main electron energy levels an atom has.
  B. Groups (families)—the vertical columns.
    1. Elements in one group have similar chemical properties.
      a. The groups (families) have similar outer electron (valence electron) configurations.
      b. Valence electrons determine most of the chemistry of an atom.
    2. Groups were once designated by a Roman numeral and letter A or B.
      a. New IUPAC system renumbers groups 1 to 18 and does not use A or B designations.
    3. Group A elements—main group elements: Members of the A group have the same number of electrons in the outermost shell.
      a. Family groups.
        1. Group 1A—Alkali Metals (highly reactive). ns^1
        2. Group 2A—Alkaline Earth Metals (moderately reactive). ns^2
        3. Group 7A—Halogens (highly reactive nonmetals). ns^2np^5
        4. Group 8A—Noble Gases (nonreactive nonmetals). ns^2np^6
    4. Group B elements—transition group elements.
      a. These elements have properties that are "transition" between those of Groups 2A and 3A as their electron configurations are more complex.
  C. Metals, nonmetals, and metalloids.
    1. Elements in the periodic table are divided into two main classes: metals and nonmetals. A heavy, stair-like line separates the two classes.
      a. Metals—elements to the left of the line.
      b. Nonmetals—elements to the right of the line.
      c. Metalloids—elements bordering the line.
    2. The characteristics of metals are: luster, good conductors of heat and electricity, solid at room temperature (except mercury, a liquid), malleable, and ductile.
    3. The characteristics of nonmetals: lack metallic properties.
      a. Most are solids or gases at room temperature.
      b. Bromine is a liquid.
    4. The characteristics of metalloids: possess properties of both metals and nonmetals.
    5. The group number for the main group elements (A groups) gives the number of electrons in the outer energy level (valence electrons).
  D. Which model to use: the model that is most helpful in understanding a particular concept.

Answers to Self-Assessment Questions

  1. b Cl and Br are in the same group, 7A.
  2. c The period number is determined by the highest main shell number that the electrons are filling.
  3. c Group 7A (the halogens) has seven valence electrons.
  4. a Group 1A are the alkali metal elements.
  5. b Bromine is in group 7A and has 7 valence electrons.
  6. c Li, Na, and K are all in group 1A.
  7. b The period number gives the number of main shells that are populated (but not necessarily filled) with electrons.

LEARNING OBJECTIVES

You should be able to ...

1. Explain the electrical properties of an atom. (3.1)

2. Describe how the properties of electricity explain the structure of atoms. (3.1)

3. Describe the experiments that led to the discovery of X-rays and an explanation of radioactivity. (3.2)

4. Distinguish the three main kinds of radioactivity: alpha, beta, and gamma. (3.3)

5. Describe Rutherford's gold-foil experiment, and explain its results. (3.4)

6. Sketch the nuclear model of the atom, and identify its parts. (3.4)

7. List the particles that make up the nucleus of an atom, and give their relative masses and electric charges (3.5)

8. Identify elements and isotopes from their nuclear particles. (3.5)

9. Define *quantum*. (3.6)

10. Arrange electrons in a given atom in energy levels (shells). (3.6)

11. Relate the idea of a quantum of energy to an orbital. (3.7)

12. Write an electron configuration (in subshell notation) for a given atom. (3.7)

13. Describe how an element's electron configuration relates to its location in the periodic table. (3.8)

14. Distinguish the conversion of solar energy into electrical energy in a solar cell from the conversion of solar energy into the chemical-bond energy of a solar fuel.

15. Explain why splitting water into the elements hydrogen and oxygen requires an energy input and producing water by the reaction of hydrogen and oxygen releases energy.

DISCUSSION

We can see the images of atoms even though they are too small to be seen by visible light. The experiments that led to the modern atomic theory started with the beginnings of electricity and radioactivity and progress through spectroscopy. The descriptions of the arrangement of electrons around the nucleus and quantum mechanics are the result of many years of the proposal of hypotheses, experimentation, and observation. Finally, we organize the periodic table to maximize our understanding of atomic structure. Applications of our understanding allow us to devise new technologies, such as solar fuels, to replace some of the nonrenewable resources and reduce pollution.

ANSWERS TO ODD-NUMBERED REVIEW QUESTIONS AND SOLUTIONS FOR ODD-NUMBERED END OF CHAPTER PROBLEMS

Review Questions

1. Many scientists contributed to our knowledge of the atom.

    a. Crookes invented the gas discharge tube. He also investigated the cathode rays and showed them to be negatively charged and light mass.

    b. Goldstein discovered positive particles (protons) in similar experiments to those of Crookes.

    c. Faraday showed that matter is electrical in nature.

    d. Thomson determined the mass-to-charge ratio for the electron.

3. Both X-rays and gamma rays are forms of energy. Gamma rays are more penetrating than X-rays.

5. Atoms A and B are not isotopes because they have different numbers of protons and are thus different elements. Atoms A and C are not isotopes, they are different atoms because they have different numbers of protons. Atoms A and D are isotopes because they differ only in the number of neutrons. Atoms B and C are isotopes because they differ only in the number of neutrons.

7. Atoms A and B have about the same masses. Protons have about the same mass as neutrons. The mass numbers (nucleon numbers) of atoms A and B are the same (35), indicating that these atoms have the same total number of protons and neutrons.

9. An atom containing 21 protons has an atomic number of 21 and is Scandium, Sc. Scandium's atomic mass is 44.956.

11. More energy is required to excite an electron from the first to the third shell than is required to excite an electron from the second to the third shell.

13. The atomic number is the same as the number of protons.

    a. Lithium has 3 protons.

    b. Magnesium has 12 protons.

    c. Chlorine has 17 protons.

    d. Fluorine has 9 protons.

    e. Aluminum has 13 protons.

    f. Phosphorus has 15 protons.

Problems

15. A nuclear symbol has the atomic number to the left as a subscript to the atomic symbol and the nucleon number to the left as a superscript. The atomic number determines the element and indicates the number of protons. The nucleon number is determined by the sum of the number of protons and neutrons.

a. $^{42}_{20}\text{Ca}$

b. $^{51}_{23}\text{V}$

17. There are four different elements listed: two isotopes of sodium (Na, atomic number 11), and one atom each of neon (Ne, atomic number 10), boron (B, atomic number 5), and magnesium (Mg, atomic number 12).

19. The number of electrons is given by the sum of the superscripts of the electron structures; this is the atomic number (assuming neutral atoms). The atomic number identifies the element.

   a. 7 electrons or atomic number 7

   b. 13 electrons or atomic number 13

   c. 19 electrons or atomic number 19

21. The order-of-filling chart tells us in which order the orbitals fill in ground-state atoms. Any pattern that violates this order represents an atom in an excited state.

   a. Possible excited state: The $1s$ orbital holds 2 electrons. In this case, one of those electrons appears to be excited into the next higher, or $2s$, orbital

   b. Incorrect. The maximum number of electrons that can populate the three p orbitals is six.

   c. Possible excited state: Two electrons have been raised to the $2p$ subshell.

   d. This atom is in its ground state.

23. F has 9 electrons. Adding one electron would give 10 electrons or atomic number 10. This is the element neon, Ne.

25. Silicon (Si) and germanium (Ge) are both in Group 4A. Each has four electrons in its outermost electron shell designated as ns^2np^2. Silicon's four valence electrons are in the third main shell, while those of germanium are in the fourth main shell.

27. In general, metals are to the left on the table and nonmetals are to the right. Most published tables have a code to identify metals and nonmetals.

   a. Manganese is a metal.

   b. Strontium is a metal.

   c. Cesium is a metal.

   d. Argon is a nonmetal.

29. Ne and Kr are noble gases.

31. Four: Ne, P, Kr, and N are nonmetals.

33. a. The atom has a total of 15 electrons, so it must have 15 protons. Its atomic number is 15.

   b. Phosphorus.

   c. Because atoms are electrically neutral, an atom of phosphorus has 15 electrons.

d. The electron configuration for phosphorus is $1s^2 2s^2 2p^6 3s^2 3p^3$. The atom has 6 s electrons.

e. According to the filling pattern (see d.), this atom has no electrons in d orbitals.

35. a. The fourth period noble gas is Kr.

   b. The third period alkali metal is Na.

   c. The fourth period halogen is Br.

   d. The metal in the fourth period and group 3B is Sc.

37. a. Fe (atomic number 26): $1s^2 2s^2 2p^6 3s^2 3p^6 3d^6 4s^2$

   b. Sn (atomic number 50): $1s^2 2s^2 2p^6 3s^2 3p^6 3d^{10} 4s^2 4p^6 4d^{10} 5s^2 5p^2$

   c. Pb (atomic number 82): $1s^2 2s^2 2p^6 3s^2 3p^6 3d^{10} 4s^2 4p^6 4d^{10} 4f^{14} 5s^2 5p^6 5d^{10} 6s^2 6p^2$

39. Both atoms are in the fifth period. Atom L must be strontium (Sr) with an electron configuration of $1s^2 2s^2 2p^6 3s^2 3p^6 3d^{10} 4s^2 4p^6 5s^2$. Atom M, which is adjacent to atom L, must be yttrium (Y), with an electron configuration of $1s^2 2s^2 2p^6 3s^2 3p^6 3d^{10} 4s^2 4p^6 4d^1 5s^2$.

41. b. Energy is required to break the bonds that hold the two H atoms to the O atom in water.

43. d. Scientists are looking for electrodes and other components that can be fabricated from more abundant materials than the platinum that is typically used.

Chemical Bonds

The Ties That Bind

CHAPTER SUMMARY

Introduction
A. Chemical bonds hold atoms together in molecules and ions together in ionic crystals.
1. The nature of bonding within the molecule determines the forces between molecules.
2. Bonds determine the shape of the molecule.

4.1 The Art of Deduction: Stable Electron Configurations
A. Atoms can gain or lose electrons to form electron configurations that are isoelectronic with (have the same electronic configuration as) the noble gases.
B. When atoms gain or lose electrons and acquire a charge, they are called ions.

Answers to Self-Assessment Questions

1. c Elements in Group 8A all have a completely filled outermost shell.
2. b Sodium loses one electron to achieve the same electron configuration as neon.
3 a K^+ and Ar both have 18 electrons and the same electron configuration.
4. a Cl^- and Ca^{2+} both have 18 electrons like Ar and the same electron configuration.

4.2 Lewis (Electron-Dot) Structures
A. Electron-dot symbols, or Lewis symbols, are a useful way to represent atoms or ions.
1. The chemical symbol represents the core (nucleus plus inner electrons).
2. Valence electrons are represented by dots.

B. Chemical Symbolism
1. Electron-dot symbols are more convenient to use than energy-level diagrams.
a. Group number of A group elements gives the number of valence electrons.
Na (1A)—one valence electron; Cl (7A)—seven valence electrons.

Answers to Self-Assessment Questions

1. a Two valence electrons because Be is in Group 2A.
2. c Seven valence electrons because F is in Group 7A.

3.   c   Li is in Group 1A and only has one valence electron.

4.   a   As is in group 5A and needs 5 valence electrons.

4.3   The Reaction of Sodium and Chlorine
   A.   Sodium is a very soft, reactive metal. Chlorine is a poisonous greenish-yellow reactive gas.
   B.   When sodium metal is added to chlorine gas, a violent reaction takes place and produces a white, stable, water-soluble solid known as sodium chloride (table salt).
   C.   Sodium reacts with chlorine by giving it an electron.
   D.   The ion products of this reaction are stable because both ions have stable noble gas type electron configurations. The ions have opposite charges, so the ions are attracted to each other, forming ionic bonds.
      1.   Compounds with ionic bonds often form crystalline solids that have well-defined regular shapes.

Answers to Self-Assessment Questions

1.   a   Both have 10 electrons and the same electron configuration.
2.   d   The Cl^- ion has 8 valence electrons and a 1$-$ charge.
3.   b   The K^+ and F^- ions form an ionic bond.

4.4   Using Lewis Symbols for Ionic Compounds
   A.   Potassium (in the same family as sodium) reacts with chlorine the same way sodium does.
   B.   Potassium reacts with bromine (same family as chlorine) the same way it reacts with chlorine.
   C.   Magnesium (Group 2A) reacts with oxygen (Group 6A) by giving up two electrons.
   D.   Metallic elements of Group 1A, 2A, and 3A react with nonmetallic elements in Group 5A, 6A, and 7A to form stable crystalline solids.
      1.   Metals give up electrons, forming (+) ions.
      2.   Nonmetals gain electrons, forming ($-$) ions.
      3.   The attraction of (+) ions for ($-$) ions is the basis of ionic bonds.
   E.   Octet rule.
      1.   All noble gases have an octet (8) of valence electrons except He, which has two.
      2.   Atoms lose or gain electrons to follow the octet rule according to their group number:
         Group 1A loses one electron to form 1+ cations.
         Group 2A loses two electrons to form 2+ cations.
         Group 3A gains two electrons to form 2$-$ anions.
         Group 7A gains one electron to form 1$-$ anions.

Answers to Self-Assessment Questions

1.   c   Generally, ionic compounds form between metals, which lose electrons, and nonmetals, which gain electrons to achieve stability. K is in group 1A and O is in group 6A. K can easily lose one electron and O can easily gain two electrons to achieve the octet rule.
2.   b   S is in group 6A and can easily gain two electrons to give an anion with a 2$-$ charge.
3.   b   Mg is in group 2A and can easily lose two electrons to give a cation with a 2+ charge.
4.   c   There are 5 valence electrons in neutral N and when 3 electrons are added, there are 8 valence electrons in the N^{3-} anion.
5.   b   Li loses one electron to become Li^+ and O gains two electrons to become O^{2-}. Two Li^+ ions are needed to balance the 2$-$ charge on the O^{2-}.
6.   c   Mg loses two electrons to become Mg^{2+} and Br gains one electron to become Br^-. Two Br^- ions are needed to balance the 2+ charge on the Mg^{2+} ion.

7.   b.   Br is in group 7A and will easily gain one electron to become Br⁻.

4.5   Formulas and Names of Binary Ionic Compounds
   A.   Binary compounds are composed of two different elements.
   B.   Names and symbols for simple ions.
      1.   To name simple cations, add "ion" to the name of the parent element.
         a. Na^+, sodium ion
      2.   To name simple anions, change the ending of the name of the element to "-ide" and add "ion."
         a. Cl^-, chloride ion
      3.   Elements in the B groups on the periodic table can form more than one ion.
   B.   Formulas and names for binary ionic compounds.
      1.   The "crossover" method is used to determine the numbers of cations and anions needed for the correct formula of an ionic compound. For aluminum sulfide, $Al^{3+} + S^{2-} \rightarrow Al_2S_3$.

Answers to Self-Assessment Questions

   1.   a   Ba in group 2A loses two electrons to become Ba^{2+}, and S in Group 6A gains two electrons to become S^{2-}.
   2.   c   Mg in group IIA loses two electrons to become Mg^{2+}, and F in group 7A gains one electron to become F^-. Two F^- ions are needed to balance the 2+ charge on Mg^{2+}. The formula should be MgF_2.
   3.   b   Al in group IIIA loses one electron to become Al^{3+}, and P in group VA gains three electrons to become P^{3-}. The formula should be AlP.
   4.   c   K, the cation, is named first and keeps the original element's name, potassium. Cl, the anion, has the suffix -ide added to the root, chlor-.
   5.   a   Al, the cation, is named first and keeps the original element's name, aluminum. S, the anion, has the suffix -ide added to the root, sulf-.
   6.   d   Li, the cation, is named first and keeps the original element's name, lithium. I, the anion, has the suffix -ide added to the root, iodid-.
   7.   b   Zn, the cation, is named first and keeps the original element's name, zinc. Cl, the anion, has the suffix -ide added to the root, chlor-.

4.6   Covalent Bonds: Shared Electron Pairs
   A.   Elements that are unable to transfer electrons completely between them achieve electronic configurations by sharing pairs of electrons.
   B.   A bond formed by sharing a pair of electrons is called a covalent bond. Covalently bonded atoms, except hydrogen, seek an arrangement that surrounds them with eight electrons (octet rule).
      1.   If one electron pair is shared, the bond formed is a single bond.
      2.   The two shared electrons forming the bond are called a bonding pair.
      3.   The electrons that stay with each atom and are not shared are the nonbonding pairs or lone pairs.
      4.   Covalent bonding can be symbolized in several ways.
   C.   Multiple bonds.
      1.   Atoms can share more than one pair of electrons, resulting in:
         a.   Double bonds (two pairs of electrons shared between two atoms).
         b.   Triple bonds (three pairs of electrons shared between two atoms).
   D.   Names of covalent (or molecular) compounds.

1. When two nonmetals form a covalently bonded compound, prefixes are used to indicate the number of atoms of each element in the molecule.

Prefix	Number
mono-	1
di-	2
tri-	3
tetra-	4

2. The prefix mono- is omitted; SO_2 is sulfur dioxide (not monosulfur dioxide).

Answers to Self-Assessment Questions

1. a   The definition of a covalent bond is the sharing of a pair of electrons by two atoms.
2. c   Each Br has one unpaired valence electron. They share to form a single covalent bond between the atoms.
3. d   Each N has three unpaired valence electrons. They share to form a triple covalent bond giving each of the N atoms an octet of electrons.
4. c   There is one phosphorus and three chlorines for the trichloride.
5. b   Disulfur designates two sulfurs and difluoride designates two fluorines.
6. b   The prefix for two N atoms is di- and the prefix for four S atoms is tetra-.
7. a   The prefix for two I atoms is di- and the prefix for five O atoms is penta-.

4.7   Unequal Sharing: Polar Covalent Bonds
  A. In a polar covalent bond the electron pair is unequally shared between the two bonded atoms.
      1. The bonding pair of electrons is more strongly attracted to the element that is the most electronegative.
      2. The chlorine atom has a partial negative charge because it attracts the electrons more strongly than the hydrogen, which has a partial positive charge.
          a. $\delta^+ \quad \delta^-$
              H—Cl
  B. Electronegativity is a measure of the attraction of an atom in a molecule for a pair of shared electrons.
      1. Nonmetals are more electronegative than metals. Fluorine (upper-right corner of the periodic table) is the most electronegative element, and metals like cesium (lower left) are the least electronegative.
  C. When the electronegativity difference is < 0.5, the bond is nonpolar covalent; when the difference is large (> 2.0), complete electron transfer occurs producing an ionic bond; when the difference is 0.5–2.0, the bond is polar covalent.

Answers to Self-Assessment Questions

1. c   The H and Cl atoms each have one unpaired electron. Those electrons are shared, producing the covalent bond between the two atoms. The bond in HCl is polar covalent, which means electrons are shared even if unevenly.
2. d   The difference in electronegativity is smallest for H and C.
3. b   The difference in electronegativity is greatest for C and F.
4. c   The atom with the greater electronegativity has the stronger attraction for electrons in a bond so the electrons (negatively charged) are closer to that atom.
5. c   The accepted line between covalent polar and ionic is an electronegativity difference of 2.0 or more.

4.8 Polyatomic Molecules: Water, Ammonia, and Methane
   A. To calculate the number of covalent bonds a nonmetallic element (Groups 6A–7A) will form, subtract the group number from 8.
      1. Hydrogen forms one bond.
      2. Oxygen in Group 6A: $8 - 6 = 2$ bonds.
      3. Nitrogen in Group 5A: $8 - 5 = 3$ bonds.
      4. Carbon in Group 4A: $8 - 4 = 4$ bonds.
   B. Water.
      1. The molecular formula for water is H_2O.
      2. The electron-dot formula for water is

$$H : \overset{..}{\underset{..}{O}} :$$
$$H$$

      3. Water is a bent molecule, rather than a linear molecule, owing to its polar nature.

$$\delta^{(+)} H \text{—} \overset{..}{O} : \quad \delta^{(-)}$$
$$|$$
$$H$$

vs.

$$H \text{—} \overset{..}{\underset{..}{O}} \text{—} H$$

   C. Ammonia.
      1. The molecular formula for ammonia is NH_3.
      2. The electron-dot formula for ammonia is

$$H : \overset{..}{N} : H$$
$$H$$

      3. The shape is pyramidal which explains its polar nature.

$$\overset{..}{N}$$
$$H \diagup \quad \diagdown H$$
$$\diagdown H$$

   D. Methane.
      1. The molecular formula for methane is CH_4.
      2. It forms a tetrahedron with each H bond pointing to a corner of the geometric figure.

$$H$$
$$|$$
$$H \text{—} C \text{—} H$$
$$|$$
$$H$$

1. d The electronegativity difference between O and H is 1.4, so the H – O bond is polar covalent.
2. d N shares electrons with 3 H atoms to obtain 8 valence electrons.
3. b C with four valence electrons requires four H atoms each with one valence electron.

4.9   Polyatomic Ions
   A. Polyatomic ions are groups of atoms that remain together during most chemical reactions. They are bonded to each other by covalent bonds and, as a unit, have an overall charge.
   B. A number of polyatomic ions are so common that they have been given names.
       1.   Examples

Name	Formula	Name	Formula
ammonium ion	NH_4^+	nitrate ion	NO_3^-
carbonate ion	CO_3^{2-}	phosphate ion	PO_4^{3-}
hydroxide ion	OH^-	sulfate ion	SO_4^{2-}

   C. In balanced formulas, the formula of the polyatomic ion is enclosed in parentheses. A subscript outside the parentheses surrounding a polyatomic ion indicates the number of those polyatomic ions required to balance the charge of the counter ion.

Answers to Self-Assessment Questions

1. c SO_3^{2-}, sulfite, is a polyatomic ion.
2. d The ammonium ion is NH_4^+ and the phosphate ion is PO_4^{3-}.
3. a Sodium is Na^+ and the hydrogen carbonate ion is HCO_3^-.
4. a Cu(I) is Cu^+ and the hydrogen sulfate ion is HSO_4^-.
5. c The calcium ion is Ca^{2+} and the nitrate ion is NO_3^-.
6. c The ammonium ion is NH_4^+ and the hydrogen carbonate ion is HCO_3^-.

4.10 Rules for Writing Lewis (Electron-Dot) Formulas
   A. Construct a skeletal structure that shows the order in which atoms are attached to each other.
       1. H atoms form only one bond, so they cannot be in the middle of a skeletal structure.
           a. H atoms are often bonded to C, N, or O.
       2. In polyatomic molecules, the central atom is surrounded by more electronegative elements.
   B. Calculate the total number of valence electrons by summing the number of valence electrons contributed by each atom.
       1. In polyatomic anions, add the number of negative charges to the valence electron total.
       2. In polyatomic cations, subtract the number of positive charges from the valence electron total.
   C. Draw single lines to represent bonds between atoms in the skeletal structure.
       1. Subtract two electrons from the total number of valence electrons for each bond drawn.
   D. Assign the remaining valence electrons so that each atom is surrounded by eight electrons in keeping with the octet rule (except H and He, which are surrounded by two electrons, duet rule).
       1. If there are not enough valence electrons to satisfy each atom, move one or more lone pairs from an outer atom to the space between atoms to form a double or triple bond between atoms.
       2. Count the electrons around each atom to make certain every atom except H (or He) has an octet of electrons.
   E. Odd-electron molecules: free radicals.
       1. A free radical is an atom or molecule with an unpaired electron.
       2. Many free radicals are highly reactive.

3. Nitrogen oxides, major components of smog, are examples of free radicals, as are chlorine atoms from the breakdown of chlorofluorocarbons in the stratosphere.

Answers to Self-Assessment Questions

1. b Each F atom has 3 lone pairs of electrons. Four F atoms have a total of 12 lone pairs.
2. b Each oxygen atom in the Lewis structure has two unshared electron pairs, so the total number of unshared electrons is 8.
3. d Each Cl atom in the Lewis structure has three unshared electron pairs, or six unshared electrons. The total number of unshared electrons is 24.
4. d There are 16 valence electrons that must be distributed between the central carbon atom and the two oxygen atoms. We can give each of the three atoms an octet of electrons by drawing two double bonds, one between the carbon atom and each of the oxygen atoms. (Can you think of two other ways of correctly drawing this structure?)
5. d Cl_2O is an exception to the rule that the least electronegative element is the central atom in a polyatomic molecule. The number of valence electrons available for the structure is $(7 + 7 + 6 = 20)$. Note that the structure in answer b has only 18. The chemical formula of the compound shown in answer c is incorrect (ClO_2).
6. a See the correct answer to problem 4 above.
7. b The compounds in answers a and c both have single bonds, while there is a double bond between the two oxygen atoms in O_2. The structure for HCN is H−C≡N:.
8. d There should be 26 valence electrons in the correct structure $[(6 \times 4) + 2]$ and answers c and d have 28 electrons. The S atom in the structure in answer a only has 6 electrons but should have an octet (8).

4.11 Molecular Shape: The VSEPR Theory
   A. VSEPR is used to predict the three-dimensional arrangement of atoms around the central atom.
       1. Electron pairs are arranged around a central atom to minimize repulsion.
           a. Two electron sets (bonding or nonbonding) are arranged so they are on opposite sides of the central atom at an angle of 180°.
           b. Three electron sets assume a triangular arrangement about the central atom forming angles of 120°.
           c. Four electron sets form a tetrahedral array around the central atom, giving angles of separation of 109.5°.
   B. To determine molecular shape:
       1. Draw a Lewis formula in which a shared electron pair (bonding pair) is indicated by a line. Indicate unshared electron pairs with dots.
       2. Count the number of electron sets around the central atom. Note: multiple bonds count as only one electron set.
       3. Draw the shape as if all bonds were bonding pairs, placing them as far as possible from each other.
       4. To visualize the shape of the molecule, erase nonbonding pairs because the molecular shape refers to the arrangement of bonded atoms only.

Answers to Self-Assessment Questions

1. b CS_2 is linear. The compound is analogous to CO_2, with the central C atom doubly bonded to each of the S atoms.
2. a H_2S has a bent shape, similar to water, because the central sulfur atom is surrounded by two bonding electron pairs and two sets of nonbonding electron pairs.

3. c There are 26 valence electrons in this structure. The central P atom is attached with single bonds to each F atom and has a nonbonded electron pair (similar to the situation around the central atom in NH_3) for a total of four electron sets.

4. d The central Si atom is attached with single bonds to each of the four F atoms, giving it four electron sets to separate.

4.12 Shapes and Properties: Polar and Nonpolar Molecules

A. A polar molecule has separate centers of positive and negative charge so both the polarities of bonds and the molecular geometry must be considered when deciding whether or not a molecule is polar.

1. Diatomic molecules.
   a. A molecule is polar if its bonds are polar.
   b. A molecule is nonpolar if its bonds are nonpolar.

2. Methane: a tetrahedral molecule.
   a. VSEPR predicts a tetrahedral shape. The four bonds (nonbonding pairs) form angles of 109.5°.
   b. Slight bond polarities are canceled by the symmetrical shape of the molecule.
   c. The molecule is nonpolar.

3. Ammonia: a pyramidal molecule.
   a. VSEPR predicts a tetrahedral shape, but the nonbonding pair in nitrogen pushes the bonds closer together, forming an angle of 107° rather than 109.5°.
   b. The shape is pyramidal.

4. Water: a bent molecule.
   a. Water acts like a dipole (a molecule with a positive and a negative end). The water molecule must be bent; otherwise the charge on the bonds would cancel each other.
   b. According to VSEPR, the two bonds and the two nonbonding pairs of electrons on water's oxygen should form a tetrahedron shape. However, the nonbonding pairs occupy a larger volume and push the two bonds closer together, forming an angle of 104.5° instead of the tetrahedral angle of 109.5°.

Answers to Self-Assessment Questions

1. d NH_3 has polar bonds and a pyramidal shape that gives a net polar molecule.
2. d PF_3 has polar bonds and a pyramidal shape that gives a net polar molecule.
3. c NF_3 has polar bonds and a pyramidal shape that gives a net polar molecule.
4. a CCl_4 has polar bonds and a tetrahedral shape that gives a net nonpolar molecule.

4.13 A Chemical Vocabulary

A. A strong chemical vocabulary makes learning chemistry a lot easier.
   a. Chapter 1 covered the symbols of the elements.
   b. Chapter 3 covered the structure of the nucleus and isotopes.
   c. Chapter 4 covered Lewis symbols and formulas as well as the prediction of shapes using the VSEPR theory.

DISCUSSION

Electrons are the glue that holds atoms together. Atoms achieve a stable octet of electron configuration by transferring electrons (forming ions) from one to another or by sharing electrons (forming covalent bonds). Because only valence electrons (electrons outside the filled electron shells) are involved in either of these processes, an abbreviated notation called Lewis symbols and formulas is used. The group number gives the number of valence electrons. For example, NaCl is formed from unstable Na metal and reactive Cl_2 gas. Electron configurations or electron-dot symbols explain the properties of Na, Cl_2, and NaCl. Covalent compounds are formed when the atoms share electrons. Reactive free radicals are exceptions to the octet rule. The VSEPR theory is used to predict shapes of molecules according to the number of electron pairs around the atoms. The shape (and polarity) of molecules can be used to explain the states of matter. The shapes of molecules become the basis for molecular recognition and the manner in which molecules interact with one another in many biological situations. Understanding molecular shape, the nature of chemical bonds, and how molecules interact with other molecules is the basis of the design of medicines and other substances that benefit society.

Many of the problems at the end of the chapter are drills. These include practice with drawing ions, putting together molecules, or naming compounds. This practice should help firmly establish the rules governing chemical structure in your mind. In case it doesn't, here is some additional help.

First, how do you know whether a compound is ionic or covalent? Just follow these rules:
1. When hydrogen bonds with other nonmetals, except for Group 7A, the compounds are covalent.
   Examples: H_2O, NH_3, and CH_4.
2. When hydrogen bonds with Group 1A or 2A metals, the compounds are ionic.
   Examples: NaH, CaH_2, and LiH.
3. When Group 1A or 2A metals bond with Group 5A, 6A, or 7A nonmetals, the compounds are ionic.
   Examples: NaCl, CaF_2, K_2S, and Na_3N.
4. When nonmetals bond with other nonmetals, the compounds are covalent.
   Examples: CO_2, CCl_4, and PCl_3.

Second, if the compound is covalent, how do you know whether it is polar or nonpolar?
1. If both (or all) of the atoms in the molecule are the same, the compound is nonpolar.
   Examples: O_2, N_2, Br_2, and S_8.
2. If the atoms in the molecule are not the same, consider each bond separately. Determine the electronegativity of the two atoms sharing the electron pair. If there is no difference in these electronegativities or if the difference is small, then the bond is nonpolar; if the difference is larger, then the bond is polar.
   Examples: NO, PCl_3, SO_2, H_2, and HCl.
3. To decide if the molecule is polar or nonpolar, you must determine its shape.
   a. If the shape is symmetrical, the molecule is nonpolar.
      Example: CO_2
   b. If the shape is not symmetrical, the molecule is polar.
      Example: HCN

LEARNING OBJECTIVES

You should be able to...

1. Determine the number of electrons in an ion.   (4.1)

2. Write the Lewis symbol for an atom or ion.   (4.2)

3. Distinguish between an ion and an atom.   (4.3)

4. Describe the nature of the attraction that leads to formation of an ionic bond.   (4.3)

5. Write symbols for common ions, and determine their charges.   (4.4)

6. Describe the relationship between the octet rule and the charge on an ion.   (4.4)

7. Name and write formulas for binary ionic compounds.   (4.5)

8. Explain the difference between a covalent bond and an ionic bond.   (4.6)

9. Name and write formulas for covalent compounds.   (4.6)

10. Classify a covalent bond as polar or nonpolar.   (4.7)

11. Use electronegativities of elements to determine bond polarity.   (4.7)

12. Predict the number of bonds formed by common nonmetals (the HONC rules).   (4.8)

13. Recognize common polyatomic ions and be able to use them in naming and writing formulas for compounds.   (4.9)

14. Write Lewis formulas for simple molecules and polyatomic ions.   (4.10)

15. Identify free radicals.   (4.10)

16. Predict the shapes of simple molecules from their Lewis formulas.   (4.11)

17. Classify a simple molecule as polar or nonpolar from its shape and the polarity of its bonds.   (4.12)

18. Explain how shape and composition change the properties of molecules.

19. Describe the concept of molecular recognition.

20. Explain the green chemistry advantages of using production methods based on molecular recognition.

ADDITIONAL PROBLEMS

1. Compounds are formed from the following pairs of elements. Indicate whether the compound would be ionic or covalent. (Note that you're not being asked to draw the compounds, just to evaluate their tendency to form ionic or covalent bonds.)

   a. Mg and O   b. F and Ca   c. Li and S   d. Br and Cl
   e. Na and H   f. S and H   g. Ba and Br   h. C and O
   i. N and O   j. Rb and F

2. You should be able to draw electron-dot symbols for any element in the A groups (1A, 2A, etc.). To do this, write the symbol for the element and surround it with dots representing the valence (outermost) electrons. The number of valence electrons is given by the group number. For practice, draw electron-dot structures for the atoms of these elements.

   a. barium   b. carbon   c. xenon   d. nitrogen
   e. silicon   f. hydrogen   g. potassium   h. chlorine
   i. sulfur   j. boron

3. Electron-dot structures for ions are drawn either by adding electron-dots to complete the octet or by removing electron dots to empty the outermost level. Electrons are added to elements with five or more valence electrons; they are subtracted from elements with three or fewer valence electrons. For the following elements, how many electron dots would you add to or remove from the electron-dot symbols of the atoms to form the ions?

   a. barium   b. chlorine   c. nitrogen   d. iodine
   e. potassium   f. magnesium   g. sulfur   h. aluminum

4. The charge is written to the upper right of the electron-dot symbol for an ion. The charge is equal to the number of electrons added to or removed from the neutral atom to form the ion. The charge is positive if electrons are removed and negative if electrons are added. Write electron-dot symbols for the ions that are formed from the eight elements listed in problem 3.

ANSWERS TO ODD-NUMBERED REVIEW QUESTIONS AND SOLUTIONS FOR ODD-NUMBERED END OF CHAPTER PROBLEMS

Review Questions

1. Na metal is a reactive, soft, silver metal. Na^+ cations are nonreactive and independently stable because, by losing one electron, they have achieved an octet of electrons.

3. a. Group 1A ions have a 1+ charge.
   b. Group 6A ions have a 2− charge.
   c. Group 5A ions have a 3− charge.
   d. Group 2A ions have a 2+ charge.

5. a. H forms 1 covalent bond.

b. In binary compounds Cl forms 1 covalent bond. In some polyatomic ions Cl forms more than one bond.

c. In binary compounds S forms 2 covalent bonds. In some polyatomic ions S forms more than 2 bonds.

d. F forms one covalent bond.

e. N forms 3 covalent bonds.

f. In binary compounds P forms 3 covalent bonds. In some polyatomic ions P forms more than 3 bonds.

Problems

7. a. $\overset{\cdot}{Ca}\cdot$ b. $:\overset{\cdot}{\underset{\cdot\cdot}{S}}\cdot$ c. $\cdot\overset{\cdot}{\underset{\cdot}{Si}}\cdot$

9. a. $Na^+ + :\overset{\cdot\cdot}{\underset{\cdot\cdot}{I}}:^-$

b. $2K^+ + :\overset{\cdot\cdot}{\underset{\cdot\cdot}{S}}:^{2-}$

c. $Ca^{2+} + 2:\overset{\cdot\cdot}{\underset{\cdot\cdot}{Cl}}:^-$

d. $Al^{3+} + 3:\overset{\cdot\cdot}{\underset{\cdot\cdot}{F}}:^-$

11. a. Mg^{2+}

b. Sodium ion

c. O^{2-}

d. Chloride ion

e. Zn^{2+}

f. Copper(I) ion

13. a. Chromium(II) ion

b. Chromium(III) ion

c. Chromium(VI) ion

15. a. V^{2+}

b. Ti^{2+}

c. Ti^{4+}

17. a. NaI

b. Potassium chloride

c. Cu_2O

d. Magnesium fluoride

e. $FeBr_2$

f. Iron(III) bromide

19. Cr_2O_3 is called chromium(III) oxide

    CrO_3 is called chromium(VI) oxide.

21. a. KOH

    b. Magnesium carbonate

    c. $Fe(CN)_3$

    d. FeC_2O_4

    e. Copper(II) sulfate

    f. Sodium dichromate

23. The Lewis dot structure for the compound formed with H and F (HF) is

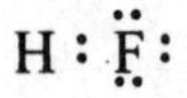

    H : F̈ :

25. The Lewis dot structure for the compound formed from P and H (PH_3) is

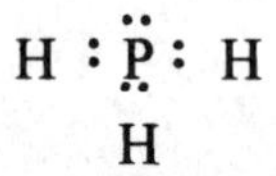

    H : P̈ : H
        H

27. The Lewis dot structure for the compound formed from C and Cl (CCl_4) is

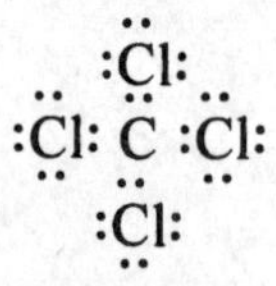

    :Cl:
    :Cl: C :Cl:
    :Cl:

29. a. N_2O_4

    b. $BrCl_3$

    c. Oxygen difluoride

    d. NI_3

    e. Carbon tetrabromide

f. Dinitrogen tetrasulfide

31. a. The Lewis dot structure for SiH_4 is:

```
        H
        ··
H  :  Si :  H
        ··
        H
```

b. The Lewis dot structure for N_2F_4 is:

c. The Lewis dot structure for CH_5N (CH_3NH_2) is:

```
   H   H
   ··  ··
H :C : N :
   ··  ··
   H   H
```

d. The Lewis dot structure for H_2CO is:

```
     ·O·
     ‖
     C
   /   \
 H       H
```

e. NOH_3

```
  :O: H
   ··
H :N: H
   ··
```

f. H_3PO_3

```
       H
       ··
      :O:
   ··   ··
H :O: P :: O
   ··   ··
       H
```

33. a. The Lewis dot structure for ClO^- is:

```
        ⁻
 ··  ··
:Cl:O:
 ··  ··
```

b. The Lewis dot structure for HPO_4^{2-} is:

c. The Lewis dot structure for BrO_3^- is

35. a. The bond between H and O is polar. The electronegativities of H and O are 2.1 and 3.5 respectively. The electronegativity difference between H and O is 1.4.

b. The bond N−F is polar. The electronegativities of N and F are 3.0 and 4.0 respectively. The electronegativity difference between N and F is 1.0.

c. The bond Cl−B is polar. The electronegativites of Cl and B are 3.0 and 2.0 respectively. The electronegativity difference between Cl and B is 1.0.

37 a. Dipole for H----O

b. Dipole for   N----F

c. Dipole for   Cl---B

39 a. $Si^{\delta+}$— $O^{\delta-}$ Si has an electronegativity of 1.8 and O has an electronegativity of 3.5.

b. F—F   The difference in electronegativity is zero so there are no partial charges.

c. $F^{\delta-}$—$N^{\delta+}$ F has an electronegativity of 4.0 and N has an electronegativity of 3.0.

41. a. The bond in K_2O is ionic. The electronegativity difference between K (0.8) and O (3.5) is 2.7, which is greater than 2.0.

b. The bond in BrCl is nonpolar covalent. The electronegativity difference between Br (2.8) and Cl (3.0) is 0.2, which is less than 0.5, the minimum electronegativity difference for a bond to be considered polar.

c. The bond in MgF_2 is ionic. The electronegativity difference between Mg (1.2) and F (4.0) is 2.8, which is greater than 2.0.

d. The bond between the two iodine atoms in I_2 is nonpolar covalent. The electronegativies of the two atoms (2.5) are identical, so the electron pair is shared equally by the bonding atoms.

43. a. Silicon in SiH_4 has four bonded atoms, four bonded electron sets, and no nonbonded electrons. It is tetrahedral.

b. Selenium in H_2Se has two bonded atoms and four electron sets counting the two shared pairs and the two lone pairs. It is bent.

c. Phosphorus in PH_3 has three bonded atoms and four sets of electrons including one lone pair. It is pyramidal.

d. Silicon in SiF_4 has four bonded electron sets of electrons and no nonbonded electrons. It is tetrahedral.

e. Oxygen in OF_2 has two bonded atoms and four electron sets counting the two shared pairs and the two lone pairs. It is bent.

f. C in H_2CO has three bonded atoms and three electron sets, one of which is a double bond between the C and O atoms. It is triangular.

45. BeF_2 is linear and therefore nonpolar because the polarity cancels out. $F^- - Be^+ - F^-$. The center of partial positive charge is on the Be atom; the center of partial negative charge is also on the Be atom.

47. a. The difference in electronegativity between Si (1.8) and H (2.1) is 0.3, so the Si—H bonds are nonpolar covalent and the molecule is nonpolar covalent. Note: even if the bonds were polar, the molecule would still be nonpolar because it is symmetrical; the centers of partial positive and partial negative change would be on the central atom (see d. below). The bond angles are 109.5°.

b. The difference in electronegativity between Se and H is 0.3. The Se—H bond is nonpolar covalent and the molecule is nonpolar covalent. The bond angles are slightly less than 109.5° because the nonbonded electrons occupy more space than do the shared electron pairs.

c. The difference in electronegativity between P and H is 0.0. The P—H bond is nonpolar covalent and the molecule is nonpolar covalent. The bond angles are slightly less than 109.5° due to the nonbonded electron pair on P.

d. The difference in electronegativity between Si and F is 2.2. The Si—F bonds are almost ionic but the molecule is nonpolar because it is symmetrical so the centers of partial positive and partial negative charge are located at the same place. The bond angles are 109.5°.

e. The difference in electronegativity between O and F is 0.5. The O—F bonds are polar covalent and the molecule is polar. The bond angles are less than 109.5° because the two lone pairs on O cause the tetrahedral bond angles to be compressed.

f. The difference in electronegativity between C and H is 0.4, and between C and O is 1.0. The C-H bonds are nonpolar covalent; the C=O bond is polar covalent. Because the molecule is not symmetrical, the partial positive charge falls on the C atom and the partial negative charge rests on the O atom. The molecule is polar and triangular in shape. The bond angles are 120°.

49. a. Br with 7 valence electrons is a free radical.

b. F_2 has no unpaired electrons and is not a free radical.

c. CCl_3 has an unpaired electron on the carbon atom and is a free radical.

51. a. Lewis dot structure for $AlBr_3$ is:

$$:\ddot{Br}:$$
$$|$$
$$Al$$
$$:\ddot{Br} \diagup \quad \diagdown \ddot{Br}:$$

b. Lewis dot structure for BeH_2 is:

$$H :Be: H$$

c. Lewis dot structure for BH_3 is:

$$H :\underset{..}{B}: H$$
$$H$$

Additional Problems

53. Ne has a complete valence shell and is stable.

55. The chemical formula of aluminum phosphide is AlP. The chemical formula of magnesium phosphide is Mg_3P_2.

57. The difference between the electronegativities of I and Cl is 0.5. The molecule is very slightly polar covalent.

59. You would not take the metal or elemental form of potassium because of its extreme reactivity (potassium, K, produces a flame when it reacts with water). You would take a salt of potassium with the stable K^+ cation as part of its structure.

61. a. The electron configuration of Ca is $1s^2 2s^2 2p^6 3s^2 3p^6 4s^2$. The Ca^{2+} ion forms when Ca loses its two valence electrons. The electron configuration of Ca^{2+} is $1s^2 2s^2 2p^6 3s^2 3p^6$.

   b. The most stable ion of Rb forms when a Rb atom loses its one valence electron. The electron configuration of Rb^+ is: $1s^2 2s^2 2p^6 3s^2 3p^6 3d^{10} 4s^2 4p^6$.

   c. The most stable ion of S is S^{2-}: $1s^2 2s^2 2p^6 3s^2 3p^6$.

   d. The most stable ion of I is I^-: $1s^2 2s^2 2p^6 3s^2 3p^6 3d^{10} 4s^2 4p^6 4d^{10} 5s^2 5p^6$.

   e. The most stable ion of N is N^{3-}: $1s^2 2s^2 2p^6$.

   f. The most stable ion of Se is Se^{2-}: $1s^2 2s^2 2p^6 3s^2 3p^6 3d^{10} 4s^2 4p^6$.

63. The halogens have 7 valence electrons, giving them three electron pairs and one unpaired valence electron available for bonding. Forming a single bond by sharing an electron with one other atom gives them an octet of electrons.

65. Two Na^+ ions are required to balance the negative charge of the tungstate ion, WO_4, so the charge on this ion must be 2− and its formula must be WO_4^{2-}. The charge on an aluminum ion is 3+ (Al^{3+}). Using the crossover method, the formula for aluminum tungstate must be $Al_2(WO_4)_3$.

67. Use the cross-over method to get $Q_3(ZX_4)_2$.

69. Molecular recognition.

71. Medicinal chemists design new medicines and drug molecules so they will resemble biological molecules and bind to enzymes or receptors in our body. Enzymes often recognize the molecules with which they interact by their shapes and partial charges.

Chemical Accounting

Mass and Volume Relationships

CHAPTER SUMMARY

5.1 Chemical Sentences: Equations
   A. A chemical equation is a shorthand notation for describing the chemical change as the reactants (shown on the left of the arrow) are converted to products (shown on the right of the arrow).
      1. Reactants → Products
      2. We can indicate the physical states of reactants and products by writing the initial letter of the state immediately following the formula: (g) indicates the substance is a gas, (l) a liquid, and (s) a solid. The label (aq) means the substance is dissolved in water (an aqueous solution).
   B. Chemical equations involve electron rearrangements as chemical bonds are broken and formed. The nuclei of all atoms remain unchanged during chemical reactions (as opposed to the process in nuclear reactions).
   C. When balancing chemical equations, make sure that the same number of each kind of atom appears on both sides of the equation.

$$2\,H_2 + O_2 \rightarrow 2\,H_2O$$

   1. When counting atoms, multiply the coefficients preceding formulas by the subscripts for a given atom in the formula.
   2. Polyatomic ions are treated as units whenever possible in the process of balancing chemical equations.

Answers to Self-Assessment Questions

1. b
   I. All elements are balanced.
   II. Al and Cl are not balanced.
   III. All elements are balanced.
   IV. O is not balanced.
2. c The balanced equation is: $4\,PH_3 + 8\,O_2 \rightarrow P_4O_{10} + 6\,H_2O$, so 6 molecules of H_2O are produced every time one P_4O_{10} molecule forms.
3. c The balanced reaction is $3\,Ca(OH)_2 + 2\,H_3PO_4 \rightarrow 6\,H_2O + Ca_3(PO_4)_2$.

2 molecules of H_3PO_4 produce 6 molecules of H_2O, so 1 molecule of H_3PO_4 produces 3 molecules of H_2O.

4. b The balanced reaction is $3\,Ca(OH)_2\ +\ 2\,H_3PO_4\ \rightarrow\ 6\,H_2O\ +\ Ca_3(PO_4)_2$.
For each $Ca_3(PO_4)_2$ that forms, two H_3PO_4 must react.

5. d The balanced reaction is $3\,Ca(OH)_2\ +\ 2\,H_3PO_4\ \rightarrow\ 6\,H_2O\ +\ Ca_3(PO_4)_2$.
We take the conversion factor from the coefficients in the balanced equation: 3 $Ca(OH)_2$ formula units are proportional to 2 H_3PO_4 molecules.
Number of formula units of $Ca(OH)_2$ = (6 H_3PO_4)(3 $Ca(OH)_2$/2 H_3PO_4) = 9 $Ca(OH)_2$.

5.2 Volume Relationships in Chemical Equations
A. Gay-Lussac's law of combining volumes: When all measurements are made at the same temperature and pressure, the volumes of gaseous reactants and products are in small whole-number ratios.
B. Avogadro's hypothesis: Equal volumes of all gases (at the same temperature and pressure) contain the same number of molecules.

Answers to Self-Assessment Questions

1. d Use the coefficients of the balanced equation, $2\,H_2\ +\ O_2\ \rightarrow\ 2\,H_2O$, for a 2 to 1 to 2 ratio of H_2 to O_2 to H_2O.
2. c Use the coefficients in the balanced equation $2\,C_8H_{18}\ +\ 25\,O_2\ \rightarrow\ 16\,CO_2\ +\ 18\,H_2O$.
number of CO_2 molecules = (50 O_2 molecules)(16 CO_2 molecules/25 O_2 molecules)
= 32 CO_2 molecules.
3   d Use the coefficients in the balanced equation, $N_2\ +\ 3\,H_2\ \rightarrow\ 2\,NH_3$.
volume of NH_3 = (4.50 L N_2)(2 L NH_3/1 L N_2) = 9.00 L NH_3.

5.3 Avogadro's Number and the Mole
A. The number of C-12 atoms in a 12.0-g sample of C-12 is called Avogadro's number and is equal to 6.02×10^{23}.
B. One mole (mol) of a substance is the amount of that substance that contains the same number of elementary units as there are atoms in exactly 12.0 g of C-12.
C. Each element has a characteristic atomic mass; the mass of a compound is the sum of the masses of its constituent atoms, called a formula mass; if the substance is a molecule, its mass is called its molecular mass.
1. For example, S has an atomic mass of 32.0 g and has 6.02×10^{23} atoms of S.
2. The formula, or molecular mass, of NO is 14.0 u + 16.0 u = 30.0 u.
D. We can calculate the percent of a formula (molecular) mass that is attributed to each of the elements in the compound by comparing the contribution of that element to the overall formula mass and then multiplying by 100.
1. This is called the mass percent composition.
2. For example, the mass percent of nitrogen in NO is (14.0 u N/30.0 u NO) x 100% = 46.7%; the mass percent of O in NO is (16.0 u O/30.0 u NO) x 100% = 53.3%. Note that, because NO contains only N and O, the sum of the two mass percents is 100% (46.7% + 53.3% = 100%).

Answers to Self-Assessment Questions

1. d 12 g of C-12 is one mole or Avogadro's number (6×10^{23} atoms/mole).
2. a By definition, the mass of 1 mole of C-12 atoms is 12 g.
3. a The molecular masses are CH_4 = 16.0 u, HF = 20.0 u, H_2O = 18.0 u, and NH_3 = 17.0 u.

4. b According to the chemical formula, there are 3 mol S atoms/1 mol $Fe_2(SO_4)_3$.
5. c (2 mol NH_3)(3 mol H atoms/1 mol NH_3) = 6 mol H atoms.
6. a The formula mass of NaCl is 58.5 u (23.0 u + 35.5 u = 58.5 u).
      The mass percent of Na in NaCl is (23.0 u/58.5 u)(100%) = 39.3%.
      The mass percent of Cl in NaCl is (35.5 u/58.5 u)(100%) = 60.7%.

5.4 Molar Mass: Mole-to-Mass and Mass-to-Mole Conversions
  A. Mole is a term that refers to 6.02×10^{23} things. It is the amount of substance containing as many
      elementary units as there are atoms in exactly 12 g of the carbon-12 isotope.
      1. One mole of Mg atoms = 6.02×10^{23} atoms.
      2. One mole of H_2O molecules = 6.02×10^{23} molecules.
  B. The molar mass is equal to the mass of 1 mol of a substance, in grams.
      1. The molecular mass of NO is 30.0 u; the molar mass of NO is 30.0 g.
  C. Calculations: grams to moles and moles to grams.
      1. The key to these problems is determining a conversion ratio between moles and grams of a
          substance.
      2. Use the periodic table to calculate the molar mass of a substance, which is the
          number of grams of the substance in 1 mole of the substance.
          a. This ratio can then be used in either type of conversion problem (moles to grams
              or grams to moles).
  D. Mole and Mass Relationships in Chemical Equations
      1. Molar masses of substances give the mole-to-gram ratio of a substance.
      2. Coefficients in balanced equations provide mole ratios of the substances in the equation.
      3. Stoichiometry: the mass relationships in chemical equations.
          a. Typically, the amount of a substance in a problem is given in grams rather than moles,
              but when you are asked for grams:
          b. Write a balanced equation.
          c. Use the periodic table to determine the molar masses of substances involved in the
              problem.
          d. Convert the quantity given to moles by using its molar mass.
          e. Use the mole ratio from the coefficients in the balanced equation to convert moles of
              the substance given to moles of the substance asked for.

Answers to Self-Assessment Questions

1. c mass of H_2SO_4 = (4.75 mol H_2SO_4)(98.1 g H_2SO_4/1 mol H_2SO_4) = 466 g H_2SO_4.
2. c For each element, divide 10.0 g by its molar mass. Si has the lowest molar mass, resulting
      in the largest number of moles.
3. c number of moles of CO_2 = (453.6 g CO_2)(1 mol CO_2/44.0 g CO_2) = 10.3 mol CO_2.
4. a number of moles of C_6H_6 = (7.81 g C_6H_6)(1 mol C_6H_6/78.1 g C_6H_6) = 0.100 mol C_6H_6.
5. c The balanced equation is 2 H_2 + O_2 → 2 H_2O. Use the coefficients in the equation to
      interpret the equation to read 2 mol of H_2 reacts with 1 mol O_2 to form 2H_2O.
6. a The balanced equation is 2 H_2 + O_2 → 2 H_2O.
      number of moles of H_2O = (0.500 mol H_2)(2 mol H_2O/2 mol H_2) = 0.500 mol H_2O.
7. a The balanced equation is 2 H_2 + O_2 → 2 H_2O.
      number of moles of O_2 = (0.222 mol H_2O)(1 mol O_2/2 mol H_2O) = 0.111 mol O_2.

Green Chemistry
A. Atom Economy (A.E.)
1. Atom economy is a calculation of the number of atoms that are conserved in the desired product rather than in waste; a measure of reaction efficiency.
2. The traditional way of describing the efficiency of a chemical reaction is to determine the ratio of the amount of product actually collected from a reaction to the amount of product that could, theoretically, have been produced, times 100. In the somewhat rare instances when reaction yields are extremely high, it is still possible that, along with the desired product, there are many byproducts that end up being discarded.
3. The green chemical approach is to minimize waste so the emphasis is to design reaction schemes in which the largest number of reactant atoms is incorporated into the desired reaction product.
4. Therefore, rather than calculate percent yield, a better way to measure reaction efficiency is to calculate percent atom economy, % A.E.

% A.E. = (molar mass of desired product/sum of the molar masses of all reactants)(100%)

5.5 Solutions
A. Solutions are homogeneous mixtures of two or more substances. The substance being dissolved is the solute, and the substance doing the dissolving is the solvent. When the solvent is water, the solutions are called aqueous.
B. Solution concentrations.
1. Molarity is defined as the number of solute moles divided by liters of solution. Molarity is abbreviated as M and has the units of moles/liter (mol/L). For example:
   a. The concentration of a solution in which 15 mol of salt are dissolved in a volume of 5 liters is 3 M.
   b. To find the molarity of 54.5 g of KBr dissolved in 3 liters of solution, first convert the grams of KBr to mol of KBr, then divide by the volume, in liters.
      1 mol of KBr = 119.0 g KBr
      number of mol of KBr = (54.5 g KBr)(1 mol KBr/119.0 g KBr) = 0.458 mol KBr
      0.458 mol of KBr/3 L = 0.153 mol/L or 0.153 M
   c. To find the number of grams in a given volume of solution, calculate the number of moles from molarity: M = mol/L and convert to grams. 300 mL is 0.3 L
      mass of LiCl = (0.40 M LiCl)(0.300 L) = 0.12 mol LiCl
      LiCl has a molar mass of 42.4 g/mol
      (0.12 mol LiCl)(42.4 g LiCl/1 mol LiCl) = 5.09 g LiCl
2. Percent concentrations.
   a. Percent is a fraction (or part/whole) times 100%.
   b. Percent by volume is the ratio of the volume of solute to the volume of solution, times 100. Note that the volume of the solution is the sum of the volumes of all its components.
   c. Percent by mass is the mass of a component divided by the mass of the solution, times 100. Note that the mass of the solution is the sum of the mass of the solute(s) and the mass of the solvent.
   d. What is the mass percent $MgCl_2$ in a solution that contains 15 g of $MgCl_2$ in 250 g of solution?
      % $MgCl_2$ = (15 g $MgCl_2$/250 g solution)(100%)
      % $MgCl_2$ = 6.0%

Answers to Self-Assessment Questions

1. b Sucrose, the solute, is dissolved in water, the solvent.
2. c molarity = 0.500 mol NaOH/0.250 L solution = 2.00 M
3. b number of moles of sugar = (4.00 L)(0.600 mol sugar/L) = 2.40 mol sugar
4. d 1 mol of NaCl = 58.5 g
      number of moles of NaCl = (2.500 L)(0.800 mol NaCl/L) = 2.00 mol NaCl
      mass of NaCl = (2.00 mol NaCl)(58.5g NaCl/mol NaCl) = 117 g NaCl
5. a M = mol/L so L = mol/M
      volume of HCl solution = 1.50 mol HCl/(6.00 mol HCl/L solution)
      volume = 0.250 L or 250 mL
6. b % = (part/whole) x 100%
      volume percent ethanol = (50.0 mL ethanol/250 mL solution)(100%) = 20%
7. b % = (part/whole) x 100%
      mass percent sucrose = (15.0 g sucrose)/(15.0 g sucrose + 60.0 g water)(100%) = 20.0%
8. d The final solution needs to have a volume of 100 mL.

LEARNING OBJECTIVES

You should be able to...

1. Identify balanced and unbalanced chemical equations, and balance equations by inspection. (5.1)

2. Determine volumes of gases that react, using a balanced equation for a reaction.   (5.2)

3. Calculate the formula mass, molecular mass, or molar mass of a substance.   (5.3)

4. Determine the percentage composition of a substance from its formula.   (5.3)

5. Convert from mass to moles and from moles to mass of a substance.   (5.4)

6. Calculate the mass or number of moles of a reactant or product from the mass or number
    of moles of another reactant or product.   (5.4)

7. Calculate the concentration (molarity, percent by volume, or percent by mass) of a solute
    in a solution.   (5.5)

8. Calculate the amount of solute or solution given the concentration and the other amount.   (5.5)

9. Explain how the concept of atom economy can be applied to pollution prevention and
    environmental protection.

10. Calculate the atom economy for chemical reactions.

DISCUSSION

Chapter 5 introduces the language of chemistry. If, instead of chemistry, English literature were our area of study, we would just be at the point of having learned to read. In earlier chapters, we learned to use chemical symbols to represent elements. The symbols are the alphabet of chemistry. In this chapter, we learn to use the "words" of chemistry— the formulas for compounds, to compose chemical "sentences"— that is, to write chemical equations. This chapter also introduces the math of chemistry.

You may never have realized how much information is contained in a chemical equation. Much of the chapter is devoted to a discussion of the concepts and terminology needed to extract every last bit of information from an equation. Therefore, one of the first things you should do is learn the key terms.

Molar mass and mole are interrelated terms. The molar mass of a compound (calculated the same as formula mass) is the mass of 1 mol of the compound expressed in grams.

$$1 \text{ formula mass} = 1 \text{ mole}$$

You can treat this relationship as a conversion factor. If you calculate the formula mass of a compound and remember the relationship, you can interconvert units expressed in grams to moles and vice versa.

Example: Conversions involving methane (CH_4)

Formula weight:

    atomic weight of C = 12.01 = 12.0
    atomic weight of H = 1.008 so 4 H atoms weigh (4)(1.008) = 4.03
    Total is the molar mass of methane or 16.0 g

    Now that we have the molar mass, we have our conversion factor: 16.0 g CH_4 = 1 mol CH_4

How many moles of CH_4 are represented by 4.0 g of CH_4?

    Number of mol of CH_4 = (4.0 g CH_4)(1 mol CH_4/16.0 g CH_4) = 0.25 mol CH_4

What is the mass of 4.0 moles of CH_4?

    Mass = (4.0 mol CH_4)(16.0 g CH_4/mol CH_4)= 64 g CH_4

There are many ways of expressing concentrations, including molarity, mass percent composition, and volume percent composition. These various concentration units are interconvertible.

Realizing the environmental concerns associated with disposal of wastes, chemical and otherwise, the green chemistry approach to help solve this problem is to revise the standard synthesis routes to maximize the atom economy of the procedure. This means that synthesis routes are chosen in which the maximum number of reactant atoms is incorporated into the desired product, not into byproducts which, ultimately, will be discarded. Reaction sequences are evaluated in terms of their percent atom economy rather than in terms of percent yield.

ADDITIONAL PROBLEMS

1. Calculate the formula masses of the following compounds. The formulas are relatively complicated just to make sure that you understand when a subscript applies to a particular atom in the formula and when it does not. You'll require a periodic table or a list of atomic masses.

    a. $CaCO_3$ b. $(NH_4)_2CO_3$ c. $Be(NO_3)_2$ d. $(NH_4)_2C_2O_4$

    e. $Al_2(C_2O_4)_3$ f. $Ca(C_2H_3O_2)_2$ g. $(CH_3)_2SO_4$

2. In this problem, all questions refer to the compound $C_5H_8O_2$.

    a. How many mol of $C_5H_8O_2$ are represented by 100 g of the compound? By 200 g of the compound? By 25 g of the compound? By 3.687 g of the compound?

    b. What is the mass of $C_5H_8O_2$, in grams, of 1 mol of the compound? Of 8 mol of the compound? Of 0.8 mol of the compound? Of 0.01 mol of the compound?

3. For additional practice in interconverting these units, answer the questions in problem 2 for the compound H_2CO_3. A calculator will be useful because these numbers will not be easy.

Let's suppose you are now totally at ease with moles and formula weights and conversions. That brings us to equations. First, determine if the equation is balanced. (We'll supply the correct reactants and products.) If the equation isn't balanced, the quantitative information derived from it will be incorrect. As we indicated in the chapter, you won't be balancing extremely complex equations, but you should be able to handle those in problem 4 below.

4. Balance the following chemical equations.

    a. $Zn + KOH \rightarrow K_2ZnO_2 + H_2$
    b. $HF + Si \rightarrow SiF_4 + H_2$
    c. $B_2O_3 + H_2O \rightarrow H_6B_4O_9$
    d. $SiCl_4 + H_2O \rightarrow SiO_2 + HCl$
    e. $SnO_2 + C \rightarrow Sn + CO$
    f. $Fe_2O_3 + CO \rightarrow FeO + CO_2$
    g. $Fe_3O_4 + C \rightarrow Fe + CO$
    h. $Fe(OH)_3 + H_2S \rightarrow Fe_2S_3 + H_2O$

Once you have a balanced equation, the coefficients in that equation give you the following information:
    a. The combining ratio of molecules (or other formula units such as ion pairs)
    b. The combining ratio of moles of molecules (or other formula units)

The coefficients *do not* give you the combining mass ratios. Thus, from the equation (below) you know that:

$$CH_4 + 2\,O_2 \rightarrow CO_2 + 2\,H_2O$$

    a. 1 molecule of methane (CH_4) reacts with 2 molecules of oxygen (O_2) to produce 1 molecule of carbon dioxide (CO_2) and 2 molecules of water (H_2O).

b. 1 mol of methane reacts with 2 mol of oxygen to give 1 mol of carbon dioxide and 2 mol of water.

The equation does *NOT* say that 1 g of methane reacts with 2 g of oxygen to produce 1 g of carbon dioxide and 2 g of water. If you want to find out how many grams of oxygen react with 1 g of methane, you must first convert mass to the equivalent number of moles and only then use the balanced chemical equation to determine the combining ratio in moles. After using the equation, you'll have the answer in moles and must then convert to grams.

The examples in the text demonstrate the use of equations to obtain information about combining ratios. Review those examples and then the problems at the end of the chapter. For more practice, try the following problems.

5. Refer to the equation

$$CS_2 + 2\,CaO \rightarrow CO_2 + 2\,CaS$$

a. How many moles of CO_2 are obtained from the reaction of 2 mol of CS_2? From the reaction of 2 mol of CaO?
b. How many moles of CaO are consumed if 0.3 mol of CS_2 react? If 0.3 mol of CaS are produced?
c. How many grams of CaS are obtained if 152 g of CS_2 are consumed in the reaction? If 7.6 g of CS_2 are consumed? If 22 g of CO_2 are produced? If 44 g of CO_2 are produced?
d. How many grams of CaO are required to react completely with 38 g of CS_2? With 152 g of CS_2? To produce 36 g of CaS?

ANSWERS TO ODD-NUMBERED QUESTIONS AND SOLUTIONS FOR ODD-NUMBERED END OF CHAPTER PROBLEMS

Review Questions

1. a. A formula unit is the smallest unit of an ionic compound.
    b. Formula mass is the sum of the masses of the atoms represented in the formula.
    c. One mole is 6.02×10^{23} particles.
    d. Avogadro's number is the name we give to the number of ^{12}C atoms in exactly 12 g of ^{12}C, or 6.02×10^{23}.
    e. Molar mass is the mass of one mole of a substance, expressed in grams.
    f. Volume occupied by Avogadro's number of atoms or molecules of a gas under specified conditions.

3. According to Avogadro's hypothesis, equal volumes of all gases, measured at the same pressure and temperature, contain the same number of molecules. Gay-Lussac's law of combining volumes says that when all measurements are made at the same temperature and pressure, the volumes of gaseous reactants and products are in small, whole-number ratios. Because there is a relationship between the volume of a gas and the number of particles it contains, it follows

that the volumes of gases would be in the same, whole-number ratios as the coefficients in the balanced chemical equation.

5. a. A solution is the homogeneous mixture of two or more substances.
    b. The solvent is the substance present in the greatest quantity in a solution.
    c. A solute is a substance dissolved in a solvent.
    d. An aqueous solution is a solution in which water is the solvent.

Problems

7. a. There are 12 oxygen atoms in $Al(H_2PO_4)_3$.
    b. There are 3 oxygen atoms in $HOC_6H_4COOCH_3$.
    c. There are 6 oxygen atoms in $(BiO)_2SO_4$.

9. One formula unit of $(NH_4)_2HPO_4$ contains 2 N atoms, 1 P atom, 9 H atoms, and 4 O atoms so 3 formula units would contain three times as many of each kind of atom or has 6 N, 3 P, 27 H, and 12 O atoms.

11. For the reaction: $2\ H_2O_2 \rightarrow 2\ H_2O + O_2$.
    a. 2 molecules of H_2O_2 produce 2 molecules of H_2O and one molecule of O_2.
    b. 2 mol of H_2O_2 produce 2 mol of H_2O and one mol of O_2.
    c. 68 g of H_2O_2 produce 36 g of H_2O and 32 g of O_2.

13. a. $2\ Mg + O_2 \rightarrow 2\ MgO$
    b. $C_3H_8 + 5\ O_2 \rightarrow 3\ CO_2 + 4\ H_2O$
    c. $3\ H_2 + Ta_2O_3 \rightarrow 2\ Ta + 3\ H_2O$

15. a. $N_2 + O_2 \rightarrow 2\ NO$
    b. $2\ O_3 \rightarrow 3\ O_2$
    c. $UO_2 + 4\ HF \rightarrow UF_4 + 2\ H_2O$

17. $2\ H_2(g) + O_2(g) \rightarrow 2\ H_2O(g)$ Sketch should show 2 volumes of hydrogen, one volume of oxygen, and two volumes of water.

19. Use the Law of Combining Volumes and the balanced equation:
    $$2\ C_6H_{14}(g) + 19\ O_2(g) \rightarrow 12\ CO_2(g) + 14\ H_2O(g).$$
    a. volume of CO_2, L = (20.6 L C_6H_{14})(12 L CO_2/2 L C_6H_{14}) = 124 L CO_2.
    b. volume C_6H_{14}, mL = (29.0 mL O_2)(2 mL C_6H_{14}/19 mL O_2) = 3.05 mL .

21. Use the Law of Combining Volumes and the balanced equation:
    $$2\ C_6H_{14} + 19\ O_2 \rightarrow 12\ CO_2 + 14\ H_2O$$
    12 mol of CO_2 are produced for every 2 mol of C_6H_{14} burned. Therefore, the ratio of the volume of CO_2 produced to the volume of C_6H_{14} reacted is 6:1.

23. a. number of S_8 molecules = (1.00 mol S_8)(6.02 x 10^{23} molecules/mol)
        = 6.02 x 10^{23} molecules of S_8.

b. number of S atoms =
(1.00 mol S_8)(6.02 x 10^{23} molecules S_8/mol S_8)(8 S atoms/molecule S_8) = 4.82 x 10^{24} S atoms.

25. The answer is c. There are two atoms of Br in Br_2 and 6.02 x 10^{23} Br_2 molecules in one mole of Br_2.
   Using the conversion factors:
   number of Br atoms = (1 mol Br_2)(6.02 x 10^{23} Br_2 molecules/mol Br_2)(2 Br atoms/Br_2 molecule)
   = 12.04 x 10^{23} Br atoms

27 a. The molar mass of $AgNO_3$ is 169.9 g/mol
   Ag (107.9 g/mol), N (14.0 g/mol), O (16.0 g/mol): 107.9 + 14.0 + (3)(16.0) = 169.9.
   b. The molar mass of $Mg(ClO)_2$ is 127.3 g/mol
   Mg (24.3 g/mol), Cl (35.5 g/mol), O (16.0 g/mol): 24.3 + (2)(35.5) + (2)(16.0) = 127.3.
   c. The molar mass of $Zn(IO_4)_2$ is 447.2 g/mol
   Zn (65.4 g/mol), I (126.9 g/mol), O (16.0 g/mol): 65.4 + (2)(126.9) + (8)(16.0) = 447.2.
   d. The molar mass of $CH_3(CH_2)_3COF$ is 104.0 g/mol.
   C (12.0 g/mol), H (1.0 g/mol), O (16.0 g/mol), F (19.0 g/mol): (5)(12.0) + (9)(1.0) + 16.0 + 19.0 = 104.0 g/mol.

29. a. The molar mass of $BaSO_4$ is 233.4 g/mol.
   mass of $BaSO_4$ = (7.57 mol $BaSO_4$)(233.4 g $BaSO_4$/mol $BaSO_4$) = 1770 g
   b. The molar mass of $CuCl_2$ is 134.5 g/mol
   mass of $CuCl_2$ = (0.0472 mol $CuCl_2$)(134.5 g $CuCl_2$/mol $CuCl_2$) = 6.35 g.
   c. The molar mass of $C_{12}H_{22}O_{11}$ is 342.0 g/mol.
   mass of $C_{12}H_{22}O_{11}$ = (0.250 mol $C_{12}H_{22}O_{11}$)(342.0 g $C_{12}H_{22}O_{11}$/mol $C_{12}/H_{22}/O_{11}$) = 85.5 g.

31. a. The molar mass of Sb_2S_3 is 340.0 g/mol.
   number of moles = (6.63 g Sb_2S_3)(1 mol Sb_2S_3/339.72 g Sb_2S_3) = 0.0195 mol.
   b. The molar mass of MoO_3 is 143.9 g/mol.
   number of moles = (19.1 g MoO_3)(1 mol MoO_3/143.9 g MoO_3) = 0.133 mol.
   c. The molar mass of $AlPO_4$ is 122.0 g/mol.
   number of moles = (434 g $AlPO_4$)(1 mol $AlPO_4$ /122 g $AlPO_4$) = 3.56 mol.

33. a. The molar mass of $NaNO_3$ is 85.0 g/mol, of which 14.0 is contributed by the N atom. The mass percent of N in $NaNO_3$ is (14.0 g/85.0 g)(100%) = 16.5%.
   b. The molar mass of NH_4Cl is 53.5 g/mol, of which 14.0 is contributed by the N atom. The mass percent of N in NH_4Cl is (14.0 g/53.5 g)(100%) = 26.2%

35. Use the coefficients of the balanced equation: $2 C_4H_{10} + 13 O_2 \rightarrow 8 CO_2 + 10 H_2O$.
   a. number of moles of CO_2 = (8.12 mol C_4H_{10})(8 mol CO_2/2 mol C_4H_{10}) = 32.5 mol.
   b. number of moles of O_2 = (3.13 mol C_4H_{10})(13 mol O_2/2 mol C_4H_{10}) = 20.3 mol.

37. The balanced chemical equation is $N_2 + 3 H_2 \rightarrow 2 NH_3$.
   a. number of moles of H_2 = (440 g H_2)(1 mol H_2/2.0 g H_2) = 220 mol H_2.
   number of moles of NH_3 = (220 mol H_2)(2 mol NH_3/3 mol H_2) = 147 mol NH_3.
   mass of NH_3 = (147 mol NH_3)(17.0 g NH_3/1 mol NH_3) = 2500 g NH_3.

Note: If you do these steps individually, rounding the answer to the appropriate number of significant figures at the end of each calculation (as shown above) the answer you will get is 2499 g NH_3. However, if you do the calculation as a continuous series of steps on your calculator and then round the answer to three significant figures at the end of the calculation, you will get 2493 g NH_3. In either case, the appropriate number of significant figures for the answer is three, and both the answers above, rounded to three significant figures are similar: 2500 g and 2490 g, respectively.

b. number of moles of N_2 = (892 g N_2)(1 mol N_2/28.0 g N_2) = 31.9 mol N_2.
number of moles of H_2 = (31.9 mol N_2)(3 mol H_2/1 mol N_2) = 95.7 mol H_2.
mass of H_2 = (95.7 mol H_2)(2.0 g H_2/1 mol H_2) = 191 g H_2.

39. M = mol of solute/L of solution
   a. molarity = 23.4 mol/10.0 L = 2.34 M
   b. molarity = 0.0875 mol/0.632 L = 0.138 M

41. M = mol of solute/L of solution; mol = M x L
   a. number of mol of NaOH = (0.500 mol NaOH/L)(3.50 L) = 1.75 mol NaOH
       mass of NaOH = (1.75 mol NaOH)(40.0 g NaOH/mol NaOH) = 70.0 g NaOH
   b. number of mol of $C_6H_{12}O_6$ = (1.45 mol $C_6H_{12}O_6$/L)(0.065 L) = 0.0943 mol $C_6H_{12}O_6$
       mass of $C_6H_{12}O_6$ = (0.0943 mol $C_6H_{12}O_6$)(180.0 g $C_6H_{12}O_6$ /mol $C_6H_{12}O_6$)
                             = 17.0 g $C_6H_{12}O_6$

43. M = mol of solute /L of solution; L = mol/M
   a. volume of solution, L = (2.50 mol NaOH)/1 L solution/6.00 mol NaOH) = 0.417 L
   b. The molar mass of KH_2AsO_4 is 180.0 g/mol.
       number of moles of KH_2AsO_4 = (8.10 g KH_2AsO_4)(1 mol KH_2AsO_4/180 g KH_2AsO_4)
                                      = 0.0450 mol KH_2AsO_4
       volume of solution = 0.0450 mol KH_2AsO_4/0.0500 M = 0.900 L.

45. V% = (V_{solute}/$V_{solution}$) x 100
   a. V% = (58.0 mL water/625 mL solution)(100%) = 9.28%
   b. V% = (79.1 mL acetone/755 mL solution)(100%) = 10.5%

47. 8.2% NaCl = 8.2 g NaCl/100 g solution.
    mass of NaCl = (3375 g solution)(8.2 g NaCl/100 g solution) = 277 g NaCl
    To prepare the solution, dissolve 277 g of NaCl in 3098 g of water.

49. 2.00% acetic acid, by volume = 2.00 L acetic acid/100 L of solution.
    volume of acetic acid = (2.00 L solution)(2.00 L acetic acid/100 L solution)
                          = 0.0400 L acetic acid
    Add enough water to 0.0400 L (40.0 mL) of acetic acid to bring the total volume of the solution to 2.00 L.

51. The first equation is correct. The second equation is not correct because it is not balanced. One of the criteria for a balanced equation in which some/all of the species are charged is that the sum of the charges on each side of the equation must be the same. In the case of the second equation, the charge on the reactant side (left side) of the equation is +2, while the charge on the product side (right side) of the equation is 3+.

53. a. $Hg(NO_3)_2(s) \rightarrow Hg(l) + 2\,NO_2(g) + O_2(g)$
    b. $Na_2CO_3(aq) + 2\,HCl\,(aq) \rightarrow H_2O(l) + CO_2(g) + 2\,NaCl(aq)$

55. a. Each mol of H_2 contains 2 mol of H atoms, so 1.00 mol of H_2 contains 2.00 mol of atoms. He is only composed of one atom, so 2.00 mol He is also 2.00 mol of He atoms. There are 4 mol of atoms/mol of C_2H_2 so 0.50 mol of C_2H_2 contains (0.50 mol)(4 mol atoms/mol C_2H_2) = 2.0 mol of atoms. All three samples contain the same number of atoms.
    b. The molar mass of H_2 is 2.0 g/mol, so 1.00 mol of H_2 has a mass of 2.0 g. The molar mass of He is 4.00 g/mol so 2.00 mol of He has a mass of 8.00 g. The molar mass of C_2H_2 is 26.0 g/mol so 0.50 mol of C_2H_2 has a mass of 13.0 g. The C_2H_2 sample has the largest mass.

57. The balanced equation is $CaCO_3 \rightarrow CaO + CO_2$.
    number of moles of $CaCO_3 = (4.72 \times 10^9\text{ g }CaCO_3)(1\text{ mol }CaCO_3/100.1\text{ g }CaCO_3)$
    $$= 4.72 \times 10^7\text{ mol .}$$
    number of moles of $CaO = (4.72 \times 10^7\text{ mol }CaCO_3)(1\text{ mol }CaO/1\text{ mol }CaCO_3)$
    $$= 4.72 \times 10^7\text{ mol.}$$
    mass of $CaO = (4.72 \times 10^7\text{ mol }CaO)(56.1\text{ g }CaO/\text{mol }CaO) = 2.65 \times 10^9\text{ g }CaO.$

59. mass of H_2O_2 solution in 1 bottle =
    (16.0 oz solution)(29.6 mL/1.00 oz)(1.00 g solution/mL solution) = 474 g solution
    mass of H_2O_2 in 1 bottle of solution = (474 g solution)(3 g H_2O_2/100 g solution) = 14.2 g
    number of mol of H_2O_2 in 1 bottle of solution = (14.2 g H_2O_2)(1 mol H_2O_2/34.0 g H_2O_2)
    $$= 0.418\text{ mol }H_2O_2$$

61. $V\% = (V_{solute}/V_{solution})(100\%)$
    a. $V\% = (567\text{ mL ethanol}/625\text{ mL solution})(100\%) = 90.7\%$
    b. $V\% = (10.00\text{ mL acetone}/1250\text{ mL solution})(100\%) = 0.800\%$

63. a. number of moles of $U = (1.00\text{ ymol U})(1 \times 10^{-24}\text{ mol}/1\text{ ymol}) = 1 \times 10^{-24}\text{ mol}$
    mass of $U = (1 \times 10^{-24}\text{ mol U})(238\text{ g U/mol U}) = 2.38 \times 10^{-22}\text{ g U}$
    $$= (2.38 \times 10^{-22}\text{ g U})(1\text{ yg}/1 \times 10^{-24}\text{ g}) = 238\text{ yg}$$

    b. number of U atoms = (1.00 zmol U)(1 $\times 10^{-21}$ mol/zmol)(6.02 $\times 10^{23}$ U atoms/mol U)
    $$= 602\text{ U atoms}$$

65. Volume of ethanol = (5.0 L blood)(1000 mL/L)(0.165 mL alcohol/100 mL blood) = 8.25 mL

67. According to Problem 25 in Chapter 1, the volume of water in all of Earth's oceans is $1.46 \times 10^9\text{ km}^3$. To evaluate the statement we need to convert the units of this volume to cm^3.

Volume, cm^3 = (1.46 x 10^9 km^3)(1000 m/km)^3(100 cm/m)^3 = 1.46 x 10^{24} cm^3

We can now calculate the number of cups of water present in all of Earth's oceans:

Number of cups = (1.46 x 10^{24} cm^3)(1 cup/236 cm^3) = 6.19 x 10^{21} cups

To calculate the number of molecules of water in 1 cup of water we use the density of water, 1.0 g/1.0 mL, to convert from volume to mass, and then we can convert the mass of water to the number of moles of water, using the molar mass of water, 18.0 g/mol. Finally, we can use Avogadro's number to calculate the number of water molecules in one cup of water.

Mass of water in 1 cup = (236 mL)(1.0 g H_2O/mL H_2O) = 236 g H_2O

Number of moles of water = (236 g H_2O)(1 mol H_2O/18.0 g H_2O) = 13.1 mol H_2O

Number of H_2O molecules = (13.1 mol H_2O)(6.02 x 10^{23} molecules/mol)
$$= 7.89 \times 10^{24} \text{ molecules}$$

The statement is valid.

69. The balanced chemical equation for the neutralization reaction is:
$$H_2SO_4 + 2\,NaHCO_3 \rightarrow Na_2SO_4 + 2\,H_2O + 2\,CO_2$$

mass of H_2SO_4 = (31,000 kg)(1000 g/1 kg) = 3.1 x 10^7 g H_2SO_4.

number of moles of H_2SO_4 spilled = (3.1 x 10^7 g H_2SO_4)(1 mol H_2SO_4/98.1 g $H_2\,SO_4$)
$$= 3.16 \times 10^5 \text{ mol } H_2\,SO_4.$$

number of moles of $NaHCO_3$ = (3.16 x 10^5 mol $H_2\,SO_4$)(2 mol $NaHCO_3$ / 1 mol H_2SO_4)
$$= 6.32 \times 10^5 \text{ mol.}$$

mass of $NaHCO_3$ required = (6.32 x 10^5 mol $NaHCO_3$)(84.0 g $NaHCO_3$/mol $NaHCO_3$)
$$= 5.31 \times 10^7 \text{ g or } 5.31 \times 10^4 \text{ kg.}$$

71. mass of water = (1 L)(1000 mL/L)(1.00 g/L) = 1000 g.

number of moles of H_2O = (1000 g H_2O)(1 mol H_2O/ 18.0 g H_2O) = 55.6 mol H_2O.

73. a. The balanced equations for each of the reactions are:
$$C_6H_{12}O_6 \rightarrow 2\,C_2H_6O + 2\,CO_2$$
$$C_2H_4 + H_2O \rightarrow C_2H_6O$$

b. For the first reaction, the molar masses of ethanol (C_2H_6O) and glucose ($C_6H_{12}O_6$) are 46.0 g/mol and 180.0 g/mol respectively.

% A.E. = [(2 mol C_2H_6O)(46.0 g C_2H_6O)/
(1 mol $C_6H_{12}O_6$)(180.0 g $C_6H_{12}O_6$/mol $C_6H_{12}O_6$)](100%) = 51.1%

For the second reaction, the molar masses of ethylene (C_2H_4) and water are 28.0 g/mol and 18.0 g/mol respectively.

% A.E. = (1 mol C_2H_6O)(46.0 g C_2H_6O/mol C_2H_6O)/
[(1 mol C_2H_4)(28.0 g C_2H_4/mol C_2H_4) + (1 mol H_2O)(18.0 g H_2O/mol H_2O)](100%)
= 100%

c. In the case of the first reaction, for every mole of ethanol produced, two moles of CO_2 are also produced and these are, in some respects, "waste." Therefore, the %A.E. for this reaction is, by definition, less than 100%. In the case of the second reaction, one mole of water is added to one mole of ethylene to form ethanol with no byproducts. Every reactant atom is incorporated into the reaction product, making the %A.E. = 100%.

d. The first preparation process is sustainable because the reactant, glucose, is obtainable from renewable crops (corn, switch grass, etc.). The second reaction is not sustainable because the reactant, ethylene, is a compound derived from a nonrenewable resource, petroleum.

60

e. For the long term, in spite of the fact that it produces CO_2, a compound that contributes to climate change, the second reaction is the reaction of choice. Finding ways of disposing or utilizing CO_2 will be a challenge if large-scale ethanol production continues, but the process has the advantage of not depleting our nonrenewable resource that is also used extensively for polymer and pharmaceutical production.

75. The balanced chemical equation is: $C_5H_{12} + 8 O_2 \rightarrow 5 CO_2 + 6 H_2O$.
   a. Percent atom economy = (molar mass of desired product/molar masses of all reactants)(100). Note that the coefficients in the balanced equation are taken into account as well. For this reaction, based on the CO_2 produced,
   mass of CO_2 = (5 mol CO_2)(44.0 g CO_2/mol CO_2) = 220 g.
   The masses of all the reactants = (1 mol C_5H_{12})(72.0 g C_5H_{12}/mol C_5H_{12}) +
   (8 mol O_2)(32.0 g O_2/mol O_2) = 328 g.
   Percent atom economy for this reaction = (220 g/328 g)(100%) = 67.1%.
   b. number of mol of C_5H_{12} reacted = (10.0 g C_5H_{12})(1 mol C_5H_{12}/72.0 g C_5H_{12}) = 0.139 mol
   number of mol of CO_2 produced = (0.139 mol C_5H_{12})(5 mol CO_2/mol C_5H_{12}) = 0.695 mol
   mass of CO_2 produced = (0.695 mol CO_2)(44.0 g CO_2/mol CO_2) = 30.6 g CO_2.
   c. percent yield = (experimental yield/theoretical yield)(100%)
   % yield = (25.4 g/30.6 g)(100%) = 83.0%.

Gases, Liquids, Solids ...

and Intermolecular Forces

CHAPTER SUMMARY

6.1 Solids, Liquids, and Gases
   A. In solids, particles are
     1. Highly ordered.
     2. Close together.
     3. Held together by ionic or intermolecular forces.
   B. In liquids, particles are
     1. More randomly arranged.
     2. Fairly close together.
     3. Less tightly held by ionic or intermolecular forces.
   C. In gases, particles
     1. Are moving rapidly in random directions.
     2. Are separated by great distances.
     3. Experience little or no attraction to one another.
   D. The three physical states can be changed into each other.
     1. Melting point: temperature at which a solid becomes a liquid.
     2. Vaporization: process of a liquid changing to a gas.
     3. Boiling point: temperature at which a liquid becomes a gas.
     4. Condensation: process of a gas changing to a liquid.
     5. Sublimation: process of a solid changing directly to a gas.

Answers to Self-Assessment Questions

1. b Molecules are farther from each other in the gas phase than in any other phase.
2. a Molecules in the liquid phase are difficult to compress because they are very close together, but have no definite shape because their organization is random.
3. d Vaporization occurs when the particles in the liquid phase gain enough energy to overcome attractions and enter the gas phase.
4. b Freezing occurs when the particles in a liquid lose energy and become more influenced by ionic or intermolecular forces.
5. c Sublimation occurs when a solid changes directly into a gas without proceeding through a liquid phase.

Green Chemistry: Supercritical Fluids
  A. Supercritical fluid.
    1. Critical point is the highest temperature and pressure at which a substance can exist in the liquid and gas phases.
    2. Above the critical point matter exists as neither a gas nor a liquid but as a hybrid called a supercritical fluid.
    3. Supercritical fluids have properties of both gases and liquids.
    4. Supercritical carbon dioxide ($scCO_2$) is particularly useful for many industrial processes including decaffeinating coffee, isolating flavors and fragrances, and as the active agent in dry cleaning.

6.2 Comparing Ionic and Molecular Compounds
  A. Compounds that experience strong intermolecular forces are either solids or liquids at room temperature and pressure. Under the same conditions, compounds without significant intermolecular forces are usually in the gas phase.
  B. Ionic compounds generally have much higher melting points and boiling points than molecular compounds.
    1. The amount of energy required to overcome ionic interactions is much greater than the amount of energy required to overcome intermolecular interactions.
  C. Many ionic compounds dissolve in water and form solutions that conduct electricity because they dissociate into ions. Molecular compounds usually form solutions that do not conduct electricity.
  D. As solids, most ionic compounds are crystalline, hard, and often brittle; solid molecular compounds are usually much softer.

Answers to Self-Assessment Questions

  1. c NaBr is an ionic compound and is not a molecule.
  2. c KBr is an ionic compound and has the strongest forces holding it together.

6.3 Forces between Molecules
  A. Dipole-dipole forces.
    1. Unsymmetrical molecules containing polar bonds are dipoles with centers of partially negative and partially positive charges.
    2. Polar molecules attract one another as the positive end of one molecule interacts with the negative end of another molecule. Dipole forces are weaker than ionic bonds but stronger than forces between nonpolar molecules of comparable size.
  B. Dispersion forces.
    1. Nonpolar compounds experience attractive intermolecular forces owing to momentary induced dipoles arising from the motions of electrons around the nuclei of atoms in the compound.
    2. These transient attractive forces, called dispersion forces, are fairly weak but are present in all molecules and increase as the size and number of electrons in the molecule increases.
    3. Dispersion forces can be substantial between large molecules, such as those in polymers.
    4. Although, individually, they are much weaker than dipole-dipole or ionic forces, dispersion forces exist between any two particles, whether polar, nonpolar, or ionic.
  C. Hydrogen bonds.
    1. Compounds containing H attached to small electronegative elements such as N, O, or F exhibit stronger intermolecular attractive forces than would be expected on the basis of dipole-dipole forces alone. These forces are called hydrogen bonds.

2. A hydrogen bond is much weaker than a covalent bond. The hydrogen bond is an interaction of the partially positive hydrogen of the donor molecule with the lone pair of nonbonding electrons on the F, O, or N of the acceptor molecule.
   a. Hydrogen bonds are usually represented by dotted lines.
   b. Hydrogen bonds are extremely important in biological molecules, including in establishing the three-dimensional structure of proteins, and the arrangement of the double strands of DNA.

Answers to Self-Assessment Questions

1. c Hydrogen bonding causes water to be held together much more strongly than is the case for other molecules of similar molar mass.
2. a Covalent bonds, which are involved in joining the atoms in a molecular structure, are much stronger than the forces which attract one molecule to another.
3. d Ethanol has an -OH group which can be involved in hydrogen bonding, as well as carbon-hydrogen bonds which can be involved in dispersion forces.
4. c Water molecules are attracted to other water molecules by intermolecular forces called hydrogen bonds.
5. c Hydrogen bonding occurs between molecules which include a hydrogen atom bonded to O, N, or F.
6. b Chloroform is a polar molecule, but its structure does not include a hydrogen atom bonded to O, N, or F.

6.4 Forces in Solutions
   A. Solutions.
      1. A solution is a homogeneous mixture of two or more substances.
      2. The solute is the substance being dissolved (the minor component).
      3. The solvent is the substance doing the dissolving (the major component).
   B. "Like dissolves like."
      1. Nonpolar substances dissolve best in nonpolar solvents; polar substances dissolve best in polar solvents.
      2. Salts dissolve in water because the ion-dipole forces overcome the ion-ion attractions.

Answers to Self-Assessment Questions

1. b Solutions are uniform throughout, or homogeneous.
2. a Ionic compounds with positive and negative charges are strongly attracted to each other. In order to dissolve in a solvent, the solvent-solute interactions must be as strong as the interactions between solute particles, and the only interactions that exist in nonpolar solvents are weak dispersion forces.
3. b Both I_2 and C_6H_{14} are non-polar covalent substances which give rise to dispersion-dispersion interactions.
4. b $CaCl_2$ is ionic and water is polar covalent, giving rise to ion-dipole interactions.
5. c Both acetic acid and water can form hydrogen bonds.
6. a Octane is a non-polar covalent substance and will dissolve non-polar covalent $CH_3(CH_2)_4CH_3$.

6.5 Gases: The Kinetic-Molecular Theory
   A. Kinetic-molecular theory.
      1. Gas particles are in rapid constant motion and move in straight lines.

2. Particles of a gas are small compared with the distances between them.
3. Because the particles of a gas are so far apart, there is very little attraction between them.
4. Particles of a gas collide with one another. Energy is conserved in these collisions; energy lost by one particle is gained by the other.
5. Temperature is a measure of the average kinetic energy (energy of motion) of the gas particles.

Answers to Self-Assessment Questions

1. b The kinetic molecular theory does not address pressure and volume relationships of a gas.
2. c The gas particles are very much smaller than the volume occupied by the gas.
3. d Energy is conserved when gas particles collide.

6.6 The Simple Gas Laws
   A. Boyle's law: For a given amount of gas at constant temperature, the volume of the gas varies inversely with its pressure ($P_1V_1 = P_2V_2$).
   B. Charles's law: The volume of a fixed amount of a gas at constant pressure is directly proportional to its absolute (Kelvin) temperature ($V_1/T_1 = V_2/T_2$).
      1. When the volume of gas reaches zero, the temperature is at absolute zero.
   C. The molar volume of a gas is equal to 22.4 L at STP.
      1. The molar volume is the volume occupied by 1 mole of any gas if measured at STP (standard temperature and pressure: 0 °C and 1 atm).
         a. Use the molar volume (22.4 L) to calculate the density of any gas for which the molecular formula is known.

Answers to Self-Assessment Questions

1. b Gas particles striking vessel walls cause pressure.
2. d Boyle's law states that the pressure of a gas is inversely proportional to its volume.
3. b $P_1V_1 = P_2V_2$, $P_2 = (2.00 \text{ atm})(6.00 \text{ L})/(1.50 \text{ L}) = 8.00$ atm.
4. d The Kelvin temperature scale must be used. To halve the volume, the Kelvin temperature must be halved.
5. b Both flasks have the same number of particles because they have the same pressure and temperature. NO has a smaller molar mass than NO_2, so flask A weighs less than Flask B.
6. a 1 mol of a gas at STP occupies 22.4 L.
      number of mol of gas = (5.60 L)(1 mol gas/22.4 L) = 0.250 mol

6.7 The Ideal Gas Law
When Boyle's law and Charles's law are combined, the equation $PV = nRT$ is obtained in which n is the number of moles of gas in the sample and R is the universal gas constant with a value of 0.0821 L ·atm/mol ·K.

Answers to Self-Assessment Questions

1. c n stands for the number of moles of gas in the sample.
2. c $P_1V_1/T_1 = P_2V_2/T_2$
      $V_2 = P_1V_1T_2/T_1P_2$
      $V_2 = (1 \text{ atm})(22.4 \text{ L})(293 \text{ K})/(273 \text{ K})(1 \text{ atm}) = 24.0$ L
      Note: you could also solve this problem using the ideal gas law:

$$PV = nRT \text{ so } V = (nRT)/P$$
$$V = [(1.00 \text{ mol})(0.0821 \text{ L·atm/mol·K})(273 + 20 \text{ K})]/1 \text{ atm} = 24.1 \text{ L}$$

3.   b $P_1V_1/T_1 = P_2V_2/T_2$

$$V_2 = P_1V_1T_2/T_1P_2$$
$$V_2 = (1 \text{ atm})(22.4 \text{ L})(546 \text{ K})/(273 \text{ K})(2 \text{ atm}) = 22.4 \text{ L}$$

Note: you could also solve this problem using the ideal gas law:
$$PV = nRT \text{ so } V = (nRT)/P$$
$$V = [(1 \text{ mol})(0.0821 \text{ L·atm/mol·K})(546 \text{ K})]/2 \text{ atm} = 22.4 \text{ L}$$

LEARNING OBJECTIVES

You should be able to…

1. Explain how the different properties of solids, liquids, and gases are related to the motion and spacing of atoms, molecules, or ions.   (6.1)

2. Identify some differences between ionic and molecular substances, and explain why these differences exist.   (6.2)

3. Classify forces between molecules as dipole-dipole forces, dispersion forces, or hydrogen bonds.   (6.3)

4. Explain why nonpolar solutes tend to dissolve in nonpolar solvents and polar and ionic solutes tend to dissolve in polar solvents.   (6.4)

5. List the five basic concepts of the kinetic-molecular theory of gases.   (6.5)

6. State the three simple gas laws, by name and mathematically.   (6.6)

7. Use any gas law to find the value of one variable if the other values are given.   (6.6)

8. State the ideal gas law, and use it to calculate one of the quantities if the others are given.   (6.7)

9. Describe how green chemistry principle 3 must be considered in designing chemical reactions and processes.

10. Identify the properties that make supercritical fluids applicable in greener chemical processes.

DISCUSSION

Chapter 6 discusses the properties of the physical states: solids, liquids, and gases. These properties are explained by the type of ionic or intermolecular attractions between particles. These forces are determined by the type of bonds within the particle: polar molecules give rise to dipole-dipole interactions; molecules including one or more hydrogen atoms bonded to oxygen, nitrogen, or fluorine atoms gives rise to hydrogen-bonding; and nonpolar molecules give rise to dispersion interactions. The gas laws summarize data concerning volume, temperature, pressure, and the number of moles of gases.

Utilization of supercritical fluids to replace otherwise hazardous solvent illustrates the green chemical approach to using less hazardous materials and recycling the materials that are used.

Sample Gas Law Problems

Boyle's law, Charles's law, and the ideal gas law quantitatively describe the behavior of gases. Here are some worked examples:

The pressure of a 4.0 L sample of He gas is increased from 5.0 atm to 7.0 atm. What is the new volume?

$$P_1V_1 = P_2V_2$$

$$V_2 = P_1V_1/P_2$$

$$V_2 = (5.0\ atm)(4.0\ L)/7.0\ atm$$

$$V_2 = 2.9\ L$$

The temperature of a 4.0 L sample of He gas is increased from 10 °C to 100 °C. What is the new volume, assuming the pressure is held constant?

First, convert the temperature to Kelvin: 10 °C = 283 K, 100 °C = 373 K

Then list your variables: $T_1 = 283$ K; $T_2 = 373$; $V_1 = 4.0$ L; and V_2 is the unknown

$$V_1/T_1 = V_2/T_2$$

$$V_2 = T_2V_1/T_1$$

$$V_2 = (373\ K)(4.0\ L)/283\ K = 5.3\ L$$

Use the ideal gas law to calculate the volume of 3.0 mol of He gas at 473 K and 2.0 atm.

Always list your variables. This helps you to know which formula to use.

V= unknown; P = 2 atm; n = 3 mol; T = 473 K, R = 0.0821 L atm/mol K

PV = nRT

V = nRT/P

V = (3.0 mol)(0.0821 L atm/mol K)(473K)/(2.0 atm) = 58 L

ANSWERS TO ODD-NUMBERED REVIEW QUESTIONS AND SOLUTIONS FOR ODD-NUMBERED END OF CHAPTER PROBLEMS

Review Questions

1. Solids and liquids are both composed of particles (atoms, molecules, and/or ions). In both cases, the particles are tightly held together, are compact, difficult to compress, and have a definite volume. But while most solids are highly ordered with particles in fixed positions, liquid particles are

randomly arranged and free to move, leading to a definite shape for solids and indefinite shape for liquids.

3. a. Ionic interactions are the forces that attract cations (positively charged ions) to anions (negatively charged ions) in ionic compounds. Sodium chloride, NaCl, is an example of an ionic compound.

    b. Dipole-dipole interactions are the attractions between nonsymmetrical polar covalent compounds. The attractions between molecules of formaldehyde, $H_2C=O$, are an example of dipole-dipole interactions.

    c. Hydrogen bonding is a special kind of dipole-dipole interaction that exists between compounds with one or more H atoms bonded to N, O, or F atoms. Water (H_2O), ethyl alcohol (CH_3CH_2OH), and ammonia (NH_3) are substances that can form hydrogen bonds.

    d. Dispersion forces are the strongest interactions that exist between nonpolar molecules. Although a dispersion force is weaker than a hydrogen bond, a dipole-dipole interaction, or an ionic interaction, when nonpolar molecules with high molar masses experience dispersion forces along their entire lengths, the sum effect of the forces can cause the substances to be solids at room temperature. Carbon tetrachloride, CCl_4, is an example of a compound that experiences dispersion forces.

5. In the combined gas law, the volume is inversely proportional to pressure. In the combined gas law, the volume is directly proportional to the absolute temperature.

Problems

7. b. and d. Both methyl amine (CH_3NH_2) and methyl alcohol (CH_3OH) can engage in hydrogen bonding. There is an N-H bond in methyl amine and an O-H bond in methyl alcohol. While c. has a F atom, it is not bonded directly to H.

9. HBr has polar covalent bonds resulting in dipole-dipole forces. Br_2 is nonpolar covalent, and NaBr is an ionic compound.

11. KNO_3 is an ionic compound which would not dissolve in hexane (C_6H_{14}). The attraction between K^+ and NO_3^- ions in KNO_3 is too strong to be broken up by the dispersion forces that exist between C_6H_{14} molecules.

13. $P_1V_1 = P_2V_2$
    a. $V_2 = P_1V_1/P_2$
       $V_2 = (719 \text{ mmHg})(1820 \text{ mL})/(752 \text{ mmHg}) = 1740 \text{ mL}$
    b. $P_2 = P_1V_1/V_2$
       $P_2 = (719 \text{ mmHg})(1820 \text{ mL})/(345 \text{ mL}) = 3790 \text{ mmHg}$

15. a. $P_1V_1 = P_2V_2$
       $V_2 = P_1V_1/P_2$
       $V_2 = (150 \text{ atm})(60.0 \text{ L})/(0.925 \text{ atm}) = 9730 \text{ L}$
    b. time $= (9730 \text{ L})(1 \text{ min}/6.00 \text{ L}) = 1620 \text{ min.}$

17. $V_1/T_1 = V_2/T_2$
    $V_2 = T_2V_1/T_1$
    $V_2 = (351 \text{ K})(5.90 \text{ L})/299 \text{ K} = 6.93 \text{ L}$

19. $V_1/T_1 = V_2/T_2$
    $T_2 = T_1 V_2/V_1$ and $V_2 = 3V_1$
    $T_2 = (T_1)(3V_1)/V_1$
    $T_2 = 3\,T_1$ or the temperature would be tripled; $3 \times 273\ K = 819\ K$.

21. a. 22.4 L
    b. $V = (1.75\ mol)(22.4\ L/mol) = 39.2\ L$.
    c. $V = (0.225\ mol)(22.4\ L/mol) = 5.04\ L$.

23. 1 mol of Rn has a mass of 222 g and a volume of 22.4 L at STP.
    The density is $222\ g/22.4\ L = 9.91\ g/L$

25. $d = mass/volume$. $mass = d \times volume$. The molar volume at STP is 22.4 L.
    a. molar mass $= (2.12\ g/L)(22.4\ L) = 47.5\ g/mol$
    b. molar mass $= (2.97\ g/L)(22.4\ L) = 66.5\ g/mol$

27. a. The volume of the gas will decrease. Volume and pressure are inversely proportional at constant
       temperature. When the pressure is increased, the volume must decrease.
    b. The volume of the gas will decrease. Volume and pressure are directly proportional to one
       another at constant temperature; when one decreases the other must also decrease.
    c. The volume of the gas will increase. The pressure decrease will cause an increase in volume, and
       the temperature increase will also cause in increase in volume. One way to test this would be to
       make up some values, for example, for one mole of a gas ($n = 1$), $V = 22.4\ L$ at $T = 273\ K$ and P
       $= 1$ atm. Then calculate a new volume for the same 1-mol sample when $T = 373$ and $P = 0.5$ atm.

29. a. If the molecules of a gas move more slowly, then the temperature will decrease.
    b. If the molecules of a gas hit the walls of a container less often, then the pressure will decrease.
31. $PV = nRT$
    a. $V = nRT/P$
       $V = (0.00600\ mol)(0.0821\cdot L\ atm/mol\cdot K)(304\ K)/(0.870\ atm) = 0.172\ L$
    b. $P = nRT/V$
       $P = (0.0108\ mol)(0.0821\cdot L\ atm/mol\cdot K)(310\ K)/(0.265\ L) = 1.04\ atm$

33. $PV = nRT$
    $n = PV/RT$
    $n = (0.918\ atm)(0.555\ L)/(0.0821\ L\cdot atm/mol\cdot K)(298\ K) = 0.0208\ mol$

35. Equal molar amounts of gases occupy the same volume, so 0.75 mol of He would occupy the same
    volume as is occupied by 0.75 mol of H_2. The mass of He in that volume would be:
    $mass = (0.75\ mol\ He)(4.0\ g\ He/mol\ He) = 3.0\ g\ He$.

37. Answers b, c, and d are correct. Option a results in an increase in volume.

39. The density of a gas is proportional to its molar mass. Each gas occupies 22.4 L/mol at STP so the
    higher the molar mass, the higher the density. Of the choices, PF_3 has the largest molar mass so it has
    the greatest density. For example: The molar mass of SO_3 is 80.1 g/mol and its density is (80.1
    g/mol)/22.4 L/mol $= 3.58\ g/L$ while the molar mass of PF_3 is 88.0 g/mol and its density is (88.0
    g/mol)/22.4 L/mol $= 3.93\ g/L$.

41. $V_1/T_1 = V_2/T_2$
    $V_2 = T_2V_1/T_1$
    $V_2 = (77 \text{ K}) (1.50 \text{ L})/(293 \text{ K}) = 0.394 \text{ L}$

43. a. Because all three flasks are the same size (volume), the number of moles of gas in each flask is the same. Because each of the samples, Ne, Ar, and Kr, are monoatomic gases, the number of atoms is the same in each flask.
    b. The gas with the greatest density is the gas with the highest molar mass. In this case that gas is Kr (flask Z).
    c. The pressure will be higher in Flask X (the one that was heated) because the molecules in it will be moving faster than those in Flask Y and will contact the flask walls at a higher velocity, creating a higher pressure.
    d. As long as the flasks are kept closed, the number of atoms in all three is identical so the same number of moles of gas will be present in all three of the flasks.

45. $P_1/T_1 = P_2/T_2$
    $P_2 = T_2P_1/T_1$
    $P_2 = (283 \text{ K}) (1.32 \text{ atm})/(298 \text{ K}) = 1.25 \text{ atm.}$

47. Use $PV = nRT$ and $n = \text{mass/molar mass}$ to get
    $PV = (\text{mass/molar mass}) RT$
    $\text{mass}/V = \text{density}$. Therefore, $d = (\text{molar mass})P/RT$
    $\text{molar mass} = dRT/P$
    Because R has units of L·atm/mol·K, P must be converted to atm.
    $P = (750 \text{ mmHg})(1 \text{ atm}/760 \text{ mmHg}) = 0.987 \text{ atm}$
    $\text{molar mass} = (2.34 \text{ g/L})(0.0821 \text{ L·atm/mol·K})(300 \text{ K})/(0.987 \text{ atm})$
    $\text{molar mass} = 58.4 \text{ g/mol}$ which is close to 58 g for C_4H_{10}.

49. The answer is e, all of the considerations listed in a–d are important. To be an effective green chemistry solvent, a substance must have the same kind of intermolecular interactions as the solute (if the solute is polar, then the solvent must be polar as well), the solute must be able to be isolated and removed from the solvent so the solvent can be reused, the solvent must be safe to use (both nonflammable and nontoxic).

51. Perchloroethylene, previously used in the dry cleaning industry, has been replaced with $scCO_2$, and methylene chloride has been replaced by $scCO_2$ for the decaffeination of coffee.

CHAPTER

7

Acids and Bases

Please Pass the Protons

CHAPTER SUMMARY

7.1   Acids and Bases: Experimental Definitions
    A. Characteristic properties of acids.
       1. Taste sour.
       2. Turn blue litmus indicator dye red.
       3. Dissolve active metals to produce H_2 gas.
       4. React with bases to produce water and ionic compounds called salts.
    B. Characteristic properties of bases.
       1. Taste bitter.
       2. Turn red litmus indicator dye blue.
       3. Feel slippery.
       4. React with acid to form water and ionic compounds called salts.

Answers to Self-Assessment Questions

1. a   Bases feel slippery on the skin.
2. b   Bases do not react with salts to form acids. Bases react with acids to form salts and water.
3. d   Acids and bases neutralize each other to form a salt (an ionic compound) and water.
4. d   Yogurt is a milk product containing lactic acid.
5. d   Citric acid is a component of grapefruit.

7.2   Acids, Bases, and Salts
    A. The Arrhenius theory of acids and bases.
       1. An acid is a molecular substance that breaks up (ionizes) in aqueous solution into hydrogen
         ions (H^+, also called protons) and anions.
         a. Chemists often indicate an acid by writing the formula with the H atom(s) first:
             $HC_2H_3O_2$, HNO_3.
       2. In water, the properties of acids are those of the H^+ ions.
       3. Bases are substances that release hydroxide ions (OH^-) in aqueous solution.

a. Ionic hydroxides (for example, NaOH, KOH) dissolve in water rather than reacting with it.
4. In water, the properties of bases are those of the OH^- ions.
5. Neutralization is the reaction of an acid and a base: the cation that was part of the base combines with the anion that was part of the acid to form a salt; the H^+ ion(s) from the acid combines with the OH^- ion(s) from the base to form water.

B. Limitations of the Arrhenius theory.
1. Free protons (H^+) do not exist in water. H^+ ions react with H_2O molecules to form H_3O^+ ions, called hydronium ions.
2. The Arrhenius theory does not explain why ammonia (NH_3) is basic.
3. The Arrhenius theory applies only to aqueous solutions and not to solutions with other kinds of solvents.

C. Bronsted-Lowry acids-base theory.
1. An acid is a proton donor.
2. A base is a proton acceptor.
a. Explains why NH_3 is basic: $NH_3 + H_2O \leftrightarrow NH_4^+ + OH^-$

D. Salts.
1. Salts are ionic compounds formed from neutralization reactions of acids and bases.
2. Salts that dissolve in water form solutions that conduct electricity.

E. Green chemistry: sustainability: it's basic (and acidic).
1. Sustainability means meeting the needs of the present generation without compromising the ability of future generations to meet their needs.
2. Example: soap making:
a. Fats are heated with aqueous lye (NaOH) forming 3 mol of soap and 1 mol of glycerol.
3. Example: biofuel production:
a. Fats are heated with methyl alcohol (CH_3OH) to form esters (biodiesel fuel).
4. Example: polylactic acid (PLA)
a. PLA is a biodegradable and renewable plastic made from chemicals derived from corn.
b. Used PLA materials can be converted into antimicrobial cleaning solution.
5. All three examples illustrate ways of recycling and using what would otherwise be waste materials.

Answers to Self-Assessment Questions

1. e CH_3COOH is acetic acid which is found in vinegar.
2. c H_3BO_3 is a mild antiseptic.
3. d HCl reacts with $CaCO_3$, the main component of boiler scale.
4. a H_2SO_4 is found in car batteries.
5. b NaOH is used in soap-making to convert fats into soaps and glycerol.
6. d When dissolved in water, HBr forms H_3O^+ and Br^- ions.
7. c An Arrhenius acid produces H^+ in water.
8. d An Arrhenius base produces OH^- in water.
9. b A Bronsted acid is a proton (H^+) donor.
10. a A Bronsted base is a proton (H^+) acceptor.

7.3 Acidic and Basic Anhydrides
A. Nonmetal oxides are called acid anhydrides. They form acids when added to water.
B. Metal oxides are called basic anhydrides. They form bases when added to water.

Answers to Self-Assessment Questions

1. c   Subtract 2 H atoms and 1 O atom from H_2SeO_4 to get SeO_3.
2. a   Subtract 2 H atoms and 1 O atom from $Zn(OH)_2$ to get ZnO.

7.4   **Strong and Weak Acids and Bases**
    A. Strong acids are those that ionize completely in aqueous solutions.
$$HCl + H_2O \rightarrow H_3O^+ + Cl^-$$
      1. Strong acids (a list worth remembering): HCl, H_2SO_4, HNO_3, HBr, HI, $HClO_4$.
      2. Note: The term "strong" relates only to the extent to which an acid ionizes in water and NOT to the concentration of the acid solution. The terms we use to denote relative concentrations are "concentrated" and "dilute."
    B. Weak acids ionize only slightly in aqueous solutions. (A mole of HCN in 1 L of water solution is only 1.0 % ionized.)
$$HCN + H_2O \leftrightarrow H_3O^+ + CN^-$$
    C. Strong bases are those that ionize completely, or nearly so, in water.
      1. Strong bases (information worth remembering): All Group 1A metal hydroxides, all Group 2A metal hydroxides except $Be(OH)_2$, remembering that both $Ca(OH)_2$ and $Mg(OH)_2$ are only slightly soluble in water so the OH^- concentrations in those solutions is not high.
      2. Note: The term "strong" relates only to the extent to which the dissolved base provides OH^- ions in solution, NOT to the concentration of the base solution. The terms we use to denote relative concentrations are "concentrated" and "dilute."
    D. Weak bases are those that yield relatively few hydroxide ions when dissolved in water.

Answers to Self-Assessment Questions

1. b $Ca(OH)_2$ is a strong base (on the list of strong bases: a Group 2A metal hydroxide).
2. c   HCN is a weak acid (not on the list of strong acids).
3. c   HF is a weak acid (not on the list of strong acids).
4. a HNO_3 is a strong acid (on the list of strong acids).
5. c H_3PO_4 is a weak acid (not on the list of strong acids).
6. b   KOH is a strong base (on the list of strong bases: a Group 1A metal hydroxide).
7. d NH_3 is a weak base (not on the list of strong bases).
8. c   The reaction is $CH_3COOH + H_2O \leftrightarrow CH_3COO^- + H_3O^+$.
9. b   The reaction is $NH_3 + H_2O \leftrightarrow NH_4^+ + OH^-$.

7.5   **Neutralization**
    A. In water, an acid will release H_3O^+. When combined with an equivalent amount of base that releases OH^-, a neutralization reaction combining H_3O^+ (acid) and OH^- (base) will produce water and a salt.

$$HCl + NaOH \rightarrow H_2O + NaCl$$
$$Acid + Base \rightarrow Water + Salt$$
$$H_3O^+ + OH^- \rightarrow H_2O$$

Answers to Self-Assessment Questions

1. d   Neutralization occurs when an acid and base are mixed.
2. b   The balanced chemical equation for the reaction of HCl with NaOH shows that 1 mol of HCl reacts with 1 mol of NaOH (HCl + NaOH → NaCl + H$_2$O). We can calculate the number of moles of HCl required using this stoichiometric ratio.
     Number of mol of HCl = (1.5 mol NaOH)(1 mol HCl)/(1 mol NaOH) = 1.5 mol HCl.

3. d   The balanced chemical equation for the neutralization of Ca(OH)$_2$ with HCl is
     2 HCl + Ca(OH)$_2$ → CaCl$_2$ + 2 H$_2$O
     We can use the stoichiometric relationship to calculate the number of moles of HCl required to neutralize 2.4 mol of Ca(OH)$_2$:
     Number of mol of HCl = (2.4 mol Ca(OH)$_2$)(2 mol HCl/mol Ca(OH)$_2$) = 4.8 mol HCl.
4. c   The balanced chemical equation for the neutralization of H$_3$PO$_4$ with NaOH is:
     H$_3$PO$_4$ + 3 NaOH → Na$_3$PO$_4$ + 3 H$_2$O
     We can use the stoichiometric relationship to calculate the number of moles of NaOH required to neutralize 1 mol of H$_3$PO$_4$:
     Number of moles of NaOH = (1 mol H$_3$PO$_4$)(3 mol NaOH/mol H$_3$PO$_4$) = 4.5 mol NaOH.

7.6   The pH Scale
   A. pH is a measure of the molar concentration (M = mol/L) of H$_3$O$^+$. We express the molar concentration of a solute by putting its chemical formula in square brackets: [H$_3$O$^+$].
      1. pH is defined as the negative logarithm of the molar concentration of hydrogen ion:
      $$pH = -\log [H^+]$$
      2. On the pH scale, a H$^+$ concentration of 1 x 10^{-7} mol/L of hydrogen ions becomes a pH of 7; a H$^+$ concentration of 1 x 10^{-10} mol/L becomes a pH of 10; and so on.
      3. Interpreting pH.
         a. Solutions with pH < 7.0 are acidic.
         b. Solutions with pH = 7.0 are neutral.
         c. Solutions with pH > 7.0 are basic.
      4. Acidic solutions contain a higher concentration of H$^+$ ions than of OH$^-$ ions.
         Basic solutions contain higher concentration of OH$^-$ ions than of H$^+$ ions.
         Neutral solutions contain equal concentrations of H$^+$ and OH$^-$ ions.

Answers to Self-Assessment Questions

1. b   HNO$_3$ is a strong acid. Change 0.0010 M HNO$_3$ to scientific notation to get 1.0 x 10^{-3} M.
2. d   The negative logarithm of 1 x 10^{-11} is 11.
3. c   Find the antilog of -8 to get 1.0 x 10^{-8}, or the molar concentration of H$^+$ in the pool water.
4. c   The concentrations of H$^+$ and OH$^-$ ions in pure water are the same: 1.0 x 10^{-7} M. The pH of pure water is 7.0.
5. b   HCl is a strong acid so the H$^+$ ion concentration in 0.15 M HCl is 0.15 M. The pH of this solution is slightly lower than the pH of a solution with [H$^+$] = 0.10 M, which would be 1.0 so pH = 0.82 makes sense.
6. d   An 0.15 M solution of NaOH should be extremely basic. pH = 13.18 is the most sensible answer.
7. e   This is close to pH 7 but slightly basic. If the H$^+$ concentration were 1.0 x 10^{-8}, the pH would be 8.0, not 7.4. Because a solution with pH = 7.4 contains a slightly higher concentration of H$^+$ ions than one of pH = 8.0, [H$^+$] = 4 x 10^{-8} M is a reasonable choice.

7.7 Buffers and Conjugate Acid-Base Pairs
  A. A conjugate acid-base pair is a pair of compounds the formulas of which differ by one proton (H^+). For example, NO_3^- is the conjugate base of the acid HNO_3, and NH_4^+ is the conjugate acid of NH_3.
  B. A buffer is a solution that resists change in pH upon addition of small amounts of acid or base.
    1. A buffer solution contains a weak acid and the salt of that weak acid (for example, HF and NaF) or
    2. A buffer solution contains a weak base and the salt of that weak base (for example, NH_3 and NH_4Cl).

Answers to Self-Assessment Questions

1. b HCN and CN^- have a common anion and differ only by H^+. HCN is a weak acid and CN^- is the conjugate base of that weak acid.
2. d Only NH_3 and H_3O^+ do not share a common ion.
3. a $HCOO^-$ is the base in this buffer and will react with added H^+ to form HCOOH.
4. a C_6H_5COOH and C_6H_5COONa share a common ion. C_6H_5COOH is a weak acid and $C_6H_5COO^-$ is the conjugate base of that weak acid.

7.8 Acids and Bases in Industry and in Daily Life
  A. Acid rain.
    1. All rain is slightly acidic because atmospheric CO_2 dissolves in the falling raindrops, forming carbonic acid, H_2CO_3, which ionizes to form H^+ and HCO_3^- ions.
  B. Antacids: a basic remedy.
    1. Antacids work to neutralize excess stomach acid.
    2. Sodium bicarbonate, $NaHCO_3$, was one of the earliest antacids. This compound works by combining with H^+ to form H_2CO_3 which breaks down to form CO_2 and H_2O.
    3. Other compounds commonly used in antacids are calcium carbonate, $CaCO_3$, aluminum hydroxide, $Al(OH)_3$, magnesium carbonate, $MgCO_3$, and magnesium hydroxide, $Mg(OH)_2$.
    4. "Acid rain" is produced when acidic pollutants such as sulfur oxides and nitrogen oxides present in the atmosphere dissolve in the rain.
  C. Why doesn't stomach acid dissolve the stomach?
    1. A mucus layer protects the cells lining the stomach from stomach acid.
    2. Bacterial infections can damage the mucus, exposing the cells to stomach acid and causing ulcer formation.
  D. Acids and bases in industry and at home.
    1. Sulfuric acid, H_2SO_4, is the leading chemical product in the US and around the world. H_2SO_4 is used to make fertilizers and other industrial chemicals, as well as in car batteries.
    2. Hydrochloric acid, HCl, is also called muriatic acid and is used in construction.
    3. Lime, calcium oxide (CaO), is the most widely used commercial base. CaO is prepared by heating limestone ($CaCO_3$) to drive off CO_2.
    4. Sodium hydroxide, NaOH, is used in such products as oven cleaners and drain cleaners, as well as to make soaps.
    5. Ammonia, NH_3, is used for fertilizers.
  E. Acids and bases in health and disease.
    1. Strong acids and bases can break down, or denature, proteins.
    2. Living cells can function properly only at an optimal pH.

Answers to Self-Assessment Questions

1. a   Calcium carbonate reacts with excess H^+ to form H_2CO_3 which then decomposes to produce CO_2 and H_2O.
2. a   Acidic solutions have low pHs. When some of the acid is neutralized, the concentration of H^+ decreases slightly, causing the stomach pH to rise slightly.
3. d H_2SO_4 is the leading chemical product not only in the US, but worldwide as well.
4. d   One of the uses of H_2SO_4 is in automobile batteries.
5. c   Aqueous solutions of lye (NaOH) are used to convert fats to soaps and glycerol.

LEARNING OBJECTIVES

You should be able to...

1. Distinguish between acids and bases using their chemical and physical properties. (7.1)

2. Explain how an acid-base indicator works. (7.1)

3. Identify Arrhenius and Bronsted-Lowry acids and bases. (7.2)

4. Write a balanced equation for a neutralization or an ionization. (7.2)

5. Identify acidic and basic anhydrides, and write equations showing their reactions with water. (7.3)

6. Define and identify strong and weak acids and bases. (7.4)

7. Identify the reactants and predict the products in a neutralization reaction. (7.5)

8. Describe the relationship between the pH of a solution and its acidity or basicity. (7.6)

9. Find the molar concentration of hydrogen ion, $[H^+]$, from a pH value or the pH value from $[H^+]$. (7.6)

10. Write the formula for the conjugate base of an acid or for the conjugate acid of a base. (7.7)

11. Describe the action of a buffer. (7.7)

12. Describe everyday uses of acids and bases and how they affect daily life. (7.8)

13. Write equations for the production of soap and of biofuel.

14. Describe ways by which acids and bases can contribute to greener production of consumer products.

DISCUSSION

We will begin by reviewing the definitions of acids. Acids are defined in the chapter in two ways: as compounds that yield hydronium ions in aqueous solutions and as compounds that act as proton donors. It is now generally accepted that a hydrogen ion does not exist in solution as an independent unit. Thus, the second definition is an attempt to be a bit more accurate in describing the action of an acid.

Since the H^+ ion is only a proton (a nuclear particle), it only exists in water associated with H_2O as the H_3O^+ ion, called the hydronium ion. There are many practical aspects of acids and bases that you should learn: their properties, their sources (acid and base anhydrides), whether strong or weak, the pH scale, and their applications. Practice writing formulas and equations for each of these.

Minimizing the environmental impacts of acids and bases, as well as finding ways to reuse what would otherwise be waste products is important to the welfare of future generations. Soap-making and biofuel synthesis create useful products from waste fats and oils. Polylactic acid disposable tableware can be recycled into cleaning products rather than sent to landfills or incinerated.

ANSWERS TO ODD-NUMBERED REVIEW QUESTIONS AND SOLUTIONS FOR ODD-NUMBERED END OF CHAPTER PROBLEMS

Review Questions

1. a. Arrhenius said an acid is a substance that donates H+ to water. Bronsted-Lowry defined an acid as a substance that donates one or more H^+ ions to a solution. H_2SO_4, sulfuric acid, is an example.
    b. An Arrhenius base is a compound that donates one or more OH^- ions to a solution. According to the Bronsted-Lowry definition, a base is a proton acceptor. KOH, potassium hydroxide, is an example.
    c. A salt is an ionic compound formed from the neutralization of an acid with a base. K_2SO_4, potassium sulfate, is the salt formed by the reaction of H_2SO_4 and KOH.

3. a. Acidic solutions turning litmus red, taste sour, dissolve active metals to produce hydrogen gas, and react with bases to form salts.
    b. Basic solutions turn litmus blue, taste bitter, feel slippery on the skin, and react with acids to form salts.

5. Strong bases ionize in water, producing OH^- to the extent that they are soluble. Weak bases also react with water to produce OH^- ions, but only 5% or less of the weak base species in solution undergo the reaction.

7. An acid anhydride is a nonmetal oxide that reacts with water to form an acid. A base anhydride is a metal oxide that reacts with water to form a base.

9. Because magnesium hydroxide is only slightly soluble, it can be safely used as an antacid.

11. Alkalosis occurs when the blood is too alkaline so its pH is too high. One circumstance that promotes alkalosis is the overuse of the antacid sodium bicarbonate.

Problems

13.
$$HClO_4 \xrightarrow{H_2O} H^+ + ClO_4^-.$$

15.
$$RbOH \xrightarrow{H_2O} Rb^+ + OH^-.$$

17. a. The N atom in $(CH_3)_2NH$ shares its nonbonded electron pair with a H^+ ion released from H_2O and is therefore a base.
   b. The N atom in $C_6H_5NH_2$ shares its nonbonded electron pair with an H^+ ion released from H_2O and is therefore a base.
   c. $C_6H_5CH_2NH_2$ shares its nonbonded electron pair with an H^+ ion released from H_2O and is therefore a base.

19. $HCl(g) + H_2O(l) \rightarrow H_3O^+(aq) + Cl^-(aq)$. The acid formed through this reaction is hydrochloric acid.

21. $$NH_3(aq) + H_2O \longrightarrow NH_4^+(aq) + OH^-(aq)$$

23. a. HCl: $HCl(g)$ is hydrogen chloride; $HCl(aq)$ is hydrochloric acid.
   b. $Sr(OH)_2$
   c. KOH is potassium hydroxide.
   d. H_3BO_3

25. a. H_3PO_4 is phosphoric acid, an acid.
   b. CsOH is cesium hydroxide, a base.
   c. H_2CO_3 is carbonic acid, an acid.

27. a. HNO_3 is nitric acid, so the formula for nitrous acid is HNO_2.
   b. H_3PO_4 is phosphoric acid, so the formula for phosphorus acid is H_3PO_3.

29. a. $SO_3 + H_2O \rightarrow H_2SO_4$. An acid is produced when a nonmetal oxide reacts with water. H_2SO_4 is sulfuric acid, an acid.
   b. $MgO + H_2O \rightarrow Mg(OH)_2$. A base is produced when a metal oxide reacts with water. $Mg(OH)_2$ is magnesium hydroxide, a base.

31. HI is a strong acid because all the HI molecules ionize and form H^+ and I^- ions when the substance is added to water.

33. CH_3NH_2 is a weak base because only a few of the dissolved molecules react with water to form $CH_3NH_3^+$ and OH^- ions.

35. a. LiOH is a strong base (it's a Group 1A hydroxide).
   b. HBr is a strong acid (it's on the list of strong acids).
   c. HNO_2 is a weak acid. It is not on the list of strong acids, although you have to look carefully because nitric acid, HNO_3, is on the list.
   d. $CuSO_4$ is copper(II) sulfate, a salt.

37. a. 0.10 M HNO_3: Nitric acid is a strong acid and ionizes completely in water. This solution has the highest concentration of H^+ ions.

b. 0.10 M NH_3: Ammonia is a weak base. When dissolved in water, NH_3 produces OH^- ions so, of the three solutions, the H^+ ion concentration in this solution is the lowest.

c. 0.10M CH_3COOH: Acetic acid is a weak acid so its ionization is not complete, but it does increase the H^+ ion concentration in aqueous solution.

39.

a. HNO_2 is an Arrhenius acid. $HNO_2(aq) \overset{H_2O}{\leftrightarrow} H^+(aq) + NO_2^-(aq)$

b. $Ba(OH)_2$ is an Arrhenius base. $Ba(OH)_2(s) \overset{H_2O}{\rightarrow} Ba^{2+}(aq) + 2\,OH^-(aq)$

c. HBr is an Arrhenius acid. $HBr(aq) \overset{H_2O}{\rightarrow} H^+(aq) + Br^-(aq)$

41.

a. $HClO(aq) + H_2O \leftrightarrow H_3O^+(aq) + ClO^-(aq)$

b. $HNO_2(aq) + H_2O \leftrightarrow H_3O^+(aq) + NO_2^-(aq)$

c. $H_2S(aq) + H_2O \leftrightarrow H_3O^+(aq) + HS^-(aq)$

43.

a. $KOH(aq) + HCl(aq) \rightarrow KCl(aq) + H_2O$

b. $LiOH(aq) + HNO_3(aq) \rightarrow LiNO_3(aq) + H_2O$

45. $H_2SO_3(aq) + Mg(OH)_2(aq) \rightarrow MgSO_3(aq) + 2\,H_2O$

47.

a. A solution with pH 4 is acidic (pH < 7.0).

b. A solution with pH 7 is neutral (pH = 7.0).

c. A solution with pH 3.5 is acidic (pH < 7.0).

d. A solution with pH 9.0 is basic (pH > 7.0).

49. The pH of the solution is 5.0. The pH is the negative logarithm of H^+ concentration, or 5.0.

51. $[H^+] = 1 \times 10^{-3}$ M. The concentration is the negative antilog of the pH.

53. The pH of milk of magnesia is between 10 and 11. The pH is the negative logarithm of H^+ concentration.

55. $HNO_3(aq) + NH_3(aq) \rightarrow NO_3^-(aq) + NH_4^+(aq)$

a. HNO_3, nitric acid, is the acid in this reaction because it releases an H^+ ion. Ammonia, NH_3, is the base in this reaction because it accepts an H^+ ion.

b. The conjugate base of $HNO_3(aq)$ is $NO_3^-(aq)$.

c. The conjugate acid of $NH_3(aq)$ is $NH_4^+(aq)$.

57. $Al(OH)_3(s) + 3\,HCl(aq) \rightarrow AlCl_3(aq) + 3\,H_2O$
$Mg(OH)_2(s) + 2\,HCl(aq) \rightarrow MgCl_2(aq) + 2\,H_2O$

59. No. To be an Arrhenius base the OH group must be paired with a metal. For example, methyl alcohol, CH_3OH, has an OH group but is not a base.

61.

a. The Cl^- ion is the conjugate base of a strong acid (HCl) and is, therefore, a weak base.

b. The CN^- ion is the conjugate base of a weak acid (HCN) and is, therefore, a strong base.

63.

a. pOH = 3 The pOH is the negative logarithm of OH^- concentration.

b. pOH = 2 The pOH is the negative logarithm of OH^- concentration.

65.   a.   When it acts as an acid, HPO_4^{2-} releases an H^+ ion to water:
$$HPO_4^{2-}(aq) + H_2O \leftrightarrow PO_4^{3-}(aq) + H_3O^+(aq)$$
When it acts as a base, HPO_4^{2-} acquires an H^+ ion from water:
$$HPO_4^{2-}(aq) + H_2O \leftrightarrow H_2PO_4^-(aq) + OH^-(aq)$$

67. $Al_2(CO_3)_3(s) + 6\ HCl(aq) \rightarrow 2\ AlCl_3(aq) + 3\ H_2O(l) + 3\ CO_2(g)$

69.   The evidence tells us that the solution produced is basic. Solutions of bases are slippery and, in basic solutions, red litmus turns blue. $HS^-(aq) + H_2O \rightarrow H_2S(g) + OH^-(aq)$

71.   Soap is made by adding lye (NaOH) to fats or oils, forming a basic solution (pH > 7.0). Adding citric acid would neutralize some of the NaOH, reducing $[OH^-]$ and decreasing the pH.

73. $HC_{16}H_{31}O_2(s) + KOH(aq) \rightarrow KC_{16}H_{31}O_2(s) + H_2O(l)$
The product of this reaction is a soap because it is the salt of a fatty acid.

CHAPTER

8

Oxidation and Reduction

Burn and Unburn

CHAPTER SUMMARY

8.1 Oxidation and Reduction: Three Views
   A. Oxidation is the <u>gain</u> of oxygen atoms.
      Reduction is the <u>loss</u> of oxygen atoms.
      1. $4\,Fe + 3\,O_2 \rightarrow 2\,Fe_2O_3$
         Fe is oxidized.
         O_2 is reduced.
      2. $2\,H_2 + O_2 \rightarrow 2\,H_2O$
         H_2 is oxidized.
         O_2 is reduced.
   B. Oxidation is a <u>loss</u> of hydrogen atoms.
      Reduction is a <u>gain</u> of hydrogen atoms.
      1. $CH_4O + \tfrac{1}{2}\,O_2 \rightarrow CH_2O + H_2O$
         CH_4O is oxidized.
      2. $CO + 2\,H_2 \rightarrow CH_4O$
         CO is reduced.
   C. Oxidation is a <u>loss</u> of electrons.
      Reduction is a <u>gain</u> of electrons.
      1. $Mg + Cl_2 \rightarrow Mg^{2+} + 2\,Cl^-$
         Mg is oxidized.
         Cl_2 is reduced.
      <u>Increase</u> in oxidation number is <u>oxidation</u>.
      <u>Decrease</u> in oxidation number is <u>reduction</u>.
         $Mg + \tfrac{1}{2}\,O_2 \rightarrow Mg^{+2}O^{-2}$.
         Mg is oxidized.
         O is reduced.

Answers to Self-Assessment Questions

1. a   "Electrons gained" is reduction, not oxidation.
2. d   N loses one electron to go from +4 to +5. Alternatively, in the reactant, there are 2 O atoms/N atom while in the product there are 5 O atoms/2 N atoms, representing a gain in O atoms.
3. b   The Cr atom in CrO_4^- loses oxygen atoms to become Cr^{3+} which represents a reduction of Cr.
4. b   The Mo atom loses oxygen atoms and so is reduced. Looked at another way, Mo gains four electrons to go from an oxidation state of +4 to an oxidation state of 0.

5. d   Cl goes from an oxidation state of zero in Cl_2 to an oxidation state of -1 in Cl^-, which is a reduction.
6. c Mn^0 loses two electrons in the oxidation to Mn^{2+}.
7. d   An example is #6 above.

8.2   Oxidizing and Reducing Agents
  A. Oxidation and reduction must occur together.
    1. Substance being <u>oxidized</u> is the <u>reducing agent</u>.
    2. Substance being <u>reduced</u> is the <u>oxidizing agent</u>.

Answers to Self-Assessment Questions

1. c   A reducing agent supplies the electrons for the substance that is reduced.
2. b Ag^+ takes the electrons released when Cu is oxidized.
3. a   Al provides the electrons required to reduce Cr^{3+}.
4. b Tl^+ takes an electron released by the oxidization of Zn.
5. a Fe^{2+} provides the electrons required to reduce I in IO_3^-.

8.3   Electrochemistry: Cells and Batteries
  A. An electric current in a wire is a flow of electrons. Oxidation-reduction reactions can be used to produce electricity, as is done in dry cell and storage batteries.
  B. When a reactive metal (zinc) is placed in contact with the ions of a less reactive metal (copper), the more active metal will give up its electrons (oxidation) to the ions of the less active metal (which are reduced).
  C. If the two metals (zinc and copper) are placed in solutions of their metal ions in separate containers, the electrons traveling between the two containers must flow through an external circuit and can be harassed to do work.
    1. The metal electrode where oxidation takes place (more active metal) is the <u>anode</u>.
    2. The metal electrode where reduction takes place (less active metal) is the <u>cathode</u>.
    3. This arrangement is an <u>electrochemical cell</u>.
  D. A battery is a series of electrochemical cells. (In everyday life, however, we refer to a single electrochemical cell, such as that used in flashlights, as a "battery.")
  E. Dry cells are the common batteries used in flashlights.
  F. Lead storage batteries are the rechargeable batteries found in cars. These batteries can be recharged but are heavy and contain sulfuric acid.
  G. Other common batteries are lithium-SO_2 cells used in submarines and rockets, lithium iodine cells used in pacemakers, lithium–FeS_2 batteries used in cameras, radios, and compact disc players, rechargeable Ni-Cad batteries for portable radios and cordless tools, and small "button" batteries used in watches, calculators, and cameras.
  H. In fuel cells, fuel is oxidized at the anode and oxygen is reduced at the cathode.
    1. Fuel cells are a much more efficient way of using fuel.
  I. Whereas the chemical reactions in batteries occur spontaneously, electrolysis reactions occur when electricity is supplied to cause a chemical reaction to occur.
    1. Aluminum is produced from Al_2O_3, chromium (for chrome plating) from Cr^{6+} solutions, and copper from Cu(II) salts by electrolysis.

Answers to Self-Assessment Questions

1. c   Zinc is oxidized at the anode, which is negative.
2. b   In a dry cell battery, zinc acts as the anode and a carbon rod is the cathode.

3.   c   The porous membrane allows ions to pass through in order to have a complete circuit.
4.   d   Mg loses two electrons to become Mg^{2+}. Loss of electrons is oxidation.
5.   d $PbSO_4$ is produced at both the cathode and anode of a lead storage battery.
6.   d. Sulfuric acid is used in lead storage batteries.
7.   c   Reduction occurs at the cathode where O_2 is reduced to O^{2-}.

8.4 Corrosion and Explosion
   A. The rusting of iron is an electrochemical process that requires water, oxygen, and an
       electrolyte.
       1. Oxidation and reduction often occur at different places on the metal's surface.
   B. Aluminum is more reactive than iron, but is protected by an aluminum oxide film on its surface
       that forms from the reaction of Al with oxygen in the air.
   C. Silver tarnish is largely silver sulfide (Ag_2S).
       1. It is formed by the reaction of silver with hydrogen sulfide (H_2S) in the air.
           a. Tarnish can be removed by reacting it with aluminum.
   D. Except for nuclear reactions, explosive reactions are oxidation-reduction reactions that occur
       very rapidly (corrosion reactions occur slowly).
       1. Ammonium nitrate mixed with fuel oil (ANFO) is used for mining, earthmoving projects,
           and demolishing buildings.

Answers to Self-Assessment Questions

1.   c   Fe is oxidized when corroded, so the corrosion reaction is an oxidation-reduction reaction.
2.   a Al_2O_3 forms on the surface of Al and protects it from further oxidation.
3.   c   Hydrogen sulfide from the air or from foods reacts with silver to produce silver sulfide, which
         is the black substance we call tarnish.
4.   c   The formation of a large volume of gas from a small volume of solid or liquid reactant creates
         enormous pressure which causes the damage of an explosion.
5.   c   The nitrate (NO_3^-) component of KNO_3 is the oxidizing agent in black powder just as NO_3^- is
         the oxidizing agent in ANFO.

8.5 Oxygen: An Abundant and Essential Oxidizing Agent
   A. Oxygen is one of the most important elements on Earth.
       1. Air: one-fifth elemental oxygen by volume.
       2. Water: 89% oxygen by mass.
       3. People: approximately two-thirds oxygen by mass.
   B. Fuels such as natural gas, gasoline, coal, and the foods we eat all require oxygen to burn and
       release their stored chemical energy.
   C. Pure oxygen is obtained by liquefying air, then allowing the nitrogen and argon to boil off.
   D. Many metals and nonmetals react with oxygen.
   E. Ozone (O_3) is a powerful oxidizing agent which is a pollutant at ground level and a beneficial
       chemical in the upper stratosphere.
   F. Other common oxidizing agents.
       1. Germicides (kill microorganisms) such as disinfectants (for nonliving tissue) and
           antiseptics (for living tissue) are oxidizing agents. Hypochlorous acid (HOCl) is used in
           swimming pools for this purpose.
       2. Hydrogen peroxide, used as a 3% or 30% aqueous solution. Hydrogen peroxide is reduced
           to water and oxygen is produced.
       3. Iodine is used as an antiseptic.
       4. Potassium dichromate is a common laboratory oxidizing agent and is used in breathalyzer
           tests which make use of the color change associated with the reduction of dichromate ions.

83

5. Acne ointments often contain benzoyl peroxide as the active ingredient.
6. Bleaches, used to whiten paper or fabrics, are usually sodium hypochlorite (NaOCl) or calcium hypochlorite, $Ca(OCl)_2$. Non-chlorine bleaches contain sodium percarbonate (a combination of Na_2CO_3 and H_2O_2) or sodium perborate (a combination of $NaBO_2$ and H_2O_2).

Answers to Self-Assessment Questions

1. d   Carbon dioxide and water are produced with efficient burning of CH_4.
2. d   The reaction is $S + O_2 \rightarrow SO_2$.
3. b H_2O_2 is a common oxidizing agent used to clean wounds and as an ingredient in nonchlorine bleach.
4. a Cl_2 is a strong oxidizing agent.
5. b. NaOCl is a common ingredient in chlorine bleach and is an oxidizing agent.
6. c   Hydrogen peroxide is commonly used to bleach hair.
7. a   Oxidation is an effective way to disinfect many surfaces.

8.6   Some Common Reducing Agents
A. Elemental carbon (coke) is used as a reducing agent for large-scale production of metals.
B. Antioxidants such as ascorbic acid (vitamin C) and vitamin E are reducing agents in food chemistry.
C. Hydrogen is an important reducing agent for metals, for reducing organic compounds, and for reducing nitrogen to ammonia (nitrogen fixing).
   1. Many reactions with H_2 require use of a catalyst, a substance that increases the rate of a reaction (by lowering the activation energy of the reaction) without being consumed by the reaction.
   2. Because of their affinity for H_2, metals such as iron, platinum, and palladium are often used as catalysts.
D. Catalysts are an important area of research in green chemistry.
   1. Catalysts increase the efficiency and efficacy of chemical and energy resources and reduce reaction time, leading to cost savings.
   2. Catalysts composed of using nontoxic materials are being designed to withstand thousands of catalytic cycles and can be effective at levels as low as 1 ppm.
E. A closer look at hydrogen.
   1. Hydrogen represents only 0.9% of the Earth's crust (by weight), but is the most abundant element in the universe.
   2. Elemental hydrogen (uncombined) is rarely found on Earth.
   3. Combined hydrogen is found in water, natural gas, petroleum products, and all foodstuffs.
   4. Hydrogen can be ignited with a spark, as occurred in 1937 when the airship Hindenburg was destroyed in a fire and explosion over Lakehurst, NJ.

Answers to Self-Assessment Questions

1. c H_2 is often used to reduce metal ores to metals.
2. a   C, often in the form of coke, is used to reduce metal ores to metals.
3. a   Al does not interact with hydrogen.
4. d   By lowering the activation energy, the catalyst speeds up the reaction.
5. d   Hydrogen is behind silicon and oxygen in abundance on Earth.
6. a   The reaction is $Zn + 2 HCl \rightarrow H_2 + ZnCl_2$.
7. a   Remember the Hindenberg!

8.7   Oxidation, Reduction, and Living Things
   A. Reduced compounds represent a form of stored potential energy. The driving force to produce reduced compounds is ultimately derived from the sun in the processes of photosynthesis.
      1. Plants and the animals that feed on plants use the glucose to make other reduced compounds such as carbohydrates. The many steps of the metabolic process that releases the energy in carbohydrates, cellular respiration, are:
$$C_6H_{12}O_6 + 6\,O_2 \rightarrow 6\,CO_2 + 6\,H_2O + energy$$
      2. The overall photosynthesis reaction, the process by which plants utilize the energy from the sun to synthesize carbohydrates, is essentially the reverse of the cellular respiration reaction, and is the only natural process that produces O_2.
$$6\,CO_2 + 6\,H_2O + energy \rightarrow C_6H_{12}O_6 + 6\,O_2$$

Answers to Self-Assessment Questions

1. b   Cellular respiration, or the oxidation of glucose, is the main process used by animals to get energy.
2. b   Photosynthesis by plants is the only natural process that produces oxygen.

LEARNING OBJECTIVES

You should be able to...

1.	Identify an oxidation-reduction reaction.	(8.1)
2.	Classify a particular change within a redox reaction as either oxidation or reduction.	(8.1)
3.	Identify the oxidizing agent and the reducing agent in a redox reaction.	(8.2)
4.	Balance redox equations.	(8.3)
5.	Identify and write the half-reactions in an electrochemical cell.	(8.3)
6.	Describe the reactions that occur when iron rusts.	(8.4)
7.	Explain why an explosive reaction is so energetic.	(8.4)
8.	Write equations for reactions in which oxygen is an oxidizing agent.	(8.5)
9	List some of the common oxidizing agents encountered in daily life.	(8.5)
10.	Identify some common reducing agents.	(8.6)
11.	List some of the important properties and uses of hydrogen.	(8.6)
12.	Write the overall equations for the metabolism of glucose and for photosynthesis.	(8.7)

13. Distinguish between the objectives of chemists producing industrial chemicals and those of chemists producing specialty chemicals.

14. Explain how green chemistry can be applied to the design of new catalysts.

DISCUSSION

It is impossible to overemphasize the importance of oxidation-reduction processes. Think of it this way: You are powered by the energy of sunlight; only you can't simply unfold solar panels, as artificial satellites do, and convert sunlight to stored electrical energy to be tapped as necessary. You are a chemical factory and not an artificial satellite, solar-powered or otherwise. So somehow you have to tap that solar energy in a chemical way. This is precisely the role of oxidation-reduction reactions in life processes—they plug you into the sun.

You should practice writing the formulas and chemical equations for the oxidation-reduction reactions. Be sure to know the common oxidation and reduction agents and their applications. These applications range from large-scale industrial uses to batteries, to household uses, and finally the source of energy for living organisms, including us.

EXAMPLE PROBLEM

1. Identify the element being oxidized, the element being reduced, the oxidizing agent, and the reducing agent in the following reactions.
   a. $2\,Mg + CO_2 \rightarrow 2\,MgO + C$
      Mg gains oxygen; therefore, it is oxidized. CO_2 loses oxygen; therefore, it is reduced. If Mg is oxidized, CO_2 must be the oxidizing agent. If CO_2 is reduced, Mg must be the reducing agent.
   b. $C_2H_4 + N_2H_2 \rightarrow C_2H_6 + N_2$
      C_2H_4 gains hydrogen; therefore, it is reduced. N_2H_2 gives up hydrogen; therefore, it is oxidized. N_2H_2 is the reducing agent (it reduces C_2H_4), and C_2H_4 is the oxidizing agent (it oxidizes N_2H_2).
   c. $Cu + 2\,Ag^+ \rightarrow Cu^{2+} + 2\,Ag$
      Cu loses electrons to become Cu^{2+}; therefore, it is oxidized (and is the reducing agent). Ag^+ gains electrons to become Ag; therefore, it is reduced (and is the oxidizing agent).

ADDITIONAL PROBLEM

1. Identify the substance oxidized, the substance reduced, the oxidizing agent, and the reducing agent in each of the following equations.
   a. $CuO + H_2 \rightarrow Cu + H_2O$
   b. $C_2H_4 + 3\,O_2 \rightarrow 2\,CO_2 + 2\,H_2O$
   c. $Fe + Cu^{2+} \rightarrow Fe^{2+} + Cu$
   d. $5\,CO + I_2O_5 \rightarrow I_2 + 5\,CO_2$
   e. $CH_3CHO + H_2O_2 \rightarrow CH_3COOH + H_2O$
   f. $C_6H_{12}O_6 + 6\,O_2 \rightarrow 6\,CO_2 + 6\,H_2O$
   g. $16\,H^+ + 2\,Cr_2O_7^{2-} + 3\,C_2H_5OH \rightarrow 4Cr^{3+} + 3\,C_2H_4O + 11\,H_2O$

ANSWERS TO ODD-NUMBERED REVIEW QUESTIONS AND SOLUTIONS FOR ODD-NUMBERED END OF CHAPTER PROBLEMS

Review Questions

1. The oxidation number is increased during oxidation and decreased in reduction.

3. The porous plate between two electrode compartments allows ions to pass through, thereby completing the electrical circuit and keeping the solutions electrically neutral.

5. The case (container) of a regular carbon-zinc dry cell battery is composed of Zn which acts as the anode in the oxidation-reduction reaction. Zn is oxidized to Zn^{2+} in the reaction.

7. The reaction that occurs during the recharging of a lead storage battery is:
$2 PbSO_4 + 2 H_2O \rightarrow Pb + PbO_2 + 2 H_2SO_4$. $PbSO_4$ is converted to Pb and PbO_2.

9. When iron corrodes in moist air, Fe is oxidized to Fe^{2+} while O_2 is reduced to O^{2-}, like a miniature battery. Road salt intensifies the process by dissolving in the moisture, creating an aqueous solution that conducts electricity because of its ionic content.

11. Ag is oxidized by H_2S to produce Ag_2S which is black. Aluminum foil can be used to reduce Ag^+ back to Ag. This way the silver remains on the object rather than being abraded off with a rough cloth.

Problems

13. a. Fe loses three electrons when it is oxidized to Fe^{3+}.
    b. The oxygen atom in H_2O loses two electrons to be oxidized to O_2. The oxidation number of O in H_2O is -2; the oxidation number of O in O_2 is zero.
    c. Sr^0 loses two electrons to be oxidized to Sr^{2+}.
    d. Each P atom in P_4 gains three electrons when it is reduced to P^{3-}.
    e. CH_4O loses two hydrogen atoms when it is oxidized to CH_2O.

15. a. $Ca \rightarrow Ca^{2+} + 2 e^-$
    b. $Al \rightarrow Al^{3+} + 3 e^-$
    c. $Cu \rightarrow Cu^+ + e^-$
       $Cu \rightarrow Cu^{2+} + 2 e^-$

17. a. Fe^{3+} in Fe_2O_3 gains three electrons when it forms Fe, so Fe_2O_3 is the oxidizing agent.
       C loses two electrons and is the reducing agent.
    b. Each O in O_2 gains two electrons so O_2 is the oxidizing agent.
       Each P in P_4 loses electrons, so P_4 is the reducing agent.
    c. Both H atoms in H_2O gain 1 electron, so H_2O is the oxidizing agent.
       Elemental carbon loses 2 electrons (oxidation number goes from zero to +2), so C is the reducing agent.
    d. H^+ gains one electron so H_2SO_4 is the oxidizing agent.
       Zn loses two electrons and is the reducing agent.

19. Ag^+ gains one electron and is the oxidizing agent. Cu loses two electrons and is the reducing agent.

21. Mn^{4+} in MnO_2 gains one electron, so MnO_2 is the oxidizing agent.
        Zn loses two electrons and is the reducing agent.

23.   a. $Fe \rightarrow Fe^{2+} + 2\,e^-$ half-reaction of oxidation.
            $2\,H^+ + 2\,e^- \rightarrow H_2$ half-reaction of reduction.
        b. $Cr^{2+}\ 2\,e^- \rightarrow Cr^0$ half-reaction of reduction.
            $Al \rightarrow Al^{3+} + 3\,e^-$ half-reaction of oxidation.

25.   a. $2\,H_2O_2 \rightarrow 2\,O_2 + 4\,H^+ + 4\,e^-$ is oxidation.
            $Fe^{3+} + e^- \rightarrow Fe^{2+}$ is reduction.
            The combined redox reaction is $4\,Fe^{3+} + 2\,H_2O_2 \rightarrow 4\,Fe^{2+} + 2\,O_2 + 4\,H^+$.
        b. $WO_3 + 6\,H^+ + 6\,e^- \rightarrow W + 3\,H_2O$ is reduction.
            $C_2H_6O \rightarrow C_2H_4O + 2H^+ + 2e^-$ is oxidation.
            The combined redox reaction is:
            $WO_3 + 3\,C_2H_6O \rightarrow W + 3\,C_2H_4O + 3\,H_2O$.

27.   a. HNO_3 is reduced to NO_2, so HNO_3 is the oxidizing agent. SO_2 is oxidized to $SO_4{}^{2-}$, so SO_2 is the reducing agent.
        b. The I^- in HI is oxidized to I_2, so HI is the reducing agent. Cr^{6+} in CrO_3 is reduced to Cr^{3+} in Cr_2O_3, so CrO_3 is the oxidizing agent.

29.   Hydrogen is added to ethylene in this reaction, so ethylene is reduced.

31. Ta^{5+} in Ta_2O_5 is reduced to Ta. The electrons for the reduction were supplied by Na, so Na is the reducing agent.

33.   Zr metal is oxidized to Zr^{4+} in ZrO_2. The electrons were used to reduce H^+ in H_2O to H_2, so H_2O is the oxidizing agent.

35. N^{3+} in $NO_2{}^-$ is reduced to N^{2+} in NO. Ascorbic acid is the reducing agent.

37.   a. $S + O_2 \rightarrow SO_2$.
        b. $2\,CH_3OH + 3\,O_2 \rightarrow 2\,CO_2 + 4\,H_2O$.
        c. $C_3H_6O + 4\,O_2 \rightarrow 3\,CO_2 + 3\,H_2O$.

39.   Indoxyl is oxidized. O_2 is the oxidizing agent.

41. $2\,Al(s) + 3\,Cu^{2+}(aq) \rightarrow 2\,Al^{3+}(aq) + 3\,Cu(s)$.

43.   a. $Pb^{2+}(aq) + H_2S(g) \rightarrow PbS(s) + 2\,H^+(aq)$.
        b. $PbS(s) + 4\,H_2O_2(aq) \rightarrow PbSO_4(s) + 4\,H_2O(l)$.

45.   volume of $O_2 = (80\ g\ fat)(2000\ L\ O_2/1000\ g\ fat) = 160\ L\ O_2$.

47. a. V^{2+} loses an electron when it is oxidized to V^{3+}.
     b. NO_2 is neither oxidized nor reduced as the N in NO_2 and N_2O_4 are both N^{4+}. Note that NO_2 is a free radical. When the two NO_2 molecules combine, each N atom has an octet of electrons.
     c. Since CO gains hydrogen when forming CH_3OH, the CO must be reduced.

49. The balanced equation is: $H_2(g) + Cl_2(g) \rightarrow 2\ HCl(g)$. Cl_2 is the oxidizing agent.

51. The balanced equation is: $2\ Al + 6\ H_2O \rightarrow 2\ Al(OH)_3 + 3\ H_2$.
     Metallic Al is the reducing agent and H_2O is the oxidizing agent.

53. a. NAD^+ is reduced to NADH and ethanol is oxidized to acetaldehyde.
         The half-reaction of reduction is: $NAD^+ + H^+ + 2\ e^- \rightarrow NADH$.
         The half-reaction of oxidation is: $CH_3CH_2OH \rightarrow CH_3CHO + 2\ H^+ + 2\ e^-$.
         The complete reaction is: $NAD^+ + CH_3CH_2OH \rightarrow CH_3CHO + H^+ + NADH$.
     b. The half-reaction of reduction is:
         $CH_3COCOOH + 2\ H^+ + 2\ e^- \rightarrow CH_3CHOHCOOH$.
         The half-reaction of oxidation is: $NADH \rightarrow NAD^+ + H^+ + 2\ e^-$.
         The complete reaction is:
         $CH_3COCOOH + NADH + H^+ \rightarrow CH_3CHOHCOOH + NAD^+$.

55. a. Industrial chemicals are produced on a large scale.
     b. Complex molecules are usually produced as specialty chemicals.
     c. Specialty chemicals usually have a higher value in the marketplace than industrial chemicals.
     d. Industrial chemicals are often the building blocks for more complex specialty chemicals.

57. Many oxidation catalysts have organic molecules built into their structures. These organic components may undergo chemical oxidation, causing the catalyst to lose effectiveness.

Organic Chemistry

The Infinite Variety of Carbon Compounds

CHAPTER SUMMARY

9.1 Aliphatic Hydrocarbons
  A. Hydrocarbons contain only hydrogen and carbon.
    1. Hydrocarbons are classified according to the type of bonding between carbon atoms.
    2. Aliphatic compounds are defined as nonaromatic (aromatic compounds are discussed in Section 9.2).
  B. Alkanes.
    1. Alkanes are hydrocarbons that contain only single bonds.
    2. Methane, CH_4, is the simplest example.
    3. The four attachments to the carbon atoms in alkanes are in a tetrahedral arrangement around the central carbon atom (see Chapter 4).
    4. Alkanes are considered to be saturated because each carbon atom is bonded to the maximum possible number of hydrogen atoms.
    5. Compounds are often represented with condensed structural formulas such as $CH_3CH_2CH_3$.
    6. Hydrocarbons are named according to the number of carbon atoms in the longest continuous chain of carbon atoms in the structure. The prefix to the name indicates the length of this chain, and the ending of the name, *ane*, indicates that the compound is a hydrocarbon. Any branching in the chain is both located with respect to its insertion into the longest chain, and described in terms of its length.
    7. It will be important to memorize the prefixes in Table 9.1, and to look carefully at the compound names in Table 9.2.

meth = 1	hex = 6
eth = 2	hept = 7
prop = 3	oct = 8
but = 4	non = 9
pent = 5	dec = 10

  C. Homologous series.
    1. A series of compounds whose properties vary in a regular and predictable manner.
    2. Example of a homologous series: CH_4, CH_3CH_3, $CH_3CH_2CH_3$, $CH_3CH_2CH_2CH_3$, where each member differs from the one on either side of it by a CH_2 unit.
    3. Sometimes members of a homologous series are branched.
  D. Isomerism.

1. Because carbon chains can be straight or branched, often there are several different compounds with the same chemical formula. These compounds are termed isomers.
2. Examples of isomers:

E. Properties of alkanes.
  1. Alkanes with 1 to 4 C's are gases at room temperature; alkanes with 5 to 16 C's are liquids; alkanes with 17 or more C's are solid.
  2. Alkanes are nonpolar and, hence, insoluble in water but dissolve other nonpolar organic substances such as fats, oils, and waxes.
  3. Alkanes are less dense than water, so they float on water.
  4. Generally, alkanes are not particularly reactive; their primary reaction is combustion. Among their most important uses is as fuels. When they burn, they release a great deal of heat.
  5. In the lungs, alkanes can lead to chemical pneumonia.
  6. Heavy alkanes (long C chains) act as emollients (skin softeners).
F. Cyclic hydrocarbons: rings and things.
  1. Compounds with closed rings of carbon atoms are called cyclic and are often represented with geometric shapes: Three carbon: cyclopropane: triangle; Four carbon: cyclobutane: square; Five carbon: cyclopentane: pentagon; Six carbon: cyclohexane: hexagon.
  2. These compounds are named in a similar fashion to the aliphatic hydrocarbons except that each name begins with the prefix "cyclo."

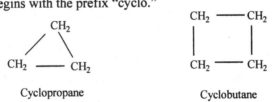

Cyclopropane   Cyclobutane

G. Unsaturated hydrocarbons: alkenes and alkynes.
  1. An alkene is a hydrocarbon that contains one or more carbon-carbon double bonds (C=C).
  2. An alkyne is a hydrocarbon that contains one or more carbon-carbon triple bonds (C≡C).
  3. Collectively, alkenes and alkynes are called unsaturated hydrocarbons because they can have more hydrogen atoms added to them.
H. Properties of alkenes and alkynes.
  1. Unsaturated hydrocarbons burn in the presence of oxygen.
  2. The carbon-carbon double bond in these compounds is reactive; many different small molecules can add to the compound at this site, including, among others, hydrogen (H_2), chlorine (Cl_2), bromine (Br_2), and water (H_2O). These reactions are called addition reactions.

Answers to Self-Assessment Questions

1. b   Oxidation is a type of chemical reaction, not an explanation for the large number of carbon compounds that exist. The other three answers do address the reasons for the large number of compounds.

2. a   Saturated compounds have a maximum number of hydrogen atoms attached to each carbon atom and have single bonds.

3. b   Each successive member of the alkane series differs by CH_2.

4. c   Isomers have different structures, but the same chemical formula.

5. b   Boiling points of alkanes increase as the molecular weights increase. Among other things, this is because the extent to which dispersion forces occur between molecules increases as their molecular masses increase.

6. c   The prefix "cyclo" indicates a cyclic compound, "hex" indicates six carbons, and the ending "ane" indicates that the compound is a hydrocarbon,

7. c   Alkynes are identified as compounds containing one or more $C \equiv C$ bond.

8. a   Because the carbon atoms in alkanes are already bonded to four different atoms, it is not possible to insert any more atoms into those structures. The carbon atoms involved in the $C=C$ bond of alkenes are bonded to three different atoms, so it is possible to break the $C=C$ bond and attach each of the carbons to one more atom.

9. a.   The reaction shows an alkene (C_2H_4 or $CH_2=CH_2$) reacting with H_2 to form an alkane (C_2H_6 or $CH_3\text{-}CH_3$).

9.2   Aromatic Hydrocarbons: Benzene and Its Relatives

A. Benzene was first isolated in 1825. It has the molecular formula C_6H_6.

B. In 1865, Kekulé proposed a cyclic structure with alternating single and double carbon-carbon bonds for benzene. However, it has been determined that all of the bonds in benzene are identical and that there are no real double bonds.
   1. Benzene doesn't react by addition reactions the way unsaturated hydrocarbons do, but rather by substitution reactions, like saturated hydrocarbons.

C. Benzene and compounds containing the benzene-type ring structure are called aromatic compounds. Many have pleasant aromas; others stink.
   1. Today aromatic means compound with rings of electrons and properties similar to benzene. It no longer refers to odor.
   2. Monosubstituted benzenes are compounds where one of the H atoms is replaced with another atom or group called a substituent.

Answers to Self-Assessment Questions

1. c   The molecular formula for benzene is C_6H_6.

2. c   Chlorobenzene is a ring structure (benzene in which one of the H atoms is replaced by a Cl atom). The other compounds do not have ring structures.

3. a   Benzene is represented as a hybrid of two structures.

4. d   Naphthalene is an aromatic compound with alternating single and double bonds in two fused rings.

5. d   The reactivity of the benzene ring reflects the spreading of six electrons over all six carbon atoms.

9.3   Chlorinated Hydrocarbons: Many Uses, Some Hazards

A. Methane derivatives.
   1. Substitution of a chlorine atom for one of the H atoms in an alkane occurs in the presence of ultraviolet light.

2. Methyl chloride (CH_3Cl): used in making silicones.
3. Methylene chloride (CH_2Cl_2): solvent, paint remover.
4. Chloroform ($CHCl_3$): early anesthetic; industrial solvent.
5. Carbon tetrachloride (CCl_4): dry-cleaning solvent.
B. Properties of chlorinated hydrocarbons.
1. Only slightly polar, thus insoluble in water.
2. These compounds dissolve fats, greases, and oils, thereby making them useful as solvents.
3. Some chlorinated compounds (DDT, PCBs, etc.) are stored in fatty animal tissue.
C. Chlorofluorocarbons and fluorocarbons.
1. CFCs: Carbon compounds containing fluorine, as well as chlorine.
2. Typical compounds are gases or low-boiling liquids at room temperature.
3. They are insoluble in water and inert toward most chemical substances.
   a. Used as propellants (for aerosol spray cans).
   b. Their inertness leads to stability in nature, meaning they break down slowly. Diffusion into the stratosphere may damage the ozone layer.
4. Perfluorinated compounds have been used as blood extenders (they dissolve large amounts of oxygen) and in Teflon.
5. Prefix "per" means all the H atoms have been replaced.

Answers to Self-Assessment Questions

1. b CH_3Cl is named methyl chloride.
2. a CF_2Cl_2 is a chlorofluorocarbon because it contains both Cl and F atoms.
3. c   1-chloropropane is an isomer of $CH_3CHClCH_3$, which is 2-chloropropane.

9.4   The Functional Group
A. Many organic compounds can be divided into two parts:
1. A functional group: an atom or group of atoms that gives a family of organic compounds its characteristic chemical and physical properties. See Table 9.4, which summarizes the functional groups' names, structure, and general formulas.
2. In many simple molecules, a functional group is attached to a hydrocarbon stem called an alkyl group.
   a. The letter "R" represents alkyl groups in general structures.
B. Alkyl groups can be derived from alkanes by removing an H atom from the alkane. They are named by replacing "-ane" with "-yl."

   methyl CH_3—   propyl CH_3—CH_2—CH_2—
   ethyl CH_3—CH_2—   isopropyl CH_3—CH—CH_3—

Answers to Self-Assessment Questions

1. c   A functional group is a specific arrangement of atoms that gives characteristic properties to an organic molecule.
2. a $CH_3CH_2CH_2$— is a three-carbon substituent called a propyl group.
3. c   There are four carbon atoms in a butyl group.
4. a   The formula $CH_3CH_2CH_2CH_2$— represents a butyl group.

9.5 Alcohols, Phenols, and Ethers
A. An alcohol has a hydroxyl group (OH) substituted for an H of the corresponding alkane.
   1. The names for alcohols are based on those of alkanes, with the ending changed from –e to –ol. A number designates the carbon to which the —OH group is attached: $CH_3CH_2CH_2CH_2OH$ is 1-butanol and $CH_3CH_2CHOHCH_3$ is 2-butanol.
   2. Many alcohols are also known by common names.
B. Methyl alcohol (methanol) is the first member of the family.
   1. Methanol is called wood alcohol and once was made by the destructive distillation of wood.
   2. Methanol, a valuable industrial solvent, is now made from carbon monoxide and hydrogen.

$$CO(g) + 2 H_2(g) \rightarrow CH_3OH(l)$$

C. Ethyl alcohol (ethanol).
   1. Ethyl alcohol (ethanol) is also called grain alcohol.
   2. Most ethyl alcohol is made by the fermentation of grain.
   3. Denatured alcohol, ethanol to which toxic substances have been added, is not fit to drink.
D. Toxicity of alcohols.
   1. Methyl alcohol can cause blindness or death.
   2. Ethyl alcohol is less toxic than methyl alcohol, but one pint rapidly ingested can cause death.
   3. "Proof" is calculated as twice the percent of alcohol.
E. Multifunctional alcohols.
   1. Some alcohols have more than one hydroxyl (OH) group.
      a. Ethylene glycol (an ingredient in some antifreeze).

```
        H       H
        |       |
  H ——— C ——— C ——— H
        |       |
        OH      OH
```

Ingestion leads to kidney damage and possible death.
      b. Glycerol is used in lotions and for making nitroglycerin.

```
        H       H       H
        |       |       |
  H ——— C ——— C ——— C ——— H
        |       |       |
        OH      OH      OH
```

F. Phenols
   1. Phenols have an —OH group attached directly to a benzene ring.
   2. Phenols are widely used as antiseptics.

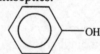

Phenol, also known as carbolic acid

G. Ethers
   1. Ethers have two hydrocarbon groups attached to the same oxygen atom (R—O—R′).
   2. Diethyl ether, once used as an anesthetic, is an important solvent. It is highly flammable.
   3. Methyl tert-butyl ether is sometimes used as an octane booster in gasoline.

Answers to Self-Assessment Questions

1. a   Only the first formula contains an OH group attached to a carbon atom.
2. b   There are three —OH groups in a glycerol molecule.
3. d   The —OH groups in ethylene glycol are on separate carbon atoms.
4. d   Phenols are compounds with an —OH group attached to a benzene ring.
5. b   Phenols are used as antiseptics and disinfectants.
6. b   Ethers have two hydrocarbon groups attached to the same oxygen atom.
7. d   The two aliphatic groups attached to the oxygen atom are both ethyl groups.
8. d   One of the aliphatic groups attached to the oxygen has four carbons (butyl) and the other has two carbons.
9. b   Isomers have the same chemical formulas but different structures.

9.6   Aldehydes and Ketones
A. Both aldehydes and ketones have a carbonyl functional group.

$$\underset{\displaystyle \overset{\displaystyle O}{\parallel}}{-\!\!\!-C-\!\!\!-}$$

B. Aldehydes
1. Aldehydes have at least one H atom attached to the carbonyl carbon atom.

$$\underset{\displaystyle \overset{\displaystyle O}{\parallel}}{-\!\!\!-C-\!\!\!-H}$$

2. Many aldehydes have common names. The systematic name of an aldehyde is based on the name of the alkane with the same number of carbon atoms, to which the ending –al is added. For example, CH_3CHO is ethanal.
3. The simplest aldehyde is formaldehyde, made by the oxidation of methanol. It is used as a preservative and to make plastics.

$$H-\!\!\!-\underset{\displaystyle \overset{\displaystyle O}{\parallel}}{C}-\!\!\!-H$$

4. The next higher aldehyde is acetaldehyde, made by the oxidation of ethanol.

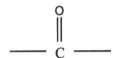

5. Benzaldehyde has an aldehyde group attached to a benzene ring. It is called oil of almond, and is used in flavors and perfumes.

C. Ketones have their carbonyl carbon atom joined to two other carbon atoms. Acetone, a common solvent, is an example.

$$\underset{\underset{\displaystyle CH_3}{|}}{\overset{\overset{\displaystyle O}{\|}}{CH_3 \longrightarrow C \longrightarrow CH_3}}$$

1. The systematic names for ketones are based on those of alkanes, with the ending changed from -e to -one. When necessary, a number is used to indicate the location of the carbonyl group. For example, $CH_3COCH_2CH_2CH_3$ is 2-pentanone.

Answers to Self-Assessment Questions

1. a   The aldehyde functional group has an H atom attached to a carbonyl group.
2. c   The ketone functional group has a carbonyl group attached to two carbon atoms.
3. c   R—CO—R' is a ketone, with alkyl groups attached to the carbonyl carbon atom.
4. c $CH_3COCH_2CH_3$ is a ketone with a methyl group on one side of the central oxygen and an ethyl group on the other side.
5. b $CH_3CH_2CH_2CHO$ is a four-carbon aldehyde.
6. a   Formaldehyde has one carbon and is produced from CH_3OH, which has one carbon.
7. d   Acetone has two carbon atoms on each side of the central oxygen atom and is produced from $CH_3CHOHCH_3$.

9.7   Carboxylic Acids and Esters
   A. Organic or carboxylic acids have the carboxyl group as their functional group.
      1. Carboxyl group.

$$\overset{\overset{\displaystyle O}{\|}}{-C-OH} \quad or \quad -COOH$$

      2. Carboxylic acids are weak acids.
   B. Common carboxylic acids include

1.	HCOOH	formic acid	in ant bites, bee stings
2.	CH_3COOH	acetic acid	in vinegar
3.	CH_3CH_2COOH	propionic acid	salts used as preservatives
4.	$CH_3CH_2CH_2COOH$	butyric acid	rancid butter (stench)
5.		benzoic acid	salts used as preservatives

   C. Carboxyl acid salts are used as food preservatives (calcium propionate, sodium benzoate).

9.8   Esters: The Sweet Smell of RCOOR'
   A. Esters are derived from the reaction of a carboxylic acid with an alcohol.
      1. General formula.

$$\overset{\overset{\displaystyle O}{\|}}{R-C-OR'}$$

   B. Although derived from carboxylic acids with unpleasant odors, many esters have pleasant odors.
      1. They are used in fragrances and flavors.

Answers to Self-Assessment Questions

1. b   The COOH in CH_3CH_2CHOOH is the carboxylic acid group.
2. d $CH_3CH_2CH_2COOH$ is a carboxylic acid with four carbon atoms.
3. a   Benzoic acid has the —COOH group bonded directly to the benzene ring.
4. a   Ethanol with two carbon atoms would be oxidized to ethanoic acid or CH_3COOH.
5. c   RCOOR′ is the general formula for an ester.
6. b   Counting the carbonyl carbon atom, $CH_3CH_2CH_2COOCH_2CH_3$ has four carbon atoms attached to the oxygen atom, followed by a two-carbon alkyl group also attached to that oxygen atom.
7. d   If the CH_3 bonded to the oxygen was replaced with an H atom, we would have propanoic acid. The H in the OH group of the acid is replaced with a CH_3 group, so $CH_3CH_2COOCH_3$ is methyl propanoate.

Green Chemistry

A. The solvents used in the synthesis of petroleum-based drugs are often flammable, toxic, and pose serious disposal problems.
1. These procedures are being modified to use greener alternatives or using no solvent at all.
2. Water is the ideal solvent, but many organic molecules are nonpolar and not soluble in water.
3. "On water" reactions have been developed for which the reactants float on water.
B. Green chemistry can also use microwaves to speed up reactions and reduce energy consumption.
C. Salicylates: pain relievers based on salicylic acid.
1. Salicylic acid is both a carboxylic acid and a phenol.
2. The compound was first isolated from willow bark and used as an antipyretic (fever reducer) and analgesic (pain reliever).
3. Salicylic acid was irritating when taken orally, so a derivative, acetylsalicylic acid, an ester formed when the phenol group of salicylic acid reacts with acetic acid, was produced.
4. Methyl salicylate, called oil of wintergreen, is used as a flavoring agent and in rub-on analgesics for sore muscles.

9.9   Nitrogen-Containing Compounds: Amines and Amides

A. Amines are basic compounds derived from ammonia (NH_3) by replacing one or more of the hydrogen atoms with an alkyl group.
1. RNH_2, R_2NH, and R_3N are amines.
2. Amines are named by naming the alkyl groups first, and adding the ending "-amine."
CH_3NH_2	$CH_3CH_2NH_2$	CH_3NHCH_3
Methylamine	Ethylamine	Dimethylamine
3. The simplest aromatic amine has the special name aniline.

4. The —NH_2 group is called an amino group.
B. Amides have a nitrogen atom attached to a carbonyl carbon atom.

1. Urea (H_2NCONH_2), the compound that helped change the understanding of organic chemistry, is an amide.
2. Nylon, silk, and wool are amides.
3. Names for simple amides are derived from the corresponding carboxylic acids or based on those of alkanes with the ending changed from *–e* to *–amide*.
C. Heterocyclic compounds: alkaloids and others.
1. Heterocyclic compounds are those having atoms other than C in a ring structure.
2. These compounds usually contain N, O, or S in the ring.
3. Pyrimidine and purine, found in DNA, are examples.
D. Alkaloids are amines, often heterocyclic, that occur naturally in plants.
1. Morphine, nicotine, caffeine, and cocaine are examples.

Answers to Self-Assessment Questions

1. b $CH_3CH_2CH_2CH_2NH_2$ has four carbon atoms in the alkyl group and two H atoms bonded to the N atom, so it is called butylamine.
2. b $CH_3CH_2NHCH_3$ has an ethyl group and a methyl group attached to the N atom.
3. a CH_3CONH_2 is acetamide (a common name) or ethanamide.
4. b   Amides have a carbonyl group attached to a nitrogen atom.
5. c   Heterocyclic compounds contain at least one atom in the ring that is not a carbon atom.
6. a   Alkaloids are cyclic organic compounds found in plants that have at least one nitrogen atom in the ring.

LEARNING OBJECTIVES

You should be able to...

1. Define *hydrocarbon*, and recognize structural features of alkanes, alkenes, and alkynes.   (9.1)

2. Identify hydrocarbon molecules as alkanes, alkenes, or alkynes, and name them.   (9.1)

3. Define *aromatic compound*, and recognize the structural feature such compounds share.   (9.2)

4. Name simple aromatic hydrocarbons.   (9.2)

5. Name a halogenated hydrocarbon given its formula, and write the formula for such a compound given its name.   (9.3)

6. Classify an organic compound according to its functional group(s), and explain why the concept of a functional group is useful in the study of organic chemistry.   (9.4)

7. Recognize and write the formulas of simple alkyl groups.   (9.4)

8. Recognize the general structure for an alcohol, a phenol, and an ether.   (9.5)

9. Name simple alcohols, phenols, and ethers.   (9.5)

10. Name simple aldehydes and ketones, and list their important properties.   (9.6)

11. Name simple carboxylic acids and esters, and list their important properties.   (9.7)

12. Name and write the formulas of simple amines and amides.   (9.8)

13. Recognize a structure as that of a heterocyclic compound.   (9.8)

14. Identify greener solvents that can replace those from nonrenewable fossil fuels, methods for incorporating renewable resources into organic synthesis, and efficient energy sources for enhancing chemical reactions.

DISCUSSION

An understanding of the chemistry of carbon and the hydrocarbons is essential for comprehension of our energy problems and associated pollution problems. Perhaps equally important, the chemistry of the hydrocarbons is the basis for most of the organic and biological chemistry that we will encounter in subsequent chapters. Organic chemistry is very extensive because carbon bonds to itself so well and in so many combinations. Focus on the characteristics of the classes (alkanes, alkenes, etc.) of organic compounds to organize your study.

Once again, you may find flash cards helpful in learning the names of the hydrocarbons. Just write the name on one side of a note card and the structure on the other. Look at the name and see if you can write the structure (or vice versa). Then flip the card to see if you got it right.

Adapting the principles of green chemistry to a wide variety of organic reactions has greatly improved the speed, cost, and safety of these processes. In addition, the amount of amount of hazardous waste produced in these reactions has been greatly reduced.

ANSWERS TO ODD-NUMBERED REVIEW QUESTIONS AND SOLUTIONS FOR ODD-NUMBERED END OF CHAPTER PROBLEMS

Review Questions

1.   Three characteristics of the carbon atom that make possible millions of organic compounds are
        a. Carbon atoms can bond strongly to each other
        b. Carbon atoms can bond strongly to other atoms
        c. Carbon atoms can form chains, rings, and other kinds of structures.

3.   Isomers have the same general formula but different structures. If you can draw two or more structures of compounds with the same general formula, they are isomers.

5.   The circle represents the six delocalized electrons from the three double bonds and that the ring is aromatic.

7.   Methane through butane are gases (C_1 through C_4)
     Pentane through hexadecane are liquids (C_5 through C_{16})
     Heptadecane (C_{17}) and larger are solids.

9. a. Grain alcohol is ethyl alcohol or ethanol.
    b. Rubbing alcohol is isopropyl alcohol or 2-propanol.
    c. Wood alcohol is methyl alcohol or methanol.

11. Diethyl ether was used as an anesthetic but is now used as solvent.

13. a. ROH is the general formula for alcohols.
    b. RCOR′ is the general formula for ketones.
    c. RCOOR′ is the general formula for esters.
    d. ROR′ is the general formula for ethers.
    e. RCOOH is the general formula for carboxylic acids.
    f. RCHO is the general formula for aldehydes.

Problems

15. Compounds a and b are organic as they contain carbon. Compounds c and d do not contain carbon and are not organic.

17. a. Hexane has six carbon atoms.
    b. Decane has ten carbon atoms.
    c. Cyclopentane has five carbon atoms.
    d. 2-pentene has five carbon atoms.

19. a. An alkane with nine carbon atoms has the general formula of C_9H_{20}.
    b. An alkane with thirteen carbon atoms has the general formula of $C_{13}H_{28}$.

21. a. $CH_3CH_2CH_2CH_3$ is butane.
    b. $CH_2=CH_2$ is ethene (or ethylene).
    c. C_2H_2 is ethyne, or commonly known as acetylene.

23. a. The molecular formula for pentane is C_5H_{12} and the condensed formula is $CH_3CH_2CH_2CH_2CH_3$.
    b. The molecular formula for nonane is C_9H_{20} and the condensed formula is $CH_3CH_2CH_2CH_2CH_2CH_2CH_2CH_2CH_3$.

25. a. CH_3— is a methyl group.
    b. CH_3CH_2CH— is a *sec*-butyl group.
        |
        CH_3

27. a. CH_3OH is methanol.
    b. $CH_3CH_2CH_2OH$ is 1-propanol.
    c. Ethanol is CH_3CH_2OH.
    d. 1-Heptanol is $CH_3CH_2CH_2CH_2CH_2CH_2CH_2OH$.

29. The structure for phenol is

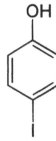

    a. The structure of 2-methyl phenol is:

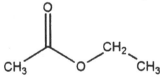

    b. The structure of 4-iodophenol is:

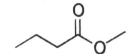

31.   a. The structure of dipropyl ether is $CH_3CH_2CH_2OCH_2CH_2CH_3$.
       b. The structure of butyl ethyl ether is $CH_3CH_2CH_2CH_2OCH_2CH_3$.

33.   a. The structure of acetone is CH_3COCH_3.
       b. The structure of formaldehyde is $HCHO$.
       c. The structure is butanal.
       d. The structure is butyl ethyl ketone or 3-heptanone.

35.   a. CH_3COOH is ethanoic or acetic acid.
       b. $CH_3CH_2CH_2CH_2COOH$ is pentanoic acid.
       c. Formic acid is $HCOOH$.
       d. Octanoic acid is $CH_3CH_2CH_2CH_2CH_2CH_2CH_2COOH$.

37.   a. The structural formula for ethyl acetate is $CH_3COOCH_2CH_3$.

       b. The structural formula for methyl butyrate is $CH_3CH_2CH_2COOCH_3$.

       c. This ester is ethyl propionate.

39.   a. The formula for methylamine is CH_3NH_2.
       b. The formula for ethylmethylamine is $CH_3CH_2NHCH_3$.

101

c. $CH_3CH_2CH_2NH_2$ is propylamine.

d. $CH_3CH_2NHCH_3$ is ethylmethylamine.

41. a. These are the same compound drawn in different directions.

b. These are the same compound drawn in different ways.

c. These are different isomers. The first is 2-methylpentane and the second is 3-methylpentane.

43. a. $CH_3CH_2CH_3$ and $CH_3CH_2CH_2CH_3$ are homologs as they differ by only one CH_2 unit.

b. These compounds are none of these because one is a cyclic compound and the other is not.

45. a. This is unsaturated and an alkene.

b. This is saturated and an alkane.

47. a. This structure is an ester (RCOOR').

b. This structure is an aldehyde (RCHO).

c. This structure is an amine (RNH_2).

d. This structure is an ether (ROR').

e. This structure is a ketone (RCOR').

f. This structure is a carboxylic acid (RCOOH).

49. a. This is a heterocyclic compound and an amine.

b. This is a cycloalkane substituted with an amine group (not heterocyclic). Its name is cyclobutylamine.

Additional Problems

51. The molecular formula for capsaicin is $C_{18}H_{27}NO_3$. Capsaicin has an alkene, a phenol group, an ether group, and an amide group.

53. a. $CH_3CH_2C{\equiv}CCH_3 + 2 H_2 \rightarrow CH_3CH_2CH_2CH_2CH_3$

b. $CH_3CH{=}C(CH_3)CH_2CH_2CH_2CH_3 + H_2 \rightarrow CH_3CH_2CH(CH_3)CH_2CH_2CH_2CH_3$

55. a. $CH_3CH_2CH_2CHO$, butanal, is produced by the oxidation of $CH_3CH_2CH_2CH_2OH$, 1-butanol.

b. $CH_3CH_2COCH_2CH_3$, 3-pentanone, is produced by the oxidation of 3 pentanol, $CH_3CH_2CH(OH)CH_2CH_3$.

c. $CH_3COCH(CH_3)_2$, 3-methyl-2-pentanone, is produced by the oxidation of 3-methyl-2-pentanol, $CH_3CHOHCH(CH_3)_2$.

d. C_6H_5CHO, benzaldehyde, is produced by the oxidation of benzyl alcohol, $C_6H_5CH_2OH$.

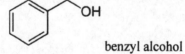

benzyl alcohol

57. These compounds are all isomers—they all have the same chemical formula ($C_4H_{10}O$), but the arrangement of the atoms in each of the molecules is different. Two of the compounds are alcohols and two are ethers, and neither of the alcohols is the same, nor are the ethers the same.

59. The balanced reaction is $CH_2{=}CH_2 + H_2O \rightarrow CH_3CH_2OH$ (it's sometimes easier to change from structures to formulas to make it easier to balance equations: $C_2H_4 + H_2O \rightarrow C_2H_6O$).
The molar masses of ethylene ($CH_2{=}CH_2$) and ethanol (CH_3CH_2OH) are 28.0 g/mol and 46.0 g/mol respectively.

mass of C_2H_6O formed = (445 g C_2H_4)(1 mol C_2H_4/28.0 g C_2H_4)(1 mol C_2H_6O/1 mol C_2H_4)
(46.0 g C_2H_6O/mol C_2H_6O) = 731 g C_2H_6O

61. a. The oxygen-carbon bonds in dimethyl ether (CH_3OCH_3) are polar covalent bonds, allowing for relatively weak dipole-dipole intermolecular forces between the molecules.
    b. All the bonds in ethanol, CH_3CH_2OH, are polar. Both the C-O and O-H bonds are polar and the O-H bond allows for hydrogen bonding interactions.
    Hydrogen bonds are much stronger than dipole-dipole forces, which is the reason ethanol is a liquid at room temperature while dimethyl ether is a gas.

63. a. The structure of hydroquinone:

HO—⟨benzene ring⟩—OH

   b. The structure of para-benzoquinone

O=⟨ring⟩=O

65. Density = mass/volume. Rearranging the ideal gas law and solving for density, d = (P)(molar mass)/RT. The molar masses of the first four gases in Table 9.3 are: methane, 16.0 g/mol; ethane, 30.0 g/mol; propane, 44.0 g/mol; and butane, 58.0 g/mol. Substituting the molar mass of each gas into the equation, we can calculate the density of each gas.

   a. Methane: d = [(1 atm)(16.0 g/mol)]/[(0.0821 L atm/mol K)(293.1 K)] = 0.655 g/L
      Converting this density, in g/mL   d = (0.655 g/L)(1 L/1000mL) = 6.55×10^{-4} g/mL

   b. Ethane: d = [(1 atm)(30.0 g/mol)]/[(0.0821 L atm/mol K)(293.1 K)] = 1.25 g/L
      Converting this density, in g/mL   d = (1.25 g/L)(1 L/1000 mL) = 1.25×10^{-3} g/mL

   c. Propane: d = [(1 atm)(44.0 g/mol)]/[(0.0821 L atm/mol K)(293.1 K)] = 1.83 g/L
      Converting this density, in g/mL   d = (1.83 g/L)(1 L/1000 mL) = 1.83×10^{-3} g/mL

   d. Butane: d = [(1 atm)(58.0 g/mol)]/[(0.0821 L atm/mol K)(293.1 K)] = 2.41 g/L
      Converting this density, in g/mL   d = (2.41 g/L)(1 L/1000 mL) = 2.41×10^{-3} g/mL
   Expressing the density of gases in units of g/L is much more convenient than expressing those densities in units of g/mL.

67. The answer is b. Because many organic molecules are nonpolar, they have limited solubility in polar solvents. Therefore, water is not a good solvent for reactions involving those compounds.

69.   First, the solvents originally used in the synthesis of sertraline, toluene, tetrahydrofuran,
        dichloromethane, and hexane, are compounds derived from petroleum, a nonrenewable
        resource. In addition, these solvents are difficult to dispose of safely. The synthesis has been
        made much greener by substituting ethanol, a solvent that can be prepared from plant materials,
        for these four petroleum-based solvents. Second, the volume of solvent used in the synthesis has
        been reduced from 60,000 gallons to 6.000 gallons per ton of sertraline prepared, which greatly
        reduces the disposal problems as well as the cost of the synthesis.

71.   The advantage of using microwaves to heat reactions is that less energy is used in the process
        than is used when other forms of heat are employed. Less energy is used because the molecules
        absorb the heat directly with less loss to the surroundings so reactions proceed more rapidly and
        are completed much more quickly than is the case when more traditional heating methods are
        used.

CHAPTER

10

Polymers

Giants Among Molecules

CHAPTER SUMMARY

10.1 Polymerization: Making Big Ones Out of Little Ones
- A. Polymer comes from the Greek term for "many parts."
  1. Polymers are macromolecules.
  2. The building blocks of polymers are small molecules called monomers ("one part").
- B. Polymerization is the process by which monomers are converted to polymers.
  1. The physical properties of the monomers are very different than those of the polymer formed from the monomer. For example, ethylene, a monomer, is a gas while polyethylene, a polymer of ethylene, is the material from which plastic bags and other familiar objects are made.
- C. Natural polymers such as proteins have served humanity for as long as we have existed. Other polymers, such as cotton and silk, have been familiar for centuries.
  1. Starch is a polymer made up of glucose units.
  2. Cotton and wool are also polymers of glucose.
  3. Proteins are polymers of amino acids.
  4. Nucleic acids are polymers in DNA.
- D. Celluloid represents the first attempt to improve on natural polymers by chemical modification.
  1. Celluloid, also called cellulose nitrate, is derived from cellulose, a polymer of glucose, treated with nitric acid.
  2. Celluloid was used as a substitute for ivory in billiard balls, and to permanently stiffen shirt collars.
  3. Because it is flammable, celluloid was removed from the market when safer substitutes became available.
  4. The first truly synthetic polymers were phenol-formaldehyde resins first made in 1909. Bakelite is an example.

Answers to Self-Assessment Questions

1. d Proteins are polymers; long chains of amino acids.
2. b Glucose, $C_6H_{12}O_6$, is a monomer that forms polymers such as starch and cellulose.
3. b Celluloid is a modification of the naturally occurring polymer cellulose that has been treated with nitric acid
4. a Bakelite, formed from phenol and formaldehyde, is not a naturally occurring polymer.

10.2 Polyethylene: From the Battle of Britain to Bread Bags
   A. Polyethylene is made from ethylene ($CH_2=CH_2$), a hydrocarbon derived from petroleum.

   B. There are three major types of polyethylene plastics.
      1. High-density polyethylene (HDPE) is made from closely packed linear polymer strands that assume a fairly well-ordered, crystalline structure. HDPEs are relatively dense and tend to be rigid, have great tensile strength, and are not deformed when placed in boiling water.
         a. Used in threaded bottle caps, toys, bottles, and milk jugs.
      2. Low-density polyethylene (LDPE) is made from branched chains that cannot pack as tightly, thus producing a more flexible, non-crystalline material which is less dense than HDPE and which is seriously deformed in boiling water.
         a. Used in plastic bags, plastic film, squeeze bottles and electric wire insulation.
      3. Linear low-density polyethylene (LLPE) is a copolymer (formed of two different monomers) of ethylene and a higher branched-chain alkene such as 4-methyl-1-pentene.
         a. Used to make plastic films for use as landfill liners, trash cans, tubing, and automotive parts.
   C. Polyethylene is a thermoplastic material; it can be softened by heat and then reformed.
      1. Some plastics are thermosetting plastics, or plastics that harden permanently when formed and cannot be softened by heat and remolded.
         a. Permanent hardness of thermosetting plastics is due to cross-linking (side-to-side connections of the polymer chains).
         b. When heated, thermosetting polymers discolor and decompose.

Answers to Self-Assessment Questions

1. d   When the polymerization occurs, one of the shared pairs of electrons in the C=C bond of the monomer is disrupted. One of the electrons in this pair is used to connect the monomer to the developing polymer; the second of the two electrons is used by the now longer polymer to connect to yet another monomer.
2. d   Because there are more branches in LDPE chains than in HDPE chains, the LDPE chains cannot pack as tightly together, resulting in materials with lower densities and lower melting points than HDPEs.
3. b   Foamed coffee cups are made of another polymer, called polystyrene, rather than polyethylene. All the other materials mentioned are made from polyethylene.
4. d   Copolymers are made from the polymerization of two different monomers.
5. d   Because of the extensive cross-linking between chains in thermosetting polymers, they harden permanently when formed and cannot be melted and reshaped.

Green Chemistry: The Many Forms of Carbon
   A. Carbon forms a variety of kinds of structures.
      1. Diamonds are pure crystalline carbon in which each carbon atom is bonded to four other carbon atoms.
      2. Graphite (used in pencil lead, for example) is formed from carbon where each carbon atom is bonded to three other carbon atoms.

      a.   Graphite is formed from many stacked layers of graphene (below).
  3. Graphene is a one-atom-thick planar sheet of carbon atoms lifted from graphite and is useful in electronics, sensing devices, and touch screens.
      a.   Geim and Novoselov were awarded the 2010 Nobel Prize in Physics for their work on graphene.
  4. Buckminster fullerene, also called buckyballs, is a spherical collection of hexagons and pentagons, like the pattern on a soccer ball, with the formula C_{60}.
      a.   The structure resembles a geodesic dome.

10.3 Addition Polymerization: One + One + One + ... Gives One!
  A. There are two general types of polymerization reactions.
    1. Addition polymerization, also called *chain-reaction polymerization*, uses an addition reaction in such a way that the polymeric product contains all of the atoms of the starting monomers.
    2. Condensation polymerization results in a product where some part of each monomer molecule is not included in the polymer chain.
  B. Polypropylene.
    1. Formed from the addition polymerization of propylene, C_3H_6.

$$CH_3-CH{=}CH_2 \xrightarrow{\text{catalyst}} \left[\!\!\begin{array}{c} CH_3 \\ | \\ (CH_2-CH) \end{array}\!\!\right]_n$$

    2. The chain of carbon atoms is called the *backbone*, while groups attached to the backbone (CH_3- in the case of polypropylene) are called *pendant groups*.
    3. Polypropylene is tough and resists moisture, oils, and solvents.
      a.   It is molded into hard-shell luggage, battery cases, and some appliance parts.
      b.   Polypropylene is also used to make packaging material, fibers for textiles such as upholstery fabrics and carpets, and ropes that float.
      c.   Because the melting point of polypropylene is 121 °C, it is used to make objects that can be sterilized with steam.
  C. Polystyrene.
    1. Formed from the addition polymerization of styrene, C_8H_8, ethylene with a benzene pendant group,

    2. Used to make transparent disposable drinking cups and, when a gas is blown into polystyrene liquid, it foams and hardens into Styrofoam® used for ice chests and disposable coffee cups.
    3. Polystyrene can be formed into shapes as packing material for shipping instruments and appliances, and is also widely used as insulation.
  D. Vinyl polymers.
    1. Formed from the addition polymerization of vinyl chloride, C_2H_3Cl, an ethylene molecule in which one of the H atoms is replaced by a chlorine atom, resulting in polyvinyl chloride (PVC).

2. Clear, transparent polymer is used in plastic wrap and clear plastic bottles. Adding color and other ingredients produces artificial leather.
3. Most floor tile and shower curtains are made from vinyl plastics, which are also widely used to simulate wood in home siding panels and window frames.
4. Vinyl chloride, the monomer from which vinyl plastics are made, is a carcinogen.
E. PTFE: the nonstick coating.
1. Made from the polymerization of tetrafluoroethylene, $CF_2=CF_2$.

2. Called Teflon, PTFE is tough, unreactive, nonflammable, strong, and heat- and chemical-resistant.
3. Used to make electric insulation, bearings, and gaskets, as well as to coat surfaces of cookware to eliminate sticking of food.
F. Processing polymers.
1. Many polymers are called plastics.
2. Plastic materials:
   a. Can be made to flow under heat and pressure.
   b. Are often made from granular polymeric material by *compression molding* or *transfer molding*.
   c. In compression molding, heat and pressure are applied directly to the granular material in the mold cavity.
   d. In transfer molding, the polymer is softened by heating before being poured into the molds to harden.
   e. Other methods of molding molten polymers are *injection molding* (plastic is melted in a heating chamber and then forced by pressure into a cold mold) and *extrusion molding* (the melted polymer is extruded through a die in continuous form to be cut into lengths or coiled).
G. Conducting polymers: polyacetylene.
1. Acetylene molecules have triple bonds and can undergo addition reactions.

$$H-C\equiv C-H$$

   a. Result is a polymer with a backbone with alternating carbon-carbon double and carbon-carbon single bonds.

   b. The alternating single and double bonds in this polymer, called a conjugated system, enable the polymer to conduct electricity.

Answers to Self-Assessment Questions

1. b Alkenes serve as the starting point for addition polymers.
2. c Polystyrene has the CH_2CH- group as a backbone with C_6H_6 as pendants.
3. c C_2H_5Cl has no double bonds and, therefore, cannot be used as a monomer for an addition polymer.

4.   a   A buckyball is a spherically-shaped carbon molecule with the formula C_{60}.

10.4 Rubber and Other Elastomers
    A. The plastics industry grew out of the need for a substitute for natural rubber during World War II.
    B. Natural rubber is a polymer of isoprene.

    C. Vulcanization is a process in which natural rubber is heated with sulfur, resulting in cross-linking of the hydrocarbon chains with sulfur atoms.
        1. Vulcanized rubber is harder than natural rubber.
        2. Elastomers are stretchable materials that return to their original structure.
    D. Synthetic rubber.
        1. Some synthetic elastomers are polybutadiene, polychloroprene (Neoprene), and styrene-butadiene rubber (SBR).
            a. Neoprene is more resistant to oil and gasoline than other elastomers are, so it is used to make gasoline hoses.
        2. Styrene-butadiene rubber (SBR) is a copolymer of styrene (~25%) and butadiene (~75%).
            a. SBR is more resistant to oxidation and abrasion than natural rubber but its mechanical properties are less satisfactory.
            b. SBR can be cross-linked by vulcanization.
            c. SBR is used mainly for making tires.
    E. Polymers are added to paint to help harden it into a continuous surface coating.
        1. This polymer is called a binder or resin.
        2. Paints made with elastomers are resistant to cracking.

Answers to Self-Assessment Questions

1.   c   Natural rubber is a polymer of isoprene.
2.   d   Isoprene has the structure $CH_2=C(CH_3)-CH=CH_2$.
3.   a   Adding sulfur to natural rubber cross-links the rubber, making it harder.
4.   d   Charles Goodyear discovered that when natural rubber was heated with sulfur, the natural rubber became cross-linked.
5.   a   Styrene-butadiene rubber is a copolymer, a polymer formed from two different kinds of monomer units.
6.   a   Paint binders are polymers.

10.5 Condensation Polymers
    A. In condensation polymerization, also called step-reaction polymerization, a small molecule, often water (sometimes methanol, ammonia, or HCl), is formed as a byproduct of the reaction.
    B. Nylon and other polyamides.

1. Nylon-6 is formed by splitting out water to join 6-aminohexanoic acid molecules into long polyamide chains.
2. An amide bond is formed between the carbonyl of one monomer and the amine group of another.
3. Water molecules are the by-products.
4. Nylon is a polyamide—amide linkages hold the molecule together.
5. Most nylon is made into fibers, some silk-like, some wool-like, and much of it used in carpeting.

C. Polyethylene terephthalate and other polyesters.
  1. A polyester is a condensation polymer made from molecules with alcohol and carboxylic acid functional groups.
  2. The most common polyester is made from ethylene glycol and terephthalic acid and is called polyethylene terephthalate (PET).

polyethylene terephthalate (polyester)

    a. PET can be molded into bottles, made into film used to laminate documents, and to make packaging tape.
  3. Polyester finishes are used on musical instruments and on the interiors of vehicles and boats. Polyester fibers are strong, quick-drying, and mildew-resistant, so they are used in home furnishings (carpets, curtains, sheets and pillow cases, and upholstery). They do not absorb water, so they are used for insulation in boots and sleeping bags. One type of polyester is the Mylar® used in balloons.

D. Phenol-formaldehyde and related resins.
  1. Bakelite, a condensation polymer of phenol and formaldehyde, is a stable, thermosetting, condensation polymer that won't soften on heating.
  2. It is a three-dimensional polymer composed of phenol units, each with three formaldehyde crosslinks.
  3. Thermosetting resins harden permanently; they cannot be softened and remolded.
  4. Bakelite is used to bind wood chips together in particle board.
  5. Melamine-formaldehyde resins are used in plastic (Melmac) dinnerware and in laminate countertops.

E. Other condensation polymers.

1. Polycarbonates—"tough as glass" polymers.
    a. Used in bullet-proof windows, protective helmets, safety glasses, clear plastic water bottles, baby bottles, and dental crowns.
    b. One polycarbonate is made from bisphenol-A (BPA) and phosgene.
2. Polyurethane
    a. Used in foam rubber in cushions, mattresses, and padded furniture, as well as for skate wheels, running shoes, and in protective gear for sports activities.
3. Epoxies
    a. Used in surface paints and coatings and on the inside of metal cans to protect from rusting.
F. Composite materials.
    1. High-strength fibers (glass, graphite, or ceramics) are held together with a polymeric matrix (usually a thermosetting condensation polymer).
    2. Composites have the strength of steel but weigh only a fraction of the weight.
        a. Powerful adhesives form when two components are mixed and polymer chains become cross-linked.
        b. Widely used in boat hulls, molded chairs, automobile panels, and sports gear such as tennis rackets.
G. Silicones—polymers of alternating silicon and oxygen atoms.
    1. Can be linear, cyclic, or cross-linked networks.
    2. Are very heat-stable and resistant to most chemicals.
    3. Used as water-proofing materials, "Silly Putty," and synthetic body parts.

Answers to Self-Assessment Questions

1. d   Water is usually the co-product with a polymer in condensation polymerization reactions.
2. d   Polyesters are the concentration products of carboxylic acids and alcohols. $HOOCCH_2CH_2CH_2CH_2COOH$ has carboxylic acid groups on both ends and $HOCH_2CH_2CH_2CH_2OH$ has hydroxyl groups on both ends, so these molecules can form condensation products proceeding from both ends of the molecules.
3. c $HOOCCH_2CH_2CH_2CH_2CH_2NH_2$ has both the needed amine and carboxylic acid groups (right and left ends of molecule, respectively) to make a polyamide.
4. c   Thermosetting polymers harden permanently when they are first formed, so they cannot be melted and remolded.
5. c   The backbone of a silicone polymer chain is repeating units of $-SiO-$.

10.6   Properties of Polymers
    A. Polymers differ from substances consisting of small molecules in three main ways.
        1. The long chains can tangle with one another, lending strength to many plastics and elastomers.
        2. The magnitude of intermolecular forces is greater in polymers than in small molecules because of the extent over which the forces exist, giving strength to the polymeric materials.
        3. Large chains have less motion than small molecules so their solutions are usually very viscous.
    B. Crystalline and amorphous polymers.
        1. Crystalline polymers: molecules line up to form long fibers of high tensile strength.
        2. Amorphous polymers: randomly orientated molecules that tangle with one another providing good elasticity.
        3. Two molecular structures can be grafted onto one polymer chain resulting in both sets of properties—flexibility and rigidity.

C. Glass transition temperature (T_g).
   1. Polymers are rubbery above their glass transition temperature (T_g) and are hard and brittle, like glass, below their T_g.
D. Fiber formation.
   1. Three-fourths of fibers and fabrics used in the United States are synthetic.
      a. Synthetic fibers can mimic silk, wool, or enhance the properties of cotton by making it wrinkle-resistant.
      b. Microfibers can be made from almost any fiber-forming polymer.

Answers to Self-Assessment Questions

1.   d   Below the glass transition temperature the polymer becomes glassy and brittle.
2.   d   The molecules in crystalline polymers lie up neatly to form long fibers of great strength.

10.7   Plastics and the Environment
   A. Most plastics break down slowly in the environment, leading to litter and solid waste problems.
      1. When disposed of in oceans, plastics pose a danger to fish by clogging their digestive tracts.
      2. The volume of plastics being disposed of puts stresses on the available space in landfills.
      3. While incinerating (burning) plastics is a source of energy, the process can cause environmental problems, such as the production of toxic gases like HCl when PVC is incinerated.
   B. Degradable plastics.
      1. One approach to solving the problem is to use biodegradable and/or photodegradable polymers in the manufacture of disposable items.
   C. Recycling.
      1. Only two kinds of plastics are recycled on a large scale, PET (28% recycled) and HDPE (29% recycled).
      2. Many plastics can be recycled, but they must be separated according to type.
      3. Code numbers specifying the type of plastic and stamped on the bottom of plastic containers help in the separation process.
         a. Only about 7% of waste plastic was recycled in 2007.
   D. Plastics and fire hazards.
      1. Because polymers are flammable and are used in so many fabrics, fire retardants, usually containing bromine and/or chlorine atoms, are incorporated into the polymeric fibers.
      2. Burning plastics often produce toxic gases, so taking safety precautions is required when anyone works with materials that could combust.
      3. Green chemists are working to make new kinds of polymers that don't burn or that don't generate toxic chemicals when they burn.
   E. Green chemistry: greener polymers.
      1. Many polymers can be recycled, especially PET (#1) and HDPE (#2), but others as well.
         a. Typically, recycled plastic is used to make different objects than the things recycled because the polymer properties are changed. For example, park benches and plastic outdoor decking material are made from recycled plastic bottles.
      2. Some polymers, including PET, can be depolymerized.
      3. Some types of plastics can be degraded into carbon dioxide and water under the right temperature and moisture conditions or in the presence of microorganisms.
      4, New kinds of polymers are being made from renewable resources such as corn, soy, grass, and other kinds of biomass.

      a. Polylactic acid (PLA) is made from corn and polyhydroxyalkanoates (PHAs) are made from plant sugars and oils.
  F. Plasticizers and pollution.
    1. Plastics are made more flexible and less brittle by adding plasticizers to lower their glass transition temperatures, T_gs.
      a. Plasticizers are liquids of low volatility which are generally lost by diffusion and evaporation as a plastic article ages, at which point the plastic becomes brittle and cracks and breaks.
      b. Polychlorinated biphenyls (PCBs), which resemble DDT in structure, were once used as plasticizers but are now banned because they bio-concentrate in the food chain and have the same general physiological effect as DDT.
      c. The most widely used plasticizers for vinyl plastics are phthalate esters which have low acute toxicity and are considered to be generally safe.
  G. Plastics and the future.
    1. In medicine, body replacement parts made from polymers have become common.
    2. PVC water pipes, siding and window frames, plastic foam insulation, and polymeric surface coatings are now used in home construction, as are lumber and wall panels fabricated from artificial wood made from recycled plastics.
    3. Synthetic polymers are used in airplane interiors. The bodies and wings of some planes and some automobile parts are made of composites.
    4. Electrically conducting polymers are used in lightweight batteries for electric automobiles.
    5. Several new types of plastics are made from non-petroleum-based monomers.

Answers to Self-Assessment Questions

1.   d Recycling is the best way to dispose of plastics.
2.   d Many plastics produce toxic gases (for example, HCl from burning polyvinyl chloride) when burned.
3.   b Plasticizers make plastics more flexible by lowering the glass transition temperature of the material.
4.   a Many flame-retardant fabrics incorporate Br and Cl atoms.
5.   c Most synthetic polymers are made from petroleum and natural gas.
6.   c Polylactic acid is made from corn, which is a renewable resource.

LEARNING OBJECTIVES

You should be able to...

1. Define *polymer* and *monomer*.   (10.1)

2. List several natural polymers including a chemically modified one.   (10.1)

3. Describe the structure and properties of the two main types of polyethylene.   (10.2)

4. Use the terms *thermoplastic* and *thermosetting* to explain how polymer structure determines properties.   (10.2)

5. Identify the monomer(s) of an addition polymer, and write the structural formula for a polymer from its monomer structure(s).   (10.3)

6. Define *cross-linking*, and explain how it changes the properties of a polymer.   (10.4)

7. Differentiate between addition and condensation polymerization.   (10.5)

8. Write the structures of the monomers that form polyesters and polyamides.   (10.5)

9. Understand the concept of the glass transition temperature.   (10.6)

10. Explain how crystallinity affects the physical properties of polymers.   (10.6)

11. Describe the environmental problems associated with plastics and plasticizers.   (10.7)

12. Name two types of sustainable, non-petroleum-derived polymers and their sources.   (10.7)

13. Describe plastic recycling, biodegradation, and production from renewable resources.

DISCUSSION

This can be called the Plastic Age (as contrasted to the Stone Age or Iron Age). Humanity has used natural polymers (rubber, wood, cotton) for millennia. Since the early 1900s, chemists have been able to produce polymers and tailor their properties by modifying their structure. Since polymers ("many units") are made out of monomers ("one unit"), the structure of the polymer is determined by the structure of the monomer.

We classify polymers by several methods or types:

1. Thermoplastic—can be reformed by softening with heat.
   Thermosetting—once made, these cannot be reformed.
2. Addition polymers—monomer needs a double (or triple) bond.
   Condensation polymers—monomer needs two functional groups and a small molecule is "condensed" out.
3. Low-density polymers—loosely packed polymer strands; soft and flexible.
   High-density polymers—tightly packed polymer strands; harder and rigid.

You should concentrate on relating the monomer structure to the polymer it makes and the properties of the polymer. The properties of the polymers are determined by their monomers but can be modified by changing their physical properties by introducing additives such as plasticizers, flame retardants, and fibers (to make composites). While there are many advantages to polymers, fire hazards and disposal issues are a problem. The research in polymers is very active with new developments occurring frequently.

ANSWERS TO ODD-NUMBERED REVIEW QUESTIONS AND SOLUTIONS FOR ODD-NUMBERED END OF CHAPTER PROBLEMS

Review Questions

1. The monomer in polyethylene is ethylene, $H_2C=CH_2$, while that in polyvinyl chloride is vinyl

chloride, $H_2C=CHCl$. Polyvinyl chloride is used for, among other things, food wrap, simulated leather, plumbing, garden hoses, and floor tile.

3. Addition polymerization is the polymerization in which all the atoms in the monomer molecules are included in the polymer. Most addition polymers are made from alkenes which contain carbon-carbon double bonds.

5. Polystyrene is used to make disposable foamed drinking cups. Polystyrene is made from styrene.

7. Bakelite is the first truly synthetic polymer and is made from phenol and formaldehyde monomers

9. Synthetic fibers are used more than natural fibers because they are cheaper and have a greater range of properties.

11. In order to be recycled, plastics must be collected, sorted, chopped, melted, and then remolded. The sorting process is simplified by the code numbers stamped on plastic containers.

Problems

13. The polymer chains in LDPE have many branches so the chains cannot pack closely together, so LDPE has a more amorphous structure than HDPE has. As a result, LDPE is less dense and more flexible than HDPE.

15. a. The structure of polyethylene monomer is $H_2C=CH_2$
    b. The structure of the monomer used to make polyacrylonitrile is $H_2C=CH-C\equiv N$

17. a. Polyvinyl chloride has the structure $-\{CH_2CHCl- CH_2CHCl- CH_2CHCl-CH_2CHCl\}-$
    b. Vinylidene has the structure $-\{CH_2CF_2- CH_2CF_2- CH_2CF_2- CH_2CF_2\}-$

19. a. 1-pentene gives a polymer with the structure
    $-CH_2CH(A)CH_2CH(A)CH_2CH(A)CH_2CH(A)-]$ where $A = (CH_3CH_2CH_2)-$
    b. Methyl cyanoacrylate gives a polymer with the structure

21 The structure of the monomer that makes polybutadiene is butadiene.

23. The long chains of polymerized isoprene are coiled and twisted and intertwined with one another, making the material elastic. When stretched, rubber's coiled molecules are straightened. When

released, the molecules coil again. Many other polymers are rigid because their chains are cross-linked or are strongly attracted to each other through intermolecular attractions.

25. SBR, styrene-butadiene rubber, is a copolymer prepared from ~25% styrene and ~75% butadiene.

27. $\left[CO(CH_2)_6\, CONH(CH_2)_8\, NHCO(CH_2)_6\, CONH(CH_2)_8\, NH \right]$

29. $\left[OCH_2COOCH_2COOCH_2COOCH_2CO \right]$

31. Three factors that give polymers properties different from materials made up of small molecules are the long chains can be entangled with one another, intermolecular forces are greatly multiplied in large molecules, and large molecules move more slowly than do small molecules.

33. The glass transition temperature, T_g, is the temperature at which the properties of the polymer change from its being hard, stiff, and brittle, to rubbery and tough. Rubbery materials such as automotive tires should have a low T_g, while glass substitutes should have a high T_g.

35. The monomer unit (a) is $CH_2=CHF$. A four-unit polymer segment (c) is -$CH_2CHF\ CH_2CHF\ CH_2CHF\ CH_2CHF$ with a repeating unit (c) of CH_2CHF. This is an addition polymer because all parts of the monomer are incorporated into the polymer.

37. The monomer structures are $CH_2=CCl_2$ and $CH_2=CHCl$.

39.

41. {-CH_2-$C(CH_3)_2$-CH_2-$C(CH_3)_2$--CH_2-$C(CH_3)_2$-CH_2-$C(CH_3)_2$-}

43. The monomer is $HOCH(CH_3)CH_2COOH$.

45. The student's structure appears to have three carbon atoms in the backbone of the monomer unit. The correct structure of propylene has two carbon atoms in the backbone and a methyl pendant group. The structure of the polymer should look like this:

47. All three balls are made of elastomers or elastic polymers. Of the three balls, the golf ball exhibits the property to the greatest degree and the SuperBall is a close second.

49. Because 1-butanol has an OH group on one end of the molecule only, the reaction cannot continue after the first ester forms on both ends of the terephthalic acid. The final product will be limited to

a trimer of butanol - terephthalic acid – butanol or $CH_3(CH_2)_3OC(O)C_6H_5C(O)O(CH_2)_3CH_3$. A polymer cannot form.

51.   a. The structure of the polymer is shown below.

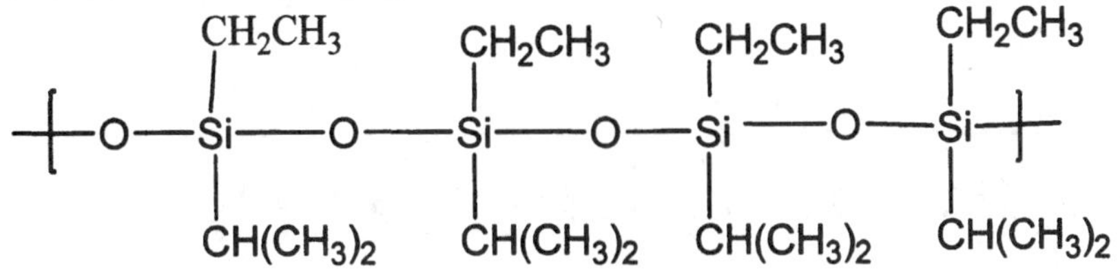

53.   a. $+CH_2CH_2OCH_2CH_2OCH_2CH_2OCH_2CH_2O+$

       b. $+CH_2CH_2SCH_2CH_2SCH_2CH_2SCH_2CH_2S+$

55.   The answer is b. Polylactic acid (PLA) is a polymer made from corn. The other three examples are made from monomers distilled from petroleum.

57.   The answer is c. Only two kinds of plastics are recycled on a large scale, PET (28% recycled) and HDPE (29% recycled).

Nuclear Chemistry

The Heart of Matter

CHAPTER SUMMARY

11.1 Natural Radioactivity
   A. Many nuclei are unstable and undergo radioactive decay. These nuclei are called radioisotopes.
   B. Background radiation: radiation from cosmic rays and natural radioactive isotopes found in air, water, soil, and rocks.
      1. Harmful effects arise from interaction of radiation with living tissue.
      2. Radiation that has sufficient energy to knock electrons from atoms and molecules, converting them into ions, is called ionizing radiation.
   C. Radiation causes damage to cells.
      1. Radiation can break up molecules and convert them into free radicals (species with an unpaired electron).
         a.   White blood cells, responsible to fight infection, are especially vulnerable.
         b.   Leukemia can be induced by exposure to radiation.
      2. Radiation causes changes in DNA that produce mutations in offspring.

Answers to Self-Assessment Questions

1.   d   According to Figure 11.1, 82% of background radiation comes from natural sources.
2.   d   According to Figure 11.1, the largest artificial source of background radiation is from medical X-rays.
3.   c   According to Figure 11.1, radon is responsible for 55% of all background radiation.

11.2 Nuclear Equations
   A. Nuclear equations differ in two ways from chemical equations.
      1. While chemical equations must have the same elements on both sides of the arrow, nuclear equations rarely do.
      2. While we balance atoms in ordinary chemical equations, we balance the nucleons (protons and neutrons) in nuclear equations.
   B. There are three common types of nuclear reactions.
      1. Alpha decay:
         a.   An alpha particle, $_2^4\text{He}$, is a helium nucleus.
         b.   The product when a Ra-226 nucleus releases an alpha particle is Rn-222. We know the equation is balanced when the sum(s) of the mass numbers on both sides of the equation are equal (226 on the left, 222 + 4 = 226 on the right) and the sum(s) of the

atomic numbers on both sides of the equation are equal (88 on the left, 86 + 2 = 88 on the right).

$$^{226}_{88}\text{Ra} \longrightarrow \, ^{222}_{86}\text{Rn} \, + \, ^{4}_{2}\text{He}$$

2. Beta decay:
   a. A beta particle, $^{0}_{-1}e$, is identical to an electron.
   b. The product when C-14 releases a beta particle is N-14. In beta decay, a neutron in the nucleus is converted into a proton (which remains in the nucleus) and an electron (which is ejected). Notice the sums of the atomic numbers (7 + (-1) = 6).

$$^{14}_{6}\text{C} \longrightarrow \, ^{14}_{7}\text{N} \, + \, ^{0}_{-1}e$$

3. Gamma decay:
   a. Gamma decay is different from alpha and beta decay because gamma radiation has no mass or charge. Neither the nucleon number nor the atomic number of the emitting atom is changed: the nucleus simply becomes less energetic.
   b. The penetrating power of gamma rays is extremely high.

C. Positron emission and electron capture are two more types of nuclear reactions.
   1. A positron, $^{0}_{+1}e$, is a particle equal in mass but opposite in charge to the electron. An example of positron emission:

$$^{11}_{6}\text{C} \longrightarrow \, ^{0}_{+1}e \, + \, ^{11}_{5}\text{B}$$

   2. Electron capture is a process in which a nucleus absorbs an electron from an inner electron shell, usually the first or second. When an electron from a higher shell drops to the level vacated by the captured electron, an X-ray is released. Once inside the nucleus, the captured electron combines with a proton to form a neutron. An example of electron capture:

$$^{195}_{79}\text{Au} \, + \, ^{0}_{-1}e \longrightarrow \, ^{195}_{78}\text{Pt}$$

D. Some differences between chemical and nuclear reactions.
   1. Atoms in chemical reactions retain their identity but may change in nuclear reactions.
   2. Chemical reactions involve electrons (usually only valence electrons), whereas nuclear reactions involve mainly protons and neutrons.
   3. Chemical reaction rates can be changed by varying the temperature while nuclear reaction rates are unaffected by temperature changes.
   4. The energy absorbed or released by chemical reactions is comparatively small when compared with the energy associated with nuclear reactions.
   5. Mass is conserved in chemical reactions while mass and energy are conserved in nuclear reactions.

Answers to Self-Assessment Questions

1. b An electron is the same as a beta particle.
2. a An alpha particle has an atomic mass of 4 u and is the same as a helium nucleus.
3. d Radioactivity is the emission of particles and energy from a nucleus.
4. c The number of protons and neutrons in an atom is the nucleon number.
5. b Gamma radiation has no charge and no mass; it is pure energy.
6. a An alpha particle, $^{4}_{2}\text{He}$, is needed to balance the atomic numbers (lower left) and nucleon numbers (upper left).

11.3 Half-Life
   A. Radioactivity is dependent on the isotope involved but is generally independent of any outside influence such as temperature or pressure.
   B. Radioactivity is a random process. Large numbers of atoms have a predictable half-life characteristic of each radioisotope.
      1. The half-life is a property of a radioactive isotope and represents the period of time required for one half of the radioactive atoms to undergo decay.
         a. Half-lives can vary in length enormously.
         b. The fraction of the original radioactive sample remaining after n half-lives is given by $1/2^n$, or 1/2, 1/4, 1/8, 1/16, and so forth.
   C. Radioisotopic dating.
      1. The half-lives of radioisotopes can be used to estimate the age of rocks and artifacts, such as the Shroud of Turin, dated to between A.D. 1260 and 1340, and the Dead Sea Scrolls, dated 2000 years ago.
      2. Many artifacts are dated by their carbon-14 content.
      3. Tritium dating is used to date items up to 100 years old.

Answers to Self-Assessment Questions

1. a   36 h is 6 half-lives. This gives the fraction $1/2^6 = 1/64$. 48 mg x 1/64 = 0.75 mg.
2. c   2.5 g is one-fourth of 10 g or $1/2^2$. This decay occurred over two half-lives so one half-life is 6.2 h.
3. d   285 years is 10 half-lives. This gives the fraction $1/2^{10}$ or 1/1024. 64.0 g x 1/1024 = 0.0625g.
4. c   The decline from 16 Bq to 2 Bq represents 3 half-lives (2 Bq is one-eighth of 16 Bq or $1/2^3$). 3 x 22.26 y = 67 y.
5. b   3.9 counts per minute is one-fourth of 15.6 counts per minute or $1/2^2$, so two half-lives have elapsed since the live wood was cut and ceased to metabolize. 2 x 5730 y = 11,460 y.

11.4 Artificial Transmutation
   A. Nuclear changes can also be brought about by the bombardment of stable nuclei with subatomic particles such as alpha particles, beta particles, or neutrons.

$$^{9}_{4}Be + ^{4}_{2}He \longrightarrow ^{12}_{6}C + ^{1}_{0}n$$

      1. A nuclear change whereby one element is changed into another is called transmutation.
   B. Transmutations carried out by Rutherford with alpha particles led to the discovery of fundamental particles such as protons.

Answers to Self-Assessment Questions

1. b   The nucleon number must be 14 and the nuclear charge must be 6 to balance the mass and charge. The new isotope is carbon-14.
2. c   The nucleon number must be 6 and the nuclear charge must be 3 to balance the mass and charge. The new isotope is lithium-6.
3. c   The nucleon number must be 242 and the nuclear charge must be 96 to balance the mass and charge. The new isotope is curium-242.

11.5 Uses of Radioisotopes
   A. Radioisotopes in industry and agriculture.
      1. Radioactive isotopes can substitute chemically for their nonradioactive counterparts but have the advantage of being easily detected; they act as tracers.

a. Radioactive I-131, with a short half-life (8.04 days) is used to detect leaks in underground pipes.
   b. Beta-emitters are used to measure the thickness of sheet metal during production.
   c. Carbon-14 is used to determine frictional wear in piston rings.
   d. Phosphorus-32, a beta-emitter with a half-life of 14.3 d, is used to study the uptake of phosphorus and its distribution in plants.
2. Radioisotopes are used to study the effectiveness of weed killers, compare the nutritional value of feeds, determine optimal methods for insect control, and monitor the fate and persistence of pesticides in soil and groundwater.
3. Radioisotopes can be used to induce heritable genetic alterations known as mutations into seeds.
4. Gamma-ray emitting radioisotopes are used in the irradiation of food to kill microorganisms.
B. Radioisotopes in medicine.
   1. Nuclear medicine involves two distinct uses of radioisotopes: therapeutic and diagnostic.
   2. An example of a therapeutic use is radiation therapy: Radiation from radioisotopes is used to treat cancer.
   3. Radioisotopes are used for diagnostic purposes to provide information about the functioning of some part of the body or about the type or extent of an illness.

Isotope	Half-life	Use
Carbon-11	20.39 min	Brain scans
Chromium-51	27.8 d	Blood volume determination
Cobalt-57	270 d	Measuring vitamin B_{12} uptake
Cobalt-60	5.271 y	Radiation cancer therapy
Gadolinium-153	242 d	Determining bone density
Gallium-67	78.1 h	Scan for lung tumors
Iodine-131	8.040 d	Thyroid diagnoses and therapy
Iridium-192	74 d	Breast cancer therapy
Iron-59	44.496 d	Detection of anemia
Phosphorus-32	14.3 d	Detection of skin cancer or eye tumors
Plutonium-238	86 y	Provision of power in pacemakers
Radium-226	1600 y	Radiation therapy for cancer
Selenium-75	120 d	Pancreas scans
Sodium-24	14.659 h	Locating obstructions in blood flow
Technetium-99m (m means metastable)	6.0 h	Imaging of brain, liver, bone marrow, kidney, lung, or heart
Thallium-201	73 h	Detecting heart problems during treadmill stress test
Tritium (H-3)	12.26 y	Determining total body water
Xenon-133	5.27 d	Lung imaging

4. Computer-aided medical imaging methods such as positron emission tomography (PET) scans use positron-emitters to generate gamma rays inside the body and measure dynamic processes such as blood flow or the rate at which oxygen or glucose is being metabolized.

Answers to Self-Assessment Questions

1. a I-131's short half-life makes it ideal for detecting leaks in underground pipes.
2. c Gamma radiation is used to irradiate foodstuffs to extend shelf life.

3. d Cobalt-60 is used in radiation therapy.
4. a Gadolinium-153 is used in determining bone density.
5. e Iodine-131 is used to treat thyroid disorders.
6. b Technetium-99m is used to create brain images.
7. c Thallium-201 is used to detect heart problems.
8. c Positrons are used in PET (Positron Emission Tomography) scans.

11.6 Penetrating Power of Radiation
A. The penetrating power of different types of radiation varies widely with gamma > beta > alpha owing in part to their masses as well as to their charges.
1. Alpha particles outside the body do little damage because they can't penetrate the skin. Inside the body, alpha particles inflict great damage because they are trapped in a small area.
2. Outside the body, beta particles are somewhat more penetrating than alpha particles; while inside the body they do their damage over a somewhat larger area because they travel further.
3. Gamma radiation is the most penetrating of all, both inside and outside the body.
B. Protection from radiation.
1. Move away from the source.
2. Use shielding between you and the source of the radiation.

Answers to Self-Assessment Questions

1. c The most penetrating type of radiation is gamma radiation and the least are alpha particles.
2. a Alpha particles cannot penetrate a sheet of paper.
3. a The reduction in Geiger counter activity indicates that most of the radiation was blocked by the piece of paper. Alpha particles are easily blocked.

11.7 Energy from the Nucleus
A. Albert Einstein (1905) derived a relationship between matter and energy, $E = mc^2$, where E is energy, m is mass, and c is the speed of light, as a part of his theory of relativity.
B. Binding energy, the energy that holds the nucleons together in the nucleus, is equivalent to the difference in mass between the individual protons and neutrons and the mass of the nucleus they form; it is related by the equation $E = mc^2$.
1. Elements with the highest binding energy per nucleon are the most stable.
2. In nuclear fission reactions, one nucleus splits into two or more smaller nuclei with higher binding energies and, therefore, with greater stability than the original nucleus that split.
3. In nuclear fusion reactions, a great deal of energy is released when small atoms with lower binding energies combine to form a larger atom with more binding energy. This is what happens when a hydrogen bomb explodes and is also the source of the sun's energy.
C. Nuclear fission.
1. In the process of bombarding U-238 nuclei with neutrons, Fermi and others discovered but couldn't explain the presence of smaller nuclei in the reaction mixture.
   a. They concluded that the uranium nucleus split into fragments.
D. Nuclear chain reaction.
1. Szilard discovered that when a uranium nucleus was bombarded with neutrons it split into two smaller fragments and, at the same time, gave off three neutrons which then could trigger the fission of other uranium atoms in a chain reaction.
E. Thermonuclear reactions.

1. The thermonuclear reactions that take place in the sun required enormously high temperatures (millions of degrees) to initiate them.
2. The intense temperatures and pressures in the sun cause small nuclei to fuse into larger ones.

Answers to Self-Assessment Questions

1. b   Helium is more stable than H and Li because of its high binding energy per nucleon.
2. c   Iron nuclei are the most stable nuclei because they have the highest binding energy per nucleon.
3. c   Nuclei with nucleon numbers above that of iron are less stable than iron because their binding energies per nucleon are lower.
4. c $E = mc^2$ gives the mass defect in a fission reaction.
5. c   Neutrons carry out the chain reaction.
6. d   In order to balance the reaction, 3 neutrons are needed.
7. d   The process involves fusing two small nuclei into one bigger nucleus, a process that is accompanied by the release of energy.
8. b. A neutron is needed to balance the nuclear reaction.

11.8 Nuclear Bombs
   A. The Manhattan Project was the research effort launched in 1939 by President Roosevelt to study atomic energy.
      1. Program involved four research teams studying how to:
         a.   sustain the nuclear fission reaction;
         b.   enrich uranium so that it contained ~90% U-235;
         c.   make plutonium-239, another fissionable isotope;
         d.   construct a bomb based on nuclear fission.
   B. Sustainable chain reaction.
      1. Studied by Enrico Fermi's group at the University of Chicago.
      2. One goal was to determine the critical mass; the amount of U-235 needed to sustain the fission reaction.
      3. On December 2, 1942, Fermi's group achieved the first sustained nuclear fission reaction using 16 kg of uranium enriched to about 94% U-235.
   C. Isotopic enrichment.
      1. Natural uranium, U-238, does not undergo fission.
      2. U-235 makes up only 0.72% of natural uranium.
      3. Chemical separation was almost impossible because the two isotopes behave almost identically.
         a.   Converted U to gaseous uranium hexafluoride, $^{235}UF_6$ and $^{238}UF_6$.
         b.   After passage through long distances, $^{235}UF_6$ ultimately moved farther than $^{238}UF_6$ because it was slightly lighter, allowing separation of the isotopes.
   D. Plutonium synthesis.
      1. Effort led by Glenn Seaborg's group at Oak Ridge (TN).
      2. Found that, although U-238 does not fission, it does decay into Pu-239, which is fissionable.
      3. A group of large reactors were built near Hanford, WA to produce Pu.
   E. Bomb construction.
      1. Construction of atomic bombs based on U-235 and on Pu-239 was done at Los Alamos, NM under the direction of J. Robert Oppenheimer.
      2. Synthesis of Pu turned out to be easier than the separation of U isotopes.
      3. First atomic bomb (a Pu device) was tested in the desert near Alamogordo, NM on July 16, 1945.

4. August 6, 1945 President Truman ordered the dropping of the U bomb "Little Boy" on Hiroshima, causing more than 100,000 casualties. Three days later, another plutonium bomb, "Fat Man," was dropped on Nagasaki. World War II ended with the surrender of Japan on August 14, 1945.
F. Radioactive fallout.
   1. The primary fission products are radioactive, as are many of the daughter isotopes.
      a. Sr-90 (half-life = 28.5 y) reaches us primarily through dairy products and vegetables and is incorporated into bone, becoming an internal radioactive source.
      b. I-131 (half-life = 8 days) is transferred up the food chain and incorporated in the thyroid gland. For healthy individuals, presence of I-131 has damaging effects.
      c. Cs-137 (half-life = 30.2 y) is similar to potassium and is taken up as part of body fluids.
   2. Concern over radiation damage from nuclear fallout led to a movement to ban atmospheric testing.
      a. Nobel laureate Linus Pauling was instrumental spokesperson for banning atmospheric tests.
   3. In 1963, a nuclear test ban treaty was signed by the major nations, with the exception of the People's Republic of China.
      a. Pauling was awarded the Nobel Peace Prize in 1962.

Answers to Self-Assessment Questions

1. c   Only U-235 undergoes fission at a level that can be used in a bomb.
2. a   Less than 1% of uranium ore is U-235.
3. a   U-238 bombarded with a neutron produces Np-239 which quickly decays into Pu-239.
4. a   Calcium and strontium are in the same group in the periodic table and have similar chemical properties.
5. b   Iodine is concentrated in the thyroid.

11.9 Uses of Nuclear Energy
A. Nuclear energy accounts for one-fifth of the energy produced in the United States.
   1. 80% of the energy in France comes from nuclear power plants.
   2. Belgium, Spain, Switzerland, and Sweden generate about one-third of their power from nuclear reactors.
B. One of the main problems with nuclear power production arises from disposal of nuclear waste and the possibility of transforming this waste into weapons-grade material.
C. Green remediation of nuclear waste.
   1. The volume of nuclear waste from the Manhattan Project, referred to as high-level liquid waste (HLLW) is in excess of 91 million gallons and is both extremely acidic and radioactive.
   2. Removal of Np, Am, and Nd produced during the fission reactions would dramatically reduce the radioactivity of the mixture.
   3. Reprocessing spent fuel rods can also reduce the radioactivity of the waste.
      a. In reprocessing, specific molecules, for example, amides, can be used to bind to the radioactive cations producing compounds that can be extracted into organic solvents and then incinerated, greatly reducing the volume of waste.
D. Nuclear proliferation and dirty bombs.
   1. A dirty bomb is a device that uses a conventional explosive, such as dynamite, to disperse radioactive material that might be stolen from a hospital or other facility that uses radioactive isotopes.
E. The nuclear age.
   1. See Figure 11.16 for examples of productive uses of nuclear energy.

LEARNING OBJECTIVES

You should be able to...

1.	Identify the sources of the natural radiation to which we are exposed.	(11.1)
2.	List the sources and dangers of ionizing radiation.	(11.1)
3.	Balance nuclear equations.	(11.2)
4.	Identify the products formed by various decay processes.	(11.2)
5.	Solve simple half-life problems.	(11.3)
6.	Use the concept of half-life to solve simple radioisotope dating problems.	(11.3)
7.	Write a nuclear equation for a transmutation, and identify the product element formed.	(11.4)
8.	List some applications of radioisotopes.	(11.5)
9.	Describe the nature of materials needed to block alpha, beta, and gamma radiation.	(11.6)
10.	Explain where nuclear energy comes from.	(11.7)
11.	Describe the difference between fission and fusion.	(11.7)
12.	Describe how uranium and plutonium bombs are made.	(11.8)
13.	Identify the most hazardous fallout isotopes, and explain why they are particularly dangerous.	(11.8)
14.	List some uses of nuclear energy.	(11.9)
15.	Identify green chemistry principles that can help solve existing problems in nuclear chemistry.	
16.	Explain how molecules used in nuclear waste processing can be designed to be safer, and give examples of such molecules.	

DISCUSSION

The nucleus is 1/100,000 the size of the atom, yet it contains all the mass and all the positive charge. Nuclear symbols summarize the information needed to describe an isotope: the number of protons (atomic number or nuclear charge) and the number of neutrons (mass number). In a nuclear equation, the atomic numbers and mass numbers are conserved; that is, they are equal before and after the reaction. The half-life of each isotope is characteristic of that isotope and a constant that cannot be changed. A half-life is the time it takes for half of the material to decay. Transmutations can be accomplished by bombarding nuclei with subatomic particles. Radioisotopes are used for their penetrating power and the amount of change they can cause in medical, food, and industrial applications. The ages of rocks and archeological artifacts are determined using half-lives. In a nuclear reaction, mass is converted into energy, producing a million times the energy of an equivalent chemical reaction. This energy is used in fission (splitting nuclei) processes such as the A-bomb and in current nuclear power plants. These processes require sophisticated technology to increase ("enrich") the amount of fissionable material and have hazards associated with radioactivity. The reaction of the sun and H-bomb is thermonuclear fusion—union of nuclei.

EXAMPLE PROBLEMS

1. Thorium-232 $\left({}^{232}_{90}Th \right)$ undergoes alpha decay. What new element is formed?

   Mass and charge are conserved. Alpha particles are helium nuclei and thus carry away 4 mass units and 2 units of charge. The new nuclei must have a mass of 232 - 4 = 228 and a nuclear charge of 90 - 2 = 88. The nuclear charge (atomic number) identifies the new element as radium. The equation for the process is

   $$ {}^{232}_{90}Th \longrightarrow {}^{4}_{2}He + {}^{228}_{88}Ra $$

2. Iodine-131 $\left({}^{131}_{53}I \right)$ undergoes beta decay. What new element is formed?

   The beta particle takes away essentially no mass (the nucleon number remains unchanged) and a charge of -1. Subtracting 1 increases the nuclear charge by one. The new element has a nuclear charge of 54, identifying it as xenon. The equation is

   $$ {}^{131}_{53}I \longrightarrow {}^{0}_{-1}e + {}^{131}_{54}Xe $$

3. Radioactive nitrogen-13 has a half-life of 10 minutes. After an hour, how much of this isotope would remain in a sample that originally contained 96 mg?

   One hour is 60 minutes or 6 half-lives (n = 6) and m_0 = 96 mg.

   $$ m_r = \left(\frac{1}{2^6} \right) \times (96 \text{ mg}) = \left(\frac{1}{64} \right) \times (96 \text{ mg}) = 1.5 \text{ mg} $$

4. Radioactive thalium-154 has a half-life of 5 seconds. After 10 seconds, how many milligrams of this isotope remain in a sample that originally contained 160 mg?

   Ten seconds is 2 half-lives (n = 2), and m_0 = 160 mg.

   $$ m_r = \left(\frac{1}{2^2} \right) \times (160 \text{ mg}) = \left(\frac{1}{4} \right) \times (160 \text{ mg}) = 40 \text{ mg} $$

ADDITIONAL PROBLEMS

1. Complete the following equations by supplying the missing component.

   a. $^{234}_{90}\text{Th} \longrightarrow \, ^{0}_{-1}e \, + \, ?$

   b. $^{222}_{86}\text{Rn} \longrightarrow \, ^{4}_{2}\text{He} \, + \, ?$

   c. $^{56}_{26}\text{Fe} \, + \, ^{2}_{1}\text{H} \longrightarrow \, ^{54}_{25}\text{Mn} \, + \, ?$

2. Protactinium-234 has a half-life of 1 minute. How much of a 400-μg sample of protactinium would remain after 1 minute? After 2 minutes? After 4 minutes?

3. The half-life of plutonium-239 is 24,300 years. About 8 kg of this isotope is released in a nuclear explosion. How many years would pass before the amount was reduced to 1 kg?

ANSWERS TO ODD-NUMBERED REVIEW QUESTIONS AND SOLUTIONS FOR ODD-NUMBERED END OF CHAPTER PROBLEMS

1. (i) The answer is b. New compounds are formed as the result of chemical reactions.
   (ii) The answer is a. New elements are formed as the result of nuclear transformations.
   (iii) The answer is c. The size, shape, appearance, or volume of a substance changes without changing its composition as the result of a physical change.

3. The symbol for protinium (or H-1) is $^{1}_{1}\text{H}$; the symbol for deuterium (H-2) is $^{2}_{1}\text{H}$; and the symbol for tritium (H-3) is $^{3}_{1}\text{H}$.

5. a. The symbol for cobalt-60 is $^{60}_{27}\text{Co}$.
   b. The symbol for iodine-127 is $^{127}_{53}\text{I}$.
   c. The symbol for sodium-22 is $^{22}_{11}\text{Na}$.
   d. The symbol for calcium-42 is $^{42}_{20}\text{Ca}$.

7. The pairs in options b and c are isotopes. Isotopes have the same nuclear charge (atomic number) but different mass. While the symbols in options a, b, and c have the same atomic number, those in option a are identical and so do not represent isotopes. The symbols in option d represent different elements.

9. Es-254 has an atomic number of 99 and a nucleon number of 254. The number of neutrons is obtained by subtracting the atomic number from the nucleon number. The number of neutrons in Es-254 = 254 - 99 = 155.

11. a. In alpha particle emission, the nucleon number is reduced by four and the atomic number decreases by two.

b.   In gamma ray emission, both the nucleon number and the atomic number stay the same.

c.   In a proton emission, both the nucleon number and atomic number decrease by one.

13.   a.   Alpha particles can be stopped by a sheet of paper or a fabric layer. Gamma rays would penetrate both these materials.

b.   Heavy lead shielding is necessary to protect workers from gamma radiation.

15.   Inside the body, alpha particles inflict their damage in a small, focused area because they do not travel far. Beta particles travel farther, so their damage is spread over a larger area.

17.   Nuclear fission is the breaking apart of nuclei while nuclear fusion is the combining of nuclei. Both produce energy as mass is lost during each reaction and the resultant product nuclei are more stable than the reactant nuclei. The mass is converted into energy.

Problems

19.   a. $^{250}_{98}\text{Cf} \rightarrow {}^{4}_{2}\text{He} + {}^{246}_{96}\text{Cm}$

b. $^{210}_{83}\text{Bi} \rightarrow {}^{210}_{84}\text{Po} + {}^{0}_{-1}e$

c. $^{117}_{53}\text{I} \rightarrow {}^{0}_{+1}e + {}^{117}_{52}\text{Te}$

21.   a. $^{179}_{79}\text{Au} \longrightarrow {}^{175}_{77}\text{Ir} + {}^{4}_{2}\text{He}$

b. $^{12}_{6}\text{C} + {}^{2}_{1}\text{H} \longrightarrow {}^{13}_{6}\text{C} + {}^{1}_{1}\text{H}$

c. $^{154}_{62}\text{Sm} + {}^{1}_{0}\text{n} \longrightarrow 2\,{}^{1}_{0}\text{n} + {}^{153}_{62}\text{Sm}$

23. $^{99}_{42}\text{Mo} \longrightarrow {}^{99m}_{43}\text{Tc} + {}^{0}_{-1}e$ A beta particle formed.

25.   Sodium-24 formed. $^{24}_{12}\text{Mg} + {}^{1}_{0}\text{n} \rightarrow {}^{1}_{1}\text{H} + {}^{24}_{11}\text{Na}$

27. $^{215}_{85}\text{At} \rightarrow {}^{4}_{2}He + {}^{211}_{83}\text{Bi}$ The original nucleus was $^{215}_{85}At$.

29. $^{210}_{85}\text{At} \rightarrow {}^{0}_{-1}e + {}^{210}_{86}\text{Rn}$; $^{210}_{86}\text{Rn} \rightarrow {}^{0}_{-1}e + {}^{210}_{87}\text{Fr}$ The nuclear symbol for B is $^{210}_{87}Fr$.

31.   5000 counts/min is one-fourth of the original 20,000 counts/min, which represents two half-lives of expired time. The half-life of Ga-67 is 78.1 hr so (2)(78.1 hr) = 156 hr (or 6.5 d) will have elapsed.

33.   The answer is b. The half-life of Mg-21 at 122 ms is very short and the sample no longer contains a significant amount of Mg-21.

35.   One quarter of the original activity is equal to $1/2^2$. The sample will have gone through two half-lives, or 26 s, to reach this level of activity.

37.   There are 8 half-lives from Friday at 4 pm to Monday at 8:30 am. 500 counts/min x $1/2^8$ = 2 counts per minute.

39. The half-life of C-14 is 5730 years. The C-14 in the artifact has gone through one half-life so it must be approximately 5730 years old.

41. If the charcoal has half the activity, then the site is 5730 years old. If the charcoal has one-fourth the activity, then the site is 11,460 years old.

43. a. $^{121}_{51}\text{Sb} + ^{4}_{2}\text{He} \rightarrow ^{124}_{53}\text{I} + ^{1}_{0}\text{n}$

    b. $^{124}_{53}\text{I} \rightarrow ^{124}_{52}\text{Te} + ^{0}_{+1}\text{e}$

45. $^{48}_{20}\text{Ca} + ^{247}_{97}\text{Bk} \rightarrow ^{293}_{117}X + 2^{1}_{0}\text{n}$; Two neutrons were released.

    $^{48}_{20}\text{Ca} + ^{247}_{97}\text{Bk} \rightarrow ^{294}_{117}X + ^{1}_{0}\text{n}$; One neutron was released.

47. $^{223}_{88}\text{Ra} \rightarrow ^{219}_{86}\text{Rn} + ^{4}_{2}\text{He}$

    $^{223}_{88}\text{Ra} \rightarrow ^{209}_{82}\text{Pb} + ^{14}_{6}\text{C}$

49. $d = m/V$
    $V = m/d$
    $V = (16{,}300 \text{ g})/19.1 \text{ g/cm}^3$
    $V = 853 \text{ cm}^3$

    $V = (2{,}500 \text{ g})/(19.1 \text{ g/cm}^3)$
    $V = 131 \text{ cm}^3$

    The equation for a sphere is $4/3\pi r^3$
        A baseball has a radius of 3.56 cm and a volume of 189 cm^3.
        A volleyball has a radius of 10.54 cm and a volume of 4905 cm^3.
        A basketball has a radius of 12.17 cm and a volume of 7750 cm^3.
    The mass of plutonium is smaller than a baseball.

51. a. Use $t = (\ln 0.795/-0.693) \times 5730 = (-0.229/-0.6930 = 0.331 \times 5730 = 1896$ or 1900
    b. Use $t = (\ln 0.175/-0.693) \times 5730 = (-1.74/-0.6930 = 2.52 \times 5730 = 14411$ or 14,400

53. $^{9}_{4}\text{Be} + ^{4}_{2}\text{He} \rightarrow ^{12}_{6}C + ^{1}_{0}\text{n}$
    This was the first experimental detection of the neutron.

55. a. $E = mc^2$; $1 \text{ g} = 0.001 \text{ kg}$
       $E = (0.001 \text{ kg})(3.00 \times 10^8 \text{ m/s})^2 = 9 \times 10^{13} \text{ kg·m}^2/\text{s}^2$ or 9×10^{13} J
       1 calorie = 4.184 J;
       number of cal released = $(9 \times 10^{13} \text{ J})/(4.184 \text{ J/cal}) = 2.2 \times 10^{13}$ cal
       number of kcal released = $(2.25 \times 10^{13} \text{ cal})(1 \text{ kcal}/1000 \text{ cal}) = 2.2 \times 10^{10}$ kcal.

    b. number of bowls of corn flakes = $(2.2 \times 10^{10} \text{ kcal})(1 \text{ bowl}/110 \text{ kcal}) = 2.0 \times 10^8$ bowls.

57. The elapsed time between March 15 and April 21 is 37 days, which represents (37 days/14.28 days) = 2.6 half-lives. Therefore, the number of P-32 atoms in the corpse at the time of death was approximately $(2^{2.6})(1.24 \times 10^{17}) = 7.5 \times 10^{17}$ atoms.

59. The statement is false. For example, green chemistry principles can be applied to the remediation of nuclear waste.

61. Having two amide groups on a molecule increases the binding power of the molecule to radioactive metal ions without losing the benefits of using this type of molecule.

CHAPTER

12

Chemistry of the Earth

Metals and Minerals

CHAPTER SUMMARY

12.1 Spaceship Earth: The Materials Manifest
  A. Structurally, the Earth is divided into three main regions: the core, the mantle, and the crust.
    1. The core is thought to be mainly iron and some nickel.
    2. The mantle is believed to consist mainly of silicates (sulfur, oxygen, and metal compounds).
    3. The crust is the outer shell of the Earth; it has three parts.
      a. The lithosphere is the solid part and is about 35 km thick under the continents and 10 km thick under the oceans.
      b. The hydrosphere is the oceans, lakes, rivers, etc.
      c. The atmosphere (air) is the gaseous part.
  B. The most abundant element in the Earth's crust by both mass and atom percent is oxygen, followed by silicon and hydrogen.
    1. In the atmosphere, oxygen occurs primarily as molecular oxygen, O_2. In the lithosphere, it occurs primarily in combination with silicon (sand is SiO_2) and some other elements, while in the hydrosphere, oxygen occurs primarily as water, H_2O.
  C. The lithosphere: organic and inorganic.
    1. The lithosphere is mainly rocks and minerals, including silicates, carbonates, oxides, and sulfides.
    2. A much smaller (in quantity) organic portion includes all living creatures, their waste and decomposition products, and fossilized minerals.
      a. Organic material always contains carbon, nearly always contains hydrogen, and often oxygen, nitrogen, and other elements.
  D. Meeting our needs: from sticks to bricks.
    1. Over the centuries people have learned to convert natural materials into products with superior properties.
    2. Fire was one of the earliest agents of chemical change.

Answers to Self-Assessment Questions

1. b   The regions of the Earth from the center to outside are the core, the mantle, and the crust.
2. b   The Earth's core is mostly iron.

3. d Oxygen is the most abundant element followed in decreasing order by silicon and hydrogen.

12.2 Silicates and the Shape of Things
  A. The basic silicate unit is the SiO_4 tetrahedron.
    1. Silicates can exist singly or be arranged linearly in fibers, in planar sheets, or in complex three-dimensional arrays.
    2. Zircon exists as simple silicate anions (SiO_4^{4-}).
  B. Quartz is pure silicon dioxide, SiO_2; however, each silicon atom in the crystal is surrounded by four oxygen atoms.
    1. Amethyst, citrine, rose, and smoky quartz contain impurities, which give them their characteristic color.
  C. Micas are composed of sheets of SiO_4 tetrahedra, giving a two-dimensional structure.
  D. Asbestos is a generic term for fibrous silicates.
    1. Chrysotile is a form of asbestos composed of a double chain of SiO_4 tetrahedra bonded to magnesium ions.
    2. Inhalation of asbestos fibers over 10 to 20 years causes asbestosis, a severe respiratory disease. After 30 to 45 years, mesothelioma or cancer may develop.
    3. Cigarette smoking and inhalation of asbestos fibers act synergistically to greatly increase the risk of lung cancer.
  E. Modified silicates: ceramics.
    1. Ceramics (modified sand, clays, and limestone) have been developed with specialized properties such as high heat resistance, magnetic properties, and computer memory capabilities.
    2. Bricks and pottery are examples of ceramics.
  F. Glass.
    1. Glass is a noncrystalline solid resulting from heating a mixture of sand, "soda" (sodium carbonate, Na_2CO_3), and limestone (calcium carbonate, $CaCO_3$).
      a. When heated, glass softens and can be blown, rolled, pressed, or molded.
      b. Properties result from an irregular three-dimensional arrangement of SiO_4 tetrahedra connected by chemical bonds of varying strength.
    2. Basic ingredients in glass can be mixed in different proportions.
    3. Glass manufacture uses no vital raw materials but the furnaces require a great deal of energy to reach high temperatures.
    4. Glass is easily recycled.
  C. Cement and concrete.
    1. Cement is a complex mixture of calcium and aluminum silicates.
      a. Raw materials are finely ground limestone and clay, heated to 1500 °C.
    2. The finished product is mixed with sand, gravel, and water to form concrete.
      a. Concrete is widely used in construction because it is inexpensive, strong, chemically inert, durable, and tolerant of a wide range of temperatures.
      b. Its production is expensive, both in terms of environmental damage and cost.
      c. Concrete can be recycled as rock fill.

Answers to Self-Assessment Questions

1. d All silicate minerals contain oxygen.
2. c Quartz is pure SiO_2.
3. c Si is at the center of a tetrahedron surrounded by four oxygen atoms.
4. a Asbestos has double chains of silicon and oxygen atoms.
5. b Mica has sheets of silicon and oxygen atoms.

6.   d   Quartz has a three-dimensional array of silicon and oxygen atoms.
7.   c   Zircon has a structure of simple anions.
8.   b   Asbestos and cigarette smoke function synergistically to cause cancer.
9.   a   Ceramics are hard and durable but break easily (brittle).
10.   d   Ordinary glass is made of mostly sand, sodium carbonate, and limestone.
11.   a   The main ingredients of ordinary cement are clay and limestone.

12.3   Metals and Ores
   A.   Copper and bronze.
        1.   Copper was probably the first metal to be separated from ore through smelting.
        2.   Bronze, a copper-tin alloy, is harder than copper.
             a. An alloy is a mixture of two or more elements, at least one of which is a metal.
   B.   Iron and steel.
        1.   Carbon reduces iron oxides to iron metal. (The actual reducing agent is carbon monoxide.)
        2.   Iron is converted to steel (an alloy of carbon with other metals) by reacting oxygen with the impurities in iron and adjusting the carbon content.
             a.   High-carbon steel is hard and strong.
             b.   Low-carbon steel is ductile and malleable.
        3.   Iron reacts with atmospheric oxygen, forming a porous, flaky coating that flakes off, allowing further oxidation.
   C.   Aluminum: abundant and light.
        1.   Unlike iron, aluminum forms an oxide film on its surface which protects the metal from further corrosion.
   D.   The environmental costs of iron and aluminum.
        1.   Aluminum is the most abundant metal in the Earth's crust, occurring as aluminum oxide (bauxite).
        2.   Making an aluminum can from bauxite requires 6.3 times as much energy as making a steel can.
        3.   When aluminum is recycled, only a fraction of the energy needed to make a steel can is required.
   E.   Other important metals.
        1.   Table 12 in your text lists other technologically important metals such as indium, lithium, and palladium.
        2.   Although atoms are conserved globally, use of metals scatters these atoms throughout the environment.

Answers to Self-Assessment Questions

1.   b   Copper is the element most likely to be found as a free element.
2.   d SO_2 is produced when Cu is produced from CuS.
3.   c   Bronze is an alloy of Cu and Sn (tin).
4.   a   Coke and limestone are the raw materials for the blast furnace production of iron from iron ore.
5.   b   Electrolysis is used to get aluminum from its ore.
6.   a   The ore composed of primarily Al_2O_3 is called bauxite.

12.4   Earth's Dwindling Resources
   A.   Most of the high-grade ores in the U.S. are gone.
        1.   It takes more energy to obtain metals from low-grade ores than from high-grade ores.

B. Land pollution: solid wastes.
 1. Once discarded, most solid goods are sent to municipal landfills. This material is called municipal solid waste (MSW).
 2. MSWs are handled in three principal ways.
   a. In 2010, 33.8% of MSW was recovered and recycled or composted.
   b. 11.9% was burned at combustion facilities (incinerators).
   c. 54.3% was disposed of in sanitary landfills.
 3. In sanitary landfills, trash is compacted and covered over.
   a. Some landfills leak and contribute to groundwater contamination.
   b. Materials in landfills decompose slowly.
   c. Land for landfills is increasingly scarce.
 4. Incineration can reduce the volume of trash, but it can lead to air pollution.
C. The three Rs of garbage: reduce, reuse, recycle.
 1. Reduce amount of throwaway material produced.
 2. Reuse materials: Durable objects can be used repeatedly and require less energy than recycling. Plastic bags are not as good as paper bags.
 3. Recycle materials: This requires less energy than making objects from ores.
D. How crowded is our spaceship?
 1. Due to medical advances, our death rate has been lowered while our birth rate has stayed the same.
 2. As a result, our birth and death rates are out of balance and our population is increasing at a very fast rate.
   a. This creates a strain on our resources.
 3. We're going to need a bigger Earth.
   a. We need to consider the atom economy of the processes used to produce goods—for example, replace steel with aluminum.
   b. We should consider the environmental friendliness of the materials we use—for example, aluminum is greener than steel. Although it takes more energy to produce, recycling aluminum saves 95% of the energy used to produce the metal.
   c. We should use non-depleting raw materials.

Answers to Self-Assessment Questions

1.   c   Paper is the largest component of the garbage put into landfills.
2.   a   Recycling aluminum requires only 5% of the energy to produce aluminum from bauxite.
3.   d   The three Rs of garbage are reuse, reduce, and recycle.

LEARNING OBJECTIVES

You should be able to...

1.   Name the regions of Earth's crust, and give the approximate composition of each.   (12.1)

2.   List the most abundant elements in Earth's crust.   (12.1)

3.   Describe the arrangement of silicate tetrahedra in common silicate minerals.   (12.2)

4.   Describe how glass differs in structure from other silicates.   (12.2)

5.   List the most important metals with their principal ores, and explain how they are extracted.   (12.3)

6.   Describe some of the environmental costs associated with metal production.   (12.3)

7.   List the main components of solid waste.   (12.4)

8.   Name and describe the three Rs of garbage.   (12.4)

9.   Identify the green chemistry principles that can guide the determination of which metal, Fe or Al, is greener.

10.   Describe how recycling supports sustainable use of natural resources.

DISCUSSION

This chapter describes the resources of planet Earth that are easily accessible to us. By far the most abundant atom is oxygen, followed by silicon and hydrogen. Combinations of silicon and oxygen (sand is SiO_2 and silicates are SiO_4) form an important part of the materials used in our everyday life. Quartz, mica, and asbestos are different forms of pure silicates; ceramics (made by heating clays) are complex silicates; glass is sand mixed with various inorganic salts; cements and concretes are aluminum silicates mixed with limestone. Most metals are found combined with oxygen and have to be reduced to produce the pure metal. Copper was the first metal to be widely used, followed by iron and steel. Although the most abundant metal, aluminum, is difficult to separate from oxygen, it is still cheaper to recycle aluminum than it is to process its ore. Since the Earth neither gains nor loses appreciable mass, and since mass is conserved, the effectiveness with which we manage our resources determines whether or not we have readily available resources and an unpolluted environment. Another factor to consider in the availability of resources and quality of the environment is the world's population.

ANSWERS TO ODD-NUMBERED REVIEW QUESTIONS AND SOLUTIONS FOR ODD-NUMBERED END OF CHAPTER PROBLEMS

Review Questions

1.   A synergistic effect is one that is greater than the sum of expected effects. The especially adverse health effects of coupling smoking and asbestos exposure is an example of a synergistic effect.

3.   Cement production requires extensive mining; the rotary kiln used in its production consumes fossil fuels; and particulate matter from the crushing operations, along with smoke and sulfur dioxide from the burning of fossil fuels, make air pollution by cement plants especially serious.

5.   The technology for manufacture of goods from copper and bronze (Cu + Sn) preceded that for iron and steel for several reasons. Copper and tin are easier to extract from ores than is iron (copper is often found in its native state while iron reacts so readily with oxygen and sulfur that it is not found uncombined in nature), coupled with the fact that iron is much higher melting than copper or bronze.

7.   Aluminum ores are thinly distributed in clays rather than localized.

9. We can run out of metal if goods produced from metal are discarded into landfills rather than being recycled. The problem is keeping the metal in a usable form and not dispersed through the environment.

Problems

11. The lithosphere is the solid portion of the Earth. The hydrosphere is the wet portion of the Earth. The atmosphere is the gaseous portion surrounding the Earth.

13. Aluminum is the third, iron the fourth, and calcium the fifth most abundant element by mass. If ranked by abundance of atoms, aluminum is fourth, iron is sixth, and calcium is seventh. The difference is caused by the differing atomic masses of these elements.

15. Galena is lead(II) sulfide, PbS. $PbS(s) + 2 HCl(aq) \rightarrow H_2S(g) + PbCl_2(s)$.

17. Quartz is a three-dimensional array of silicon dioxide, SiO_2. The basic unit of quartz is the SiO_4 tetrahedron with each Si atom surrounded by four oxygen atoms. The tetrahedra are arranged in a complex, three-dimensional array.

19. In mica, the SiO_4 tetrahedra are arranged in two-dimensional sheet-like arrays with stronger bonding (or attractions) within the sheets than from sheet to sheet.

21. Sand (SiO_2), sodium carbonate (soda, Na_2CO_3), and limestone ($CaCO_3$) are the three raw materials used for making glass.

23. The properties of glass can be modified by adding metal oxides to the basic mixture.

25. Cement is made out of limestone (calcium carbonate, $CaCO_3$) and clay (aluminum silicates).

27. Iron ore, coke, and limestone are used in modern iron production. Iron ore (or scrap iron) is the source of the iron. Coke is used to reduce the iron oxide to elemental iron. Limestone is used to combine with the silicates in the iron ore to remove the impurities in the form of slag.

29. Metal ores are usually oxides and they are reduced to make the pure metal. For example,
$Fe_2O_3 + 3 CO \longrightarrow 2 Fe + 3 CO_2$. Aluminum ore ($Al_2O_3$) is reduced by electrolysis to Al.

31. Limestone reacts with impurities to form slag.

33. Cast iron, or pig iron, is the iron drawn off at the bottom of a blast furnace. It is contaminated with phosphorus, silicon, and excess carbon.

35. $V_2O_5(s) + 5 Ca(s) \rightarrow 2 V(s) + 5 CaO(s)$
a. The vanadium in V_2O_5 is reduced (loses oxygen).
b. The reducing agent is the substance that was oxidized and provided electrons to the vanadium. That substance is Ca.
c. Calcium is oxidized in this reaction (gains oxygen).
d. The oxidizing agent is the substance that is reduced, which is the vanadium in V_2O_5.

37. $Al_2O_3(s) + 3 C(s) + 3 Cl_2(g) \rightarrow 2 AlCl_3(s) + 3 CO(g)$

136

a. The chlorine, Cl_2, is reduced (gains electrons).

b. The reducing agent is carbon, the substance that provided electrons to the chlorine.

c. Carbon is oxidized in this reaction (gains oxygen).

d. The oxidizing agent is the substance that is reduced, which is Cl_2.

39. The molar mass of NdF_3 is 201.24 g/mol and the molar mass of Nd is 144.24 g/mol.

mass of Nd = (143 g NdF_3)(1 mol NdF_3/201.24 g NdF_3)(2 mol Nd/2 mol NdF_3)
$\qquad$ (144.24 g Nd/mol Nd) = 102 g Nd

41. The molar masses of Al and Al_2O_3 are 26.98 g/mol and 101.96 g/mol, respectively.

mass of Al_2O_3 = (7.2 x 10^7 kg Al)(1000 g/1 kg)(1 mol Al/26.98 g Al)
$\qquad$ (1 mol Al_2O_3/2 mol Al)(101.96 g Al_2O_3/mol Al_2O_3)
$\qquad$ = 1.4 x 10^{11} g Al_2O_3 or 1.4 x 10^8 kg Al_2O_3

mass of bauxite required = (1.4 x 10^8 kg Al_2O_3)(2.1 kg bauxite/1.0 kg Al_2O_3)
$\qquad$ = 2.9 x 10^8 kg bauxite

43. mass of gold mined, g = (165,000 t)(1000 kg/t)(1000 g/kg) = 1.65 x 10^{11} g

volume of gold, cm^3 = (1.65 x 10^{11} g)(1 cm^3/19.3 g) = 8.55 x 10^9 cm^3

1 m^3 = 100^3 cm^3 so volume of the cube in m^3 = (8.55 x 10^9 cm^3)(1 m^3/100^3 cm^3) = 8.55 x 10^3 m^3

The length of the side of the cube, in meters = $\sqrt[3]{8.55 \times 10^3 \ m^3}$ = 20.4 m

45. mass of Fe ore, kg/day = (1.0 x 10^7 kg pig iron/day)(95 kg Fe/100 kg pig iron)
$\qquad$ (100 kg ore/82 kg Fe_2O_3)(159.7 kg Fe_2O_3/111.70 kg Fe)
$\qquad$ = 1.7 x 10^7 kg ore/day

47. Mass of trash/y = (14,000 people)(4.5 lb trash/person day)(365 days/y) = 2.3 x 10^7 lb/y

Volume of trash/y = (2.3 x 10^7 lb/y)(1 ft^3/85 lb) = 2.7 x 10^5 ft^3

Depth of trash, ft = volume/area = 2.7 x 10^5 ft^3/[(100 ft)(100 ft)] = 27 ft deep.

49. a. $Fe_2O_3 + 3 H_2 \rightarrow 2 Fe + 3 H_2O$

b. $Fe_2O_3 + 3 CO \rightarrow 2 Fe + 3 CO_2$

51. Assuming only paper and cardboard (28.2%) and wood (6.5%) can be burned with a minimum of pollution, 34.7% of municipal waste can be burned as fuel. If you count paper and cardboard (28.2%), wood (6.5%), yard wastes (13.7%), and plastics (12.3%) the percentage is 60.7%.

53. a. mass = (5 x 10^{11} bags)(1 lb/67 bags)(1 kg/ 2.20 lb) = 3.4 x 10^9 lbs.

b. km traveled = (1 lb bags)(67 bags/lb)(1 km/8.7 bags) = 7.7 km.

c. km traveled = (5 x 10^{11} bags)(1 km/8.7 bags) = 5.7 x 10^{10} km.

55. a. Recall the formula for % A.E. (Chapter 5):

% A.E. = (molar mass of desired product/molar masses of all reactants)(100%)

For the reaction: $Fe_2O_3 + 3\,CO \rightarrow 2\,Fe + 3\,CO_2$ the mass of two moles of Fe produced = 2(55.85 g Fe/mol Fe) = 111.7 g Fe. The total mass of all reactants is the mass of one mole of Fe_2O_3 plus the mass of 3 mol of CO or 159.70 g + 84.03 g = 243.73 g. So: % A.E. = (111.7 g/243.73 g)(100%) = 45.83%.

b.   According to the discussion of Green Chemistry, there are two methods for converting magnetite (Fe_3O_4) to Fe, one using carbon monoxide for which the % A.E. is 49% and the other using H_2 for which the % A.E. is 70%. Either of these methods would be preferable based on their atom economy.

57.   Recycling aluminum saves 95% of the energy required to produce aluminum from bauxite which saves both the fossil fuels used to supply the energy and the bauxite used to supply the aluminum.

Air

The Breath of Life

CHAPTER SUMMARY

13.1   Earth's Atmosphere: Divisions and Composition
  A. The atmosphere is divided into layers.
    1. The troposphere is the layer next to the Earth's surface where nearly all life exists.
    2. The next layer is the stratosphere, where the Earth's protective ozone layer is located.
    3. Above the stratosphere is the mesosphere and, above that are the thermosphere followed by the exosphere.
  B. Air is a mixture of gases. Dry air, by volume, is
    1. 78.08% nitrogen (N_2).
    2. 20.94% oxygen (O_2).
    3. 0.93% argon (Ar).
    4. 0.039% carbon dioxide (CO_2).
    5. 0.002% trace gases.
  C. Variable components of air include
    1. 0% to 4% water vapor.
    2. About 390 ppm carbon dioxide and rising by approximately 2 ppm each year.

Answers to Self-Assessment Questions

1.   d   The part of the atmosphere enveloping virtually all human activity is called the troposphere.
2.   b   The ozone layer is found in the stratosphere.
3.   a   The atmosphere blends into outer space.
4.   d   The approximate percentage of nitrogen in the atmosphere is 78%.
5.   a   After nitrogen and oxygen, the most abundant gas in dry air is argon.

13.2   Chemistry of the Atmosphere
  A. The nitrogen cycle.
    1. Plants need nitrogen as a nutrient, but cannot use nitrogen in the form of N_2 molecules.
    2. Fixed nitrogen is atmospheric nitrogen combined with other elements.
    3. Lightning fixes nitrogen by causing it to combine with oxygen to make nitrogen oxides.
      a. The latter react with water to form nitric acid.
    4. Nitrogen is also fixed industrially to make nitrogen fertilizers.
    5. Some bacteria fix nitrogen; others convert it back to N_2. This establishes a nitrogen cycle.
  B. The oxygen cycle.

1. In the troposphere our supply of oxygen is constantly replenished by green plants and consumed by animals and plants in the metabolism of foods.
2. In the stratosphere, oxygen is formed by the action of ultraviolet rays on water molecules.
    a. Some oxygen is converted to ozone.
    b. Ozone shields us from harmful ultraviolet radiation.
C. Temperature inversions.
    1. Lower stagnant cold air is trapped by warmer air above it.
        a. Pollutants in the cold air are trapped near the ground, sometimes for several days.

Answers to Self-Assessment Questions

1. c Lightning can convert N_2 into nitrogen oxides.
2. b Nitrogen fixation is the conversion of nitrogen (N_2) into biologically useful forms of nitrogen.
3. a Hydrogen (H_2) and nitrogen (N_2) are used in the industrial process to make ammonia.
4. a Carbon dioxide is removed from the atmosphere by photosynthesis.
5. b The corrosion of metals consumes oxygen (O_2).
6. c Thermal inversions concentrate air pollutants.

13.3 Pollution Through the Ages
A. Volcanoes spew ash and sulfur dioxide into the atmosphere.
B. Dust storms add enormous amounts of particulate matter to the air.
C. Swamps and marshes emit noxious gases.
D. The air our ancestors breathed:
    1. Early people made fires, which added smoke to the atmosphere, and cleared land, which made dust storms worse.
    2. Rome was afflicted with stinking air and soot in A.D. 61.
    3. Heavy smoke promoted regulation of emissions from burning coal in England in the thirteenth century.
    4. The Industrial Revolution caused terrible pollution from burning coal in factory towns.
    5. The level of air pollution today is much more complex than at other times in history.
E. Pollution goes global.
    1. Huge urban areas today are afflicted with air pollution that drifts from one area to another.
    2. Pollution from Midwestern power plants leads to acid rain in the Northeast.
    3. Norway is afflicted with pollution from Germany and England.
    4. Most major cities around the world have suffered serious episodes of air pollution.
    5. Cities in China, Iran, Mexico, and Indonesia have experienced serious episodes of air pollution.
    6. A pollutant is too much of any chemical in the wrong place or at the wrong time.
F. Coal + fire → industrial (sulfurous) smog.
    1. The term "smog" is a contraction of the words smoke and fog.
    2. There are two basic types of smog, industrial smog and photochemical smog.
        a. Polluted air associated with industrial activities is called industrial smog.
        b. Industrial smog consists of smoke, fog, sulfur oxides, sulfuric acid, ash, and soot and derives primarily from burning coal.
        c. When burned, the carbon in coal winds up as carbon dioxide, carbon monoxide, and soot (unburned carbon).
        d. The sulfur in coal is oxidized to sulfur dioxide (an acrid, choking gas), and then to sulfur trioxide, which reacts with water to form sulfuric acid.
    3. Particulate matter (solid and liquid particles of greater than molecular size) consists of minerals (fly ash) and soot.

140

  a. Visible particulate matter consists of dust and smoke.

  b. Invisible particulates are called aerosols (a dispersion of liquid particles in air).

  c. Unburned minerals in coal are known as clinkers.

    i. When clinkers are carried aloft in smokestacks, they are called fly ash.

 G. Health and environmental effects of industrial smog.

  1. Sulfur dioxide and particulates such as ammonium sulfate act synergistically to cause far greater harm than either would alone.

  2. Air pollution contributes to the development of respiratory diseases such as emphysema. (Cigarette smoking is a far larger contributor.)

  3. Sulfur oxides and sulfuric acid also damage plants, causing crop losses.

 H. What to do about industrial smog.

  1. There are several ways to remove particulate matter from smokestack gases.

   a. Electrostatic precipitators induce electric charges on the particles, which then are attracted to oppositely charged plates.

   b. Bag filtration works much like a vacuum cleaner to clean the smokestack gases.

   c. Cyclone separators cause the gas to spiral upward; particles hit the walls and settle out.

   d. Wet scrubbers pass the stack gases through water, from which the particulates are removed.

  2. Ash removed from stack gases can be used

   a. To replace clay in making cement.

   b. The rest is stored in ponds and landfills.

  3. It is difficult to remove sulfur oxides.

   a. Sulfur can be removed from coal before burning

    i. By flotation.

    ii. By gasification or liquefaction.

   b. Sulfur can be removed after burning by scrubbing the stack gases with a suspension of limestone or dolomite.

    i. The calcium sulfite formed can be converted to the more useful calcium sulfate.

Answers to Self-Assessment Questions

1. c The air in thirteenth century England was smoky from coal burning.

2. b Oxides of nitrogen are not usually released from burning fossil fuels.

3. d Carbon monoxide is produced by the partial combustion of fossil fuels.

4. c Examples of particulates are ash, soot, and dust.

5. d SO_2 and particulates combine synergistically to cause lung damage.

6. c An electrostatic precipitator cleans smoke from flue gases by producing static charges.

7. d Wet scrubbers remove SO_2 from flue gases.

8. b $CaSO_4$ is a common by-product of sulfur removal from flue gases.

13.4 Automobile Emissions

 A. The main components of automotive exhaust are water vapor, carbon dioxide, and unreacted nitrogen gas (from the atmosphere) that result from the complete combustion of hydrocarbons.

  1. If combustion is not complete, side reactions occur which produce small quantities of harmful products.

   a. Carbon monoxide (CO), a colorless, odorless, poisonous gas formed by incomplete combustion of fuels.

   b. Nitrogen oxides (NO_x), formed when sunlight breaks down NO_2 to form NO and O atoms, contribute to smog and acid rain and cause lung irritation.

      c. Volatile organic compounds (VOCs) come mainly from unburned fuel or evaporating fuel and react with oxygen atoms to form ground-level ozone (O_3), aldehydes, and peroxyacetyl nitrate (PAN).

B. Carbon monoxide: the quiet killer.
1. Carbon monoxide forms when a hydrocarbon burns in an insufficient amount of oxygen.
    a. About 75% of the carbon monoxide that we dump into the atmosphere comes from transportation sources.
2. Carbon monoxide is odorless, tasteless, and invisible and can only be detected using CO detectors or test reagents.
3. Carbon monoxide reacts with hemoglobin in the blood, hindering the transport of oxygen.
    a. Chronic exposure to low levels of carbon monoxide adds stress to the cardiovascular system and may increase the chance of a heart attack.
    b. Exposure to higher levels of carbon monoxide can cause drowsiness and death.
    c. The best antidote is the administration of pure oxygen.

C. Nitrogen oxides: some chemistry of amber air.
1. Any time combustion occurs in air, some of the nitrogen combines with oxygen to form nitrogen oxides. The higher the temperature, the more nitrogen oxides are formed.
2. Nitric oxide is slowly oxidized in air to amber-colored nitrogen dioxide.

$$2\ NO + O_2 \rightarrow 2\ NO_2$$

3. Photons from the sun split nitrogen dioxide into NO and reactive oxygen atoms.
    a. The oxygen atoms produce a variety of irritating and toxic chemicals.
4. Nitrogen oxides produce smog and form nitric acid, which contributes to acid rain.

D. Volatile organic compounds (VOCs).
1. VOCs are organic substances that vaporize significantly at ordinary temperatures and pressures and are major contributors to smog formation.
1. Natural sources release hydrocarbons; only 15% of those in the atmosphere are there as the result of human activity.
2. In urban areas, the processing and use of gasoline contribute substantially to atmospheric hydrocarbons.
3. Hydrocarbons react with
    a. Atomic oxygen or ozone to form aldehydes.
    b. Oxygen and nitrogen dioxide to form peroxyacetyl nitrate (PAN).

Answers to Self-Assessment Questions

1.   a   CO, carbon monoxide, is a dangerous colorless, odorless, and tasteless pollutant.
2.   a   Addiction is not a problem caused by NO_x emissions.
3.   a   VOCs are almost always composed of molecules containing carbon and hydrogen.
4.   d   VOCs come mainly from natural sources.
5.   b   Alkenes react with oxygen atoms to form aldehydes.

13.5   Photochemical Smog: Making Haze while the Sun Shines
A. Photochemical smog.
1. Photochemical smog is produced by a complex series of reactions that starts with nitrogen oxides and unburned hydrocarbons from automobiles.
B. Solutions to photochemical smog.
1. Modified gas tanks and crankcase ventilation systems have reduced evaporative emissions from automobiles.
2. Catalytic converters, which reduce hydrocarbon and carbon monoxide emissions in automotive exhausts, are the principle approach to reduce photochemical smog.

3. Lowering the operating temperature of an engine helps reduce NO_x emissions but lowers engine efficiency.
4. Driving hybrid vehicles saves gasoline and helps the environment.

Answers to Self-Assessment Questions

1. d   Nitrogen oxides and hydrocarbons combine in the presence of sunlight to produce photochemical smog.
2. c   An amber haze is an indication of NO_2.
3. b   Photochemical smog occurs mainly in dry, sunny weather.
4. a   The main source of photochemical smog is automobiles.
5. c   A reduction catalyst is required to remove NO_x.

13.6   Acid Rain: Air Pollution → Water Pollution
  A. Sulfur oxides become sulfuric acid and nitrogen oxides become nitric acid. These acids lower the pH of rainwater.
     a. Rain with a pH below 5.6 is called acid rain.
     b. Normal rainwater is slightly acidic due to dissolved CO_2.
  B. Good evidence indicates that acid rain comes from sulfur oxides and nitrogen oxides emitted from power plants, smelters, and automobiles.
  C. Acid rain corrodes metals and destroys marble and limestone buildings and statuary.

Answers to Self-Assessment Questions

1. c   Acid rain has a pH below 5.6.
2. d   The oxidation of S ($S + O_2 \rightarrow SO_2$) leads to acid rain.

13.7   The Inside Story: Indoor Air Pollution
  A. Home: no haven from air pollution.
     1. Indoor air is often as bad as or worse than that outside.
        a. Gas ranges and kerosene heaters produce nitrogen oxides.
        b. Formaldehyde is slowly released from building materials and new furniture.
  B. Cigarette smoke.
     1. Cigarette smoke is the most prevalent indoor air pollutant.
     2. More than 40 carcinogens have been found in cigarette smoke.
     3. Carbon monoxide levels often exceed standards for ambient air.
     4. Nonsmokers are also exposed to tars, nicotine, and allergy-triggering substances in cigarette smoke.
  C. Radon and its dirty daughters.
     1. Radon is a colorless, odorless, tasteless, chemically unreactive, radioactive gas found in rocks (granite and shale) and minerals.
        a. Radon decays to the daughter isotopes polonium-218, lead-214, and bismuth-214, which are trapped in the lungs and damage tissue.
        b. Trapped inside well-insulated houses, radon levels build up and exceed EPA limits.
  D. Other indoor pollutants.
     1. Unvented natural gas heaters and kerosene heaters can produce carbon monoxide.
     2. Mold can be produced by excessive moisture.
     3. Some electronic air cleaners produce ozone.
  E. Green chemistry solutions have to be carefully studied for their environmental effects.
     1. Liquid crystal displays (LCD) replaced cathode ray tube (CRT) displays to remove need for lead shielding and to reduce the energy required for operation.

a. Producing LCDs leads to unwanted materials that can harm the environment. For example, ~16% of the nitrogen trifluoride (NF_3) used for LCDs and solar panel manufacture escapes into the environment where it is 17,000 times more efficient at trapping atmospheric heat than CO_2.

b. Replacing NF_3 with F_2 is problematic because F_2 is highly toxic.

Answers to Self-Assessment Questions

1. b   Gas ranges in kitchens are a major source of NO_x.
2. b   Carbon monoxide is the most immediate threat from indoor air contaminants.
3. d   Radon in homes comes from the uranium present in soil and rocks.
4. c   Polonium-218 is a radioactive daughter of radon.

13.8   Stratospheric Ozone: Earth's Vital Shield
A. Ozone (O_3) is an allotrope, or different elemental form, of oxygen (O_2).
B. Ozone as an air pollutant.
 1. In the stratosphere, ozone protects us from lethal ultraviolet radiation.
 2. In the troposphere, ozone is a constituent of photochemical smog and is highly toxic when inhaled.
C. The stratospheric ozone shield.
 1. Oxygen in the mesosphere absorbs short wavelength ultraviolet radiation, breaking the bond between the oxygen atoms.
 2. Oxygen atoms migrate into the stratosphere where they form O_3.
 3. Ozone molecules absorb longer wavelength ultraviolet radiation which separates an oxygen atom from O_3, producing O_2 and O.
 4. Undisturbed, ozone is formed and destroyed in a cyclic process in the stratosphere. Levels fluctuate, but human activities may contribute to the destructive part of the cycle.
D. Chlorofluorocarbons and the ozone hole.
 1. Chlorofluorocarbons are insoluble in water and inert toward most substances. They persist in the environment for a long time.
 2. Chlorofluorocarbons are broken down by ultraviolet light in the stratosphere to fragments including chlorine atoms.
 3. These chlorine atoms catalyze the destruction of ozone.
 4. U.S. National Research Council predicts a 2–5% increase in skin cancer for each 1% depletion of the ozone layer.
 5. In 1974, Mario Molina and F. Sherwood Rowland proposed a mechanism for the enhanced ozone depletion by CFCs in the stratosphere for which they received the 1995 Nobel Prize.
   a. They found that one CFC molecule can lead to the destruction of thousands of O_3 molecules.
 6. CFCs were used as the dispersing gases in aerosol cans, as foaming agents for plastics, and as refrigerants.
E. International cooperation.
 1. The United Nations addressed the problem of ozone depletion through the 1987 Montreal Protocol, an international agreement enforcing the reduction and eventual elimination of the production and use of ozone-depleting substances.
 2. Hydrofluorocarbons (HFCs) have been suggested as substitutes.

Answers to Self-Assessment Questions

1. c   Ozone is produced from oxygen in the stratosphere.
2. d   Ozone is an allotrope of oxygen.
3. d   Ozone in the troposphere is harmful while the O_3 in the stratosphere protects life by helping absorb harmful ultraviolet radiation before it reaches the troposphere and living things on the land.
4. d   Automobiles emit NO_x and VOCs that react in the sunlight to produce ozone.
5. d   Oxygen atoms are produced in the mesosphere by the splitting of oxygen molecules by short wavelength ultraviolet radiation.
6. d   Energy with wavelengths in the ultraviolet region of the spectrum are absorbed by ozone.
7. d   Ultraviolet radiation reacts with chlorofluorocarbons to produce chlorine atoms which destroy ozone.

13.9   Carbon Dioxide and Climate Change
   A.   Nearly all combustible processes yield carbon dioxide as one of the reaction products.
      1.   Carbon dioxide levels increased nearly 40% between 1832 and 2008; they are increasing at a rate of 2 ppm per year since 2000.
   B.   The sun radiates different types of radiation, of which visible, infrared, and ultraviolet are most prominent.
      1.   About half of this energy is either reflected or absorbed by the atmosphere.
      2.   The light that gets through (primarily visible radiation) acts to heat the surface of Earth.
   C.   Molecules that absorb infrared energy.
      1.   The three main constituents of the atmosphere—N_2, O_2, and Ar—are small, nonpolar molecules and do not absorb much infrared energy.
      2.   Carbon dioxide and some other gases produce a greenhouse effect: they let the sun's visible light pass through the atmosphere to warm the surface but when the Earth radiates infrared energy back toward space, these greenhouse gases absorb and trap the energy.
      3.   Some greenhouse effect is necessary to life—without an atmosphere, all the radiated heat would be lost to outer space and Earth would be much colder than it is.
   D.   Greenhouse gases and global warming.
      1.   An enhanced greenhouse effect is caused by increased concentration of carbon dioxide and other greenhouse gases in the atmosphere.
      2.   Enhancement could result in an increase in the Earth's average temperature, an effect called global warming.
      3.   Methane and other trace gases contribute to the greenhouse effect; methane concentrations are rising.
         a.   Methane is 20 to 30 times more efficient at trapping heat than CO_2.
         b.   Chlorofluorocarbons are 5000–14,000 times more efficient at trapping heat than carbon dioxide and HCFCs are up to 11,700 times more efficient at trapping heat than CO_2.
   E.   Predictions and consequences.
      1.   Many scientists believe that global warming is melting the ice caps and causing oceans to rise.
   F.   Mitigation of global warming.
      1.   Technologically advanced countries must make quick and dramatic cuts in emissions.
      2.   Technology transfer must occur to developing countries so that those countries can continue to develop their economies without heavy use of coal-fired power plants.
      3.   More energy-efficient cars, appliances, and home heating and cooling systems need to be designed and used.

4. Capture of carbon dioxide from smoke stack emissions by carbon sequestration should be explored.

Answers to Self-Assessment Questions

1.   b   Infrared radiation is trapped on the Earth's surface by the greenhouse effect.
2.   b   The global average air temperature increased by 0.75°C in the twentieth century.
3.   a   The main cause of global warming is CO_2 from factories, power plants, and automobiles.
4.   b CO_2 dissolving in the ocean forms an acid that dissolves the shells of sea creatures.
5.   d   Planting trees is one way a person can help combat global warming.

13.10   Who Pollutes? Who Pays?
     A. The EPA lists six criteria pollutants, so called because scientific criteria are employed to determine their health effects.
         1. Carbon monoxide.
         2. Nitrogen dioxide.
         3. Ozone.
         4. Particulate matter.
         5. Sulfur dioxide.
         6. Lead.
     B. Where does the pollution come from?
         1. Our transportation system accounts for ~85% of urban carbon monoxide emission, 40% of hydrocarbon emissions, and 40% of nitrogen oxide emissions.
         2. ~40% of PM comes from power plants and ~45% from industrial processes.
         3. More than 80% of sulfur oxide emissions come from power plants, with 15% more coming from other industries.
         4. Power plants alone contribute ~55% of nitrogen oxide emissions.
         5. Carbon monoxide is toxic but is deadly only in concentrations approaching 4000 ppm, so the World Health Organization rates sulfur oxides as the worst pollutants.
     C. Paying the price.
         1. Air pollution costs us tens of billions of dollars each year due to health problems, crop destruction, livestock health issues, and its effects on machines and buildings.
         2. Costs increase rapidly as we try to remove larger percentages of pollutants.

Answers to Self-Assessment Questions

1.   a   The EPA is responsible for gathering and analyzing air pollution data.
2.   c   Increased pollution controls are the reason air pollutants have decreased significantly since 1970.
3.   c   Motor vehicles are the largest source of carbon monoxide.
4.   c   Electric power plants are the largest source of sulfur dioxide (SO_2) pollution.
5.   d   The World Health Organization cites sulfur dioxide as the worst pollutant in terms of health effects.
6.   a   The largest sources of NO_x pollution are electric power plants and motor vehicles.
7.   b   The largest sources of particulate pollution are electric power plants and industry.

LEARNING OBJECTIVES

You should be able to...

1. List and describe the layers of the atmosphere. (13.1)

2. Give the proportions of N_2, O_2, Ar, and CO_2 in Earth's atmosphere. (13.1)

3. Describe the nitrogen and oxygen cycles. (13.2)

4. Describe the origin and effects of temperature inversions. (13.2)

5. List some natural sources of air pollution. (13.3)

6. List the main pollutants formed by burning coal, and describe some technologies used to clean up these pollutants. (13.3)

7. List the main gases in automobile emissions, and describe how catalytic converters reduce these gaseous pollutants. (13.4)

8. Explain how carbon monoxide acts as a poison. (13.4)

9. Distinguish the origin of photochemical smog from the origin of sulfurous smog. (13.5)

10. Describe the technologies used to alleviate photochemical smog. (13.5)

11. Name the air pollutants that contribute to acid rain. (13.6)

12. List the major industrial and consumer sources of acid-rain producing pollutants. (13.6)

13. List the main indoor air pollutants and their sources. (13.7)

14. Explain where radon comes from and why it is hazardous. (13.7)

15. Explain the link between CFCs and depletion of the ozone layer. (13.8)

16. Describe the consequences of stratospheric ozone depletion. (13.8)

17. List the important greenhouse gases, and describe the mechanism and significance of the greenhouse effect. (13.9)

18. Describe some strategies for reducing the amount of CO_2 released into the atmosphere. (13.9)

19. List the EPA's criteria pollutants and the major air pollutants that come mainly from automobiles and mostly from industry. (13.10)

20. Identify that green chemistry assessment includes evaluation of the safety of substances as well as awareness of long-term effects.

21. Explain how the green chemistry principles can be applied in the development of manufacturing processes.

EXAMPLE PROBLEMS

1. There is 0.36 L of carbon dioxide in 1000 L of air. What is the concentration of CO_2 in air in parts per million (by volume)? Parts per million means the number of a particular item (or volume) in a mixture containing one million total items (or volumes). To find out the answer to this problem, multiply both the numerator and denominator of the ratio
    Concentration, ppm = (0.36 L CO_2/1000 L air)(1000/1000) = 360 L CO_2/1 x 10^6 L air
    We now have 360 L CO_2 per 1,000,000 L air, or 360 parts CO_2 per million parts air, or simply 360 ppm CO_2.

2. What mass of particulate matter would be inhaled each day by a person breathing 20,000 L of city air containing 230 µg/m^3 of particulate matter? (1 m^3 = 1000 L)

    Mass of particulate matter = (2.0 x 10^4 L air)(230 µg particulate matter/m^3 air)(1 m^3/1000 L)
    = 4.6 x 10^3 µg

ADDITIONAL PROBLEMS

1. At present, the atmosphere contains about 2.5 quadrillion kilograms (2.5 x 10^{15} kg) of carbon dioxide. By burning fossil carbon, we add about 22 trillion kilograms (22 x 10^{12} kg) of CO_2 to the atmosphere each year. If half of this CO_2 remains in the atmosphere, how many years will it take, at the present rate, to double the amount of CO_2 in the atmosphere?

2. A supersonic transport (SST) burns 60,000 kg of fuel per hour. What weight of carbon dioxide and of water vapor will be produced? A (representative) equation is
    $$C_{15}H_{32} + 46\ O_2 \rightarrow 15\ CO_2 + 16\ H_2O$$

3. In 10,000 L of air there are 3 L of argon. What is the concentration of argon in parts per million (by volume)?

DISCUSSION

While nitrogen is 80% of the atmosphere, it needs to be combined with other elements (fixed) in order to be useful. The Earth naturally produces out a number of pollutants via volcanoes, dust storms, swamps, and marshes. However, since human beings started living in cities, man-made pollution has been a serious problem. Burning coal produces industrial (London) smog which is a combination of smoke, fog, sulfur oxides, and particulate matter. To reduce industrial smog requires the removal of sulfur from the fuel and smoke that produces particulates. Photochemical (Los Angeles) smog is produced by automobiles and contains carbon monoxide, nitrogen oxides, and unburned hydrocarbons. The best way to reduce photochemical smog is through the use of catalytic converters. Ozone is a pollutant at ground level but needed as a protective screen against UV rays in the upper atmosphere. CFCs threaten to diminish this protective layer of ozone. Acid rain occurs when sulfur oxides and nitrogen oxides combine with water to lower its pH. The United States successfully removed lead as an air pollutant by banning tetraethyllead as a gasoline additive. Tighter insulation has increased the level of indoor air pollution. Indoor air pollutants include nitrogen oxides from gas ranges, cigarette smoke, and radon. Carbon dioxide produced by burning coal or hydrocarbons may contribute to global warming. "Waste" heat produced as a by-product during the conversion of one type of energy to another may contribute to global warming in the future.

ANSWERS TO ODD-NUMBERED REVIEW QUESTIONS AND SOLUTIONS FOR ODD-NUMBERED END OF CHAPTER PROBLEMS

Review Questions

1.   CFCs were used as refrigerants and in the molding of plastic foams.

3.   Bottom ash is the mineral matter that is left behind when coal is burned in power plants or factories. Fly ash is unburned minerals that are airborne due to the drafts created by the fire and that settle over the surrounding area, covering everything with dust. Fly ash can be used in concrete or as a soil modifier.

5.   A greenhouse gas increases the retention of the sun's heat energy. Three examples of greenhouse gases are carbon dioxide (CO_2), methane (CH_4), and water (H_2O).

7.   Smog is the combination of smoke and fog which often results from polluted air.

Problems

9.   Nitrogen fixation is combining nitrogen with another element to make it available to plants. One very useful form of "fixed" nitrogen is ammonia (NH_3). Nitrogen fixation has greatly increased food production.

11.   1 km = 0.6214 mi so height reached by aircraft, km = (67 mi)(1 km/0.6214 mi) = 110 km
       According to Figure 13.1 the aircraft reached the thermosphere.

13.   a. $4\,Fe + 3\,O_2 \rightarrow 2\,Fe_2O_3$
       b. $4\,Cr + 3\,O_2 \rightarrow 2\,Cr_2O_3$

15.   The weather conditions associated with industrial smog are cool/cold temperatures, high humidity, and often fog.

17. $S + O_2 \rightarrow SO_2$.

19. $SO_2 + 2\,H_2S \rightarrow 3\,S + 2\,H_2O$.

21.   The solid lime (CaO) reacts with SO_2 gas, causing it to form a solid product, $CaSO_3$, which is easy to collect. Some scrubbers react the $CaSO_3$ with oxygen to form a more useful product, $CaSO_4$.
       The reactions for this are: $CaCO_3(s) \rightarrow CaO(s) + CO_2(g)$
                                      $CaO(s) + SO_2(g) \rightarrow CaSO_3(s)$
       And, in the case of formation of $CaSO_4(s)$: $2\,CaSO_3(s) + O_2(g) \rightarrow 2\,CaSO_4(g)$.

23.   The reaction of N_2 and O_2 requires high temperatures. Otherwise, the two main components of the atmosphere would react at ambient temperatures. $N_2 + O_2 \rightarrow 2\,NO$.

25. PAN stands for peroxyacetyl nitrate ($CH_3COOONO_2$). PAN, which is formed from hydrocarbons, oxygen, and nitrogen dioxide, makes breathing difficult and causes eye irritation.

27. The answers are a and c. Consumer products such as paints and aerosol sprays are sources of VOCs, as are petroleum fumes.

29. NO is a free radical. NO has 11 valence electrons, so not all of them can be paired. The other compounds have even numbers of valence electrons, so their valence electrons can occur in pairs.

31. Carbon monoxide binds to hemoglobin, preventing the hemoglobin from carrying O_2.

33. Ozone is an allotrope of oxygen.

35. HCFCs are effective greenhouse gases, so leakage of them into the atmosphere contributes to global warming. They are more reactive than CFCs, so they break down while in use and can cause corrosion of the components of compressors and refrigeration coils.

37. Sulfuric acid (H_2SO_4) and nitric acid (HNO_3) are the primary acids responsible for acid rain.

39. $6\ HNO_3(aq) + 2\ Fe(s) \rightarrow 2\ Fe(NO_3)_3(aq) + 3\ H_2(g)$.

41. Carbon monoxide is a pollutant both indoors and outdoors. Indoors it results from the use of woodstoves, gas stoves, cigarette smokers, and unvented gas and kerosene space heaters. Outdoors it results primarily from the incomplete combustion of hydrocarbon fuels.

43. In a house built with a crawl space, radon migrating from the nuclear decomposition of rock beneath the house becomes concentrated in the crawl space, which is an uninhabited space in a house. The radon dissipates through vents. In houses built on concrete slabs, the radon migrates through the slab and into the first floor rooms of the house, posing a greater health risk for the inhabitants of the house.

45. Radon is a radioactive gas that can be breathed into a person's lungs. If the radon nucleus undergoes a nuclear decomposition by alpha emission while it is in a person's lungs, the daughter product, polonium, is a solid which deposits on the lung tissue where it remains while it continues to go through its decomposition sequence.

47. The greenhouse effect is the slow warming of the Earth caused by the trapping of infrared energy.

49. There are too many natural pollutants and there are too many people on the planet to eliminate all processes that produce pollutants as a by-product. Also, some waste heat is formed every time energy is transferred from one form into another (the second law of thermodynamics).

51. mass of particulates/day = $(22\ m^3\ air/day)(312\ \mu g\ PM/m^3)(1\ mg/1000\ \mu g) = 6.9\ mg/day$.

53. Water vapor will form clouds and may even lead to cooling by reflecting sunlight back to space.

55. According to the data from problem 54:

number of mol of molecules in the universe = $(5.2 \times 10^{21}$ g$)(1$ mol/29 g$) = 1.8 \times 10^{20}$ mol

mass of 1 breath = $(0.50$ L/breath$)(1.3$ g/L$) = 0.65$ g/breath

number of molecules in Buddha's last breath = $(0.65$ g/breath$)(1$ mol/29 g$)$
$$(6.02 \times 10^{23} \text{ molecules/mol})$$
$$= 1.4 \times 10^{22} \text{ molecules}$$

number of breaths in atmosphere = $(1.8 \times 10^{20}$ mol$)(1$ breath/0.022 mol$) = 8.0 \times 10^{21}$ breaths

There are more molecules from Buddha's last breath than there are breaths in the atmosphere so, with even distribution, there should be at least one molecule from Buddha's last breath in the breath any one of us just took.

57. $3 NO_2 + H_2O \rightarrow 2 HNO_3 + NO.$

$2 NO + O_2 \rightarrow 2 NO_2.$

59. The answer is a. One NF_3 molecule is 17,000 times more effective trapping infrared radiation than one CO_2 molecule, so 1,000 t of NF_3 is equal to 17 million t of CO_2.

61. The answer is 5.4×10^7 t CO_2.

amount of CO_2 = $(20,000$ t NF_3 produced$)(16$ t NF_3 escaped/100 t NF_3 produced$)$
$$(17,000 \text{ t } CO_2/\text{t } NF_3) = 5.4 \times 10^7 \text{ t } CO_2$$

Water

Rivers of Life, Seas of Sorrows

CHAPTER SUMMARY

14.1   Water: Some Unusual Properties
   A.   Water is the only common liquid on the surface of planet Earth.
   B.   Solid water (ice) is less dense than liquid water.
   C.   Water has a higher density than most other familiar liquids.
   D.   Water has an unusually high specific heat.
        1.   Specific heat is the quantity of heat required to raise the temperature of 1 g of a substance by 1 °C.
        2.   The vast amounts of water on the surface of Earth act as a giant heat reservoir to moderate daily temperature variations.
   E.   Water has an unusually high heat of vaporization. (Amount of heat required to evaporate a small amount of water.)
   F.   The properties of water are explained by its structure.
        1.   Liquid water is strongly associated through hydrogen bonding, but the molecules are randomly organized.
        2.   In ice, molecules have a more ordered arrangement where each water molecule forms hydrogen bonds with four other water molecules, producing a well-defined structure with large hexagonal holes.

Answers to Self-Assessment Questions

1.   b   Water has a high specific heat which allows it to absorb (or release) a relatively large amount of heat before its temperature rises (or falls.)
2.   b   The presence of the hydrogen bonds that attract water molecules to each other account for its unusual properties.
3.   a   Hydrogen bonds form between the partially positive H atom in one H_2O molecule and the partially negative O atom in another H_2O molecule.
4.   b   Ice has an open structure with large hexagonal holes.

14.2   Water in Nature
   A.   Three-fourths of the surface of Earth is covered with water, but 98% of the water on the surface of the Earth is seawater, which is not suitable for drinking.
   B.   Water is polar; it tends to dissolve ionic substances.
   C.   Water dissolves minerals that are carried to the sea by rivers.
        1.   Water evaporates from the oceans, leaving the salts behind.

2. The oceans are ever so slowly becoming more salty.
D. The water cycle and natural contaminants.
    1. Although the percentages of water apportioned to the oceans, ice caps, rivers, lakes, and streams remain fairly constant, water is dynamically cycled among these various repositories through the water (hydrological) cycle.
    2. Water evaporates from water and land surfaces, condenses into clouds, and returns to Earth as rain, sleet, and snow.
    3. The precipitation becomes part of the ice caps, runs off in streams and rivers, and fills both lakes and underground pools of water in rocks and sand called aquifers.
E. Gases.
    1. Natural water isn't all H_2O.
       a. Rainwater contains dust, dissolved gases (carbon dioxide, oxygen, nitrogen), and, in thunderstorms, nitric acid.
       b. Carbon dioxide makes natural rainwater slightly acidic because it reacts with water to form carbonic acid (H_2CO_3).
       c. Groundwater also contains the radioactive gas radon.
F. Dissolved minerals.
    1. Groundwater contains dissolved ions.
       a. The principal positive ions are sodium, potassium, calcium, magnesium, and sometimes iron.
       b. Calcium, magnesium, and iron ions are responsible for hard water.
       b. The principal negative ions are sulfate, bicarbonate, and chloride.
G. Organic matter.
    1. Rainwater dissolves matter from decaying plants and animals.
    2. Organic matter in the form of traces of lubricants, fuels, some fertilizers, and pesticides can contaminate water.
    3. Bacteria, other microorganisms, and animal wastes are potential contaminants of natural waters.
H. Some biblical chemistry.
    1. Moses purified bitter water by throwing a tree into it.
       a. The oxidized cellulose of the tree may have neutralized the alkali in the water.

Answers to Self-Assessment Questions

1.   c   The sun is the source of energy to power the water cycle.
2.   a   Rainwater becomes acidic when carbon dioxide dissolves in it, forming carbonic acid.
3.   c   The principal cations in water are Na^+, K^+, Ca^{2+}, and Mg^{2+}.
4.   c   Hard water is not caused by the presence of K^+ ions.

14.3   Chemical and Biological Contamination
A. Water-borne diseases (cholera, typhoid fever, dysentery) plagued the entire world until about 100 years ago.
    1. Today in developed nations, unlike in developing nations, chemical treatment has made municipal water supplies generally safe.
    2. The threat of biological contamination has not been totally eliminated from developed nations.
       a. *Cryptosporidium* and *Giardia*, excreted in human and animal feces, resist standard chemical disinfection.
    3. People with waterborne diseases fill half of the world's hospital beds.
    4. The recreational safety of water is also decreased by biological contaminants.

B. Acid waters.
1. Sulfur oxides (SO_x) and nitrogen oxides (NO_x) emitted into the air are converted to acids by moisture and come down from the sky as acid rain.
2. The major sources of sulfur and nitrogen oxides are coal power plants, other industries, and automobile emissions.
3. Acid rain decreases the viability of life in lakes, dissolves limestone and marble, and ruins the finish of automobiles.
4. Acids are not a threat to life in lakes and streams where limestone (calcium carbonate) is plentiful because limestone can neutralize excess acid.
C. Sewage and dying lakes.
1. Pathogenic microorganisms cause disease.
2. Breakdown of sewage by bacteria depletes dissolved oxygen (DO) and adds plant nutrients to water.
    a. Degradation can be aerobic (using dissolved oxygen from the air) or anaerobic (without air).
    b. Biochemical oxygen demand (BOD) is a measure of the amount of oxygen required to degrade the organic material in water.
3. With adequate dissolved oxygen, aerobic bacteria degrade organic wastes to carbon dioxide, water, nitrates, phosphates, and sulfates.
    a. Nitrates and phosphates fertilize the water, stimulating algae growth.
    b. When the algae die, their decomposition requires oxygen (increases the BOD), a process called eutrophication.
4. With the oxygen depleted, anaerobic bacteria flourish. Anaerobic decay leads to foul-smelling sulfur compounds, ammonia, and amines.
5. The ecology of waterways is also affected by fertilizer runoff from farm fields, golf courses, and lawns, as well as from seepage from feedlots.
6. Water quality is affected by introduction of substances from modern industrial and consumer society: pesticides, radioisotopes, detergents, drugs, toxic metals, and industrial chemicals.

Answers to Self-Assessment Questions

1. a Half the world's hospital beds are filled by individuals suffering from diseases caused by waterborne microorganisms.
2. a Acidic lakes are often clear.
3. d The survival of aquatic animals is dependent upon the level of dissolved oxygen (DO).
4. b Biochemical oxygen demand (BOD) of a water sample measures organic matter levels.
5. c A high BOD causes the amount of dissolved oxygen (DO) to fall as organic matter decays.
6. c Anaerobic oxidation (without air) produces non-oxygenated products, CH_4, NH_3, and H_2S as plant materials decay.
7. b Eutrophication in a lake or river is caused by excess nitrates or phosphates.

14.4   Water: Who Uses It and How Much?
A. The average American uses ~400 L of water a day.
B. It takes several hundred kilograms of steel to produce a typical automobile and 100 metric tons (t) of water to produce 1 t of steel.
C. Porous materials are used in water remediation.
1. Zeolites are a class of both natural and synthetic solids.
    a. They can have a variety of different three-dimensional structures, all of which have a well-defined network of pores and a large surface area.

    b. Zeolites found in nature are minerals with Al and Si atoms bonded to four O atoms shared by other Al and Si atoms.

    c. Al atoms in zeolites cause a buildup of negative charge, which attracts positively charged ions, such as Na^+ and K^+ which are easily exchanged for Ca^{2+} and Mg^{2+} to soften water.

    d. Zeolites that have the natural cations replaced by H^+ ions can act as solid acid catalysts to speed up reactions.

    e. Zeolites are microporous, which can limit their effectiveness in applications involving larger molecules.

    f. This problem was solved with the synthesis of mesoporous materials and zeolite applications can now be extended to larger molecules.

    g. Sulfur-containing molecules can be anchored to the surfaces of mesoporous solids to create a sponge that will bind and remove heavy metals from water.

D. There are a lot of pollutants added to the water during the manufacturing process but most of these can be partially eliminated.

E. Almost 70% of the freshwater supply is used in agriculture, primarily for irrigation.

Answers to Self-Assessment Questions

1.   a About 70% of the freshwater supply is used in agriculture, primarily for irrigation.

2.   c Except for the water that is lost through evaporation, most of the water used in the manufacture of steel is recycled.

14.5   Groundwater Contamination → Tainted Tap Water

A. Half of the people in the United States depend upon groundwater for drinking water.

   1. Toxic substances have been found in many community and private wells. Poisons in the wells include

    a. Methyl *tert*-butyl ether (MTBE), a gasoline additive.

    b. Industrial wastes.

    c. Perfluorooctanoic acid (PFOA) and related compounds used in the processing of polymers.

B. Nitrates.

   1. In many agricultural areas, well water is contaminated with nitrates (from fertilizer).

   2. Water high in nitrates is dangerous to infants, causing methemoglobinemia (blue baby syndrome).

   3. Only expensive advanced treatment can remove highly soluble nitrates from water.

C. Volatile organic chemicals.

   1. Volatile organic chemicals are used in homes and factories as solvents, cleaners, and fuels.

    a. Common volatile organic compounds (VOCs) are hydrocarbons (benzene and toluene) and chlorinated hydrocarbons (carbon tetrachloride, chloroform, methylene chloride, and trichloroethylene).

    b. Except for toluene, all are suspected carcinogens.

   2. Only traces of commonly used volatile organic chemicals dissolve in water, so amounts of contaminants are often in the parts per million, parts per billion, or parts per trillion ranges.

D. Leaking underground storage tanks.

   1. Underground storage tanks (USTs) at service stations often rust and leak gasoline into the surrounding soil and water.

Answers to Self-Assessment Questions

1.   c   Methemoglobinemia is caused by the nitrate ion (NO_3^-).
2.   d   Toluene, a component of gasoline, is an example of a volatile organic compound (VOC) that contaminates groundwater.

14.6   Making Water Fit to Drink
A. Safe drinking water act.
   1. Gives the EPA the power to set, monitor, and enforce national health-based standards for contaminants in municipal water supplies.
   2. Modern analytical techniques allow identification of smaller and smaller concentrations of potentially harmful substances.
   3. The number of regulated substances with maximum contaminant levels (MCLs) has increased.
B. Calculations of parts per million and parts per billion.
   1. 1 ppm = 1 g solute/1 x 10^6 g solution or 1 mg solute/ Liter of solution and 1 ppb = 1 g solute/1 x 10^9 g solution.
      Change 4.2 mg Cl⁻/L to ppm and ppb
      Assume density of water = 1.00 g/mL so we have 4.2 mg Cl⁻/1000 g H_2O
      (4.2 mg Cl⁻/1000 g water)(1 g water/1000 mg water) =
         4.2 mg Cl⁻/1,000,000 mg water or 4.2 ppm Cl⁻
      1000 ppb = 1ppm so   (4.2 ppm)(1000 ppb/1 ppm) = 4200 ppb Cl⁻
C. Water treatment.
   1. Water from reservoirs, rivers, and lakes must be treated to make it safe for drinking.
      a. Water is treated with slaked lime and aluminum sulfate.
         1. The aluminum hydroxide formed carries down dirt and bacteria.
      b. The water is then filtered through sand and gravel.
      c. Sometimes the water is aerated to remove odors and improve the taste.
      d. Sometimes the water is filtered through charcoal to remove colored and odorous compounds.
      e. Finally, the water is chlorinated to kill harmful bacteria.
D. Chemical disinfection.
   1. In the final step of water treatment, chlorine is added to kill any remaining bacteria, a treatment that can produce some unwanted byproducts.
   2. Ozone can also be used to disinfect water but does not provide the residual protection against microorganisms that chlorine provides.
E. UV irradiation.
   1. UV irradiation can purify water containing *Cryptosporidium* and other microorganisms but leaves no residual protection and does not correct for taste and odor issues.
F. Fluorides.
   1. Fluorides are poisonous in moderate to high concentrations.
   2. In concentrations of 0.7 to 1.0 ppm, fluorides in drinking water lead to a reduction in the incidence of tooth decay (dental caries).
      a. Fluorides strengthen tooth enamel by converting hydroxyapatite to fluorapatite.
      b. Excessive fluorides can cause a mottling of tooth enamel and interfere with calcium metabolism, kidney action, and thyroid function.

Answers to Self-Assessment Questions

1. c   About 90 substances are regulated under the U.S. EPA drinking water standards.
2. a   A value of 3 ppm of dissolved oxygen means that 3 mg O_2/L H_2O.
3. a   Flocculation helps remove dirt and bacteria in the treatment of public water.
4. a   The taste of water is improved by aeration.
5. b   Chlorine is added to water to kill bacteria.
6. c   Ozonation has the advantage that the oxygenated byproducts are generally less toxic than chlorinated byproducts.
7. c   Fluoridation of drinking water converts hydroxyapatite to fluorapatite.

14.7   Waste Water Treatment
   A. Primary sewage treatment plants remove 40–60% of suspended solids as sludge and ~30% of organic matter.
      1. The effluent water has a high Biochemical Oxygen Demand (BOD).
      2. None of the nitrates and phosphates are removed in this process.
   B. Secondary sewage treatment plants pass the effluent through sand and gravel filters.
      1. The water is aerated, to aid the action of aerobic bacteria which metabolize organic contaminants.
      2. BOD is lowered by ~90%, but most nitrates and phosphates remain in the water.
   C. The activated sludge method combines primary and secondary treatment.
      1. Sewage is aerated with large blowers, forming large porous floes.
      2. Part of the sludge is recycled.
   D. Advanced, or tertiary, treatments are increasingly used but are expensive.
      1. If charcoal filtration is used, charcoal adsorbs certain organic molecules that are difficult to remove otherwise.
      2. If reverse osmosis is used, pressure forces wastewater through a semipermeable membrane, leaving the contaminants behind.
      3. If phytoremediation is used, the effluent is passed into large natural or constructed lagoons for storage, allowing plants such as reeds to remove metals and other contaminants.
   E. Sewage effluent is chlorinated to kill pathogenic bacteria.
      1. Excess chlorine provides residual protection.
         a. Chlorine is not effective against some viruses.
         b. Chlorine reacts with organic compounds to form chlorinated hydrocarbons, some of which are carcinogens.
      2. Some European cities use ozone rather than chlorine to kill pathogens.
         a. Ozone is more effective against viruses.
         b. Ozone yields oxidized, not chlorinated, hydrocarbons.
         c. Ozone imparts no "chemical" taste to the water.
         d. Unlike chlorine, ozone provides no residual protection.
   F. Water pollution and the future.
      1. Each person in the U.S. flushes ~35,000 L of drinking-quality water each year.
      2. Nutrients from wastes could be returned to the soil instead of dumped into water.
      3. In many societies, human and animal wastes are returned directly to the soil.
      4. Sludge is used as fertilizer in some parts of the United States.
      5. Toilets are available that use no water; they compost wastes.
   G. Some disadvantages of using sludge as fertilizer.
      1. Pathogenic organisms may survive and spread disease.
      2. The sludge is often contaminated with toxic metal ions.

H. We're the solution to water pollution.
    1. There are between 4,000 and 40,000 cases of waterborne illnesses in the U.S. each year.
    2. 20,000,000 people have no running water and more still obtain water from suspect sources.
    3. 10% of public water supplies do not meet one or more of the EPA standards.
    4. 30,000,000 people draw their water from individual wells or springs whose water is often of unknown quality.
I. The newest soft drink: bottled water.
    1. Bottled water is the fastest growing and most profitable segment of the beverage industry.
    2. Bottled water is regarded as a food and regulated by FDA and not EPA.
    3. 25% of bottled water comes from municipal water supplies.
    4. Bottled water is not necessarily safer, but convenience, taste, and the promise for improved health are driving sales for bottled water.
    5. In general, both municipal and bottled water are safe.

Answers to Self-Assessment Questions

1.   c   Bacteria consume dissolved substances during the secondary treatment of wastewater.
2.   b   Trihalomethanes are the reaction products when chlorine reacts with dissolved organic compounds.
3.   a   The charcoal filtration method of advanced treatment can be used to remove trihalomethanes and chloroform from water.
4.   c   Reverse osmosis uses pressure to force water through a semipermeable membrane.
5.   b   weight of sewage = (500,000 gal)(8 lb/gal) = 4,000,000 lb.
            16 lb chlorine/4,000,000 lb sewage = 4 ppm Cl_2 in the wastewater.

LEARNING OBJECTIVES

You should be able to...

1. Relate water's unique properties to the polarity and the hydrogen bonding of its molecules.   (14.1)

2. Explain how water on the surface of Earth acts to moderate daily temperature variations.   (14.1)

3. Explain why humans can use less than 1% of all the water on Earth.   (14.2)

4. Describe how human activities affect water quality.   (14.3)

5. Give an example of a biological water contaminant.   (14.3)

6. List the major uses of water.   (14.4)

7. List some groundwater contaminants.   (14.5)

8. Identify the sources of nitrates in groundwater.   (14.5)

9. Describe how water is purified for drinking and other household uses.   (14.6)

10. Describe primary, secondary, and tertiary treatment of wastewater.   (14.7)

11.　Describe the structures of zeolites and mesoporous materials.

12.　Explain how zeolites and mesoporous materials can be used to clean up contaminated water.

EXAMPLE PROBLEMS

1.　The U.S. Food and Drug Administration (FDA) limit for mercury in food is 0.5 ppm. On a seafood diet, a person might consume 340 g (12 oz) of tuna per day. How much mercury would the person get each day if the tuna contained the maximum of mercury? (One microgram is 1×10^{-6} g.)

Mass of mercury = (340 g tuna)(0.5 g Hg/1 x 10^6 g tuna)(1 µg/1x 10^{-6} g) = 200 µg

(The lowest level at which toxicity symptoms have been observed is about 300 microgram/day.)

2.　Every 3 parts of organic matter in water require about 8 parts of oxygen for its degradation. How much organic matter is needed to deplete the 10 ppm of oxygen in (a) 1 L (which weighs 1 kg) of water? (b) A small lake containing 1,000,000,000 kg of water?
a.　mass of organic matter = (1 kg H_2O)(1000 g/kg)(10 g O_2/1 x 10^6 g H_2O)
(3 g organic matter/8 g O_2)(1000 µg/g)
= 4 µg organic matter
b.　mass of organic matter = (1 x 10^9 kg H_2O)(1000 g/kg)(10 g O_2/1 x 10^6 g H_2O)
(3 g organic matter/8 g O_2)
= 4 x 10^6 g organic matter

ADDITIONAL PROBLEMS

1.　Sewage discharged by each person each day in the United States consumes, on the average, 60 g of oxygen. How many kilograms of water, at 10 ppm O_2, are depleted daily by the raw sewage from a city of 100,000 people?

2.　Arizona has estimated recoverable groundwater of 8.7 x 10^{14} kg. At present, the water is being used at a net rate of 5.0 x 10^{12} kg/year. At this rate, how long will the water last?

DISCUSSION

Water has some very unusual properties that make life possible. Although three-fourths of the Earth is covered with water, only 1% of the world's water is fresh water. The water cycle (evaporation and condensation) cleans water. Until 100 years ago, the leading cause of death was from contamination of water by human waste. Even now 80% of the world's sickness is caused by contaminated water. Biochemical oxygen demand (BOD) measures the amount of organic material dissolved. Groundwater can be contaminated by volatile organic chemicals (VOCs) and leakage from underground storage tanks (USTs). Recent abilities to detect lower and lower concentrations have led to over dramatization of pollution problems. Acid rain and runoff from abandoned mines can cause lakes to become acidic. Industry uses large amounts of water in its processes with multiple chances to pollute. Wastewater can be treated by settling (primary), settling and filtering (secondary), and settling, filtering, and advanced treatment (tertiary) methods. Drinking water is often treated with aeration and chlorination. Fluoridation is used to reduce tooth decay but the concentrations must be carefully monitored. In rural areas, nitrates from farming operations are a problem.

ANSWERS TO ODD-NUMBERED REVIEW QUESTIONS AND SOLUTIONS FOR ODD-NUMBERED END OF CHAPTER PROBLEMS

Review Questions

1. Crude oil will not dissolve in water because gasoline is nonpolar and water is polar. The oil will float because it is less dense than water.

3. Pathogenic microorganisms are microorganisms that cause disease.

5. Leaking underground storage tanks are a major source of groundwater contamination. Groundwater may also be contaminated with nitrates from farm fertilizer runoff and with volatile organic chemicals, or chemicals buried in dumps which have infiltrated the groundwater.

7. Chlorinated hydrocarbons are unreactive and do not break down easily.

Problems

9. The hydrogen bonding between water molecules in ice create larger holes than exist in the liquid phase, causing water to expand when it freezes. Thus, solid water is less dense than liquid water, so ice floats. Fish and other aquatic species can survive winter in the temperate zones because the ice forms a layer on top of the water rather than sinking to the bottom and allowing the water to freeze solid.

11. Heat required = $(875 \text{ g } H_2O)(37.0 \text{ °C} - 3.0 \text{ °C})(1 \text{ cal/g °C}) = 3.0 \times 10^4$ cal.

13. The high heat of vaporization of water means that large amounts of heat can be dissipated by the evaporation of small amounts of water (perspiration) from the skin.

15. Water evaporates from the skin. The heat required for the evaporation is removed from the skin, cooling it.

17. Rainwater picks up dust and dissolves atmospheric gases such as carbon dioxide and oxygen as it passes through the atmosphere. During thunderstorms, the water reacts with fixed nitrogen to form nitric acid.

19. Hardness, mg/L = (3 gr/gal)(64.8 mg/gr)(1 gal/3.78 L) = 51 mg/L

21. Bodies of water gain acidity from acid rain formed when sulfur oxides and nitrogen oxides dissolve in rain, fog, and snow. Acids also flow into streams from abandoned mines.

23. Hard water contains relatively high amounts of Ca^{2+} and Mg^{2+} ions. These ions enter the water when acidic water reacts with limestone to produce water soluble calcium and magnesium salts which contribute to water hardness.

25. Aluminum ions, usually tightly bound in clays and other minerals, are released by acid. These ions have low toxicity to humans but can be deadly to young fish.

27. The optimal level of fluoride in drinking water is 0.7 to 1.0 ppm (by mass).

29. Yes, ultraviolet radiation can be used to disinfect water because it kills microorganisms.

31. Primary sewage treatment allows heavy materials to sink to the bottom of a tank holding the sewage and removing the effluent. This process removes 40%–60% of suspended solids as sludge in settling tanks as well as 30% of organic matter.

33. Nitrites and phosphates are not removed by secondary wastewater treatment.

35. a. Charcoal filtration is a form of tertiary (or advanced) wastewater treatment.
     b. A settling pond is used as a form of primary wastewater treatment.
     c. Trickling filters are used as a secondary wastewater treatment process.

37. $2\ HNO_3(aq) + CaCO_3(s) \rightarrow Ca^{2+}(aq) + 2\ NO_3^-(aq) + H_2O(l) + CO_2(g)$

39. a. $11\ \mu g/L = 11 \times 10^{-6}$ g benzene/1×10^3 g solution $= 11 \times 10^{-9}$ g benzene/g solution.
        ppb benzene $= (11 \times 10^{-9}$ g benzene/g solution$)(1 \times 10^9$ g solution$) = 11$ ppb benzene.
     b. 0.014% $BaCO_3 = 0.014$ g $BaCO_3$/100 g solution $= 0.00014$ g $BaCO_3$/g solution.
        $= (0.00014$ g $BaCO_3$/g solution$)(1 \times 10^6$ g solution$) = 140$ ppm $BaCO_3$.

41. The maximum allowable concentrations for copper and nitrate in water are 1.3 mg/L and 45 mg/L respectively. $18\ \mu g/2\ L = 9\ \mu g$ copper/L or 9.0×10^{-3} mg copper/L and $16\ \mu g/2\ L = 8\ \mu g$ nitrate/L or 8.0×10^{-3} mg nitrate/L. The levels of both substances are lower than the acceptable upper limit.

43. a. Activated charcoal removes $CHCl_3$.
     b. Distillation removes NaCl, phosphate ion, and sand.
     c. Filtration removes sand from the water.

45. It takes more energy to boil water (give water molecules enough energy to overcome all hydrogen bonding attractions between them so that they can move independently from one another and remain at some distance from each other) than it does to melt ice (give water molecules enough energy to move out of the rigid crystalline structure and to move from attractions with some water molecules to attractions with other water molecules).

47. Chlorine gains electrons (is reduced) in going from Cl_2 to $2\ Cl^-$; it is the oxidizing agent. Sulfur dioxide is oxidized (gains oxygen) in going from SO_2 to SO_4^{2-}; it is the reducing agent.

49. A positron is emitted. $^{26}_{13}Al \rightarrow\ ^{0}_{+1}e +\ ^{26}_{12}Mg$

51. a. heat, kcal = (50 gal)(3.8 L/gal)(1000 g/1L)(60 °C - 12 °C)(1.00 cal/g °C)(1 kcal/1000 cal)
        $= 9.12 \times 10^3$ kcal
     b. mass of CH_4, g $= (9.12 \times 10^3$ kcal)(4.184 kJ/kcal)(16.04 g CH_4/890 kJ) $= 688$ g CH_4

c. volume CH_4, ft^3 = (688 g CH_4)(1 mol CH_4/16.04 g CH_4)(22.4 L/mol CH_4)(1 ft^3/28.3 L) = 34.0 ft^3

d. cost = (15-min)(2.5 gal/min)(9.12 x 10^3 kcal/50 gal)(612 g CH_4/9.12 x 10^3 kcal)

(30.2 ft^3/612 g CH_4)(1 therm/100 ft^3)($1.50/therm) = $0.34

53. The answer is c. Zeolites are solids in which one cation can be replaced by another. Therefore, the cations Ca^{2+}, Mg^{2+}, and K^+ can be replaced. The anion, PO_4^{3-}, cannot be exchanged by the zeolite.

55. The answer is a. To maintain charge balance in zeolite frameworks, negative charge build-up is offset by cations. 1+ satisfies the charge balance in the formula Al (+3) 3 Si (+12), 8 O (-16) = −1.

57. Microporous materials means have pores less than 2 nm in diameter, while mesoporous materials have pores whose diameters are between 2 and 50 nm. Macroporous materials would have pores with diameters greater than 50 nm.

CHAPTER

15

Energy

A Fuel's Paradise

CHAPTER SUMMARY

15.1 Energy: Starring Our Sun
A. Nearly all the energy available to us on Earth comes from the sun (173,000 TW), where it is generated by nuclear fusion.
1. The SI unit for energy is the joule (J).
2. The SI unit for power is the watt (W).
3. 1 watt = 1 joule/second.
B. There are two forms of energy: potential (energy stored in the form of position or arrangement) and kinetic (energy of motion).
C. Energy and the life-support system.
1. The energy the Earth receives from the sun is
a. reflected back into space (30%).
b. converted to heat and warms the planet (~50%).
c. used to power the water cycle (23%).
2. Green plants use sunlight (less than 0.02%) to convert solar energy to chemical energy (photosynthesis).
a. The sunlight is absorbed by green plant pigments called chlorophylls.
b. The energy is used to convert carbon dioxide and water to glucose (an energy-rich simple sugar) and oxygen.
c. Glucose can be stored, or it can be converted to more complex foods and structural materials.

Answers to Self-Assessment Questions

1. b Energy is defined as the ability or capacity to do work.
2. c The industrial sector uses the largest fraction of the nation's energy.
3. d The U.S. uses about one-fifth, or 20%, of the world's energy.
4. c An apple hanging on a branch above Isaac Newton's head has potential energy.
5. b The largest portion (~50%) of Earth's incident solar radiation is converted to heat and warms the planet.
6. a About 0.02% of Earth's incident solar radiation is used in photosynthesis.

15.2   Energy and Chemical Reactions
        A. Two areas of chemistry that focus on energy are kinetics and thermodynamics.
            1. Chemical kinetics describes the rate at which a chemical reaction occurs which depends
                on temperature, concentration of reactants, and the presence of catalysts.
                a. *Temperature*: Generally, the higher the temperature, the faster the reaction. At higher
                    temperatures, molecules move faster and collide more often. Also, more energy is
                    available for breaking chemical bonds.
                b. *Concentration of reactants*: The more molecules there are in a given volume of space,
                    the more likely they are to collide; the more collisions there are, the more reactions
                    are likely to occur.
                c. *Catalysts*: These substances speed up reactions without being used up in the process.
                    i.   Enzymes are biological catalysts that mediate the reactions in living cells.
        B. Thermochemistry: the study of energy changes that occur during chemical reactions and
            physical processes.
            1. Energy changes and chemical reactions are quantitatively related to the amounts of
                chemicals undergoing change (see EXAMPLE PROBLEMs).
                a. *Exothermic* reactions are those that release heat or energy.
                b. *Endothermic* reactions are those that require a net input of heat or energy.

Answers to Self-Assessment Questions

1.   c   The rate of a chemical reaction usually decreases when reactant concentrations are decreased
           because the number of collisions between reactant species decreases.
2.   b   When water goes from liquid $\{H_2O(l)\}$ to solid $\{H_2O(s)\}$, energy is given off, so the process
           is exothermic (think about the reverse process, heating liquid water to put the molecules into
           the gas phase—in this case the heat the molecules absorbed is released when they return to
           the liquid phase).
3.   b   The equation indicates that 624.7 kJ of energy is required when one mole of SiO_2 reacts.
           Because only one-tenth of one mole of SiO_2 reacts, only one-tenth of the energy, or 62.47 kJ,
           is consumed.
4.   d   Any reaction or process that releases heat is exothermic.

15.3   The Laws of Thermodynamics
        A. The first law of thermodynamics (also called the law of conservation of energy) states that
            energy is neither created nor destroyed (although it can be changed in form).
        B. The second law of thermodynamics states that the energy available for work in the universe is
            continually decreasing, or that energy does not flow spontaneously from a cold object to a hot
            one.
            1. No engine can operate at 100% efficiency; some energy is converted to heat or friction.
            2. Not all forms of energy are equal; high-grade forms are constantly degraded to low-grade
                forms.
                a. Mechanical energy (high grade) is eventually changed to heat energy (low grade).
            3. Natural processes tend toward greater entropy (more disorder).
                a. We can reverse the tendency toward disorder, but it costs energy to do it.
                b. The more the energy is spread out, the higher the entropy of the system and the less
                    likely it is that this energy can be harnessed to do useful work.
                c. Spontaneous processes tend toward greater entropy or are exothermic, or both.

Answers to Self-Assessment Questions

1. a The first law of thermodynamics is also known as the law of conservation of energy.
2. c The second law of thermodynamics states that energy goes from more useful to less useful forms of energy.
3. d The second law of thermodynamics states that the total entropy always increases for an isolated system.
4. c Because liquids are more organized than gases, the entropy increases when a substance goes from the liquid to the gaseous state.

15.4   Power: People, Horses, and Fossils
      A. A fuel is a substance that burns readily with the release of significant amounts of energy.
          1. Primitive people obtained their energy (food and fuel) by hunting and gathering.
          2. Domestication of animals increased available energy somewhat; people gained horsepower and oxpower.
          3. Windmills and waterwheels further increased available energy by converting energy to useful work.
          4. Since 1850 and the Industrial Revolution, steam engines and other mechanical devices have provided us with 10,000 times as much energy as was available to primitive people.
          5. Today, more than 85% of the energy used to support our way of life comes from fossil fuels—coal, petroleum, and natural gas that formed during Earth's Carboniferous period around 300 million years ago.
      B. Fuels are reduced forms of matter, and the burning process is an oxidation.
      C. Reserves and consumption rates of fossil fuels.
          1. Fossil fuel reserves are rapidly being depleted.

Answers to Self-Assessment Questions

1. d Coal, petroleum, and natural gas are fossil fuels because they were formed over millennia from the remains of ancient plants and animals.
2. d CO_2 is not a fuel. The carbon in CO_2 is in its most oxidized form.
3. d Fuels are reduced forms of matter and release their energy when they are burned.

15.5   Coal: The Carbon Rock of Ages
      A. Coal is a complex combination of organic materials that burn and inorganic materials that produce ash; its energy content is closely related to its carbon content.
          1. Coal was formed millions of years ago from plant material buried under mud.
              a. Cellulose of plants was compressed; it broke down, releasing small hydrogen- and oxygen-rich molecules and leaving behind a material rich in carbon.
          2. Of all the fossil fuels that ever existed, we will have used about 90% in 300 years
      B. Coal is an abundant but inconvenient fuel.
          1. Coal is our most plentiful fossil fuel; the United States is estimated to have 25% of the world's reserves.
          2. Electric utilities burn one billion metric tons of coal per year to generate 45% of our electricity.
          3. Coal is inconvenient to use and dangerous to mine.
              a. Most is obtained by strip mining.
      C. Source of pollution.
          1. Burning coal produces carbon dioxide, carbon monoxide, sulfur oxides (and sulfuric acid), and particulate matter.
          2. Coal can be cleaned before burning by the flotation method.

a. Coal has a density of 1.3 g/cm³. It can be floated away, leaving denser sulfur-containing minerals behind.
D. Coke and coal tar.
1. When coal is heated in the absence of air, volatile material is driven off leaving behind coke, which is mostly carbon and is used in the production of iron and steel.
2. Coal tar (a source of chemicals) is made by heating coal to drive off volatile matter.
a. Coal tar and liquid coal oil are good sources of organic chemicals for medical and industrial use.

Answers to Self-Assessment Questions

1. b Bituminous coal is 90% carbon.
2. a After burning, the inorganic constituents of coal end up as ash.
3. a Coal is the most plentiful fossil fuel.
4. a Of the fossil fuels, coal contributes the most to SO_x pollution because much of it has a relatively high sulfur content.
5. a The flotation method of cleaning coal takes advantage of the fact that coal is less dense than its major impurities.

15.6 Natural Gas and Petroleum
A. Composition of natural gas in the North American pipeline.
1. Methane   82%
2. Ethane   6%
3. Propane   2%
4. Butane and pentane   smaller amounts
B. Most natural gas is burned as fuel, but some is separated into fractions.
1. The fractions are cracked to produce ethylene, propylene, and other valuable chemical intermediates.
a. Ethylene, propylene, and four-carbon compounds are also made by cracking the alkane mixture.
b. Natural gas is the starting material for many one-carbon compounds.
C. Natural gas is the cleanest fossil fuel in regards to pollution.
D. Petroleum is a complex liquid mixture of organic compounds.
1. Petroleum is thought to be formed mainly from the fats of ocean-dwelling, microscopic animals.
2. When efficiently burned (when they undergo complete combustion and produce CO_2 and H_2O rather than incomplete combustion and produce CO and H_2O), petroleum products are relatively clean fuels.
3. Burning petroleum reserves depletes the reserves also used as starting materials for most industrial organic chemicals.
E. Obtaining and refining petroleum.
1. Crude oil is a liquid which can be pumped through pipelines.
2. To improve its use, crude oil is separated into fractions by boiling in a distillation column.
a. Lighter hydrocarbon molecules come off the top of the column and heavier ones come off at the bottom.
3. Fractions that boil at higher temperatures are often converted to gasoline by cracking, or breaking the long molecules into shorter ones, illustrating the way chemists modify nature's materials to meet human needs and desires.
F. Gasoline is a mixture of hydrocarbons.

1. A typical gasoline sample might have, by volume, 4–8% straight-chain alkanes, 25–40% branched-chain alkanes, 2–5% alkenes, 3–7% cycloalkanes, 1–4% cycloalkenes, and 20–50% aromatic hydrocarbons (0.5–2.5% benzene), as well as small amounts of some sulfur- and nitrogen-containing compounds.
   a. The gasoline fraction of petroleum as it comes from a distillation column is called straight-run gasoline.
G. Octane ratings of gasolines indicate the extent to which the gasoline will cause knocking.
   1. In 1927, isooctane was assigned an octane rating of 100 and heptane, a straight-chain compound, was assigned an octane rating of zero. Gasoline rated 90 octane would perform the same as a mixture that was 90% isooctane and 10% heptane.
   2. During the 1930s chemists discovered that the octane rating of gasoline could be improved by heating it in the presence of a catalyst to isomerize some of the unbranched molecules to highly branched molecules with higher octane numbers.
   3. Certain additives also improve the antiknock quality of gasoline.
      a. Tetraethyllead was especially effective, but lead fouls catalytic converters and can lead to learning disabilities in children. Unleaded gasoline became available in the U.S. in 1974.
      b. Refineries use catalytic reforming to convert low-octane alkanes to high-octane aromatic compounds.
      c. Octane boosters such as ethanol, methanol, *tert*-butyl alcohol, and methyl *tert*-butyl ether (MTBE) have replaced tetraethyllead in gasoline.
      d. MTBE from leaded gasoline storage tanks has polluted groundwater in some areas.
H. Alternative fuels.
   1. An automobile engine can be made to run on nearly any liquid or gaseous fuel.
   2. Examples are natural gas, propane, diesel fuel, and ethanol.
   3. Fuel cells and batteries are also being used.
I. Energy return on energy invested (EROEI).
   1. Evaluating an energy source involves comparing the amount of energy required to produce the energy source with the amount of energy it releases.

Answers to Self-Assessment Questions

1.	a	Methane, CH_4, is the principal constituent in natural gas.
2.	d	Natural gas is the simplest fossil fuel in composition.
3.	a	United States oil production peaked in 1970.
4.	a	Cracking converts larger hydrocarbons into smaller, more useful ones.
5.	a	An alkylation unit is used to convert smaller molecules into larger ones.
6.	d.	An isomerization unit improves the octane rating by converting straight-chain alkanes to branched-chain alkanes.
7.	c.	A catalytic reforming unit converts low octane straight-chain molecules into high octane aromatic ones.
8.	d.	The octane rating for gasoline is a measure of a fuel's tendency to cause knocking or premature firing in an engine.
9.	c.	E15 fuel contains 15% ethanol and 85% gasoline.

15.7   Convenient Energy
   A. Electricity is perhaps the most convenient form of energy.
      1. It flows through wires and can be converted into light, heat, or mechanical energy.
      2. Electricity can be generated by any fuel that can be burned to boil water so the steam produced can turn a turbine.

3. ~45% of U.S. electric energy comes from coal-burning plants, any one of which is only ~40% efficient; the rest of the energy is generally wasted as heat (thermal pollution).

B. Coal gasification and liquefaction.

1. Coal can be converted to gas or oil, which are easy to transport and freer of sulfur and minerals than the coal from which they came.

2. The process involves reduction of carbon by hydrogen to form methane:

$$C + 2 H_2 \rightarrow CH_4$$

3. The hydrogen is produced by passing steam over hot charcoal to produce synthesis gas, a mixture of hydrogen and carbon monoxide.

   a. Some of the CO in the synthesis gas reacts with water to produce CO_2 and H_2.

   b. Some of the CO in the synthesis gas reacts with H_2 to form methanol (CH_3OH) which can be used directly or reacted to form larger hydrocarbons.

3. Coal liquefaction and gasification require large amounts of energy.

   a. Up to one-third of the energy is wasted in the conversion process.

   b. Liquid fuels made from coal contain sulfur, nitrogen, and arsenic compounds, which contribute to air pollution.

   c. Coal conversions also require large amounts of water and are messy, often resulting in air and water pollution.

4. The Bergius and Fischer-Tropsch methods are also used to make liquid fuel from coal.

Answers to Self-Assessment Questions

1. c About 45% of the electricity produced in the United States comes from coal burning plants.
2. b Natural gas is transported mainly by pipelines.
3. c Methane, CH_4, is the main fuel produced by coal gasification.
4. d The convenience of a fuel depends upon its physical state which relates to its ease of transportation and use.

15.8 Nuclear Energy

A. Energy released during fission is used to produce steam, which turns a turbine, generating electricity.

1. In the United States, nuclear power plants produce ~20% of the nation's electricity.

B. Nuclear power plants.

1. Pressurized water reactors are common in the United States although boiling water reactors have been used in the past.

2. Nuclear power plants use the same fission reactions as employed in nuclear bombs, but the uranium used in power plants is enriched to only 3–4% U-235 while a bomb requires ~90% U-235.

3. A *moderator*, such as water or graphite, is used to slow down the fission neutrons so they can be absorbed by the U-235 nuclei. Water often serves as a moderator.

4. *Control rods*, made of boron steel or cadmium, are inserted to absorb neutrons and slow the fission reaction. Partial removal of the rods starts the chain reaction.

C. The nuclear advantage: minimal air pollution.

1. Advantages: No soot, fly ash, sulfur dioxide, or other chemical air pollutants are emitted.

   a. Nuclear power does not contribute to global warming, air pollution, or acid rain.

D. Problems with nuclear power.

1. Elaborate safety precautions are required.

2. Runaway nuclear reactions are unlikely, but possible.

3. Nuclear wastes are highly radioactive and must be isolated for centuries.

     a.   Tailings from uranium mines are mildly radioactive and contaminate wide areas.

     b.   Slightly more thermal pollution is generated from nuclear power plants than from fossil fuel burning plants.

E. Nuclear accidents.

   1.   Three incidents heightened public fear of nuclear power: the 1979 accident at the Three Mile Island nuclear power plant near Harrisburg, PA; the 1986 accident at Chernobyl, Ukraine; and the Fukushima accident resulting from the earthquake and tsunami in Japan in March, 2011.

F. Breeder reactors: making more fuel than they burn.

   1.   Less than 1% of natural uranium is the fissionable uranium-235 isotope; the rest is nonfissionable uranium-238.

   2.   Breeder reactors have a core of fissionable plutonium surrounded by uranium-238. Neutrons from the core convert the uranium-238 to fissionable plutonium-239. The process breeds more fuel than it consumes.

     a.   Advantage: There is enough uranium-238 to last for a few centuries.

     b.   Disadvantages: Plutonium melts at 640 °C; plant operation is inefficient because it is limited to rather cool operating temperatures.

         i.   Molten sodium metal, which reacts violently with both air and water, is used as a coolant.

        ii.   Core meltdown is more likely than with uranium-235 fuel.

       iii.   Plutonium is toxic.

       iv.   Reactor-grade plutonium can be converted to nuclear bombs.

   3.   Breeder reactors can also convert nonfissionable thorium-232 to fissionable uranium-233.

     a.   Uranium-233 emits biologically damaging alpha particles.

   4.   No breeder reactors are operating in the United States.

G. Nuclear fusion: the sun in a magnetic bottle

   1.   Thermonuclear reactions power the sun and hydrogen bombs, but controlled, sustainable fusion reactions are yet to be achieved.

   2.   Controlled fusion would have several advantages.

     a.   The principal fuel, deuterium (^{2}H), is plentiful and is obtained from fractional electrolysis (splitting apart by means of electricity) of water.

     b.   The product, helium, is biologically inert; radioactive wastes are minimized.

   3.   Some possible disadvantages.

     a.   Radioactive tritium (^{3}H) might be released and incorporated into living organisms.

     b.   Temperatures of $1 \times 10^6 - 2 \times 10^6$ °C are required.

     c.   The plasma, which is a mixture of electrons and nuclei, must be contained by a magnetic field or other nonmaterial device.

   4.   It is unlikely that electricity from fusion will be available for decades.

Answers to Self-Assessment Questions

1.   c   In a fission reactor, uranium-235 nuclei absorb a neutron and split into two smaller nuclei, releasing large amounts of energy.

2.   b   The control rods in a nuclear reactor absorb neutrons, preventing them from causing fission and thus controlling the rate of the fission reaction.

3.   c   Nuclear power plants produce about 20% of the electricity in the United States.

4.   a   Breeder reactors produce more nuclear fuel than they consume.

5.   b   There are about 100 nuclear power plants in operation in the United States.

6.   c   An advantage of nuclear power is that it produces no greenhouse gases.

7.   c $^2_1\text{H} + {}^3_1H \rightarrow {}^1_0\text{n} + {}^4_2He$

169

Copyright © 2013 Pearson Education, Inc.

8.   d   Fusion is not currently used in nuclear power plants because it requires temperatures of millions of degrees, which makes the reaction difficult to contain.

15.9   Renewable Energy Sources
   A. Renewable energy sources account for 8–11% of the energy production in the United States.
   B. Solar heating: solar collectors can be used to heat homes and water for bathing, laundry, etc.
   C. Solar cells: electricity from sunlight.
       1. Photovoltaic cells (solar cells) can convert sunlight directly to electricity.
       2. Solar cells based on silicon have
           a. donor crystals doped with arsenic to provide extra electrons (silicon has four valence electrons, arsenic, five).
               i.   The material has extra electrons, is negatively charged, and is called an *n-type* (negative) semiconductor.
           b. acceptor crystals doped with boron (three valence electrons) create positive holes.
               i.   The material has a shortage of electrons, leaving a positive hole in the crystal so these materials are called *p-type* semiconductors.
           c. Joining the *n*-type and *p*-type crystals forms a photovoltaic cell in which electrons flow from the *n*-type region to the *p*-type region.
           d. Sunlight dislodges electrons from donor crystals, creating a current flow from donor cell to receptor crystals.
       3. Solar cells have low efficiency (about 12–18%).
       4. Solar energy is not available at night or on cloudy days, but it can be stored as heat.
   D. Biomass: photosynthesis for fuel.
       1. Biomass (plants grown for fuel) has several advantages.
           a. It is a renewable resource.
           b. Energy for biomass production comes from the sun.
       2. Disadvantages.
           a. Most of the land available for farming biomass is needed for food production.
           b. Plants must be harvested and hauled to where the energy is needed, often over long distances.
       3. Biomass can be burned directly as fuel or converted to other fuels.
           a. Plants high in starches and sugars can be used to produce ethanol.
           b. Wood can be used to produce methanol.
           c. Bacteria can convert plant material to methane.
       4. Biomass and biofuels currently provide about half of the renewable energy used in the United States, or about 5% of the country's overall energy needs.
   E. Green chemistry: have we got the energy?
       1. Energy return on energy invested (EROEI) is a useful way to evaluate technology for fuel production but does not tell the entire story.
           a. EROEI measures only the energy inputs and outputs, and does not reflect the waste produced.
               i.   Fracking (hydraulic fracturing) to obtain natural gas requires adding chemicals to water which contaminate the aquifers in the area of the activity.
               ii. Methanol that enters the atmosphere from the wells is 25 times more effective as a greenhouse gas than CO_2.
   F. Hydrogen: light and powerful.
       1. Gram for gram, H_2 yields more energy than any other chemical fuel.
       2. Hydrogen is clean, yielding only water as a chemical product.
   G. Fuel cells.
       1. A fuel cell is a device in which fuel is oxidized in an electrochemical cell and produces energy directly.

a. They differ from electrochemical cells in two ways.
      i. Fuel and oxygen are fed in continuously.
      ii. The electrodes are an inert material such as platinum that does not enter the reaction.
   b. In a hydrogen fuel cell, hydrogen is oxidized at the anode, and oxygen is reduced at the cathode.
   c. Fuel cells are used on spacecraft, but they contribute little to the production of electricity on Earth because cheap catalysts have not yet been developed.
H. Other renewable energy sources.
   1. Wind power and water power could help solve the energy crisis.
      a. The sun causes the wind to blow and water to evaporate and condense to fall later as rain.
      b. Blowing wind and flowing water can be used as energy sources.
   2. About 7% of our electricity comes from hydroelectric plants, but nearly all the good dam sites are in use.
   3. Windmills can be used to provide mechanical energy or to generate electricity.
      a. Windmills could meet up to 10% of our electricity needs, but provide an almost negligible amount at present.
   4. Wind and water provide relatively clean energy, but suffer from some disadvantages.
      a. Dams flood valuable land. Reservoirs silt up. Sometimes dams break, causing devastating floods.
      b. The wind doesn't always blow; energy storage or an alternative source is needed. Windmills limit the use of the land on which they are placed.
I. Geothermal energy.
   1. The interior of Earth is heated by immense gravitational forces and by natural radioactivity. The heat comes to the surface in some areas through geysers and volcanoes.
   2. One drawback of geothermal energy is that the wastewater is quite salty, and its disposal could be a problem.
J. Oceans of energy.
   1. Ocean thermal energy takes advantage of the 20 °C difference in temperature between the surface and the depths of the oceans, which is enough to evaporate a liquid and use the vapor to drive a turbine.
   2. The liquid is then condensed by the cold from the ocean depths and the cycle repeats.
   3. Tides possess great energy. At high tide, water fills a reservoir or bay; at low tide, the water escapes through a turbine to generate electricity.
K. Energy: how much is too much?
   1. The Energy Information Administration of the U.S. Department of Energy projected that world energy consumption will increase by 50% from 2007 to 2035.
   2. Over the past three decades, we have made significant progress in energy conservation: Overall, U.S. industry has reduced its energy consumption per product by almost 30%.

Answers to Self-Assessment Questions

1.   c   Silicon doped with arsenic is an *n*-type semiconductor.
2.   c   *p*-Type semiconductors feature crystal sites with positive holes.
3.   a   Biomass is a renewable source of energy because it is material from living plants which can be grown in a short amount of time.
4.   a   Biodiesel cannot be made from corn starch. Biodiesel is made from the reaction of fats or oils with methyl alcohol.
5.   c   Water is the major product from burning hydrogen gas.
6.   b   Hydrogen has the lowest EROEI (Energy Return on Energy Invested).

7.   c   Nuclear power does not originate in the sun.
8.   b   Hydrogen is used in almost all present-day fuel cells.
9.   a   Fuel cells are dependent on fuels from other sources. They often use hydrogen and oxygen.
10. b   Hydroelectric is the renewable energy source that provides the most electrical energy ($\sim$7%) in the United States today.
11. b   Geothermal energy comes from the internal heat of the Earth, which comes to the surface as geysers or volcanoes.

LEARNING OBJECTIVES

You should be able to...

1.   Perform power and energy calculations. (15.1)

2.   Classify chemical reactions and physical processes as exothermic or endothermic. (15.2)

3.   List factors that affect the rates of chemical reactions. (15.2)

4.   State the first and second laws of thermodynamics, and discuss their implications for energy production and use. (15.3)

5.   List the common fossil fuels, and describe how modern society is based on their use. (15.4)

6.   List advantages and disadvantages of coal as a fuel. (15.5)

7.   List the characteristics of natural gas and petroleum. (15.6)

8.   List advantages and disadvantages of natural gas and petroleum as fuels. (15.6)

9.   Explain why gaseous and liquid fuels are more convenient to use than solid fuels. (15.7)

10. List advantages and disadvantages of nuclear energy. (15.8)

11. Describe how a nuclear power plant generates electricity. (15.8)

12. List important characteristics of renewable energy sources. (15.9)

13. List advantages and disadvantages of various kinds of renewable energy. (15.9)

14. Explain how applying the green chemistry principles can help identify improved methods for energy generation.

15. Identify waste products from some current energy-generation processes.

EXAMPLE PROBLEMS

1. Complete combustion of 16.0 g of methane yields 192 kcal of energy. How much energy is obtained by the combustion of 96.0 g of methane?
    Energy released, kcal = (96.0 g methane)(192 kcal/16.0 g methane) = 1150 kcal

2. Splitting 36.0 g of water into hydrogen and oxygen requires the input of 137 kcal of energy. How much energy is required to split 180 g of water?
    Energy required, kcal = (180 g water)(137 kcal/36.0 g water) = 685 kcal

ADDITIONAL PROBLEMS

1. Burning 4.00 g of hydrogen in sufficient oxygen produces 137 kcal of heat. How much heat is released by the combustion of 20.0 g of hydrogen?

2. How much carbon dioxide is formed by the complete combustion of 78 g of carbon? The equation is $C + O_2 \rightarrow CO_2$.

3. Complete combustion of 16.0 g of methane yields 192 kcal of energy. How many grams of methane are needed to produce 1850 kcal of energy?

4. Most coal contains 3.0% sulfur. How much sulfur is there in a metric ton (1000 kg) of coal? How much sulfur dioxide is formed by burning this coal? The equation is $S + O_2 \rightarrow SO_2$.

5. In 1975, nuclear power accounted for about 2×10^{10} W of electricity and the formation of tritium, with an activity of about 7.5×10^{15} disintegrations per second. By the year 2000, it is estimated that nuclear power will produce 1×10^{12} W of electricity per year. What activity of tritium will be produced?

6. Nuclear power plants producing 1×10^{12} W of electricity will produce 9000 kg of strontium-90 waste. The half-life of this isotope is 28 years. If 9000 kg was produced in the year 2000, how much of that strontium-90 will remain in 2028? In 2056? In 2112?

7. A large power plant will burn 25 million kg of coal per day. If the coal is 8% inorganic ash, how much ash is produced per day? Per year? Per decade?

8. If the coal in problem 7 contains 0.2 ppm of mercury (that is, 0.2 kg of mercury in 1,000,000 kg of coal), how much mercury is released into the environment each day? Each year?

DISCUSSION

Energy, the ability to do work, ultimately comes from the sun. All the food for life comes from photosynthesis that is powered by the sun. Rates of chemical reactions are increased with increases in temperature, increases in concentration, and in the presence of a catalyst. Almost all chemical reactions either require energy (are endothermic) or give off energy (are exothermic). The first law of thermodynamics states that energy is conserved. The second law of thermodynamics states that energy flows from regions of high energy to regions of low energy and that disorder increases. Since the 1850s, humanity has experienced a tremendous increase in the amount of energy available to them so that now people have 10,000 times as much total energy as their ancestors. Ninety percent of our energy comes from fossil fuels. The fossil fuels are coal, petroleum, and natural gas, and these are composed of organic compounds that are burned to produce energy. Each has its advantages and disadvantages. A great deal of energy is converted to electricity, a convenient secondary energy source. Although nuclear power is cleaner, radioactive material and wastes have serious handling and disposal issues. There are a number of alternative energy sources, each with its pros and cons: solar energy, biomass energy, wind and water power, geothermal energy, oil shale, and tar sands. Oil can be made from seeds, solid coal can be transformed into more convenient physical states by gasification and liquefaction, hydrogen can be used as a secondary energy source, alcohols can be made from corn, and fuel cells can be a clean secondary energy source. Because the production of any form of energy has its negative consequences, wise stewardship of energy is necessary.

ANSWERS TO ODD-NUMBERED REVIEW QUESTIONS AND SOLUTIONS FOR ODD-NUMBERED END OF CHAPTER PROBLEMS

Review Questions

1. The energy on the sun comes from the nuclear fusion of hydrogen to form helium.

3. Coal was the principle fuel used in the United States between 1850 and 1950. Petroleum has been the principle fuel used since 1950.

Problems

5. a. (sucrose), and b. (acetylene) are both fuels.

7. a. Combustion of fructose ($C_6H_{12}O_6$): $C_6H_{12}O_6(s) + 6\ O_2(g) \rightarrow 6\ CO_2(g) + 6\ H_2O(l)$ + energy
   b. Combustion of propane, (C_3H_8): $C_3H_8(g) + 5\ O_2(g) \rightarrow 3\ CO_2(g) + 4\ H_2O(l)$ + energy

9. $C(s) + O_2(g) \rightarrow CO_2(g)$

11. $CH_4(g) + 2\ O_2(g) \rightarrow CO_2(g) + 2\ H_2O(l)$

13. Water gas can serve as a fuel because both H_2 and CO are readily oxidized (burn).

15. Generally, increasing the temperature of a reaction increases the rate of reaction.

17. Amount of energy released = (24.5 mol CH_4)(803 kJ/mol) = 1.97×10^4 kJ.

19. 1 calorie = 4.184 joules.
    Number of kJ released/1.00 g gasoline = (1060 cal/g gasoline)(4.184 joules/cal)(1 kJ/1000 J)
    = 4.44 kJ.

21. The amount of energy required to reverse a reaction is the same as the amount of energy released by the reaction, 803 kJ.

23. The first law of thermodynamics says that energy is conserved, which means that the amount of energy in the universe is a constant.

25. Entropy is the measure of the degree of distribution of energy (disorder) in a system. Entropy is increased when a fossil fuel is burned because larger molecules (the fuel) are converted into a larger number of smaller molecules.

27. This essentially means that it isn't possible to create energy.

29. The advantages of coal as a fuel are that it is plentiful and burning it produces a lot of energy. The disadvantages of coal as a fuel are that as a solid, it is difficult to transport, and it produces a significant amount of pollution (SO_x, particulates, and CO) when it burns.

31. Number of years = (1342 billion barrels)(1 year/31.1 billion barrels) = 43.2 years

33. Number of years = (6254 trillion ft^3)(1 year/103.8 trillion ft^3)year = 60.3 yrs.

35. $2 C_2H_6(g) + 7 O_2(g) \rightarrow 4 CO_2(g) + 6 H_2O(l)$

37. Ancient marine animals are thought to be the origin of petroleum.

39. The compounds that make up gasoline are hydrocarbons with chemical formulas ranging from C_5H_{12} to $C_{12}H_{26}$. The compounds that make up diesel fuel are hydrocarbons with chemical formulas ranging from $C_{12}H_{26}$ to $C_{16}H_{34}$. Therefore, the molecules in a sample of diesel fuel are larger than those in a sample of gasoline and, therefore, the molecular masses of the molecules in diesel fuel are larger than the molecular masses of the molecules in gasoline.

41. Asphalt is the residue of the processing of petroleum. Using it in paving roads and highways provides a use for an otherwise "waste" product.

43. About 20% of U.S. electricity is produced by nuclear power plants.

45. The same fission reaction is used in both nuclear power plants and nuclear bombs, but the uranium used in power plants is enriched to only 3–4% U-235 whereas the uranium used in a nuclear bomb is about 90% U-235. Therefore, a power plant uses nuclear material far below the required concentration needed to create a nuclear explosion so a power plant will not explode.

47. No. The concentration required for an atomic bomb is much higher (90% vs. 3–4%) than the concentration required for a fission reactor.

49. Uranium-238 can be converted to fissionable plutonium-239 by bombardment with neutrons. If a reactor is built with a core of fissionable plutonium surrounded by uranium-238, neutrons from the fission of plutonium convert the uranium-238 shield to more plutonium, effectively producing more fuel than it consumes. Even though plutonium is created from uranium-238, the process still requires energy, so the law of conservation of energy is not violated.

51. The main fuel in fusion reactors is deuterium, which is plentiful and can be obtained from fractional electrolysis of water. Also, the primary waste product is helium, which is stable and biologically inert. Plasma is a hot, gaseous mixture of charged particles (nuclei and electrons) made from atoms that have been stripped of their electrons,

53. $^{232}_{90}Th + ^{1}_{0}n \rightarrow ^{233}_{90}Th \rightarrow ^{0}_{-1}e + ^{233}_{91}Pa$

$^{233}_{91}Pa \rightarrow ^{233}_{92}U + ^{0}_{-1}e$

55. Number of mol of CH_4 = $(1.8 \times 10^{10}$ kJ)(1 mol CH_4/803 kJ) = 2.24×10^7 mol CH_4
    Mass of CH_4, t = $(2.24 \times 10^7$ mol CH_4)(16.04 g CH_4/mol CH_4)(1 kg/1000 g)(1 t/1000 kg) = 360 t

57. A photovoltaic cell converts sunlight directly into electricity.

59. 1.2 kW = 1200 W.
    Area of solar cell, m^2 = (1200 W)(1 m^2/100 W) = 12 m^2.
    Solar cells are not very efficient and need a very large surface area. There also needs to be a means of energy storage for nighttime and very cloudy days.

61. Biomass is plant material used as fuel.

63. Fuel cells differ from electrochemical cells in that fuel cells have fuel continuously fed to the electrodes, and the electrodes in the fuel cells serve as a surface for the chemical reaction but are not used up. The cells do not stop functioning as long as reactants are supplied.

65. a. $C(s) + 2 H_2(g) \rightarrow CH_4(g)$
    b. $C(s) + H_2O(g) \rightarrow CO(g) + H_2(g)$

67. This process is endothermic because the reactants absorb heat from the surroundings when they are mixed.

69. a. number of watts = (2100 kcal)(4.184 kJ/kcal)(1 kW/3600 kJ)(1000 W/1 kW) = 2.44×10^3 W
    b. Domesticated horses increased the availability of energy somewhat; 1 hp = 7.45 humanpower

71. a. Power (W) is energy (J) per second (s). In the case of the banana,
       energy = (170 kcal)(1000 cal/kcal)(4.184 J/cal) = 7.11×10^5 J
       Time, in seconds = (2 hr)(60 min/hr)(60 s/min) = 7200 s
       Power = $(7.11 \times 10^5$ J/7200 s) = 99 W
    b. Power = $(7.11 \times 10^5$ J/0.0012 s) = 5.9×10^8 W.
       Although both the banana and the hand grenade provide the same amount of energy, the hand grenade is 6×10^6 times more powerful than the banana because of the amount of time over which the same energy is dispelled.

73. a. Carbon atoms are removed from the atmosphere by photosynthesis.
    b. Carbon atoms are returned to the atmosphere by animal respiration or the burning of fossil fuels.
    c. Carbon atoms are effectively withdrawn from the carbon cycle by conversion into insoluble carbonates.

75. mass SO_2 = (2500 tons coal)(0.65 tons S/100 tons coal)(2000 lb/t)(454 g/lb)(64.07 g SO_2/32.07 g S)
         = 2.95×10^7 g SO_2
    volume = (45000 m)(60000 m)(400 m) = 1.08×10^{12} m^3
    concentration of SO_2, $\mu g/m^3$ = $(2.95 \times 10^7$ g SO_2)(1 $\times 10^6$ $\mu g/g$)/1.08 $\times 10^{12}$ m^3 = 27.3 μg SO_2/m^3
    The SO_2 concentration does not exceed the primary national air quality standard.

77. a. number of years = $(9.92 \times 10^6$ TWh)(1 yr/1.32 $\times 10^5$ TWh) = 75.2 yr.
    b. Americans represent roughly 4.5% of the world population. If the per capita consumption for the rest of the world increased to the per capita level in the U.S., the population would be consuming roughly $(4)(1.32 \times 10^5$ TWh) = 5.28×10^5 TWh. If this were the case, the available energy would last for $(9.92 \times 10^6$ TWh)(1 yr/5.28 $\times 10^5$ TWh) = less than 19 years.

In either case, we are not using the energy in a sustainable way and need to find ways of replacing nonrenewable energy resources with renewable energy resources, as well as reducing our reliance on energy.

c. The rate of energy use will likely grow instead of remaining the same, so reserves might not last the 75 y calculated in part (a). Worldwide use is unlikely to reach the U.S. level anytime soon, if ever, and so the estimate in part (b) is not at all realistic.

79. The answer is d. All the aspects of a process listed in answers a, b, and c are looked at when green chemistry principles are used to evaluate energy-generation processes.

CHAPTER

16

Biochemistry

A Molecular View of Life

CHAPTER SUMMARY

16.1 Energy and the Living Cell
    A. Biochemistry is the chemistry of living things and life processes.
        1. The structural unit of all living things is the cell.
            a. Cells are enclosed in membranes; plant cells also have cell walls.
            b. The cell gains nutrients and gets rid of wastes through the cell membrane.
            c. The cell nucleus contains nucleic acids that control heredity.
            d. Ribosomes are the location of protein synthesis.
            e. Energy is produced in the mitochondria.
            f. Plant cells (but not animal cells) contain chloroplasts in which energy from the sun is converted into chemical energy which is stored in the plant in the form of carbohydrates.
    B. Energy in biological systems.
        1. Living organisms can use only certain forms of energy.
        2. Plants' chloroplasts convert radiant energy into chemical energy stored as carbohydrates.
        3. Plant cells can also convert carbohydrates to fats and, with proper inorganic nutrients, to proteins.
        4. Animals cannot use sunlight directly. Animals obtain energy from carbohydrates, fats, and proteins.
        5. Metabolism—the series of coordinated chemical reactions that keep cells alive.
            a. Catabolism is the degradation of molecules to provide energy.
            b. Anabolism is the synthesis of biomolecules.

Answers to Self-Assessment Questions

1. c We obtain energy from carbohydrates, fats, and proteins.
2. b Catabolism is the process of chemically breaking down molecules to access the energy that is stored in their chemical bonds.
3. c Metabolism is the entire series of coordinated chemical reactions that keep cells alive.

16.2 Carbohydrates: A Storehouse of Energy
    A. Carbohydrates are polyhydroxy aldehydes or ketones or compounds that can be hydrolyzed (split by water) to form such aldehydes or ketones.
        1. Carbohydrates are composed of carbon, hydrogen, and oxygen.

178
Copyright © 2013 Pearson Education, Inc.

2. Usually, the C, H, and O atoms are present in a ratio expressed by the formula $C_x(H_2O)_y$.
B. Some simple sugars.
   1. Sugars can be classified in terms of their functional group: aldoses are polyhydroxy aldehydes and ketoses are polyhydroxy ketones.
   2. Monosaccharides cannot be hydrolyzed (split apart by water).
      a. Some examples are glucose (also called dextrose, an aldose), fructose (fruit sugar, a ketose), and galactose (a component of lactose, milk sugar, and an aldose).
   3. Disaccharides can be hydrolyzed into two monosaccharides.
      a. Examples:
         i. Sucrose + H_2O → glucose + fructose
         ii. Lactose + H_2O → glucose + galactose
C. Polysaccharides: starch and cellulose.
   1. Polysaccharides are large molecules that yield many monosaccharide units upon hydrolysis.
      a. Examples: starch and cellulose.
         i. Both starch and cellulose are polymers of glucose.
   2. In starch, glucose molecules are connected through an alpha linkage in which the oxygen atom joining the glucose molecules is pointing downward.
      a. Two kinds of plant starch are:
         i. Amylose, in which glucose units are joined in a continuous chain.
         ii. Amylopectin, in which glucose units are joined in a branched chain.
      b. Animal starch is called glycogen.
         i. In glycogen, glucose units are joined in a branched chain.
   3. In cellulose, glucose molecules are connected through a beta linkage in which the oxygen atom joining the glucose molecules is pointing upward.

Answers to Self-Assessment Questions

1.   b An aldose is a monosaccharide with an aldehyde group.
2.   d A ketose is a polyhydroxy ketone.
3.   c Ring structures are formed by most monosaccharides when they dissolve in water.
4.   d Lactose, or milk sugar, is a disaccharide composed of glucose and galactose.
5.   d Amylopectin and glycogen are polysaccharide molecules with branched chains of glucose units.
6.   d Carbohydrates are stored in the liver and muscle tissue in the form of glycogen.

16.3   Fats and Other Lipids
A. Lipids are defined by their solubility, not their structures.
   1. Lipids are cellular components that are not soluble in water but are soluble in organic solvents.
   2. Some examples of lipids are fats, fatty acids (long-chain carboxylic acids), steroids such as cholesterol, sex hormones, and fat-soluble vitamins.
B. Fats are esters of fatty acids and glycerol (a trihydroxy alcohol).
   1. Fats are classified according to the number of fatty acid chains attached to glycerol: if one fatty acid chain is attached, the compound is a monoglyceride; if two fatty acid chains are attached, the compound is a diglyceride; and if three fatty acid chains are attached, the compound is a triglyceride.
      a. Naturally occurring fatty acids almost always have an even number of carbon atoms.
      b. Saturated fatty acids do not contain any carbon to carbon double bonds (C=C).
      c. Monounsaturated fatty acids contain one C=C bond in the chain.
      d. Polyunsaturated fatty acids contain two or more C=C bonds.

2. Animal fats are usually solid at room temperature because they are composed of a higher proportion of saturated fatty acids.
3. Vegetable fats (oils) are liquid at room temperature and have a higher proportion of mono- and polyunsaturated fatty acids.
    a. Molecules of polyunsaturated fats include mainly polyunsaturated fatty acids.
4. The degree of unsaturation of a fat is measured by the *iodine number*.
    a. The iodine number is the number of grams of iodine that can add to the double bonds of 100 g of fat.
    b. The higher the iodine number, the more unsaturated the fat.
5. Fats and oils are insoluble in water, and because they are less dense than water, they float on water.

Answers to Self-Assessment Questions

1. d   Lipids are cellular components that are insoluble in water (and other polar solvents).
2. a   S and T are saturated fatty acids, fatty acids with no C=C bonds.
3. c   U is a monosaturated fatty acid.
4. d   V is a polyunsaturated fatty acid.
5. a   Saturated fats often have a high proportion of S and T.
6. d   Polyunsaturated fats (oils) often have a high proportion of V.
7. c   The iodine number measures the degree of unsaturation in a compound.
8. c   In general, animal fats have fewer C=C double bonds than vegetable oils.

16.4   Proteins: Polymers of Amino Acids
    A. All living parts of humans and other organisms contain protein.
        1. Proteins serve as the structural material of animals.
            a. Proteins are composed of carbon, hydrogen, oxygen, nitrogen, and often sulfur.
    B. Proteins are copolymers of 20 different amino acids (see Table 16.3 in the text).
        1. Amino acids have two functional groups, an amino group (—NH$_2$) located on the carbon next to the carbon of the carboxyl group (—COOH), which is called the *alpha* (α) carbon.

$$\begin{array}{c} R \\ | \\ H_2N-C-COOH \\ | \\ H \end{array}$$

            a. The carboxyl group is acidic and donates an H$^+$ to the amino group, which is basic and accepts the H$^+$. This structure is a *zwitterion*.

α-carbon atom

            b. A zwitterion is a molecule containing a positive and negative charge on different parts of the same molecule.
            c. Amino acids differ in the variety of other groups attached to the central carbon atom.
    C. Plants synthesize proteins from CO$_2$, water, and minerals (supplying N and S). Animals must take in proteins as food.

D. The peptide bond: peptides and proteins.
   1. Proteins are polyamides: amino acids linked by many peptide bonds (amide linkages).
      a. A peptide bond (amide linkage) links the $-NH_3^+$ of one amino acid with the $-COO^-$ of another amino acid.

$$^+H_3N-\underset{\underset{R_1}{|}}{\overset{\overset{H}{|}}{C}}-C\overset{O}{\underset{O^-}{\diagdown}} \;+\; ^+H_3N-\underset{\underset{R_2}{|}}{\overset{\overset{H}{|}}{C}}-C\overset{O}{\underset{O^-}{\diagdown}} \;\rightleftharpoons\; ^+H_3N-\underset{\underset{R_1}{|}}{\overset{\overset{H}{|}}{C}}-\overset{\overset{O}{\parallel}}{C}-\underset{\underset{H}{|}}{N}-\underset{\underset{R_2}{|}}{\overset{\overset{H}{|}}{C}}-C\overset{O}{\underset{O^-}{\diagdown}} \;+\; H_2O$$

Peptide bond

      b. This arrangement leaves a free carboxyl group ($-COO^-$) at one end of the protein called the C terminal, and a free amino group ($-NH_3^+$) at the other end, called the N-terminal.
      c. Dipeptides are two linked amino acids, tripeptides are three linked amino acids, and polypeptides are formed when 10 or more amino acids link together.
      d. A protein is a polypeptide that has a molecular weight of more than 10,000 amu.
   2. The sequence of amino acids.
      a. The sequence in which the amino acids are connected in peptides is of critical importance.
         i. Sequences are written using three-letter abbreviations for the amino acids and arranging them with the N-terminal to the left of the sequence and the C-terminal to the right.
         ii. A minor change in the amino acid sequence of a protein may have disastrous effects for the organism.
         iii. *Example*: Sickle-cell anemia is caused by one incorrect amino acid in a 300-unit sequence.

Answers to Self-Assessment Questions

1.   a   Proteins are polymers of amino acids.
2.   d   The 20 amino acids making up proteins differ mainly in their side chains, groups attached to the α-C atom.
3.   d $H_2NCH_2CH_2COOH$ is not an alpha amino acid because the NH_2 group is not attached to the α-C atom.
4.   d $^+H_3NCH_2COO^-$ is a zwitterion or a structure with positive and negative charges in different parts of the same molecule.
5.   a   Two amino acids are joined through an amide linkage to form a dipeptide.
6.   b   The N-terminal amino acid and the C-terminal amino acid of the peptide Met-Ile-Val-Glu-Cys-Tyr-Gln-Trp-Asp are the amino acids on the left end (Met) and on the right end (Asp), respectively.
7.   c   Six different tripeptides can be formed from alanine, valine, and lysine when each appears only once in each product (Ala-Val-Lys, Ala-Lys-Val, Val-Ala-Lys, Val-Lys-Ala, Lys-Val-Ala, and Lys-Ala-Val).
8.   d   The tripeptides represented as Ala-Val-Lys and Lys-Val-Ala are two different peptides.

Green Chemistry and Biochemistry
   A. Virent Energy Systems received a Presidential Green Chemistry Challenge Award for its process to transform plant carbohydrates into gasoline.
   B. Liao and coworkers (UCLA and Easel Biotechnologies) have engineered bacteria to turn carbohydrates and carbon dioxide into alcohols that can be used as fuels.
   C. The LS9 company developed microorganisms that directly produce hydrocarbon fuels.

D. There are advantages using biochemistry to make molecules compared with traditional chemical synthesis.
   1. Biochemical reactions normally occur in water, which is nonflammable and nontoxic.
   2. Nonpolar reaction products can often be easily separated from more polar water.
   3. Reaction conditions (temperature, pressure) are much less extreme for biochemical reactions, reducing energy costs and potential hazards.
   4. The atom economy of biochemical reactions is very high.
   5. Use of toxic reagents can be avoided in most cases.
   6. Biological reactions are frequently catalytic, using a single enzyme for thousands or millions of repeated reactions.
   7. Reaction products are generally biodegradable.
   8. Production of specific isomers of molecules is more efficient than in traditional reactions because of the specificity of biological reactions.

16.5   Structure and Function of Proteins
   A. The structures of proteins have four organizational levels.
      1. The *primary structure* of a protein is its amino acid sequence, which is specified from the amino end (N-terminal) to the carboxyl end (C-terminal).
      2. *Secondary structure:* Polypeptide chains can fold into regular structures such as the alpha helix and the beta pleated sheet.
         a. In a *pleated-sheet structure,* molecules are stacked in extended arrays with hydrogen bonds holding adjacent chains together. (An example is silk.)
         b. In an *alpha-helix structure,* a right-handed helix formed when the amino group (NH_3^+) of one amino acid in one turn of the chain forms hydrogen bonds with the carboxyl (COO^-) group of another amino acid. This arrangement allows the protein to be stretched and then regain its shape, like a spring. (An example is wool.)
      3. *Tertiary structure:* Protein folding creates spatial relationships between amino acid units that are relatively far apart in the protein chain.
         a. An example is globular proteins.
      4. *Quaternary structure:* Two or more polypeptide chains can assemble into a multiunit structure. An example is hemoglobin.
   B. Four ways to link protein chains.
      1. Peptide (covalent) bonds fix the primary protein structure.
      2. Four other forces hold the protein in a structural arrangement.
         a. In *hydrogen bonding,* the carbonyl oxygen of one peptide may form a hydrogen bond to an amide hydrogen (N—H).
            i.   *Examples:* alpha helix structure of wool protein and pleated-sheet structure of silk protein.
         b. A *salt bridge* (ionic bond) is formed when a proton (H^+) transfer between the acidic side chain of one amino acid and the basic side chain of another results in opposite charges, which then attract each other.
         c. A *disulfide linkage* is formed when two cysteine units (SH) are oxidized. The resulting disulfide bond between the two cysteine units is a covalent bond that is much stronger than a hydrogen bond.
         d. *Hydrophobic interactions* (dispersion forces) are the weak attractive forces between nonpolar side chains.
            i.   Significant in the absence of other forces.
            ii. Nonpolar side chains cluster together on the inside folds of proteins, forming several hydrophobic interactions in a given region of the protein.
   C. Enzymes: exquisite precision machines.
      1. Enzymes are specialized proteins that act as highly specific biological catalysts.

a. Enzymes enable reactions to occur at convenient rates and at lower temperatures by changing the reaction path.

b. The enzyme attaches to a compound (substrate) to form an enzyme-substrate complex which then decomposes into the reaction product and the liberated enzyme.

    i. The substrate must fit a portion of the enzyme (active site) precisely for the reaction to occur; this fit occurs when the flexible configuration of the enzyme accommodates the substrate (the induced-fit model) much like a glove accommodates the structure of the hand of the person wearing it.

    ii. The substrate and enzyme are held together by bonds between complementary charged groups on the two.

    iii. The formation of new bonds weakens the old bonds to the substrate and facilitates the breaking of old bonds and the formation of new products.

2. An enzyme can be made ineffective or its rate of catalysis slowed down when inhibitor molecules bond to the enzyme at positions remote from the active site, thus changing the shape of the enzyme and preventing further bonding with the substrate.

3. Inorganic ions serve as *cofactors* necessary for proper functioning of some enzymes.

    a. The protein part of an enzyme is called the *apoenzyme*.

4. Organic nonprotein cofactors are called coenzymes.

    a. Many coenzymes are vitamins or substances derived from vitamin molecules.

5. Enzymes are essential to the function of every living cell.

D. Applications of enzymes.

1. Enzymes are used in medicine in test strips for diabetes, and to break up blood clots after a heart attack.

2. Clinical analysis for enzymes in body fluids or tissues is a common diagnostic technique in medicine.

3. Enzymes are widely used in a variety of industries, from baby foods to beer, and intact microorganisms are used to make bread, beer, wine, yogurt, and cheese.

4. Enzymes are components in some detergents where they attack fats, grease, and proteins responsible for stains.

Answers to Self-Assessment Questions

1. c The alpha-helix or beta-pleated sheet produced from hydrogen bonds between N-H and C=O groups are examples of secondary protein structures.

2. d The folding of protein chains into a globular form represents the tertiary structure of a protein.

3. b The arrangement of protein subunits into a specific pattern such as in hemoglobin is an example of quaternary structure in proteins.

4. b Disulfide links are the covalent cross-links between cysteine units in protein chains of fibrous proteins such as hair.

5. d Salt bridges are formed when an acidic side chain of an amino acid on a protein chain reacts with a basic side chain of an amino acid on another chain, forming ions which are attracted to one another.

6. a Dispersion forces exist between a nonpolar side chain of one amino acid on a protein chain and a nonpolar side chain of an amino acid some distance away on the same chain or on another chain.

7. d The substrate is the molecule upon which an enzyme acts; it is the reactant in the reaction catalyzed by the enzyme.

8. d The induced-fit model of enzyme action holds that shapes of active sites can change somewhat to fit a substance.

9.	c	Coenzymes are organic, nonprotein compounds required for some enzyme molecules to function.

10.	c	Enzyme cofactors are ions such as Ca^{2+}, Mg^{2+}, and K^+ or nonprotein organic molecules (called coenzymes).

11.	a	An apoenzyme is the purely protein part of an enzyme.

16.6	Nucleic Acids: Parts, Structure, and Function
   A. Nucleic acids are the information and control centers of the cell.
   B. There are two kinds of nucleic acids: deoxyribonucleic acid (DNA), which provides a mechanism for heredity and serves as the blueprint for all proteins in an organism, and ribonucleic acid (RNA), which carries out protein assembly.
      1. DNA is found in the cell nucleus and RNA is found in all parts of the cell.
      2. Nucleic acids are chains of repeating nucleotides.
         a. Nucleotides contain a pentose (sugar), a heterocyclic amine base, and a phosphate unit.
         b. The sugar is either ribose (found in RNA) or deoxyribose (found in DNA).
            i. The two sugars differ in the presence of an oxygen atom on the second carbon. Ribose has an oxygen in this position. Deoxyribose does not.
      3. The bases are either purines (two fused rings), including adenine and guanine, or pyrimidines (one ring), including cytosine, thymine, and uracil.
      4. The phosphate groups (P_i) are attached to the fifth carbon of the sugar.
      5. The phosphate groups of nucleotides form ester linkages to the hydroxyl groups of sugars of adjoining nucleotides to form nucleic acid chains.
      6. The chain is then composed of a phosphate-sugar backbone with branching heterocyclic bases.
      7. In DNA, the sugar is deoxyribose, and the bases are adenine, guanine, cytosine, and thymine.
      8. In RNA, the sugar is ribose, and the bases are adenine, guanine, cytosine, and uracil.
      9. The sequence of bases, or primary structure of the nucleic acid strand, stores all the information needed to build living organisms.
   C. The double helix.
      1. The bases in DNA are paired, (adenine to thymine) and (guanine to cytosine), through hydrogen bonding.
         a. Watson and Crick determined that DNA was composed of two helixes wound around each other and held in place by base pairing.
      2. In base pairing, a pyrimidine base is paired with a purine base.
         a. In the pyrimidine-purine pair guanine and cytosine, three hydrogen bonds can form. No other such pairing provides such extensive interaction.
   D. Structure of RNA.
      1. RNA is a single strand of nucleic acid with some internal base pairing in which the molecule folds back on itself.
   E. DNA: self-replication.
      1. Chromosomes, found in cell nuclei, contain the hereditary material.
         a. The number of chromosomes varies with species. Human cells have 46 chromosomes with egg and sperm cells providing half of these chromosomes each.
         b. Chromosomes are composed of DNA and proteins.
      2. Genes are sections of the DNA molecule.
         a. The complete set of genes of an organism is called its genome.
      3. During cell division, each chromosome replicates (produces an exact duplicate of) itself.
      4. When cell division occurs, the DNA is replicated.

a. Two chains of double helix are pulled apart, and each chain directs synthesis of a new DNA chain.

b. The chains run antiparallel to one another.

c. Synthesis begins with a nucleotide from the surrounding cellular fluid pairing with its complementary base on the DNA strand.

d. As nucleotides align, the enzymes connect them to form the sugar-phosphate backbone of the new chain.

5. When the cell divides, each daughter cell receives one of the original DNA strands.

6. The sequence of bases along the DNA strand encodes all the information for building a new organism.

a. These four bases in the genetic code can form many different combinations.

Answers to Self-Assessment Questions

1. d   Nucleotides are the monomer units of nucleic acids.
2. c   A DNA nucleotide could contain T, P_i, and deoxyribose.
3. b   A possible base pair in DNA is A-T.
4. c   A possible base pair in RNA is A-U (uracil replaces thymine in RNA).
5. d   Nucleic acid base pairs are joined by hydrogen bonds.
6. a   Replication of a DNA molecule involves breaking the hydrogen bonds between base pairs in the double helix.
7. d   The first step of DNA replication involves the unzipping of the DNA molecule by breaking hydrogen bonds.
8. a   The complementary 5' → 3' strand to the 3' → 5' base sequence T-A-G-C is A-T-C-G.
9. b   When the portion of a gene with the base sequence 3'-T-C-G-A-A-T-5' is replicated, the complementary DNA base sequence is 5'-A-G-C-T-T-A-3'.

16.7   RNA: Protein Synthesis and the Genetic Code

A. RNA carries the information from DNA to other parts of the cell.

1. *Transcription* involves the transfer of DNA information to mRNA (messenger RNA) through base pairing.

a. In RNA, uracil takes the place of thymine, so the allowed base pairing between DNA and mRNA is T-A, C-G, A-U.

2. *Translation* of the code in mRNA into a protein structure takes place in the ribosomes. The mRNA becomes attached to a ribosome, and the genetic code is deciphered.

B. Transfer RNA (tRNA), located in the cytoplasm, translates the base sequence of mRNA into the amino acid sequence of a protein.

1. tRNA has a base triplet that determines which amino acid will attach to the end of tRNA. This amino acid can then be moved into position when the tRNA base pairs with the appropriate bases on mRNA.

2. When amino acids have been moved into position by tRNAs, these amino acids then bond to each other, forming a peptide chain. In this way, a protein is built up.

3. The base triplet on the mRNA is called a *codon,* it pairs with its complementary base triplet on tRNA called an *anticodon.*

4. Some amino acids are specified by several different codons: Others are specified by only one codon.

a. Three codons are stop signals, calling for the termination of a proton chain.

Answers to Self-Assessment Questions

1. b   The synthesis of RNA from a strand of DNA is called transcription.
2. a   The base sequence of a strand of mRNA that is transcribed from an original strand of DNA that has the base sequence of 5'-T-A-C-G-3' is 3'-A-U-G-C-5'.
3. d   The anticodon triplet is found on the tRNA.
4. b   The genetic code consists of 20 amino acids and 64 codons.
5. b   The fact that each amino acid except for tryptophan and methionine is coded for by more than one codon is an example of redundancy.
6. c   The codon UUA codes for Leu only.

16.8   The Human Genome
   A.   DNA is sequenced by using enzymes to cleave it into segments of a few to several hundred nucleotides each.
      1.   The pieces are duplicated and amplified using the polymerase chain reaction (PCR), which employs enzymes called DNA polymerases to make millions of copies of the fragment.
      2.   An electric current is used to sort the DNA segments by length and the base at the end of each fragment is identified.
      3.   Computers are used to compile the short sequences into longer segments that recreate the original sequence of bases in the fragment.
   B.   Recombinant DNA: using organisms as chemical factories.
      1.   A gene from one organism can be substituted for a defective or missing gene in another organism.
         a.   The gene is identified, isolated using the RFLP process, and placed in a separate piece of DNA.
         b.   The recombined DNA is then transferred into a bacteria DNA (plasmid). The bacteria are cloned, and large amounts of protein coded by the genes are produced.
            i.   Human growth hormone, epidermal growth factor, and insulin are produced using recombinant DNA.
   C.   Gene therapy.
      1.   A functioning gene is introduced into a person's cells to correct the action of a defective gene.

Answers to Self-Assessment Questions

1. a   Recombinant DNA cloning involves combining DNA from two different organisms to make a single new organism.
2. c   In recombinant DNA cloning, the DNA is cut with restriction enzymes.
3. d   Recombinant DNA is presently used in the biotechnology industry to synthesize insulin, interferon, and human growth hormone.
4. b   Transferring some photosynthesis genes from an efficient crop to a less efficient one, thus producing a new plant variety with greater productivity, would involve genetic engineering.

LEARNING OBJECTIVES

You should be able to...

1. List the major parts of a cell, and describe the function of each part. (16.1)

2. Name the primary source of energy for plants and three classes of substances that are sources of energy for animals. (16.1)

3. Compare and contrast starch, glycogen, and cellulose. (16.2)

4. Describe the fundamental structure of a fatty acid and of a fat. (16.3)

5. Classify fats as saturated, monounsaturated, or polyunsaturated. (16.3)

6. Draw the fundamental structure of an amino acid, and show how amino acids combine to make proteins. (16.4)

7. Describe the four levels of protein structure, and give an example of each. (16.5)

8. Describe how enzymes work as catalysts. (16.5)

9. Name the two types of nucleic acids, and describe the function of each type. (16.6)

10. Explain complementary base pairing, and describe how a copy of DNA is synthesized. (16.6)

11. Explain how mRNA is synthesized from DNA and how a protein is synthesized from mRNA. (16.7)

12. List important characteristics of the genetic code. (16.7)

13. Describe recombinant DNA technology, and explain how it is used. (16.8)

14. Name some advantages of using biochemistry to create useful molecules.

15. Give examples of the use of biochemistry for energy production and other applications.

DISCUSSION

The cell is the structural unit of life. Biochemistry, the chemistry of life, is organized into classes of compounds. Carbohydrates (sugars and starches) are the products of photosynthesis and are the source of energy for living things. Fats and lipids are water-insoluble compounds with important members such as steroids (cholesterol and sex hormones). Proteins, polymers of amino acids, are the structural unit of animals. There are about 20 amino acids found in life on Earth. They are bonded with the peptide link to form polymers. They also serve as enzymes or biochemical catalysts. There are three structures for each protein: primary (the sequence of amino acids), secondary (the regular patterns of folding in short portions of the chain), and tertiary (the overall folding pattern of the entire chain). Sometimes there is a quaternary structure (details the relationship between two or more chains and/or cofactors). Nucleic acids (RNA, DNA) determine the heredity of life. RNA and DNA consist of repeating units of nucleotides that are made up of a sugar, a heterocyclic base, and a phosphate group. The sugar is either ribose (in RNA) or deoxyribose (in DNA). The sequence of bases in the chain determines the genetic code. The two strands of DNA (RNA) are held together with hydrogen bonding. These are broken and new ones formed during replication (reproduction). Recent advances in identifying DNA (DNA fingerprinting) and modifying DNA (recombinant DNA) are modern issues.

ANSWERS TO ODD-NUMBERED REVIEW QUESTIONS AND SOLUTIONS FOR ODD-NUMBERED END OF CHAPTER PROBLEMS

Review Questions

1. Photosynthesis is the process by which plants are able to capture the sun's energy in the form of carbohydrates which serve as an energy source for themselves and other species. Plants can convert the carbohydrates (initially glucose) into structural material and fats. If sufficient resources are available, plants can also convert glucose into proteins. Animals require a constant input of energy to survive. The source of this energy is ultimately the chemical compounds created by plants.

3. Proteins are found in every cell. Muscles, skin, hair, and nails are mostly proteins.

5. Proteins are polyamides, polymers formed from the joining of amino acids through peptide linkages.

7. If the molar mass of a polypeptide exceeds 10,000 g/mol the polypeptide is called a protein.

9. Hydrogen bonding is the intermolecular force holding base pairs together.

11. DNA is a double helix while RNA is a single helix with some loops. The pentose in DNA is deoxyribose while the pentose in RNA is ribose. The four nitrogenous bases in DNA are thymine, adenine, guanine, and cytosine. The four nitrogenous bases in RNA are uracil, adenine, guanine, and cytosine.

13. The polymerase chain reaction (PCR) duplicates and produces millions of copies of any specific DNA sequence.

15. Step 1: After scientists determine the base sequence of the gene that codes for a particular protein, they isolate it and amplify it by PCR.
Step 2: The gene is spliced into a special kind of bacterial DNA called a plasmid.
Step 3: The recombined plasmid is inserted into a host organism, the bacteria from which the plasmids came.
Step 4: The plasmids replicate, making multiple exact copies of themselves, a process called cloning.

Problems

17. Monosaccharides are carbohydrates that cannot be further hydrolyzed. Glucose, fructose, and galactose are common monosaccharides.

19. Glycogen is animal starch. Amylose is a plant starch with glucose units joined in a continuous chain. Amylopectin is a plant starch with branched chains of glucose units.

21. The answer is c and d. Mannose and glucose are monosaccharides.

23. None of the substances listed in problem 21 are disaccharides. Sucrose and lactose (problem 22) are disaccharides.

25. a. Amylose is hydrolyzed into glucose molecules.
    b. Glycogen is hydrolyzed into glucose molecules.

27. The open chain form of fructose includes both ketone and alcohol (hydroxyl) functional groups.

29. Aldehyde and alcohol (hydroxyl) functional groups are present in the open-chain form of galactose. The structures of glucose and galactose are identical except for the orientation of the -OH and -H groups on the fourth carbon (C-4) in the six-carbon chains.

31. At room temperature, most animal fats are solids while oils are liquids. Oils are obtained principally from vegetable (plant) sources. Structurally, oils are identical with fats, except that oils incorporate a larger proportion of unsaturated (C to C double bonds) fatty acid units than are present in fats.

33. Palmitic acid (a) and stearic acid (d) are both saturated fatty acids. Oleic acid (c) is monounsaturated, while linoleic acid (b) is polyunsaturated.

35. a. Linoleic acid has 18 carbon atoms.
    b. Palmitic acid has 16 carbon atoms.
    c. Stearic acid has 18 carbon atoms.

37. Corn oil (the image on the right) and other plant oils generally have higher iodine numbers than solid animal fats (lard, the image on the left). This is because oils have more sites of unsaturation (C=C bonds) in the fatty acid chains, and iodine adds to C=C bonds.

39. Amino acids contain an amino group and a carboxylic acid group. A zwitterion is a compound that carries both a positive and a negative charge in different parts of its structure.

41. Lycine and leucine are essential amino acids.

43. Structural formulas
    a. Alanine

$$H_3N^+-CH-C\underset{O^-}{\overset{O}{\diagup}}$$
$$\quad\quad\ |$$
$$\quad\quad CH_3$$

    b. Cysteine

$$H_3N^+-CH-C\underset{O^-}{\overset{O}{\diagup}}$$
$$\quad\quad\ |$$
$$\quad\quad CH_2SH$$

45. Structural formulas
    a. glyclalanine

$$H_3N^+CH_2CO-NH\,C\,HCOO^-$$
$$\quad\quad\quad\quad\quad\quad\quad\ |$$
$$\quad\quad\quad\quad\quad\quad\quad CH_3$$

b. alanylserine

$$H_3N^+ \underset{\underset{CH_3}{|}}{C}HCO—NH\underset{\underset{CH_2OH}{|}}{C}HCOO^-$$

47. The dipeptide is a combination of aspartic acid and phenylalanine: aspartylphenylalanine

49. Proteins are bonded to each other by hydrogen bonds, ionic bonds, disulfide linkages, and dispersion forces.

51. Nucleotide a appears in DNA while nucleotides b and c appear in RNA. In these cases the distinguishing feature is the sugar: the sugar in DNA nucleotides is deoxyribose (see choice a.) while the sugar in RNA nucleotides is ribose (see choices b. and c.).

53. The sugar is ribose and the base is uracil.

55. a. Guanine pairs with cytosine in DNA.
    b. Thymine pairs with adenine in DNA.
    c. Cytosine pairs with guanine in DNA.
    d. Adenine pairs with thymine in DNA.

57. Each strand of the parent DNA becomes incorporated in one of the daughter double helices. Therefore, one strand will end up in one of the daughter cell's nucleus; the other strand will end up in the other daughter cell's nucleus.

59. a. DNA and mRNA are involved in transcription.
    b. mRNA and tRNA are involved in translation.

61. 3'-TACTCGCTGAAACGCCCTAAT-5' is the complementary strand to
    5'-ATGAGCGACTTTGCGGGATTA-3' in DNA.

63. 5'-AGGCTA-3' is the DNA template sequence for the mRNA strand 3'-UCCGAU-5'.

65. a. 3'-AAC-5' is the complementary base triplet on mRNA for the tRNA triplet 5'-UUG-3'.
    b. 3'-CUU-5' is the complementary base triplet on mRNA for the tRNA triplet 5'-GAA-3'.
    c. 3'-AGG-5' is the complementary base triplet on mRNA for the tRNA triplet 5'-UCC-3'.

67. The codons need to be read from the 5' to the 3' direction. So 3'-AAC-5' is actually a 5'-CAA-3' codon. Codon B would be read 5'-UUC-3' and Codon C would be read 5'-GGA-3'
    a. glutamine b. phenylalanine c. glycine

69. a. The one-letter abbreviations give a primary protein structure, which is the specific order of amino acids in each of the chains.
    b. The descriptions of the loop and chain linkages give information about the secondary protein structure.

71. a. The base is a pyrimidine because it has a single ring structure.
    b. The base is a pyrimidine because it has a single ring structure.

73. a. The base is a purine because it has a fused ring structure.
    b. This compound would be found in RNA because the sugar is ribose.

75. a. The amino acid sequence for ACC-AGC-AUG-GCG is ~Thr-Ser-Met-Ala~.

    b. The amino acid sequence for ACC-AGC-GCG-GCG is ~Thr-Ser-Ala-Ala~.

77. The mRNA codon would have the three-letter base pair of 3'-AUG-5' (the sequences must be antiparallel).

79. Water is the solvent typically used in biochemical reactions.

81. The answer is d. The methods listed in answers a., b., and c. are all goals designed to produce renewable fuels.

Food

Molecular Gastronomy

CHAPTER SUMMARY

17.1 Carbohydrates in the Diet
  A. Carbohydrates include sugars and starches.
  B. Sweet chemicals: the sugars.
   1. Monosaccharides.
      a. Glucose (dextrose), often called *blood sugar*, is used by cells to provide energy.
      b. Fructose, called *fruit sugar*, is found in fruit or made from glucose with the help of enzymes.
         i. Fructose is sweeter than glucose.
         ii. High-fructose corn syrup (HFCS) is made by treating corn syrup with enzymes to convert much of the glucose to fructose.
  C. Digestion and metabolism of carbohydrates.
   1. Glucose and fructose are absorbed directly into the blood stream from the digestive tract.
   2. Sucrose and lactose are hydrolyzed with the help of enzymes to form simpler sugars.
      Sucrose + H_2O → Glucose + Fructose
      Lactose + H_2O → Glucose + Galactose
      a. Lactose intolerance is a condition in which a person lacks the correct enzyme to break down lactose.
   3. All monosaccharides are converted to glucose during metabolism.
      a. Galactosemia is a condition due to a deficiency of the enzyme that converts the monosaccharide galactose to glucose.
  D. Complex carbohydrates: starch and cellulose.
   1. Starch and cellulose are both polymers of glucose, but the connecting links between the glucose units are different.
      a. The glucose units are connected with alpha linkages in starch, and with beta linkages in cellulose.
      b. Because of the spatial differences in linkage, humans can digest starch, but not cellulose.
   2. Starch is hydrolyzed to glucose during digestion.
      a. More than 50 chemical reactions are needed to produce CO_2, water, and energy from starch. This process is the reverse of photosynthesis.

3. Carbohydrates supply ~4 kcal of energy per gram.
    a. Excess carbohydrates are stored as glycogen and fat.
    b. Carbohydrates are the body's preferred fuel.
4. Cellulose is the most abundant carbohydrate: it is present in all plants, forming their cell walls and other structural features.
    a. Most animals lack the enzymes needed to break the beta linkages in the polymer but certain bacteria can produce these enzymes.
    b. Cellulose plays an important role in human digestion, providing dietary fiber that absorbs water and helps move food through the digestive tract.

Answers to Self-Assessment Questions

1. b About 1 in 7 people in the world are hungry today.
2. b Digestion of lactose produces galactose and glucose.
3. a People who have lactose intolerance are deficient in the enzyme that catalyzes the hydrolysis of lactose to galactose and glucose.
4. b Galactosemia is an inherited disease in which the child is deficient in the enzyme that catalyzes the conversion of galactose to glucose.
5. b The monomer units of starch and cellulose, respectively, are alpha and beta glucose.
6. d Small quantities of carbohydrates can be stored in liver and muscle tissue as glycogen.
7. c Humans cannot digest cellulose because they lack enzymes for the hydrolysis of beta-glucose linkages.

17.2 Fats and Cholesterol
    A. Digestion and metabolism of fats.
        1. Dietary fats are mainly triacylglycerols, commonly called triglycerides, esters of glycerol and fatty acids.
        2. Fats are digested with the help of enzymes called lipases.
        3. Once they are absorbed, the products of digestion are reassembled as triglycerides (esters of glycerol and fatty acids) which are attached to proteins for transport through the blood.
        4. Fats are stored in adipose tissue to serve as a protective cushion and as insulation.
        5. When needed for energy, fats are hydrolyzed to glycerol and fatty acids. Glycerol can be "burned" to produce energy.
    B. Fats, cholesterol, and human health.
        1. Saturated fats and cholesterol are associated with arteriosclerosis, which can result in heart attack and strokes.
        2. Saturated fats have a large proportion of saturated fatty acids (palmitic and stearic acid).
            a. Unsaturated fats (oils) have a large proportion of unsaturated fatty acids (linoleic and linolenic acids).
        3. Cholesterol is transported in blood by water-soluble proteins.
            a. A lipoprotein is a complex of cholesterol or fat with protein and is classified by its density.
            b. Very-low-density lipoproteins (VLDL) transport triglycerides.
            c. Low-density lipoproteins (LDL) transport cholesterol to cells for use.
            d. High-density lipoproteins (HDL) transport cholesterol to the liver for eventual excretion.
            e. High levels of LDL increase risk of heart attack and stroke.
            f. Exercise increases levels of HDL.
            g. Fish oil tends to lower cholesterol and triglyceride levels.

4. Omega-3 fatty acids have carbon to carbon double bonds beginning at the third carbon from the end opposite the COOH group, the omega end.
   a. Adding omega-3 fatty acids to the diet leads to lower blood cholesterol and triglyceride levels.
5. Fats and oils containing C=C bonds can be hydrogenated by adding H_2 to the double bond.
   a. The arrangement around C=C bonds in naturally occurring fatty acid is *cis*.
   b. Hydrogenation of vegetable oils to produce semisolid fats is an important process in the food industry.
   c. During hydrogenation, the arrangement around some of the C=C bonds is changed from *cis* to *trans*.
   d. Like saturated fatty acids, *trans* fatty acids tend to raise blood levels of LDL cholesterol, which has negative health impacts.
6. Fats yield ~9 kcal of energy per gram.
7. Fats are used as fuel and to build and maintain parts of cells, and are stored as fuel reserves.
8. Health professionals recommend that no more than 30% of total calories should come from fats and no more than one-third of the fat should be saturated.

Answers to Self-Assessment Questions

1. a Fats are esters of glycerol and fatty acids.
2. a Among lipoproteins, LDLs carry cholesterol to the cells for use and are the ones that deposit cholesterol in arteries, leading to cardiovascular disease.
3. a $CH_3(CH_2)_{16}COOH$ is a saturated fatty acid (it has no C=C bonds).
4. c $CH_3(CH_2)_3(CH_2CH=CH)_2(CH_2)_7COOH$ is a polyunsaturated fatty acid but not an omega-3 fatty acid.
5. d $CH_3(CH_2CH=CH)_3(CH_2)_7COOH$ is a polyunsaturated omega-3 fatty acid.
6. d With respect to their shape, *trans* fatty acid molecules resemble saturated fatty acids.
7. c Most health professionals recommend that fat represent no more than 30% of our daily caloric intake, and that no more than one-third of the fat intake should be saturated fat.

17.3 Proteins: Muscle and Much More
A. Proteins are polymers of amino acids. They are needed to make muscles, hair, and enzymes.
B. Protein metabolism: essential amino acids.
   1. Proteins are broken down in the digestive tract into their component amino acids, which are used to synthesize proteins for growth and repair of tissues.

      a. Excess protein can be used as an energy source, supplying ~4 kcal/g.
   2. The human body can synthesize 11 of the 20 amino acids. The other 9 (called essential amino acids) must be supplied by the diet.
   3. People whose diets fail to provide all the essential amino acids in the needed quantities may suffer from malnutrition even though adequate calories are provided in the diet.
   4. Most protein from animal sources contains all the essential amino acids. Gelatin is an example of an inadequate animal protein because it contains almost no tryptophan and has only small amounts of threonine, methionine, and isoleucine.
C. Protein deficiency in young and old.
   1. Our requirement for protein is 0.8 g/kg of body weight.
      a. Kwashiorkor is a protein deficiency disease common in parts of Africa and in the U.S., mainly among elderly people in nursing homes.
D. Vegetarian diets.

194

1. Vegetarian diets are easier on the world's energy needs since it takes less energy to produce plant protein than animal protein.
2. Many ethnic foods provide good protein by combining a legume (deficient in methionine) with a cereal grain (deficient in tryptophan and lysine).
3. A strict vegetarian diet is also likely to be low in vitamin B_{12}, calcium, iron, and riboflavin. Milk, eggs, cheese, fish, and supplements can correct this deficiency.

Answers to Self-Assessment Questions

1. c The numbers of kcal/g provided by carbohydrate, fat, and protein, respectively, are 4, 9, and 4.
2. a Amino acids are the end products of the hydrolysis of a protein.
3. d An essential amino acid must be included in the diet.
4. b Eggs furnish complete protein. Brown rice and tofu are plant products and not complete proteins. Gelatin is one of the small number of animal products that is not a complete protein.
5. c The daily protein requirement for an individual is ~0.8 g/kg weight.
      Mass of protein = (80 kg body weight)(0.8 g protein/kg body weight) = 64 g protein
6. c One can get complete protein by combining whole wheat bread and peanut butter.
7. c Strict vegetarian diets are often deficient in vitamin B_{12} and iron.

17.4 Minerals, Vitamins, and Other Essentials
  A. A variety of inorganic compounds and dietary minerals are necessary for proper growth and repair of body tissues.
  B. Dietary minerals.
    1. Inorganic substances, called dietary minerals, represent ~4% of the weight of a human body.
    2. Macrominerals: sodium, potassium, calcium, magnesium, chlorine, phosphorus, and sulfur.
       Ca: bones, teeth, blood clotting, milk formation
       P: bones, teeth, nucleic acids, cell membranes
       K: intracellular cation, muscle contraction
       S: amino acids methionine and cysteine
       Na: extracellular cation, fluid pressure
       Mg: enzyme cofactor, nerve impulses
    3. Trace elements (iron, copper, and zinc) are needed in smaller amounts but are equally important.
    4. Ultratrace elements: manganese, molybdenum, chromium, cobalt, vanadium, nickel, cadmium, tin, lead, lithium, fluorine, iodine, selenium, silicon, arsenic, boron.
       a. Fe: hemoglobin for O_2 transport.
       b. Iodine: proper functioning of thyroid.
  C. The vitamins: vital, but not all are amines.
    1. Vitamins are organic substances that our bodies need for good health but cannot synthesize; they must be included in the diet.
    2. Some vitamins were discovered early because of vitamin-deficiency diseases such as scurvy (vitamin C deficiency) and beriberi (thiamine or vitamin B_1 deficiency). The first such compounds characterized were amines, hence the name "vitamin."
    3. Vitamins are divided into two broad categories.
       a. Fat-soluble vitamins: A, D, E, and K.
       b. Water-soluble vitamins: B complex and C.

4. Large doses of fat-soluble vitamins can be toxic; excess water-soluble vitamins are excreted in the urine.
   a. Vitamins E and K are fat soluble but metabolized (not stored) and excreted.
5. The body can store fat-soluble vitamins for future use; water-soluble vitamins are needed almost daily.
D. Other essentials: fiber and water.
   1. Dietary fiber may be soluble or insoluble.
      a. Insoluble fiber is usually cellulose.
      b. Soluble fiber generally consists of sticky materials called *gums* and *pectins*.
   2. Water.
      a. We need between 1.0 L and 1.5 L of water every day, in addition to the water we get from food.

Answers to Self-Assessment Questions

1. b   About 4% of our body weight is minerals.
2. b   A deficiency of iodide results in goiter.
3. b   Iron in red blood cells is found mainly in hemoglobin.
4. a   Iron is swiftly depleted from the body by blood loss.
5. b   Most of the calcium and phosphorus in the body are in the bones and teeth.
6. c   People with high blood pressure are usually told to restrict intake of Na^+.
7. c   Vitamins are specific organic compounds required in the diet to prevent diseases.
8. b   Along with the B vitamins, vitamin C is water soluble.
9. c   Eating foods high in fiber helps fill you up without adding to caloric intake.
10. b   Soluble dietary fiber helps lower cholesterol levels, perhaps by removing bile acids that digest fat.

17.5 Starvation, Fasting, and Malnutrition
A. A body totally deprived of food soon uses up its glycogen reserves and needs to convert to fat metabolism.
   1. Increased dependence on stored fats for energy can result in ketosis, a condition characterized by the appearance of ketone bodies (acetoacetic acid, ß-hydroxybutyric acid, and acetone) in the blood and urine.
      a. Ketosis rapidly develops into acidosis; the blood pH drops, and oxygen transport is hindered, leading to depression and lethargy.
      b. Acidosis is also associated with diabetes.
   2. During the early stages of a total fast, the body will also break down its own proteins to try to meet its metabolic needs and to provide glucose to the brain.
B. Processed food: less nutrition.
   1. Making white flour from wheat removes protein, minerals, vitamins, and fiber (bran).
   2. Fruit peels are rich in vitamins and fiber.
   3. Some vitamins are (partially) destroyed by heat; water-soluble vitamins are leached out and discarded in the cooking water.
   4. Over 90% of the food budget of an average U.S. family goes to buy processed foods.

Answers to Self-Assessment Questions

1. b   Glycogen stores are depleted in about 1 day.
2. b   In the intermediate stages of starvation (1 to 4 days), the body draws on its reserves of fat.
3. d   In prolonged starvation (a few weeks), the body uses structural proteins.

4. c $CH_3CHOCH_2CHOHCH_3$ is not a ketone body (its structure does not include a ketone functional group).

17.6 Food Additives

A. Food additives are substances other than basic foodstuffs that are intentionally put in products for various reasons related to production, processing, packaging, or storage.
   1. In the U.S., food additives are regulated by the Food and Drug Administration (FDA).
      a. Since 1958, the food industry must prove that food additives are safe for the intended use.

B. Additives that improve nutrition.
   1. Potassium iodide was the first nutrient supplement approved.
      a. Iodine is lacking in foods in some land regions; small amounts of potassium iodide (KI) are added to table salt to prevent goiter (enlargement of the thyroid gland).
   2. Vitamin B_1 (thiamine) is added to polished rice to prevent beriberi.
   3. Iron, in the form of ferrous carbonate, is added to flour for enrichment.
   4. Vitamin C is added to fruit drinks to match the vitamin content found in real fruit juices.
   5. Vitamin D is added to milk to prevent rickets.
   6. Vitamin A is added to margarine to match the quantity of vitamin A found in butter.
   7. Processed foods, even those with added nutrients, seldom match the nutritional value of fresh foods because only some of the nutrients lost in processing are replaced.

C. Additives that taste good.
   1. Some foods (for example, spice cake, soft drinks, sausage) depend almost entirely on additives for flavor.
   2. Natural flavors include spices and substances extracted from fruits and other plant materials (vanilla extract, lemon extract).
      a. Chemists analyze natural flavors. Artificial flavors match the (major) components of natural ones.
      b. Imitation flavors contain fewer chemicals than natural ones.
      c. Flavors generally present little hazard when used in moderation.

D. Artificial sweeteners.
   1. Cyclamates were banned in the United States in 1970; they are not banned in Canada.
   2. In 1977, saccharin was shown to cause cancer in laboratory animals. The FDA moved to ban it, but the move was blocked by the U.S. Congress.
   3. Aspartame, a dipeptide (the methyl ester of aspartylphenylalanine) is another low-calorie sweetener.
   4. Acesulfame K is a low-calorie sweetener that can survive the high temperatures of cooking.
   5. Stevia, a South American herb, is at least 30 times as sweet as sucrose.
   6. Glycerol and propylene glycol are sweet; they are used as humectants (moistening agents).
   7. Sorbitol and xylitol are sweet. They have the same caloric content as sugar but don't cause tooth decay.

E. Flavor enhancers.
   1. Some substances, not particularly flavorful themselves, enhance other flavors.
      a. Sodium chloride (table salt) is an example.
   2. Monosodium glutamate (MSG) imparts a meaty flavor to foods that contain only small amounts of meat.
      a. Overindulgence in foods high in MSG may cause neurological problems, and it may be teratogenic (cause birth defects when eaten in large amounts by pregnant women).

F. Additives that retard spoilage.

1. Propionic acid, benzoic acid, sorbic acid, and salts of these acids retard spoilage by inhibiting the growth of molds.
2. Sodium nitrite inhibits the growth of bacteria, including those that cause botulism, and is used to maintain the pink color of smoked hams and bologna.
   a. Only 10% of the amount used as a color enhancer is needed to inhibit the growth of botulism.
   b. Nitrites react with HCl in stomach acid and with amines to form carcinogenic nitrosamines, but this reaction is inhibited by ascorbic acid (vitamin C).
3. Sulfur dioxide and sulfite salts are used as disinfectants and preservatives, as bleaching agents, and as a means to prevent foods from turning brown on standing. These substances cause severe allergic reactions in some people.

G. Antioxidants: BHA and BHT.
   1. Antioxidants prevent foods containing fats and oils from becoming rancid.
   2. BHA and BHT are free-radical reaction inhibitors.
      a. Rancidity involves the reactions of fats and oils with oxygen to form free radicals.
      b. These radicals react with other fat molecules to form new free radicals in a chain reaction.
      c. BHT and BHA react with the radicals, halting the chain process.
   3. BHT and BHA cause allergic reactions in some people and fetal abnormalities in rats. Overall, though, BHT has been shown to increase the life span of rats.
   4. Vitamin E is a natural antioxidant. Lack of vitamin E causes sterility in rats, but human diets almost always have sufficient vitamin E.
      a. The action of vitamin E as an antioxidant is similar to that of BHT.

H. Color additives.
   1. Some foods are naturally colored.
      a. β-Carotene from carrots (provitamin A)—yellow
      b. Beet juice—red
      c. Grape-hull extract—blue

I. The GRAS list.
   1. Under the 1958 food additives amendment, the FDA has established a list of long-used additives "generally recognized as safe" (GRAS).
   2. Improved instruments and better experimental design have led to the banning of some GRAS substances on reexamination.

J. Nanoscience in foods.
   1. Nanoscience and nanotechnology involve the production and use of materials at a nanometer scale—billionth of a meter.
      a. Nano foods such as drinks and ice cream are being explored to improve color, flavor, and texture.
      b. Nano packaging is being developed to extend shelf life.
   2. Nano security devices are nanosensors being developed for pathogen and contamination detection.

Answers to Self-Assessment Questions

1. c   A manufacturer must provide the FDA with evidence that the ingredient is safe for its intended use.
2. d   Compared to synthetic flavors, natural flavors contain a wider variety of chemicals than make up the synthetic flavorings.
3. a   MSG is structurally related to an amino acid.
4. c   Calcium propionate is added to bread to inhibit the growth of mold.
5. d   Sodium nitrite is added to food to inhibit formation of the botulin toxin.

6.   d   Antioxidants trap free radicals.

7.   b   BHT is an example of an antioxidant and is added to foods containing fats to protect them from becoming rancid.

8.   b   Vitamin C, vitamin E, BHA, BHT, and propyl gallate are all antioxidants that are added to prevent fat-containing foods from becoming rancid.

17.7   Problems with Our Food
- A. Many plants and animals are poisonous: such as some mushrooms, rhubarb leaves (oxalic acid), and puffer fish.
    1. One of the most poisonous substances known is the botulin toxin, produced by anaerobic bacteria in improperly canned food.
- B. Carcinogens.
    1. Carcinogens occur naturally in food.
        a. Charcoal-broiled foods contain 3, 4-benzopyrene, a carcinogen.
        b. Cinnamon and nutmeg contain safrole, a carcinogen.
        c. Aflatoxins are produced by molds that grow on peanuts and grains.
- C. Food contaminants.
    1. Come from many sources and can occur at any step between producer and consumer.
        a. For example, antibiotics in animal feed often show up in the meat we eat.
        b. Today's food contamination problems are usually biological, not chemical.
        c. Bacteria from fecal material sometimes found in raw meat or dairy products and, occasionally, in raw fruits and vegetables are responsible for food poisoning.
        d. Viruses such as hepatitis A cause about 50% of all outbreaks of foodborne gastroenteritis in the U.S. and can be spread by infected food workers.
        e. Parasites are rare in developed countries but are common in developing countries and can be transmitted by eating raw or undercooked pork and fish.
- D. A world without food additives.
    1. Food additives seem to be a necessary part of modern society.
        a. Use of some food additives poses potential hazards, but the major problem with our food supply is still contamination by harmful microorganisms, rodents, and insects.
- E. Greener ways to isolate nutrients from food.
    1. Ethanol and supercritical carbon dioxide are two solvents most widely used to extract natural products, bioactive food components, and essential oils.

Answers to Self-Assessment Questions

1.   b   Aflatoxins are carcinogens.

2.   c   According to the CDC, about 48 million illnesses and 3000 deaths result each year in the United States from food poisoning caused by bacteria, viruses, and parasites.

3.   c   Microorganisms pose the major source of food contamination.

LEARNING OBJECTIVES

You should be able to...

1.   Identify dietary carbohydrates, and state their function.   (17.1)

2.   Identify dietary lipids, and state their function.   (17.2)

3.   List the essential amino acids, and explain why they are essential.   (17.3)

4.   Describe some protein deficiency diseases and their causes.   (17.3)

5.   Identify the vitamins and the bulk dietary minerals, and state their functions.   (17.4)

6.   Describe the effects of starvation, fasting, and malnutrition.   (17.5)

7.   List some common food additives and their purposes.   (17.6)

8.   Identify and describe some of the main problems with harmful substances in our food.   (17.7)

9.   Identify common molecules derived from food sources.

10.   Distinguish polar molecules from nonpolar molecules and predict which can be extracted with ethanol or supercritical carbon dioxide.

11.   Describe how green chemistry has made the extraction of natural products, bioactive food components, and essential oils from plants safer and less hazardous.

DISCUSSION

We are now ready to apply our knowledge of bonding and of molecules to the chemicals that we eat—to food. Keep in mind that a chemical compound—regardless of where it came from or how it was made—has a constant composition, structure, and properties. With these chemical principles in mind, you can go a long way toward seeing through advertising claims, fad diets, and other food-related phenomena.

Food additives serve a variety of functions. Having a knowledge of chemistry can help you to understand what the additives are and how they work. Chemistry alone cannot determine whether the benefit obtained is worth the risk involved. Whether or not an additive should be used involves a value judgment. Knowledge of chemistry may help you, however, to make a more rational judgment.

ANSWERS TO ODD-NUMBERED REVIEW QUESTIONS AND SOLUTIONS FOR ODD-NUMBERED END OF CHAPTER PROBLEMS

Review Questions

1.   Carbohydrates are used primarily as an energy source. They also provide thermal insulation and protect organs.

3.   Vitamins are organic; minerals are inorganic.

5.   Taking an excess of a fat-soluble vitamin is more dangerous than taking an excess of a water-soluble vitamin. The unused portion of the fat-soluble vitamin will be stored and accumulated in adipose tissue while the unused portion of the water-soluble vitamin will be excreted in the urine.

7. Food additives are substances that are present in food as a result of some aspect of production, processing, packaging, or storage.

9. MSG is monosodium glutamate, a sodium salt of glutamic acid, and is used as a flavor enhancer.

11. Vitamin E (α-tocopherol) is a fat-soluble antioxidant.

13. Aspartame is the methyl ester of the dipeptide aspartylphenylalanine.

15. Some food additives are added to increase the nutritional value of the substance, others are added to enhance color and flavor, others to retard spoilage, to ripen or prevent ripening, or to control moisture levels.

Problems

17. a. Blood sugar is glucose.
    b. Table sugar is sucrose.
    c. Fruit sugar is fructose.

19. Starch is a polymer of glucose. The glucose monomers are released from the chain when starch is hydrolyzed.

21. When fat is digested, the fat is hydrolyzed, producing a combination of fatty acids, glycerol, and mono- and diglycerides.

23. Most animal fats are solids. Most vegetable oils are liquids. Animal fats generally have fewer C to C double bonds than vegetable oils.

25. An adequate (or complete) protein is one that supplies all of the essential amino acids in quantities needed for the growth and repair of body tissues. Proteins from animal sources (meat, eggs, and milk) are almost all complete proteins.

27. Corn is likely to be lacking in lysine and tryptophan, while beans are likely to be deficient in methionine.

29. Yes, the combination of wheat, barley, beans, lentils, and millet will provide all the essential amino acids because it represents a combination of grains and beans.

31. a. Iodine is necessary for the thyroid gland.
    b. Iron is necessary for the proper functioning of the oxygen-transporting compound, hemoglobin.
    c. Calcium is necessary for the proper development of bones and teeth, coagulation of the blood, and the maintenance of the heartbeat rhythm.
    d. Phosphorus is necessary for the proper development of bones and teeth. It is used in nucleic acids and for ATP, which obtains, stores, and uses energy from foods.

33. Pantothenic acid and biotin are water soluble and phylloquinone is fat soluble.

35. Ascorbic acid is another name for Vitamin C; calciferol is another name for Vitamin D_2; cyanocobalamin is known as Vitamin B_{12}; retinol is known as Vitamin A; and tocopherol is known as Vitamin E.

37. a. Pellagra is caused by the deficiency of niacin (vitamin B_3).
     b. Beriberi is caused by the deficiency of thiamin (vitamin B_1).
     c. Pernicious anemia is caused by the deficiency of cyanocobalamin (vitamin B_{12}).

39. a. Vitamin A (calciferol) is fat soluble.
     b. Vitamin B_6 (pyridoxine) is water soluble.
     c. Vitamin B_{12} (cyanocobalamin) is water soluble.
     d. Vitamin C (ascorbic acid) is water soluble.
     e. Vitamin K (phylloquinone) is fat soluble.

41. a. $FeCO_3$ improves nutrition.
     b. SO_2 is a disinfectant.
     c. Potassium sorbate is a spoilage inhibitor.

43. a. BHA is an antioxidant.
     b. FD&C Yellow No. 5 is a colorant.
     c. Saccharin is an artificial sweetener.

45. d. None of the statements are true about a dietary supplement labeled "natural."

47. Antioxidants are reducing agents, usually free-radical scavengers added to foods to prevent fats and oils from becoming rancid. An example is when a fat molecule reacts with oxygen to form a free radical, then the free radical reacts with another fat molecule, and the reaction repeats indefinitely. Antioxidants stop the chain reaction by reacting with the free radical. Vitamins C and E are naturally occurring antioxidants. BHA and BHT are two examples of synthetic antioxidants.

49. Number of kcal from carbohydrates = (16 g carbohydrates)(4 kcal/g carbohydrate) = 64 kcal
        Percent of calories from carbohydrates = (64 kcal/120 kcal)(100%) = 53%
     Number of kcal from fat = (3 g fat)(9 kcal/g fat) = 27 kcal
        Percent of calories from fats = (27 kcal/120 kcal)(100%) = 23%
     Number of kcal from protein = (8 g protein) (4 kcal/g protein) = 32 kcal
        Percent of calories from proteins = (32 kcal/120 kcal)(100%) = 27%
     Note: the fact that these percentages add up to slightly more than 100% indicates that the kcal
        equivalents per gram of carbohydrate, fat, and protein are approximations rather than exact
        numbers.

51. kcal from fat = (5 g fat)(9 kcal/g fat) = 45 kcal
     kcal from carbohydrate = (6 g carbohydrate)(4 kcal/g carbohydrate) = 24 kcal
     kcal from protein = (3 g protein)(4 kcal/g protein) = 12 kcal
     Total kcal/serving = 45 kcal + 24 kcal + 12 kcal = 81 kcal
     Percent of kcal/serving from fat = (45 kcal/81 kcal)(100%) = 56%

53. 25% of 1200 kcal = 300 kcal
     Mass of fat = (300 kcal)(1 g fat/9 kcal) = 33 g of combined saturated and unsaturated fat
     Mass of saturated fat = (33 g fat)(30 g saturated fat/100 g fat) = 11 g saturated fat

55. Omega-6 fatty acids are c. linoleic acid, and e. arachidonic acid.

57. Number of kcal fat in whole milk = (8 g fat)(9 kcal/g fat) = 72 kcal
Percent of energy from fat = (72 kcal/160 kcal)(100%) = 45%

59. According to the label, 25%.

61. a. (12 g sugar)(4 kcal/g sugar) = 48 kcal. (48 kcal/80 kcal)(100%) = 60% kcal from sugar.
b. (8 g protein)(4 kcal/g protein) = 32 kcal. (32 kcal/80 kcal)(100%) = 40% kcal from
protein.

63. Water-soluble vitamins are readily excreted and so are not stored in the body for long. Because
riboflavin, niacin, and cyanocobalamin are water soluble, they are most likely to be needed on a
daily basis.

65. Carbon-carbon double bonds are more reactive than carbon-carbon single bonds. Because their
fatty acids have more C=C bonds than is the case for fats, oils are much more likely to spoil
(become rancid) faster than solids.

67. The thick polymeric starch in the soup is broken down into smaller, more soluble molecules by
enzymes from your saliva, making the soup seem thinner.

69. a. The answer is 3. Lycopene can be found in tomatoes, grapefruit, and watermelon.
b. The answer is 2. Resveratrol can be found in plums and red grapes.
c. The answer is 4. Allicin can be found in garlic.
d. The answer is 1. Chlorophyll can be found in algae and green vegetables.

71. Supercritical carbon dioxide is less toxic than methylene chloride, not flammable, and very easily
removed from the reaction mixture.

CHAPTER

18

Drugs

Chemical Cures, Comforts, and Cautions

CHAPTER SUMMARY

18.1   Scientific Drug Design
   A.   Chemists make semisynthetic drugs by modifying molecules from natural sources to improve their properties.
       1.   Examples include conversion of salicylic acid from willow bark to acetylsalicylic acid (aspirin), conversion of morphine from opium poppies to heroin, and conversion of lysergic acid from ergot fungus to LSD.
   B.   There are completely synthetic drugs on the market.
   C.   Humans in all cultures have used drugs since prehistoric times.
   D.   Paul Ehrlich (1854–1915) realized that certain chemicals were more toxic to disease organisms than to human cells and could therefore be used to control or cure infectious diseases.
       1.   Ehrlich coined the term chemotherapy ("chemical therapy")
       2.   Ehrlich was awarded the Nobel Prize in Physiology or Medicine in 1908.

Answers to Self-Assessment Questions

1.   a   Digitalis, from a natural source, has been converted into digoxin, a semisynthetic drug used to treat heart disorders.
2.   b   Heroin is a semisynthetic drug prepared from morphine from opium poppies.
3.   a   Morphine is a natural component of opium poppies.
4.   d   The term chemotherapy was first used by Paul Ehrlich to mean "chemical therapy."

18.2   Pain Relievers: From Aspirin to Oxycodone
   A.   Aspirin (acetylsalicylic acid) was introduced in 1893 as one of the first successful synthetic pain relievers and has become the largest-selling drug in the world.
   B.   Nonsteroidal anti-inflammatory drugs (NSAIDs).
       1.   The NSAID designation distinguishes these drugs from the more potent steroidal anti-inflammatory drugs such as cortisone and prednisone.
       2.   In addition to aspirin, other NSAIDs include ibuprofen (Advil®, Motrin®), naproxen (Aleve®), and ketoprofen (Orudis®).
           a.   Acetaminophen, like aspirin, relieves minor aches and reduces fever but is not anti-inflammatory and is not an NSAID.

3. NSAIDs relieve pain and reduce inflammation by inhibiting the production of prostaglandins, hormone-like lipids derived from a fatty acid.
   a. NSAIDs do not cure the source of the pain but only dull the pain.
   b. Inflammation is caused by an overproduction of prostaglandin derivatives, so inhibition of their synthesis reduces the inflammatory process.
   c. NSAIDs produce side effects such as stomach problems in some individuals.
   d. NSAIDs act as anticoagulants.
   e. NSAIDs reduce body temperature and fevers induced by pyrogens, compounds produced by and released from leukocytes (white blood cells) and other circulating cells.
C. Green pharmaceuticals.
   1. E-factor: environmental factor for chemical production.
      a. E-factor = kilograms of waste generated for each kilogram of product manufactured.
         i. Drugs that exist as stereoisomers almost always require dosage in a single isomeric form.
         ii. Only one isomer of Pregabalin (Lyrica®) used to treat fibromyalgia and neuropathic pain is effective so the other isomer was discarded leading to an E-factor > 85.
   2. New synthetic pathways can reduce E-factors.
      a. New synthesis of pregabalin using the enzyme lipolase reduced the E-factor to 12.
   3. Biocatalytic evolution of enzymes has improved the efficiency of enzyme catalysis and the efficiency of drug production.
D. How NSAIDs work.
   1. Prostaglandins are produced from the cell membrane component arachidonic acid.
      a. The reaction is catalyzed by cyclooxygenase (COX) enzymes.
   2. Aspirin works by inhibiting the production of prostaglandins.
      a. Prostaglandins are responsible for sending pain messages to the brain.
      b. Inflammation results from overproduction of prostaglandin derivatives.
      c. The anti-inflammatory action of aspirin results from inhibition of prostaglandin synthesis.
E. Acetaminophen: a COX-3 inhibitor.
   1. Acetaminophen (in Tylenol® among other products)
      a. It is an analgesic; it reduces pain.
      b. It is an antipyretic; it reduces fevers.
      c. It is not an anti-inflammatory so it is of little use to arthritis sufferers.
      d. It does not promote bleeding so it can be used by surgical patients.
      e. Overuse is linked to liver and kidney damage.
F. Chemistry, allergies, and the common cold.
   1. Many cold medicines contain antihistamines to relieve symptoms of allergies, sneezing, itchy eyes, and runny nose.
   2. Allergens bind to surfaces of certain cells, triggering the release of histamine which causes allergic symptoms.
G. Combination pain relievers.
   1. Anacin®, Excedrin®, and other products are available in various formulations, some of which include caffeine and substances for pain relief, allergy symptoms, and cold and flu treatment.
H. Narcotics.
   1. Narcotics are used to treat pain that does not respond to OTC analgesics.
      a. Narcotics produce narcosis (stupor or general anesthesia) and analgesia (pain relief).
      b. In the U.S., only those drugs that produce narcotic effects and are addictive are called narcotics.

2. Several narcotics are products of opium, products of the opium poppy.
    a. Morphine was first isolated from opium in 1805 and was used as treatment of dysentery in the Civil War, leading to many instances of addiction.
    b. Morphine and other narcotics were placed under control of the federal government by the Harrison Act of 1914.
3. Structural modifications of morphine produce narcotics with various physiological properties.
    a. Codeine, small amounts of which are naturally present in opium, is usually synthesized by methylating morphine.
        i. Codeine is less potent than morphine, and less addictive.
    b. Heroin is produced by converting both OH groups of morphine to acetate esters.
        i. Heroin is more addictive and the addiction is harder to cure than that of morphine.
4. Deaths from heroin and other narcotics are usually attributed to overdoses, but can also be caused by the quality of the drugs bought on the street.
5. Oxycodone is a semisynthetic opioid related to codeine used for relief of moderate to severe pain.
6. Hydrocodone, a synthetic narcotic, is combined with acetaminophen or another medication.
7. Methadone, a synthetic narcotic, is used to treat heroin addiction.

I. Morphine agonists and antagonists.
    1. A molecule with morphine-like action is called a morphine agonist.
    2. A morphine antagonist inhibits the action of morphine by blocking hormone receptors.
J. Endorphins are naturally produced morphine-like substances.
    1. Endorphins are thought to be released during strenuous exercise and in response to pain.
    2. Capsaicin, the active compound in chili peppers, can also stimulate endorphin release.

Answers to Self-Assessment Questions

1. b An antipyretic is a fever reducer.
2. d NSAIDs act by inhibiting the production of prostaglandins.
3. a Acetaminophen does not act as an anticoagulant.
4. b Allergens trigger the release of histamines.
5. c There is no cure for the common cold.
6. b Small amounts of codeine occur naturally in opium.
7. a Heroin is a semisynthetic opiate produced by forming acetate esters from the phenolic OH groups in morphine.
8. c Methadone satisfies an addict's drug craving while, at the same time, allowing him or her to function in society.
9. a Endorphins are naturally produced substances whose effects resemble the effects of opiates.

18.3 Drugs and Infectious Diseases
    A. Antibacterial drugs.
        1. A century ago, infectious diseases were the principal cause of death.
        2. Antibacterial drugs have dramatically altered that situation.
        3 Gerhard Domagk discovered sulfa drugs (the first antibacterial drugs) in 1935.
            a. Used extensively in WWII to prevent wound infections.
            b. Sulfa compounds inhibit the growth of bacteria by mimicking *para*-aminobenzoic acid (PABA), a nutrient needed by bacteria for proper growth.
            c. Bacteria mistake the sulfa drug (sulfanilamide) for PABA and produce molecules that cannot perform growth-enhancing functions.

4. Penicillin, the first antibiotic (substances derived from molds or bacteria that inhibit the growth of other microorganisms), was discovered by Alexander Fleming in 1928.
   a. Florey and Chain purified penicillin for use in medicine.
   b. There are several penicillins that vary in structure and properties.
   c. Penicillin inhibits the synthesis of bacterial cell walls; without the walls, the cells collapse and die. (Human cells don't have cell walls.)
   d. Disadvantages of penicillin.
      i. Many people are allergic to it.
      ii. Many kinds of bacteria have developed strains that are resistant to penicillins.
5. Penicillins have been partially replaced by related compounds called cephalosporins.
   a. Keflex® is an example of a cephalosporin.
   b. Some bacterial strains are resistant to cephalosporins.
6. Tetracyclines: Broad-spectrum antibiotics effective against a wide variety of bacteria.
   a. The tetracycline antibiotics are characterized by four rings joined side to side.

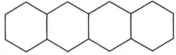

      i. Aureomycin® (chlorotetracycline) was isolated in 1948.
      ii. Terramycin® was isolated in 1950.
      iii. Tetracycline® (the parent compound) was isolated in 1953.
   b. They bind to bacterial ribosomes, inhibiting bacterial protein synthesis and blocking bacterial growth.
   c. Disadvantage: They can cause discoloration of teeth in children.
B. Viruses and antiviral drugs.
   1. Viral diseases (colds, flu, herpes, AIDS) cannot be cured with antibiotics.
   2. Viral diseases are best dealt with by prevention. Vaccination prevents mumps, measles, and other dread viral diseases.
C. DNA viruses and RNA viruses.
   1. Viruses are composed of nucleic acids and proteins.
      a. The genetic material may be DNA or RNA.
   2. DNA viruses replicate in host cells and direct production of viral proteins, which together with the viral DNA assemble into new viruses.
      a. These viruses then invade other cells.
   3. RNA virus replication is similar to DNA virus replication.
      a. Some RNA viruses, called retroviruses, synthesize DNA in host cells.
         i. The AIDS virus HIV is a retrovirus that destroys T cells, which protect the body from infections.
D. Antiviral drugs.
   1. A few modestly effective antiviral drugs have been found.
      a. Acyclovir® helps control (but does not cure) chickenpox, shingles, cold sores, and genital herpes infections.
   2. Antiretroviral drugs prevent the reproduction of retroviruses such as HIV and are used against AIDS.
      a. Azidothymidine® (AZT) slows the onslaught of AIDS.
E. Basic research and drug development.
   1. Gertrude Elion, George Hitchings, and James Black helped design antiviral drugs that block receptors in infected cells.

Answers to Self-Assessment Questions

1. a Bacteria must synthesize *para*-aminobenzoic acid rather than obtaining it in their diet.
2. a Pencillins inhibit the synthesis of bacteria cell walls.
3. b Antibiotics kill bacteria but not viruses.
4. b Taking antibiotics for a stomach virus will increase the chance of developing drug-resistant bacteria.
5. b Viruses consist of a protein coat surrounding a core of nucleic acid.
6. d Most RNA viruses replicate in host cells by replicating RNA strands and synthesizing viral proteins.
7. c Retroviruses replicate in host cells by synthesizing DNA and forming new viruses.
8. c Reverse transcriptase catalyzes the formation of a DNA copy of the viral genome inside the host cell.
9. d The best treatment for viral diseases such as diphtheria, mumps, and smallpox is vaccinations.

18.4   Chemicals Against Cancer
    A. Antimetabolites: inhibition of nucleic acid synthesis.
        1. Anticancer metabolites block DNA synthesis which blocks an increase in the number of cancer cells.
            a. Cancer cells that are dividing rapidly need large quantities of DNA and, therefore, are greatly affected by the DNA shortage.
                i. 6-Mercaptopurine substitutes for adenine and guanine and thus inhibits the synthesis of nucleotides incorporating adenine and guanine, slowing DNA synthesis.
                ii. 5-Fluorouracil and 5-fluorodeoxyuridine inhibit the formation of a thymine-containing nucleotide required for DNA synthesis.
    B. Alkylating agents: turning old weapons into anticancer drugs.
        1. Alkylating agents can transfer alkyl groups to important biological compounds.
        2. Some alkylating agents are used against cancer.
            a. Mustard "gas" is a sulfur-containing blister agent used in chemical warfare in World War I.
            b. Nitrogen mustards were developed about 1935 as chemical warfare agents.
            c. Nitrogen mustards such as cyclophosphamide are effective anticancer drugs.
    C. Cisplatin: the platinum standard of cancer treatment.
        1. Cisplatin, an alkylating agent, binds to DNA and blocks its replication, inhibiting cell division.
    D. Other anticancer agents.
        1. Alkaloids from vinca plants are effective against leukemia and Hodgkin's disease.
        2. Actinomycin from molds is used against Hodgkin's disease and other cancers.
            a. It binds to the double helix of DNA, blocking the formation of RNA on the DNA template. Protein synthesis is inhibited.

Answers to Self-Assessment Questions

1. d 5-Fluorouracil inhibits the formation of nucleotides containing the base of thymine.
2. b 6-Mercaptopurine mimics the base adenine, forming a false nucleotide, and thus slowing DNA synthesis.
3. a Methotrexate acts as a folic acid antagonist, slowing cell division.
4. b Cisplatin inhibits cell division by binding to DNA and blocking its replication.
5. c The anticancer drugs nitrogen mustards were once used as a chemical warfare agent.

6.   b   Cyclophosphamide acts by cross-linking DNA chains and blocking replication.

18.5   Hormones: The Regulators
    A. Hormones are chemical messengers produced in the endocrine glands.
        1. Hormones cause profound changes in parts of the body often far removed from the gland that secretes the substance.
        2. Table 18.2 in the text lists a variety of hormones and their physiological effects.
    B. Prostaglandins: hormone mediators.
        1. Prostaglandins are synthesized from unsaturated fatty acids that contain 20 carbon atoms (such as arachidonic acid).
        2. Prostaglandins act together with hormones to regulate smooth-muscle activity and blood flow.
        3. Medically, prostaglandins and derivatives are used to
           a. induce labor.
           b. lower or raise blood pressure.
           c. inhibit stomach secretions.
           d. relieve nasal congestion.
           e. relieve asthma.
           f. inhibit the formation of blood clots.
    C. Diabetes.
        1. Pancreas produces the hormone insulin, which allows the body to increase cellular usage of glucose.
        2. Diabetes occurs when the pancreas does not produce enough insulin (Type 1) or when the insulin is not properly used by the body (Type 2).
    D. Steroids.
        1. All steroids have the same skeletal four-ring structure.

        2. Not all steroids have hormonal activity.
           a. Cholesterol is a steroid but not a hormone.
           b. Cortisol is a steroid hormone produced by the adrenal glands.
               i. Medically, cortisol and related compounds such as prednisone are anti-inflammatory drugs.
    E. Sex hormones.
        1. Androgens are compounds that stimulate the development or control the maintenance of masculine characteristics and are secreted by the testes.
        2. Estrogens are compounds that control female sexual functions, such as the menstrual cycle and the development of breasts.
        3. Two important groups of female hormones are the estrogens and progesterones.
           a. Estrogens, produced in the ovaries, are female hormones.
           b. Two important estrogens are estradiol and estrone.
        4. Sex hormones are used therapeutically.
    F. Chemistry and social revolution: the pill.
        1. Progesterone is an effective birth control drug when injected.
        2. Synthetic analogs of progesterone, called progestins, are effective birth control drugs.
        3. Oral progestins incorporate an ethynyl group ($-C\equiv CH$).
        4. Oral birth control pills usually combine an estrogen (to regulate the menstrual cycle) with a progestin that signals a state of false pregnancy so that ovulation does not occur.

G. Emergency contraceptives.
   1. Several products, called emergency contraceptives or morning-after pills, can be used to prevent pregnancy after unprotected intercourse.
   2. There are two kinds of emergency contraception pills (ECPs): combination pills with both estrogen and progestin (synthetic analogs of the natural substances), and pills containing only progestin.
   3. An inter-uterine device (IUD) is also used for emergency contraception.
   4. ECPs are not the same as the so-called medical abortion pills such as mifepristone (or RU-486) which works after a woman becomes pregnant and the fertilized egg has attached to the uterine wall.
H. Risks of taking birth control pills.
   1. Side effects are mostly minor.
   2. FDA advises all women who smoke, especially those over 40, to use some other method of contraception.
I. The minipill.
   1. Minipills are available that contain only small amounts of progestin and no estrogen.
   2. Minipills are not quite as effective as the combination pills, but have fewer side effects.
J. A pill for males?
   1. Women usually bear the responsibility for contraception because:
      a. It is easier to interfere with a once-a-month event (ovulation) than a continuous process (sperm production).
      b. In males, the pituitary hormones FSH and LG are required for continued production of sperm and of the male hormone testosterone.
      c. Several research groups have developed what may be a safe, effective, and reversible contraceptive for males, a pill containing progestin and testosterone.

Answers to Self-Assessment Questions

1. d Hormones are produced in the endocrine glands and act throughout the body.
2. a Prostaglandins are synthesized in the body from arachidonic acid.
3. c Prolactin is a protein and not a steroid.
4. b The gonads are stimulated to produce sex hormones and eggs or sperm by FSH and LH.
5. c The "pregnancy hormone" is progesterone.
6. c The group that makes a birth control drug effective orally is the ethynyl group which contains a triple bond.

18.6 Drugs for the Heart
   A. Lowering blood pressure.
      1. Hypertension, or high blood pressure, is defined as pressure, in mmHg above 140/90; normal blood pressure is defined as less than 120/80.
      2. Hypertension is the most common cardiovascular disease, affecting one in four adults in the U.S.
      3. There are four major categories of drugs for lowering blood pressure.
         a. *Diuretics* which cause the kidneys to excrete more water, thus lowering the blood volume.
         b. *Beta blockers* which slow the heart rate and reduce the force of the heartbeat.
         c. *Calcium channel blockers* which are vasodilators, inducing muscles around the blood vessels to relax.
         d. *Angiotensin-converting enzyme (ACE) inhibitors* which inhibit the action of an enzyme that causes blood vessels to contract.
   B. Treating coronary artery disease.

1.   Angina pectoris, a common symptom of coronary artery disease, is caused by an insufficient supply of oxygen to the heart, usually due to partial blockage of the coronary arteries by lipid-containing plaque (arteriosclerosis).
2.   Medical treatment usually involves dilation of the blood vessels to increase blood flow and slowing the heart rate to decrease its demand for oxygen.
3.   Some drugs used to treat high blood pressure are effective, as are some organic nitro compounds, especially amyl nitrite and nitroglycerin.
    a.   These compounds act by releasing nitric oxide (NO), which relaxes constricted vessels.
4.   The foxglove plant was used by ancient Egyptians and Romans to treat heart failure.
    a.   Foxglove contains a mixture of glycosides, one of which is digoxin which produces the steroid digitoxigenin, which affects the rhythm and strength of the heart muscles' contractions.
    b.   Digoxin is still used to treat patients with heart failure.

Answers to Self-Assessment Questions

1.   b   A diuretic is one type of treatment for hypertension (high blood pressure).
2.   d   Drugs called beta blockers slow and reduce the force of the heartbeat.
3.   c   Nitric oxide is released by amyl nitrite and nitroglycerin to relax the smooth muscles in blood vessels.

18.7   Drugs and the Mind
   A. Psychotropic drugs affect the mind. There are three classes of these drugs:
      1. *Stimulants* increase alertness, speed mental processes, and elevate the mood.
         a. Amphetamines, caffeine, and cocaine are stimulants.
      2. *Depressants* reduce the level of consciousness and the intensity of reactions to environmental stimuli.
         a. Ethanol, barbiturates, opiates, and tranquilizers are depressants.
      3. *Hallucinogenic* (psychotomimetic, psychedelic) drugs alter qualitatively a person's perception of the surroundings.
         a. LSD, mescaline, and marijuana are hallucinogens.
   B. Chemistry of the nervous system.
      1. Nerve cells (neurons) carry messages between the brain and other parts of the body.
         a. *Axons* of a nerve cell can be very long; however, the nerve impulse must be transmitted to the next dendrite across short fluid-filled gaps (synapses) via chemical messengers called *neurotransmitters*.
         b. Neurotransmitters determine to a large degree how you think, feel, and move about.
         c. Each type of neurotransmitter binds to a specific type of receptor site to complete the intended action.
      2. Many drugs (and poisons) act either by blocking or mimicking the action of these natural neurotransmitters.
      3.   Many neurotransmitters are amines.
   C. Biochemical theories of brain diseases.
      1. Epinephrine, often called adrenaline, is secreted by the adrenal glands when a person is under stress or is frightened.
      2. Norepinephrine (NE) is a relative of epinephrine.
         a. NE causes euphoria or, in large excess, a manic state.
      3. Serotonin, a brain amine, is involved in sleep, appetite, memory, learning, sensory perception, mood, sexual behavior, and regulation of body temperature.
      4. NE and related compounds fall into several general categories:

a. NE agonists, or drugs that enhance or mimic the action of NE, are stimulants.

b. NE antagonists, or drugs that block the action of NE, slow down various processes.

c. Serotonin agonists are used to treat depression, anxiety, and obsessive-compulsive disorder; serotonin antagonists are used to treat migraine headaches and to relieve the nausea caused by cancer chemotherapy.

D. Brain amines and diet: you feel what you eat.

1. Serotonin is synthesized from the amino acid tryptophan.

   a. A high-carbohydrate meal allows maximum tryptophan to reach the brain (where it is converted to serotonin).

   b. Protein-rich diets lower the level of serotonin in the brain.

2. Norepinephrine is synthesized from the amino acid tyrosine.

E. Right-handed and left-handed molecules.

1. Stereoisomers are isomers having the same structural formula but differ in the arrangement of atoms or groups of atoms in three-dimensional space.

2. Enantiomers are nonsuperimposable mirror images.

   a. Enantiomers have a chiral carbon, a carbon atom to which four different groups are attached.

   b. Enantiomers fit enzymes differently and they have different effects.

F. Anesthetics.

1. Anesthetics are substances that cause lack of feeling or awareness.

   a. General anesthetics act on the brain to produce unconsciousness and general insensitivity to pain.

   b. Local anesthetics cause loss of feeling in a part of the body.

2. Diethyl ether (ether) was the first general anesthetic (1846).

   a. Ether is relatively safe, but causes nausea.

   b. Ether is highly flammable.

3. Nitrous oxide is a quick-acting anesthetic. It is administered with oxygen to prevent brain damage.

4. Chloroform was once used as an anesthetic.

   a. It has a narrow safety margin; the effective dose is close to the lethal dose.

   b. It causes liver damage.

   c. It can react with oxygen to form deadly phosgene gas.

   d. It is nonflammable.

5. Modern anesthetics include fluorine-containing compounds such as sevoflurane, desflurane, and isoflurane.

   a. These compounds are nonflammable and relatively safe for the patient.

   b. Women who work in operating rooms where halothane is used have higher rates of miscarriage than the general population.

6. Modern surgical practice often combines the following:

   a. A tranquilizer to decrease anxiety.

   b. An intravenous anesthetic to produce unconsciousness quickly.

   c. A narcotic pain medication to block pain.

   d. An inhalant anesthetic to provide insensitivity to pain and keep the patient unconscious, often combined with oxygen and nitrous oxide to support life.

   e. A relaxant to relax the muscles and make it easier to insert a breathing tube.

G. Local anesthetics.

1. Local anesthetics render one part of the body insensitive to pain but leave the patient conscious.

   a. Cocaine was the first local anesthetic.

2. Many local anesthetics are ester derivatives of, or related to, *p*-aminobenzoic acid.

   a. Procaine (Novocain) was introduced in 1905.

      b.   Lidocaine and mepivicaine are widely used today.

H. Dissociative anesthetics: ketamine and PCP.
    1. Ketamine is a dissociative anesthetic because it disconnects a person's perceptions from his or her sensations.
        a.   Ketamine is widely used in veterinary medicine.
    2. PCP (phencyclidine) is a dangerous drug but has found use as an animal tranquilizer.
        a.   PCP is fat soluble. Stored in body fat, it is mobilized when fat is metabolized, causing flashbacks.

I. Depressant drugs.
    1. Ethyl alcohol, obtained from the fermentation of the sugars in fruits and grains, has been used by humans for centuries.
        a.   Although people sometimes think of alcohol as a stimulant, it is actually a depressant, slowing down physical and mental activity.
        b.   The mechanism of intoxication is not well known but researchers have found that ethanol disrupts receptors for two neurotransmitters, one which inhibits impulsiveness and the other which excites certain nerve cells.

J. Barbiturates.
    1. Barbiturates can be used to produce mild sedation, deep sleep, or even death.
    2. While more than 2500 barbiturates have been synthesized, only a few have found widespread use in medicine.
        a.   Pentobarbital (Nembutal®) is a short-acting hypnotic drug used to calm anxiety.
        b.   Phenobarbital (Luminal®) is a long-acting barbiturate used as an anticonvulsant for people suffering from seizure disorders such as epilepsy.
        c.   Thiopental (Pentothal®) is used as an anesthetic.
    3. Large doses of barbiturates serve as sleeping pills.
    4. Barbiturates are especially dangerous when ingested along with ethyl alcohol.
        a.   The combination produces an effect ten times greater than the sum of the effects of two depressants, called synergism, or a synergistic effect.
    5. Barbiturates, like ethanol, are intoxicating and they are strongly addictive.
    6. Barbiturates are cyclic amides that resemble thymine.

K. Antianxiety agents.
    1. Antidepressant drugs are now the most commonly prescribed drugs.
    2. One class of antianxiety drugs (anxiolytics) is the *benzodiazepines*, compounds that feature seven-member heterocyclic rings.
        a.   Diazepam (Valium®) is a classic antianxiety agent.
        b.   Clonazepam is an anticonvulsant as well as an antianxiety drug.
        c.   Lorazepam is used to treat insomnia.
    3. The first antipsychotic drugs, sometimes called *major tranquilizers*, were compounds called phenothiazines.
        a.   Phenothiazines act in part as dopamine antagonists, blocking postsynaptic receptors for dopamine, a neurotransmitter important in the control of detailed motion, memory and emotions, and in exciting brain cells
    4. A second generation of antipsychotics, called *atypical antipsychotics*, includes drugs used to treat schizophrenia, acute manic episodes of bipolar disorder, and depression.
        a.   These drugs have served to greatly reduce the number of patients confined to mental hospitals.
    5. Oldest class of antidepressants is the tricyclic antidepressants that block reabsorption of neurotransmitters such as norepinephrine and serotonin.
        a.   These drugs have serious side effects and have been largely replaced by newer drugs.

6. Antidepressants commonly prescribed today include *selective serotonin-reuptake inhibitors* (SSRIs) which are prescribed for anxiety syndromes such as panic disorder, obsessive-compulsive disorders, and premenstrual syndrome.
L. Stimulant drugs.
  1. Amphetamines, a variety of synthetic amines related to β-phenylethylamine, are similar in structure to epinephrine and norepinephrine.
    a. Amphetamine and methamphetamine are inexpensive and have been widely abused.
    b. Methamphetamine has a more pronounced psychological effect than amphetamine and is readily prepared from an antihistamine and household chemicals.
    c. Amphetamine exists as enantiomers.
      i. Benzedrine® is a mixture of the two isomers.
      ii. Dexedrine® is the pure dextro isomer.
M. Cocaine, caffeine, and nicotine.
  1. Cocaine is obtained from the leaves of a shrub that grows almost exclusively on the eastern slopes of the Andes Mountains.
    a. Cocaine arrives illegally in this country as broken lumps of the free base (crack cocaine).
    b. Cocaine acts by preventing the neurotransmitter dopamine from being taken back up from the synapse after it is released by nerve cells so the cells fire wildly, depleting the dopamine supply.
    c. Cocaine is a stimulant, which increases stamina and reduces fatigue but the stimulant effects are short-lived, followed by depression.
  2. Coffee, tea, and cola soft drinks naturally contain caffeine, a mild stimulant.
  3. Nicotine is a drug found in smoking and chewing tobacco.
    a. The lethal dose (when injected) for humans is estimated at about 50 mg.
    b. Nicotine is powerfully addictive.
N. Hallucinogenic drugs.
  1. Hallucinogenic drugs are consciousness-altering substances that induce changes in sensory perception, qualitatively altering the way users perceive things.
    a. LSD is a semisynthetic drug that is a powerful hallucinogen whose powers were discovered by Hofmann in 1943.
  2. It is a hallucinogen related to lysergic acid and other ergot fungus alkaloids.
  3. As little as 10 μg of this powerful drug can cause hallucinations.
  4. Psilocybin and mescaline are compounds found in mushrooms and peyote cactus, respectively. The effects of these drugs are shorter-lasting than those of LSD.
O. Marijuana.
  1. Marijuana is the leaves, flowers, seeds, and small stems of the *Cannabis sativa* plant.
  2. The principal active ingredient is tetrahydrocannabinol (THC).
  3. Marijuana reduces pressure in the eyes of glaucoma patients and relieves nausea of cancer patients undergoing radiation and chemotherapy.

Answers to Self-Assessment Questions

1.   a   Neurotransmitters are chemicals that carry messages across the synapse between an axon and a dendrite.
2.   c   Serotonin is formed in the brain from the dietary amino acid tryptophan.
3.   d   Depression may be the result of abnormal metabolism of serotonin.
4.   a   When used as an anesthetic, nitrous oxide can cause brain damage if it is not combined with O_2.
5.   b   Ethyl alcohol is a depressant.
6.   b   Benzodiazepines are commonly used as anti-anxiety medications.

7.   d   Several stimulant drugs are chemical derivatives of β-phenylethylamine.
8.   d   Dextroamphetamine is composed of molecules that are all the right-handed isomer of the two enantiomers.
9.   d   LSD acts on the serotonin receptors.
10.   a   Anandamide is structurally similar to THC and is produced in the brain.

18.8   Drugs and Society
       A. *Drug abuse*: using a drug for its intoxicating effect.
       B. *Drug misuse*: inappropriate use of a drug to treat a specific illness.
       C. Placebo and nocebo effects.
           1. A placebo is an inactive substance given in the form of medication to a patient.
           2. A nocebo is a substance that is harmless but that produces harmful effects because the person involved thinks it's harmful.

Answers to Self-Assessment Questions

1.   c   Using an antibiotic to treat a cold is an example of drug misuse.
2.   b   Using Oxycontin for its intoxicating effect is an example of drug abuse.
3.   b   A placebo is an inactive drug that looks like real medication.
4.   d   In a double blind experiment, some patients are given the drug being tested and others are given a placebo.

LEARNING OBJECTIVES

You should be able to...

1. Identify common drugs as natural, semisynthetic, or synthetic.   (18.1)

2. Define *chemotherapy*, and explain its origin.   (18.1)

3. List the common OTC analgesics, antipyretics, and anti-inflammatory drugs, and describe how each works.   (18.2)

4. Name several common narcotics, describe how each functions, and state its potential for addiction.   (18.2)

5. List the common antibacterial drugs, and describe the action of each.   (18.3)

6. Name the common antiviral drugs, and describe the action of each.   (18.3)

7. Describe the action of the common types of anticancer drugs.   (18.4)

8. Define the terms *hormone*, *prostaglandin*, and *steroid*, and explain the function of each.   (18.5)

9. List the three types of sex hormones, and explain how each acts, and how birth control drugs work.   (18.5)

10. Describe the action of four types of drugs used to treat heart disease.   (18.6)

11. Explain how the brain amines norepinephrine and serotonin affect the mind and how various drugs change their action. (18.7)

12. Identify some stimulant drugs, depressant drugs, and psychotropic drugs, and describe how they affect the mind. (18.7)

13. Differentiate between drug abuse and drug misuse. (18.8)

14. Differentiate between a placebo and a nocebo. (18.8)

15. Explain how green chemistry can be applied to the manufacture of drugs.

16. Identify green chemistry principles that contribute to improving the E-factor of a chemical synthesis.

DISCUSSION

The first half of this chapter concentrates on chemical substances that are used to relieve pain or distress, to cure or alleviate disease, to prevent pregnancy, and for a variety of other purposes. Once again, keep in mind that a chemical substance has a specific set of properties that are invariant. Each compound may have some properties that are desirable and some that are undesirable; drugs may have nasty side effects as well as desired therapeutic properties.

The second half of this chapter is devoted to drugs that affect our mental state. It is important to realize that our moods, our sense of feeling "up" or "down," and our sense of and tolerance of pain are all influenced by the presence or absence of chemical molecules that help regulate our body functions. We now know that many of the drugs that have been used and abused for centuries are capable of eliciting certain effects because they somehow mimic a natural neurotransmitter or body regulator molecule. This mimicking usually involves some structural similarity that allows the drug molecule to bind to a receptor site intended for the normal body regulator molecule.

ANSWERS TO ODD-NUMBERED REVIEW QUESTIONS AND SOLUTIONS FOR ODD-NUMBERED END OF CHAPTER PROBLEMS

Review Questions

1. An antibiotic is a drug that kills or slows the growth of bacteria; originally limited to formulations derived from living organisms.

3. Cortisol is a hormone released in the body during stressed or agitated states. Prednisone is a synthetic hormone similar to cortisone.

5. Prostaglandins act as mediators of hormone action. Prostaglandins act near the site where they were produced, they are rapidly metabolized, and they have different effects on different tissues. Hormones act throughout the body.

7. Two dissociative anesthetics are Ketamine and PCP.

9. A narcotic is a drug that produces stupor and relief of pain.

11. Brain amines are made from dietary amino acids; for example, high carbohydrate diets produce high serotonin levels in the brain.

13. No, tranquilizers are not a cure for schizophrenia. These drugs relieve the symptoms, but the symptoms return once use of the drugs is terminated.

Problems

15. Acetylsalicylic acid is the chemical name for aspirin.

17. Aspirin provides pain relief and reduces fever but it is also an anticoagulant and has anti-inflammatory effects; acetaminophen provides pain relief and reduces fever, but is not an anticoagulant (nor an anti-inflammatory drug) so it does not promote bleeding, making healing from surgical procedures proceed more smoothly.

19. The acetaminophen molecule includes a phenolic group (-OH on a benzene ring) and an amide group.

21. Morphine and heroin are both narcotics used for pain relief. Morphine also induces lethargy, drowsiness, confusion, euphoria, chronic constipation, and respiratory system depression, and is addictive. Heroin is a semisynthetic drug produced by converting both OH groups of morphine to acetate esters. The physiological action of heroin is similar to that of morphine. Because heroin is less polar than morphine, it enters the fatty tissues of the brain more rapidly and seems to produce stronger euphoric sensations. Heroin is more addictive than morphine.

23. a. Endorphins, or morphine-like substances, are produced by the brain. Acupuncture may cause the release of brain opiates that relieve pain.
    b. A soldier, wounded in battle, may feel no pain until the skirmish is over because his body has secreted its own painkiller.

25. Sulfanilamide H_2N—〇—SO_2NH_2 H_2N—〇—$COOH$ *para*-aminobenzoic acid

27. Broad-spectrum antibiotics are effective against a wide variety of bacteria.

29. Antiviral drugs do not cure viral diseases. The best way to deal with viral diseases is by vaccination.

31. Two major classes of anticancer drugs are antimetabolites, which inhibit nucleic acid synthesis, and alkylating agents, which can transfer alkyl groups to biologically important compounds to block their action.

33. An estrogen is a female hormone that controls female sexual functions, such as the menstrual cycle, the development of breasts, and other secondary sexual characteristics. An androgen is a male hormone that stimulates the development or controls the maintenance of masculine characteristics.

35.   Addition of an ethynyl group ($-C\equiv CH$) to a compound such as 19-norprogesterone allowed it to be taken orally when, initially, it could only be given by injection.

37.   A psychotropic drug is one that affects the human mind and the way we perceive things. Psychotropic drugs are generally divided into three classes: stimulants, depressants, and hallucinogens.

39.   The answer is a. Diethyl ether is highly flammable.

41.   a. (cholesterol), b. (prednisone), and c. (progesterone) are steroids.

43.   a. daily dose, g = (140 lb)(0.454 kg/lb)(40 mg ampicillin/kg body weight)(1 g/1000 mg)
                    = 2.5 g
        If the medicine is given three times a day, each dose is 2.5 g/3 doses = 0.83 g/dose.
        number of capsules/dose = (0.83 g/dose)(1000 mg/g)(1 capsule/500 mg) = 1.7 capsule/dose
        847 mg/dose or about 1.7 pills for a pill containing 500 mg of active ingredient.

45.   The structure shared by all steroids is four fused rings.

47.   A compound with the chemical formula $C_{17}H_{21}NO$ would not be soluble in water because it is nonpolar, and water is polar. This compound would be soluble in fat because fat is nonpolar and the fact that this molecule has only one oxygen atom and one nitrogen atom in a structure containing 17 carbon and 21 hydrogen atoms means that the large majority of bonds in the structure are nonpolar.

49.   The structure of cyclohexylamine

51.   The LD_{50} of the timber rattlesnake is lower than the LD_{50} for the Southern copperhead. This means that the toxin from the timber rattlesnake is more toxic than the toxin from the Southern copperhead snake because less of it will cause a fatal reaction.

53.   Nicotine is more toxic than procaine because it has a lower LD_{50}.
        Lethal dose of procaine = (50 mg/kg)(50 kg) = 2500 mg
        Lethal dose of nicotine = (1.0 mg/kg)(50 kg) = 50 mg.

55. The structure of codeine is

57. The structure of oxycodone is

59. *Gamma*-butyrolactone (GBL) contains a cyclic ester. Hydrolyzing the ester will convert GBL to the open chain structure $HOCH_2CH_2CH_2COOH$.

61. The compound is 6-mercaptopurine. It is an antimetabolite.

63. a. Removal of the *para*-hydroxyl group would decrease the solubility in water.
    b. Removal of the *para*-hydroxyl group would increase the solubility in fat.

65. a. The palmitate ester would be less soluble in water because of the long hydrocarbon chain.
    b. The sodium succinate would be more soluble in water because of the salt of the acid.

67. The answer is c. The structure is a steroid because it is based on the four fused-ring system characteristics of steroids.

69. Use of lipolase allows the wrong enantiomer to be recycled and used instead of being discarded. Also, small amino acid catalysts are being used as replacements for larger expensive enzymes.

Fitness and Health

The Chemistry of Wellness

CHAPTER SUMMARY

19.1 Calories: Quantity and Quality
    A. Total calorie intake is important, but the distribution of calories is even more important.
        1. The 2000-calorie-per-day diet is an average, depending on weight, age, and level of activity
        2. Adults should keep fat intake between 20–35% of all calories.
            a. Only 7–10% of fat calories should come from saturated fats
            b. A minimum of fat calories should come from *trans*-fatty acids.
            c. Cholesterol intake should be less than 300 mg/day.
    B. Nutrition and the athlete.
        1. Recommended ranges for energy nutrients for most people are 20–35% of calories from fat, 45–65% of calories from carbohydrates, and 10–35% of calories from protein.
        2. Athletes generally need more calories because they expend more energy than the average sedentary individual.
            a. Those calories should come mainly from carbohydrates.
        3. Athletes do not need extra protein in their diets.
            a. Muscles are built through exercise, not from eating protein.
            b. Protein metabolism produces toxic wastes that tax the liver and kidneys.
            c. Athletes need the Dietary Reference Intake (DRI) quantity of 0.8 g protein/kg body weight.
        4. When muscle contracts against resistance, creatine (an amino acid) is released.
            a. Creatine stimulates production of protein (myosin), thus building muscle.
            b. If exercise is ended, the muscle begins to shrink after about two days.

Answers to Self-Assessment Questions

1.   c   Good nutrition and exercise are needed for good health and fitness.
2.   c   Undereating has been shown to extend the life span of mice.
3.   d   Saturated and *trans* fats are the most detrimental to health.
4.   b   Maximum fat intake is 35%, so 35% of 2200 kcal is 770 kcal.
            Mass of fat $=$ (770 kcal)(1 g fat/9 kcal) $=$ 86 g fat.
5.   b   Maximum saturated fat intake is 20%, so 20% of 2000 kcal is 200 kcal.
            Mass of saturated fat $=$ (200 kcal)(1 g fat/9 kcal) $=$ 22 g saturated fat.
6.   a   Most saturated fats in our diets come from animal products.

7. c   Dietary Reference Intakes (DRIs) are nutrient recommendations that are useful primarily for planning and assessing diets.

8. c   A 66-kg athlete requires a daily protein intake of about 0.8 g of protein/kg body weight, or 53 g of protein each day.

19.2   Vitamins, Minerals, Fluids, and Electrolytes
   A. Good nutrition requires sufficient carbohydrates, fats, and proteins; proper proportions of essential minerals and vitamins; and adequate water.
      1. Vitamins are organic substances that the human body needs but cannot manufacture in sufficient quantities, so they must be included in the diet.
      2. Minerals are inorganic elements that the body needs, so they must be included in the diet.
      3. The DRI values for vitamins and minerals set by the Food and Nutrition Board are the amounts that will prevent deficiency diseases and are readily supplied by any well-balanced diet.
         a. Vitamin A, a fat-soluble vitamin, is essential for good vision, bone development, and skin maintenance, and may confer resistance to some cancers.
         b. Vitamin B complex includes eight compounds, several of which serve as coenzymes and are important in maintaining skin and the nervous system.
            i.   Vitamin B_6 (pyridoxine) is a coenzyme for more than 100 different enzymes and helps people with arthritis by shrinking the connective tissue membranes that line the joints.
            ii. B_3 (niacin) offers relief from arthritis and lowers cholesterol levels.
            iii. Vitamin B_{12} deficiency can lead to pernicious anemia. Because vitamin B_{12} is not found in plants, this deficiency can be a problem for vegetarians unless they take supplements.
            iv. Folic acid, a B vitamin, is critical to the development of the nervous system of a fetus, but taken in excess of 1000 µg can cause nerve damage.
         c. Vitamin C is essential for efficient functioning of the immune system.
         d. Vitamin D is a steroid hormone that protects children against rickets by promoting adsorption of calcium and phosphorus from foods to produce and maintain healthy bones.
            i.   Too much vitamin D can lead to excessive calcium and phosphorus adsorption.
            ii. DRI for vitamin D increases with age; the recommended upper limit is 2000 IU.
         e. Vitamin E is a mixture of tocopherols, phenols with hydrocarbon side chains.
            i.   Its antioxidant activity helps maintain the cardiovascular system.
            ii. Low levels are associated with sterility and muscular dystrophy.
            iii. Upper limit for vitamin E is 400–800 IU/day depending on side effects. Higher levels bring the risk of excessive bleeding.
   B. Body fluids and electrolytes.
      1. An electrolyte is a substance that conducts electricity when dissolved in water.
      2. In the body, electrolytes are ions required by cells to maintain their internal and external electric charge and thus control the flow of water molecules across the cell membrane.
         a. The main electrolytes are Na^+, K^+, and Cl^-. Others include Ca^{2+}, Mg^{2+}, sulfate (SO_4^{2-}), hydrogen phosphate (HPO_4^{2-}), and bicarbonate (HCO_3^-).
      3. Water is an essential nutrient which is best replaced after respiration, sweating, and urination by drinking water rather than other beverages.
         a. Dehydration can be serious or even deadly.

Answers to Self-Assessment Questions

1.   d   Vitamins cannot be synthesized by the body and must be included in the diet.
2.   a   Beta-carotene is a precursor of vitamin A.
3.   c   Large doses of vitamin A are most likely to be harmful because vitamin A is fat soluble and excesses are stored in the adipose tissue.
4.   b   All B vitamins are water soluble.
5.   d   Vitamin C is a water-soluble antioxidant.
6.   c   The major electrolytes in body fluids are Na^+, K^+, and Cl^-.
7.   c   Plain water is the best replacement for water lost except in prolonged exercise.
8.   a   As little as 2% of the body weight lost in fluids can cause impaired performance by an individual.

19.3   Weight Loss: Diets and Exercise
- A. Diets with fewer than 1200 kcal/day are likely to be deficient in necessary nutrients, particularly the B vitamins and iron.
- B. Biochemistry of hunger.
  1. Two peptide hormones, *ghrelin* and *peptide YY* are produced by the digestive tract and are linked to short-term eating behaviors.
     - a. Ghrelin is an appetite stimulant produced by the stomach; PYY acts as an appetite suppressant.
  2. The hormone insulin and a substance called *leptin*, produced by fat cells, determine longer-term weight balance.
     - a. Leptin, a protein consisting of 146 amino acid units, is produced by fat cells.
  3. Other substances involved in weight control include *cholecystokinin (CCK)*, a peptide formed in the intestine that signals that we have eaten enough food, and a class of compounds called *melanocortins*, which act on the brain to regulate food intake.
- C. Crash diets: quick = quack.
  1. Any weight-loss program that promises a loss of more than a pound or two a week is likely to be dangerous quackery.
     - a. Many use a diuretic to increase urine output. Weight loss is water loss, which is quickly regained when the body is rehydrated.
     - b. Other diets, low in carbohydrates, depend on glycogen depletion.
       - i. Glycogen molecules have many OH groups that are attached to water molecules through hydrogen bonding. Each pound of glycogen carries about 3 lb of water. Depleting one pound of glycogen results in a weight loss of 4 lb.
       - ii. The weight is quickly regained when carbohydrates are returned to the diet.
  2. The largest amount of fat an individual can lose in a day, even with a total fast, is about 0.69 lb.
     - a. The body won't burn just fat; if carbohydrates are not supplied in the diet, the body will break down muscle tissue to make glucose.
     - b. Any diet that restricts carbohydrate intake results in a loss of muscle mass as well as fat.
     - c. Weight loss through dieting includes loss of muscle mass as well as fat; weight regained (without exercise) is pure fat.
- D. Exercise for weight loss.
  1. The most sensible weight-loss program is to follow a balanced low-calorie diet that meets the DRI for essential nutrients and to engage in a reasonable exercise program.

Answers to Self-Assessment Questions

1. c   There are 3500 kilocalories of energy stored in 1 pound of adipose tissue.
2. c   To lose 1 pound per week, you need to burn 500 kilocalories (3500 kcal/7 days) each day more than you eat.
3. b   The hormone ghrelin is an appetite stimulant.
4. c   The hormone insulin lowers blood glucose levels.
5. a   Cholecystokinin (CCK) seems to tell the brain that it is time to stop eating.
6. b   The adult body can store about 1 pound of glycogen.
7. b   Crash diets depend upon glycogen depletion for quick weight loss.

19.4   Measuring Fitness
    A. The male body requires about 3% body fat, while the average female body needs 10–12%.
        1. One way to estimate body fat is by measuring a person's density.
        2. A simpler way is by measuring the waist and hips and dividing the waist measurement by the hip measurement.
            a. The waist/hip ratio should be ≤ 1 for males and ≤ 0.8 for females.
        3. Newer scales provide a measure of body fat content using *bioelectric impedance analysis* which involves passing a small electric current through the body.
            a. Fat has a greater impedance (resistance to varying current) than does muscle.
    B. Body mass index.
        1. *Body mass index (BMI)* is a commonly used measure of fatness defined as weight (in kg) divided by the square of the height (in meters).
            a. A BMI < 18.5 indicates that a person is underweight.
            b. A BMI from 25–29.9 indicates that a person is overweight.
            c. A BMI > 30 indicates a person is obese.
        2. When measuring in pounds and inches, the equation is:
$$BMI = [(705)(\text{body weight, lb})]/(\text{height, in})^2$$
    C. V_{O2} max: a measure of fitness.
        1. V_{O2} max is the maximum amount, in mL/kg body weight, of oxygen that a person can use in 1 minute.
            a. The higher the V_{O2} max, the greater is the fitness.
    D. Your fitness benefits the planet.
        1. Although the chemical reactions that power your body when you walk or bike produce CO_2, they are based on renewable fuels—the carbohydrates in your food.
        2. The reaction of carbohydrates with oxygen powers your body and leads to CO_2 as a byproduct.
        3. The plants that produced the carbohydrates you eat incorporated CO_2 from the atmosphere through photosynthesis so your energy source is carbon-neutral because the CO_2 that you produce is balanced by the CO_2 used to make the fuel your body uses.

Answers to Self-Assessment Questions

1. d   Body mass index (BMI) is calculated by weight (kg) $\div$ [height (m)]^2.
2. a   A person with a body mass index (BMI) of 35 is obese.
3. d V_{O2} max is the maximum amount of oxygen used during one minute of exercise.

19.5   Some Muscular Chemistry
    A. Energy for muscle contraction: ATP.

1. Some of the energy from glucose or fatty-acid metabolism is stored as adenosine triphosphate (ATP).
   a. Muscle contains the proteins actin and myosin in a loose complex called actomyosin.
B. Aerobic exercise: plenty of oxygen.
   1. When muscle contraction begins, glycogen is converted to pyruvic acid.
   2. If sufficient oxygen is present (as in aerobic exercise), the pyruvic acid is oxidized to carbon dioxide and water.
C. Anaerobic exercise and oxygen debt.
   1. If sufficient oxygen is not available (as in anaerobic exercise), pyruvic acid is reduced to lactic acid.
   2. This lactic acid buildup leads to a pH drop and deactivation of muscle enzymes, described as "muscle fatigue."
   3. The overworked muscles incur an oxygen debt that needs to be repaid after the strenuous exercise is over.
   4. When glycogen stores are depleted, muscle cells can switch to fat metabolism.
      a. Fats are the main source of energy for sustained activity of low to moderate intensity.
D. Muscle fibers: twitch kind do you have?
   1. There are two classes of muscle fibers.
      a. Fast-twitch (Type IIB) for anaerobic activity.
      b. Slow-twitch (Type I) for aerobic activity.
   2. Slow-twitch fibers (Type I): endurance activities.
      a. These are best suited for aerobic work of light or moderate intensity for sustained periods of time.
      b. High respiratory capacity and myoglobin levels of slow-twitch fibers help supply oxygen for sustained exercise, like long-distance running.
      c. Slow-twitch fibers have a low ability to hydrolyze glycogen and low actomyosin catalytic activity.
   3. Fast-twitch fibers (type IIB): allow for bursts of power.
      a. These are best suited for anaerobic short bursts.
      b. Low respiratory capacity and myoglobin levels of fast-twitch fibers are designed for quick bursts of energy like sprints.
      c. Fast-twitch fibers have high capacity for glycogen hydrolysis and high catalytic activity of actomyosin, which facilitate rapid ATP production and ability to hydrolyze ATP quickly.
E. Building muscles.
   1. Endurance training increases myoglobin levels in muscles (slow-twitch).
   2. Weight training develops fast-twitch muscles. Muscles increase in size.

Answers to Self-Assessment Questions

1.	b	ATP is the high-energy compound used directly by muscles when contracting.
2.	d	Glycogen is converted to pyruvic acid when muscle contraction begins.
3.	a	Pyruvic acid is converted to CO_2 and H_2O during aerobic exercise.
4.	c	Pyruvic acid is converted to lactic acid during anaerobic exercise.
5.	c	Lactic acid production results in oxygen debt.
6.	c	Fast-twitch muscle fiber is classified as type IIB.
7.	c	The presence of myoglobin causes the reddish color of slow-twitch muscle fibers.

19.6 Drugs, Athletic Performance, and the Brain
   A. Restorative drugs are used to remedy the effects of performance—pain, soreness, and injury.

1. Painkillers include aspirin, acetaminophen, ibuprofen, and methyl salicylate.
   2. Anti-inflammatory drugs include aspirin and ibuprofen and cortisone derivatives.
B. Stimulant drugs.
   1. Caffeine can conserve glycogen, speed heart rate, and increase metabolism, but the effect is small.
   2. Cocaine, like amphetamines, stimulates the central nervous system and increases alertness and muscle tension. It can also mask fatigue and give a sense of increased stamina.
C. Anabolic steroids.
   1. Anabolic steroid hormones increase muscle mass.
   2. Side effects in males include testicular atrophy and loss of function, impotence, acne, liver damage (including liver cancer), edema, elevated cholesterol levels, and growth of breasts.
   3. Anabolic steroids (derived from male sex hormones) make women more masculine. In addition to muscles, they develop baldness, extra body and facial hair, a deepened voice, and menstrual irregularities.
D. Drugs, athletic performance, and drug screening.
   1. Use of drugs to increase athletic performance is illegal and physically dangerous.
      a. Stimulants give a short-lived and false sense of confidence.
      b. Following the high of stimulants is extreme depression.
   2. Blood and urine screening for illegal drugs is becoming standard practice.
E. Exercise and the brain.
   1. Vigorous exercise causes the body to produce its own painkillers, endorphins.
   2. These substances can produce euphoric highs.
   3. Endorphins are addictive; athletes suffer withdrawal symptoms when they can't exercise.
   4. Exercise also directly affects the brain by increasing its blood supply and by producing neurotrophins, substances that enhance the growth of brain cells.
F. No smoking.
   1. Cigarette smoking is the chief preventable cause of premature death in the U.S.
      a. At every age, the death rate is higher among smokers than among nonsmokers.

Answers to Self-Assessment Questions

1.	a	Aspirin is a restorative drug.
2.	d	Caffeine is thought to aid endurance athletes by stimulating the release of fatty acids.
3.	c	Anabolic steroids help build larger muscles.
4.	a	Endorphins are chemicals produced by the body that are similar to morphine.
5.	c	Exercise is thought to help relieve depression by increasing the levels of neurotrophins.
6.	a	CO in cigarette smoke makes breathing less efficient because it blocks oxygen transport by hemoglobin.
7.	d	About 5000 chemicals have been identified in cigarette smoke.

LEARNING OBJECTIVES

You should be able to...

1. List the recommendations (sources and percentages) for calories from fats and other sources in the American diet. (19.1)

2. Describe the special dietary requirements of athletes. (19.1)

3. Describe the dietary requirements for vitamins, minerals, and water. (19.2)

4. Explain how weight is lost through diet and exercise. (19.3)

5. Calculate weight loss due to calorie reduction and to exercise. (19.3)

6. Describe several ways to measure fitness. (19.4)

7. Calculate BMI values. (19.4)

8. Differentiate between aerobic exercise and anaerobic exercise, and describe the chemistry that occurs during each. (19.5)

9. Describe how muscles are built and how they work. (19.5)

10. Describe the physiological effects of restorative drugs, stimulant drugs, and anabolic steroids. (19.6)

11. Explain how endorphins, neurotrophins, and tobacco can affect the brain and body. (19.6)

12. Explain how green chemistry principles can help us make transportation choices.

13. Describe the relationship between walking or biking and personal health, especially the implications for weight loss.

DISCUSSION

In this chapter, we consider the application of chemistry to healthy living, with emphasis on sports and athletics. Science has transformed many athletic events. We now have a better understanding of the action of muscles and of the effects of diet and exercise. Chemistry has provided a plethora of new materials for clothing and equipment. It also has provided drugs that help (and harm) athletes. Chemical principles can help you to separate fact from fancy and to guard against quackery and harmful practices.

ANSWERS TO ODD-NUMBERED REVIEW QUESTIONS AND SOLUTIONS FOR ODD-NUMBERED END OF CHAPTER PROBLEMS

Review Questions

1. Meat and other animal products are the main dietary source of saturated fats.

3. This type of weight loss is due to depletion of glycogen stores and water (dehydration). It is not a useful way to lose weight and keep it off because the weight is quickly regained when carbohydrates and liquids return to the diet.

5. Three ways that chemistry has had an impact on sports are
    a.   the development of a better understanding of muscle physiology
    b.   the better understanding of drugs
    c.   the development of improved sporting equipment.

7. One method involves measuring a person's density (mass to volume ratio). Measuring mass with a scale is relatively easy, but measuring volume with a dunk tank is subject to considerable error and does not take into account the volume of air in the lungs. A second method involves using bioelectric impedance analysis where a person stands on the scale in bare feet and a small electric current is sent through the body. By measuring the impedance of the body, the percentage of body fat can be calculated based on height and weight. Problems with this method involve taking into account many variables such as bone density, water content, and location of fat.

9. Low calorie diets are often deficient in the B vitamins, iron, and other nutrients. In addition, these diets slow the person's metabolism, often making future dieting more difficult and weight gain easier.

Problems

11. No, most athletes do not need more protein than non-athletes. Protein metabolism produces more toxic wastes that tax the liver and kidneys. The added energy they require is best obtained through the consumption of additional carbohydrates.

13. The benefit derived from vitamin B_{12} is that, by taking it, the individual can avoid having pernicious anemia.

15. Arthritis is helped by vitamin B_6 (pyridoxine) because this compound shrinks the connective tissue membranes that line the joints. Vitamin B_6 is a cofactor for more than 100 different enzymes.

17. Vitamin D promotes adsorption of calcium and phosphorus. Taking too much vitamin D (more than 2000 IU) causes absorption of excessive amounts of calcium and phosphorus which leads to formation of calcium deposits in various soft body tissues, including those of the heart.

19. A diuretic promotes water loss through urine production. The antidiuretic hormone ADH keeps water in the body.

21. Thirst is not a good indicator of dehydration because it is a delayed response to water loss and may be masked by symptoms of dehydration such as exhaustion, confusion, headache, and nausea. You are not always thirsty when you are dehydrated.

23. Fad diets often include a diuretic which promotes water loss. The weight is regained as soon as the body is rehydrated. Other quick-weight-loss diets depend on depleting the body's stores of glycogen. No fat is lost, and the weight is quickly regained when the dieter resumes eating carbohydrates.

25. Walking time required = (420 kcal)(1 hr/210 kcal) = 2.0 hr.

27. 1 lb = 0.454 kg
     mass of protein, g = (253 lb player)(0.454 kg/lb)(0.8 g protein/kg body weight) = 92 g

29. distance run = (2000 kcal)(1 km/100 kcal) = 20 km

31. a. Leptin is produced by the fat cells. It causes weight loss in mice by decreasing their appetite and increasing their metabolic rates. Letpin's main role seems to be to protect against weight loss in times of scarcity rather than against weight gain in times of plentiful food.
     b. Ghrelin is an appetite stimulant produced by the stomach.

33. BMI = [(705)(body weight, lb)]/(height, in)^2.
     BMI = [(705)(182 lb)]/(81 in)^2 = 20

35. The human body has about 600 muscles.

37. No, eating more protein does not result in larger muscles. Aerobic exercise is the best means of increasing muscle mass.

39. a. Anaerobic metabolism provides energy for intense bursts of vigorous activity.
     b. Aerobic metabolism provides energy for prolonged low levels of activity.

41. High levels of myoglobin are appropriate for muscle tissue geared to aerobic oxidation because they store the oxygen needed for aerobic oxidation.

43. A high capacity for glycogen use and a high catalytic activity of actomyosin allow tissue rich in fast-twitch (Type IIB) fibers to generate ATP rapidly and also to hydrolyze this ATP rapidly during intense muscle activity.

45. No, the best way to build muscles is by weightlifting and other exercise.

47. Cortisone derivatives reduce swelling (inflammation) in damaged joints and tissues. Side effects include increased fluid retention, hypertension, ulcers, and a disturbance of the sex hormone balance.

49. In runner's high, endorphins that block pain are produced in the body.

51. The athlete may perform better for a short period, but the stimulant effect is brief and is usually followed by exhaustion and depression.

53. Some of the health problems related to smoking are heart disease, stroke, lung cancer, emphysema, pneumonia, and cancer of the pancreas, bladder, breast, kidney, and cervix.

55. number of kcal/day = (160 lb)(15 kcal/lb) = 2400 kcal/day

57. Mass, g = (85 kg)(1000 g/kg) = 85000 g; volume, mL = (80 L)(1000 mL/L) = 80000 mL
density = mass/volume = 85000 g/80000 mL = 1.1 g/mL.
The person is lean.

59.

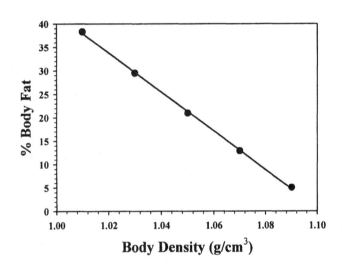

a. From the graph, a body density of 1.037 g/cm^3 is approximately equivalent to 27% body fat.

b. mass of individual, kg = (165 lb)(0.454 kg/lb) = 74.9 kg
mass of water displaced, kg = (14 lb)(0.454 kg/lb) = 6.4 kg
volume of water displaced, L = (74.9 kg – 6.4 kg)(1 L/0.9951 kg) = 68.8 L
density = 74.9 kg/68.8 L = 1.09 g/cm^3
From the graph, the individual has about 5% body fat.

c. Person B is more likely to be an athlete because the density of person A is less than that of person B, so person A's constitution likely contains a higher percentage of fat than that of person B.

d. The 5.30 kg underwater is obtained with 1.57 L of air, which displaces 1.562 kg of water. The mass of the individual when he's underwater is greater is greater than 5.30 kg by 1.562 kg, making a 'real' mass underwater of6.86 kg. Therefore, his density is:
Density = [(89.34)/89.34 – 6.86)] = 1.083 g/cm^3
The air in the lungs helps keep a person afloat.

61. a. 8 ft 11 inches = 107 inches. (199 kg)(1 lb/0.454 kg) = 438 lb
BMI = $[(705)(438\ lb)]/[107\ in]^2 = 27$

b. (487 kg)(1 lb/0.454 kg) = 1070 lbs. (184 cm)(1 in/2.54 cm) = 72.4 in.
BMI = $[(705)(1070\ lb)]/[72.4]^2 = 144$

63.   a.   volume of O_2 = (100 mL blood)(15 g hemoglobin/100 mL blood)
                           (1.34 mL O_2/1 g hemoglobin) = 20.1 mL O_2

       b.   volume of O_2 = (6.0 L blood)(1000 mL/L)(15 g hemoglobin/100 mL blood)
                           (1.34 mL O_2/1 g hemoglobin) = 1200 mL O_2

65.   pounds lost = (45 kcal/mi)(2 mi/day)(80 days)(1 lb/3500 kcal) = 2.1 lb
       The individual will lose 2.1 pounds by riding a bike rather than driving to school.

67.   The answer is c. Carbon dioxide is a greenhouse gas that contributes to global warming.

Chemistry Down on the Farm

...and in the Garden and on the Lawn

CHAPTER SUMMARY

Plants: Sun-Powered Food-Making Machines
    A. Green plants use photosynthesis to make sugars from carbon dioxide and water. The reaction also produces oxygen, replenishing the atmosphere.
    B. Structural elements of plants (carbon, hydrogen, oxygen) are derived from air and water. Other nutrients come from the soil. Energy is supplied by the sun.
        1. Using other nutrients, particularly compounds of nitrogen and phosphorus, plants can convert the sugars produced by photosynthesis to proteins, fats, and other chemicals that we use as food.
    C. In early agricultural societies nearly all the energy used came from renewable resources.
        1. Much of the energy obtained from food was used to produce food.
        2. One unit of human work energy might produce 10 units of food energy.
    D. Early societies usually recycled nutrients by returning wastes to the soil.
        1. Properly practiced, this kind of agriculture could be continued for centuries without seriously depleting the soil, but farming on this level supports relatively few people.
        2. Making use of fertilizers, pesticides, and energy from fossil fuels, modern high-production farming has greatly expanded yields.

20.1   Farming with Chemicals: Fertilizers
    A. The three primary plant nutrients are nitrogen, phosphorus, and potassium.
        1. Plants cannot use N_2 directly, but some bacteria can fix nitrogen (convert it to a combined, soluble form).
            a. Lightning also "fixes" nitrogen.
        2. Plants take up nitrogen as nitrate (NO_3^-) or ammonium ions (NH_4^+) which combine with carbon compounds from photosynthesis to form the amino acids that make up proteins.
        3. Population growth in the late nineteenth century led to an increased demand for fertilizers.
    B. Fritz Haber developed a process for combining nitrogen and hydrogen to make ammonia.
    C. By oxidizing part of the ammonia molecule to nitric acid and reacting the acid with ammonia, the Germans were able to make ammonium nitrate, an explosive.
        1. Ammonium nitrate is a valuable nitrogen fertilizer.
        2. Ammonia can also be combined with carbon dioxide to make urea.
    D. Phosphorus fertilizers.
        1. The limiting factor in plant growth is often the availability of phosphorus.

a. Plants incorporate phosphates into DNA and RNA and other compounds essential to plant growth.

b. In the 1840s, chemists learned how to treat animal bones with sulfuric acid to form soluble superphosphate.

c. Most modern phosphate fertilizers are produced by treating phosphate rock with phosphoric acid, which produces water-soluble calcium dihydrogen phosphate.

2. Phosphate reserves are limited and not renewable; phosphates are scattered and lost through use.

E. Potassium fertilizers.

1. Plants use potassium as the K^+ ion.

2. The role of potassium ions, along with sodium ions, in plants is related to fluid balance in cells, the formation and transport of carbohydrates, and the assembly of proteins from amino acids.

3. Uptake of potassium ions from the soil leaves the soil acidic.

a. Each time a potassium ion enters the root tip, a hydronium ion enters the soil to maintain electrical balance.

4. The potassium in fertilizers is usually in the form of potassium chloride (KCl), which is mined in many parts of the world.

5. Potassium salts are a nonrenewable resource; they are scattered and lost through use.

F. Other essential elements.

1. Three secondary nutrients (magnesium, calcium, and sulfur) are needed in moderate amounts.

a. Calcium, in the form of lime (CaO), is used primarily to neutralize acidic soils.

b. Magnesium ions (Mg^{2+}) are incorporated into chlorophyll molecules which are necessary for photosynthesis.

c. Sulfur is a constituent of several amino acids and is necessary for protein synthesis.

2. Plants need eight other micronutrients (boron, copper, iron, manganese, molybdenum, nickel, zinc, and chloride) in small amounts.

G. Fertilizers: a mixed bag.

1. Complete fertilizers contain the three main nutrients.

a. The first number on the fertilizer represents the percent nitrogen.

b. The second is phosphorus calculated as percent P_2O_5.

c. The third is potassium calculated as percent K_2O.

2. To be used by plants, nutrients must be soluble in water.

a. Nutrients are washed into streams and lakes, where they stimulate algal blooms.

b. Nitrates also enter the groundwater.

H. Organic fertilizers.

1. "Organic" means the fertilizers come from natural animal and plant products.

2. Organic fertilizers generally must be broken down by soil organisms to release the actual nutrients that the plants use, which can be a slow process.

3. Organic material has the advantage of providing humus, a substance consisting of partially decayed plant or animal matter.

a. Humus improves the texture of soils, thus improving water retention, reducing the loss of nutrients through leaching, and helping to resist erosion.

b. Fresh human manure should not be used to fertilize fruits and vegetables to avoid the possibility of transmitting human pathogens.

c. Pig, dog, and cat feces should not be used as fertilizers because they can carry internal parasitic worms from those animals to humans.

Answers to Self-Assessment Questions

1. d   Nitrogen is taken up in the form of NO_3^-.
2. c   In fertilizer labels, N P K means nitrogen, phosphorus, and potassium.
3. c   The third number in the fertilizer label 24-5-10 represents 10% K_2O.
4. b $(NH_4)_2HPO_4$ furnishes two primary plant nutrients, nitrogen and phosphorus.
5. a   Anhydrous ammonia is made from H_2 and N_2.
6. c   Phosphate rock is treated with H_2SO_4 to make it more available to plants.
7. b   The secondary plant nutrients are Ca, Mg, and S.
8. d Mg^{2+} is essential to the function of chlorophyll.

20.2   The War against Pests
   A. Since the earliest recorded days, insect pests have destroyed crops and spread disease.
      1. The use of modern chemical pesticides (substances that kill organisms that we consider pests) may be all that stands between us and some insect-borne plagues.
      2. Pesticides prevent consumption of a major portion of our food supply by insects and other pests.
   B. Early insecticides included lead and arsenic compounds, pyrethrum, and nicotine sulfate.
      1. Only a few insects are harmful; many are beneficial.
         a. Most pesticides are indiscriminate; they kill both harmful and beneficial insects.
         b. Because pesticides kill living things, they should be classified as biocides (substances that kill living things) rather than insecticides (substances that kill insects).
   C. DDT: the dream insecticide.
      1. DDT, a chlorinated hydrocarbon, was found to be effective against a variety of insects and of low toxicity to humans.
      2. DDT is easily synthesized from cheap, readily available chemicals.
         a. Chlorobenzene and chloral hydrate are warmed in the presence of sulfuric acid to produce DDT.
      3. The World Health Organization estimates that chlorinated hydrocarbon pesticides such as DDT have saved 25 million lives and prevented hundreds of millions of illnesses.
      4. It was soon found that many insects developed a resistance to DDT; they are able to detoxify it.
         a. DDT has been banned in most developed countries, but it is still used in many developing countries.
      5. DDT is especially toxic to fish and birds. It interferes with calcium metabolism, making eggshells weak and easily broken. This was described by Rachel Carson in *Silent Spring*.
      6. DDT and its metabolites break down very slowly in the environment, a situation known as pesticide persistence.
      7. Chlorinated hydrocarbons, such as DDT and PCBs, are generally unreactive, so they remain on plants for long periods of time.
   D. Safer pesticides through green chemistry.
      1. Chemists are aiming to reduce the environmental impact of processes for making pesticides, including less hazardous chemical synthesis through use of catalytic reagents, energy-efficient processes, and safer solvents.
      2. Many pesticides are designed to be biodegradable.
   E. Biological magnification: concentration in fatty tissues.
      1. Because they are fat-soluble, chlorinated hydrocarbons tend to become concentrated in animals higher on the food chain, a process known as biological magnification.
      2. DDT and other chlorinated hydrocarbons such as PCBs are nerve poisons, and DDT interferes with calcium metabolism essential to the formation of healthy bones and teeth.
      3. DDT is still used in some countries where malaria and typhus are great health problems.

a. It is applied mainly on the inside walls of houses, so the environmental impact is much less than that of the earlier widespread use of DDT in agriculture.

b. In 2000, more than 120 countries signed a treaty to phase out persistent organic pollutants (POPs), a group of chemicals that includes DDT.

F. Organophosphorus compounds.

1. Chlorinated hydrocarbon pesticides have been replaced in part by organic phosphorus compounds such as malathion, parathion, and diazinon.

2. Organophosphorus compounds are nerve poisons; they interfere with the conduction of nerve signals in insects.

3. These compounds generally are more toxic to mammals but less persistent in the environment, therefore, residues are seldom found in food.

    a. Malathion is an exception in that it is less toxic than DDT.

G. Carbamates: targeting the pest.

1. Like phosphorus compounds, carbamates are nerve poisons, but they act over a shorter span of time.

2. Most carbamates, such as carbaryl, carbofuran, and aldicarb, are narrow-spectrum insecticides, directed against only a few insect species.

    a. Chlorinated hydrocarbons and organic phosphorus compounds are broad-spectrum insecticides; they are effective against many species.

       i. Carbaryl is especially harmful to honeybees.

3. Carbamates break down rapidly in the environment and do not accumulate in fatty tissue.

H. Organic pesticides.

1. Organic pesticides (use of materials derived from natural sources rather than made synthetically) include:

    a. Insecticidal soap which breaks down the insect's outer covering.

    b. Pyrethrins obtained from the perennial plant pyrethrum, which are low in toxicity to most mammals.

    c. Rotenone, a natural product obtained from the roots and stems of several tropical and subtropical plants.

    d. Boric acid, used mainly to control ants and cockroaches, but is moderately toxic to humans.

    e. Cryolite, used on food crops and ornamental plants to block caterpillars and other grazing insects from feeding.

    f. Diatomaceous earth, the fossilized remains of a type of algae whose shells consist largely of silica.

    g. Rania, a botanical insecticide obtained from a tropical plant which is highly toxic to caterpillars of fruit moths, codling moths, and corn earworms.

2. Just because a product is considered organic doesn't mean it is safe.

    a. Some insecticides are as toxic as, or more so than some synthetic pesticides.

I. Biological insect controls.

1. The use of natural enemies is another way of controlling pests.

    a. These biological controls include predatory insects, mites, and mollusks; parasitic insects; and microbial controls which are insect pathogens such as bacteria, viruses, fungi, and nematodes.

2. One highly successful biological approach is the breeding of insect- and fungus-resistant plants.

J. Sterile insect technique.

1. *Sterile insect technique (SIT)* is a method of insect control that involves rearing large numbers of males, sterilizing them with radiation or chemicals or by cross-breeding, and then releasing them in areas of infestation.

      a.   Successful SIT programs have been conducted against screwworm, the Mediterranean fruit fly, and the codling moth.

   K. Pheromones: the sex trap.
      1. A pheromone is a chemical that is secreted externally by an insect to mark a trail, send an alarm, or attract a mate.
         a.   Insect sex attractants are usually secreted by females to attract males.
      2. Most sex attractants have complicated structures, and all are secreted in extremely tiny amounts.
      3. Pheronomes are usually too expensive to play a huge role in insect control, though the use of recombinant DNA methods to synthesize them holds promise for future work.
   L. Juvenile hormones.
      1. Juvenile hormones control the rate of development of young insects.
      2. Synthesis of juvenile hormones is difficult and expensive, and they can only be used against insects that are pests at the adult stage.

Answers to Self-Assessment Questions

1.	c	A pesticide is a product that kills other organisms as well as the target.
2.	d	Spraying pesticides may result in pesticides ending up in rivers and lakes.
3.	d	Through the process of biomagnification, osprey will have the highest level of pesticides.
4.	b	Compared to DDT, organic phosphorus insecticides are less persistent and more toxic.
5.	c	The SIT method of insect control works best when large numbers of males can be sterilized and then released in areas of infestation.
6.	d	A pheromone, or sex attractant, is usually produced by a female to attract a male.
7.	b	Using ladybugs and praying mantises to control insect pests is a way of allowing natural enemies to control insect populations.

20.3   Herbicides and Defoliants
   A. Herbicides are used to kill weeds.
      1. Some herbicides are defoliants, which cause leaves to fall off plants.
   B. 2,4-D and 2,4,5-T.
      1. It wasn't until the introduction of 2,4-D in 1945 that the use of herbicides became common.
      2. 2,4-D and its derivatives are growth-regulator herbicides, which are especially effective against newly emerged, rapidly growing broad-leaved plants.
         a.   One 2,4-D derivative, 2,4,5-T, is especially effective against woody plants and works by defoliation.
      3. Agent Orange, a mixture of 2,4-D and 2,4,5-T, was used in Vietnam to remove enemy cover and destroy crops.
      4. Herbicide contaminants called dioxins are thought to cause birth defects.
      5. Continuing concern about dioxin contamination led the EPA to ban 2,4,5-T in 1985.
   C. Atrazine and glyphosate.
      1. Atrazine kills plants by stopping the electron transfer reactions of photosynthesis.
         a.   When atrazine is used in corn fields, the corn plants deactivate atrazine and are not killed. Weeds cannot deactivate atrazine and are killed.
      2. Glyphosate, a derivative of the amino acid glycine, kills all vegetation.
         a.   Genetically modified soybeans, corn, alfalfa, and other plants that are resistant to glyphosate have been developed.
         b.   Widespread use of glyphosate has resulted in many glyphosate-resistant weeds.
   D. Paraquat: a preemergent herbicide.
      1. A preemergent herbicide is one used to kill weed plants before crop seedlings emerge.

2. Paraquat inhibits photosynthesis in all plants but is rapidly broken down in the soil.
E. Organic herbicides.
   1. Herbicides made from natural ingredients do not work as rapidly or as well as synthetic herbicides, and may need to be used in fairly high concentrations, making them expensive for widespread use.

Answers to Self-Assessment Questions

1.   d   The harmful component in Agent Orange was dioxin found in 2,4,5-T.
2.   d   The herbicide atrazine acts by inhibiting photosynthesis.
3.   b   Glyphosate can be used to kill grasses shortly before other plants are sown because it is metabolized by soil bacteria.

20.4   Sustainable Agriculture
A. Sustainable agriculture is the ability of a farm to produce food and fiber indefinitely, without causing irreparable damage to the ecosystem.
   1. Sustainable agriculture has three main goals: a healthy environment, farm profitability, and social and economic equity.
   2. Sustainable agriculture is similar to the practices that organic farmers and gardeners have followed for generations.
   3. Modern agriculture is energy intensive.
   4. Organic farming is carried out without synthetic fertilizers or pesticides.
   5. Organic farms use less energy, but they require more human labor (a renewable resource) than conventional farms.
   6. In addition to organic practices, sustainable agriculture involves buying local products and using local services when possible, cutting down transportation costs.

Answers to Self-Assessment Questions

1.   d   Sustainable agriculture is farming that meets human needs without degrading or depleting the environment.
2.   d   Organic farming differs from conventional agriculture in that organic farmers use no synthetic pesticides.

20.5   Some Malthusian Mathematics
A. In 1830, Thomas Malthus predicted that population would increase faster than the food supply, and that unless the birth rate was controlled, poverty and war would have to serve as restrictions on the increase.
   1. In arithmetic growth, a constant amount is added in each time period.
   2. In geometric growth, the increment increases in size for each time period.
   3. The doubling time for a population growing geometrically can be calculated using the Rule of 72: Doubling time = 72/percentage of annual growth
B. Can we feed a hungry world?
   1. The United Nations Population Division project that Earth's population will reach 9 billion in 2045.
   2. Food production can be increased through genetic engineering.
   3. Even quadrupling current food production would meet our needs for only a few decades.
      a. Virtually all the world's available arable land is now under cultivation.
      b. We lose farmland every day to housing, roads, erosion, encroaching deserts, and increasing salt content of irrigated soils.

4. Despite a growing movement toward sustainable agriculture, we are still greatly dependent on a high-energy form of agriculture that uses synthetic fertilizers, pesticides, and herbicides and depends on machinery that burns fossil fuels.

Answers to Self-Assessment Questions

1. c   The rapid population growth that has occurred since 1500 is due in large part to the use of scientific agricultural practices.
2. b   Use the rule of 72 to solve this: doubling time = 72/3.59 = 20 years. At the current rate of population growth, Uganda's population will double in 20 years.

LEARNING OBJECTIVES

You should be able to...

1.   List the three primary plant nutrients as well as several secondary nutrients and micronutrients, and describe the function of each.   (20.1)

2.   Differentiate between organic fertilizers and conventional fertilizers.   (20.1)

3.   Name and describe the action of the main kinds of pesticides.   (20.2)

4.   List several biological pest controls, and explain how they work.   (20.2)

5.   Name and describe the action of the major herbicides and defoliants.   (20.3)

6.   Describe sustainable agriculture and organic farming.   (20.4)

7.   Calculate the doubling time for a population using the rule of 72.   (20.5)

8.   Identify the benefits of pesticides to humans and the challenges in their use.

9.   Give examples of pesticides that have been designed to reduce the hazards to humans and the environment.

DISCUSSION

In this chapter we consider the chemical requirements for healthy plants, and describe some of the threats to successful agriculture, in the form of pests and weeds. The use of modern of pesticides and herbicides has helped increase crop production but has also presented environmental challenges. Organic farming avoids the use of synthetic pesticides and herbicides, allowing for much more sustainable agricultural practices. According to Malthus, food production grows arithmetically while population grows geometrically so food production cannot keep up with population growth into the future. Additional scientific and technical advances may help increase food production or control population growth but, at present, the prospect of food shortages is real. Applying green chemistry principles to the development of pesticides and herbicides has reduced the environmental threats caused by use of those crop-enhancing products.

EXAMPLE PROBLEMS

1. The LD_{50} of the herbicide paraquat is 150 mg/kg orally in rats. If its toxicity in humans is comparable, what is the lethal dose for a 50-kg (110-lb.) person?

    Lethal dose = (50 kg person)(150 mg paraquat/kg person) = 7500 mg paraquat

2. In 1986 it was estimated that world population growth had dropped to an annual rate of 1.7%. At this rate, how long will it be before the world population has doubled? Use the Rule of 72:

$$\frac{72}{1.7} = 42 \text{ years}$$

ADDITIONAL PROBLEMS

1. The United States population was estimated in 1986 to be increasing at a rate of 0.8% per year (excluding illegal immigration). At that rate, when will the population have doubled?

2. The LD_{50} of pyrethrins is 1.2 g/kg orally in rats. If its toxicity in humans is similar, what is the lethal dose for a 70-kg person?

ANSWERS TO ODD-NUMBERED REVIEW QUESTIONS AND SOLUTIONS FOR ODD-NUMBERED END OF CHAPTER PROBLEMS

Review Questions

1. Most of the matter of a growing plant comes from carbon dioxide and water.

3. A preemergent herbicide is one used to kill weed plants before crop seedlings emerge.

5. Malthus predicted that population would increase faster than the food supply. He stated that unless the birthrate was controlled, poverty and wars would serve as population restrictions.

Problems

7. The three structural elements of a plant are carbon, hydrogen, and oxygen.

9. Nitrogen (N_2) can be converted into a soluble form such as ammonia by lightning, bacterial action, and industrial production from hydrogen and nitrogen using the Haber process.

11. Anhydrous ammonia is gaseous ammonia that has been compressed until it liquefies ("anhydrous" means "without water"). Anhydrous ammonia is compressed and stored in tanks from which it is applied directly to the soil as fertilizer.

13. Phosphate fertilizers are made from phosphate rock treated with phosphoric acid to make calcium dihydrogen phosphate. Phosphorus plays an important role in the energy-transfer processes of photosynthesis.

15. DDT is easily synthesized from cheap, readily available chemicals and is very effective against a variety of insect pests. Following its use, DDT-resistant houseflies were reported, as was DDT's toxicity to fish. In addition, DDT causes birds to produce eggs with thin shells, and very low concentrations of DDT interfere with the growth of plankton and the reproduction of crustaceans such as shrimp. Finally, DDT remains toxic long after its initial application.

17. Chlorinated hydrocarbons are soluble in fats and bioaccumulate as one species feeds on those lower in the food chain.

19. Pheromones are chemicals secreted to mark a trail, send an alarm, or attract a mate. They attract male insects into traps, allowing a determination of which pests are present and the level of the infestation. Workers can then undertake measures to minimize crop damage.

21. Sterile insect technique (SIT) is a method of insect control that involves rearing large numbers of males, sterilizing them with radiation, chemicals or by cross-breeding, and then releasing them in areas of infestation. SIT is not widely used because it is very expensive and time consuming.

23. mass of DDT that would kill a 70-kg individual = (70 kg)(0.5 g DDT/kg body weight) = 35 g.

25. Arithmetic growth occurs when a constant amount is added each growth period. For example, adding $10.00 to a savings account each week.

27. number of months = ($1000)(1 month/$50) = 20 months. This is an example of arithmetic growth.

29. Apply the rule of 72. Doubling time, yr = 72/1.344 = 53.6 years. Factors likely to change this rate are changes in birth rate or death rate (war, famine, etc.)

31. $6 CO_2 + 6 H_2O \rightarrow C_6H_{12}O_6 + 6 O_2$.

33.
1. Boric acid is an example of (b) – it is not an organic compound but is used in organic farming.
2. diatomaceous earth is (b) used in organic farming but not an organic chemical.
3. lead arsenate is (d) – neither organic and not used in organic farming.
4. malathion is (a) – organic in a chemical sense but not used in organic farming.
5. rotenone is (c) – an organic compound used in organic farming.

35.
a. Ammonium monohydrogen phosphate supplies nitrogen and phosphorus.
b. $2 NH_3 + H_3PO_4 \rightarrow (NH_4)_2HPO_4$

37.
a. The sex attractant for codling moths contains two C=C bonds (alkene) and an alcohol.
b. The juvenile hormone molecule contains an epoxide (a cyclic ether), two C=C bonds (alkene), and an ester group.
c. A methoprene molecule contains an ether, two C=C bonds (alkene), and an ester group.

39. You would receive 1 +2 +4 +8 +16 +32 +64 +128 +256 +512 +1,024 +2,048 +4,096 +8,192 +16,384 +32,768 +65,536 +131,072 +262,144 +524,288 +1,048,576 +2,097,152 +4,194,304 +8,388,608 +16,777,216 +33,554,432 +67,108,864 +134,217,728 +268,435,456 +536,870,912 =1,073,741,824 cents, or $10,737,418.24. Note: another way of calculating this is to compute 2^{30}.

41. The reactions are

$$K_2CO_3 + CO_2 + H_2O \rightarrow 2\,KHCO_3$$
$$\text{Electrolysis: } 2\,KCl(aq) + 2H_2O(l) \rightarrow 2\,KOH(aq) + H_2(g) + Cl_2(g)$$
$$2\,KOH + CO_2 \rightarrow K_2CO_3 + H_2O$$

Because these reactions do not occur in nature, potassium bicarbonate made by these reactions is not organic.

43. Use the rule of 72. Doubling time = $72/4.31 = 16.7$ years. Factors likely to change this rate are changes in birth rate or death rate (war, famine, etc.)

45. The answers are a and b. Farmers use pesticides both to increase food production and to reduce the chance of crop failure.

47. The answer is d. All of the benefits listed in choices a, b, and c are gained through the application of green chemistry principles to the design of pesticides.

Household Chemicals

Helps and Hazards

CHAPTER SUMMARY

21.1 Cleaning with Soap
   A. Personal cleanliness.
      1. In developing societies, clothes were cleaned by beating them with rocks in a stream.
         a. Sometimes saponins, soapy compounds found in the leaves of soapworts and soapberry plants, were used as the first detergents.
      2. Plant ashes contain potassium carbonate and sodium carbonate, compounds that react with water to form an alkaline solution with detergent properties.
         a. These alkaline ashes were used by Babylonians 4,000 years ago.
         b. Europeans used plant ashes to wash their clothes as recently as 100 years ago.
         c. Sodium carbonate is still sold today as washing soda.
   B. Fat + lye → soap.
      1. Sodium hydroxide, also called lye, is produced by heating sodium carbonate (produced by the evaporation of alkaline water) with lime (from limestone or seashells).
         $$Na_2CO_3 + Ca(OH)_2 \rightarrow 2\,NaOH + CaCO_3$$
      2. Sodium hydroxide was heated with animal fats or vegetable oils to produce soap.
         a. Soaps are the salts of a long-chain carboxylic acid.
         b. In modern commercial soap-making, fats and oils are often hydrolyzed to fatty acids and glycerol with superheated steam and the fatty acids are then neutralized to make soaps.
            i. Hand soaps usually contain additives such as dyes, perfumes, creams, and oils.
            ii. Scouring soaps contain abrasives such as silica and pumice.
            iii. Some soaps have air blown in before they solidify to lower their density so they float.
            iv. Potassium soaps are softer than sodium soaps and produce a finer lather, so they are used alone or in combination with sodium soaps in liquid soaps and shaving creams.
      3. Soaps used in shampoos and other cosmetics are also made by reacting fatty acids with triethanolamine.
   C. How soap works.
      1. Oil and greases hold dirt to skin and fabrics.
      2. Soap has an ionic (water-soluble) end and a hydrocarbon (oil-soluble) end.
         a. Soap molecules break oils into tiny globules called micelles by sticking their hydrocarbon tails into the oil while the ionic heads remain in the aqueous phase.

        b.   The oil droplets don't coalesce owing to the repulsion of the charged groups.
    3.   The oil and water form an emulsion, with soap acting as the emulsifying agent.
    4.   Any agent, including soap that stabilizes the suspension of nonpolar substances, such as oil and grease, in water is called a surface-active agent (or surfactant).
  D. Disadvantage and advantages of soaps.
    1.   "Hard" water contains calcium, magnesium, or iron ions, which form insoluble salts with the fatty acid anions that precipitate as "bathtub ring."
    2.   Soap is an excellent cleanser in soft water, it is relatively nontoxic, it is derived from renewable resources (animal fats and vegetable oils), and it is biodegradable.
  E. Water softeners.
    1.   Water softeners are used to remove calcium, magnesium, and iron ions from water.
    2.   Sodium carbonate (washing soda) acts in two ways.
        a.   It makes the water basic so that the fatty acids won't precipitate.
        b.   The carbonate ions precipitate the hard-water ions and keep them from forming soap scum.
    3.   Trisodium phosphate acts similarly to sodium carbonate.
        a.   It makes the water basic.
        b.   The phosphate ions precipitate calcium and magnesium ions.
    4.   Water softening tanks absorb the calcium, magnesium, and iron ions on polymeric resins, exchanging them with sodium ions to soften the water.

Answers to Self-Assessment Questions

1.   b   Saponins are plant materials that lather in water.
2.   c $CH_3(CH_2)_{14}COONa$ is a soap formula.
3.   c   The reaction of tripalmitin with NaOH gives $CH_3(CH_2)_{14}COONa$.
4.   c   The formula for sodium stearate is $CH_3(CH_2)_{16}COONa$.
5.   b   The hydrocarbon portion of a surfactant molecule is hydrophobic.
6.   d   When used in cleaning, soap removes oily dirt by forming micelles.
7.   a   In the cleansing action of soap, the nonpolar hydrocarbon tail intermingles with the nonpolar oily dirt, and the ionic head with the polar water.
8.   d   Hard water contains Ca^{2+}, Mg^{2+}, and Fe^{2+} ions. These are exchanged for Na^+ ions (which do not precipitate soaps) in a water softener.
9.   d   The calcium and magnesium salts of soaps are insoluble in water, so they precipitate out and are not available to clean.

  21.2   Synthetic Detergents
  A. ABS detergents: nondegradable.
    1.   Alkylbenzenesulfonate (ABS) detergents were derived from propylene, benzene, and sulfuric acid, followed by neutralization.
        a.   ABS detergents worked well in acidic and hard waters but were not degraded by microorganisms in wastewater treatment plants or in nature, threatening the groundwater supply.
        b.   Foaming rivers led to their ban and replacement with biodegradable detergents.
  B. LAS detergents: biodegradable.
    1.   Linear alkylsulfonates (LAS) are derived from ethylene, benzene, and sulfuric acid, followed by neutralization.
        a.   LAS detergents are biodegradable.
        b.   They work better than soap in acidic solution and in hard water.
           i.   Their calcium and magnesium salts are soluble and do not precipitate out, even in extremely hard water.

C. Laundry detergent formulations.
   1. Detergent products used in homes and commercial laundries usually contain a variety of ingredients.
      a. Surface-active agents (surfactants) are substances that stabilize the suspension of nonpolar substances in water.
      b. In addition to surfactants, modern detergent formulations contain builders (substances such as phosphates and sodium carbonate that increase the detergency of phosphates), brighteners, fabric softeners, and other substances that lessen the redeposition of dirt or reduce the cost.
      c. Surfactants enable the cleaning solution to wet the surface to be cleaned.
         i. They loosen and remove soil.
         ii. They emulsify oily soils to keep them dispersed and suspended so that they do not settle back on the surface.
   2. Surfactants are classified according to the ionic charge, if any, on their working part.
      a. Soaps and ABS and LAS detergents are all anionic surfactants; they have a negative charge on the active part.
         i. Anionic surfactants are used in laundry and hand dishwashing detergents, household cleaners, and personal cleansing products.
      b. Nonionic surfactants have no electrical charge.
         i. They are low sudsing and are not affected by water hardness.
         ii. They are typically used in laundry and automatic dishwasher formulations.
      c. Cationic surfactants have a positive charge on the active part.
         i. These surfactants are not particularly good detergents but they do have germicidal properties.
         ii. They are used as cleansers and disinfectants in the food and dairy industries and as sanitizing agents in some household cleaners.
      d. Amphoteric surfactants carry both a positive and a negative charge.
         i. They react with other acids and bases and are noted for their mildness, sudsing, and stability.
         ii. They are used in personal cleansing products such as shampoos for babies and in household cleaning products such as liquid hand-washing soaps.
   3. Any substance added to a surfactant to increase its detergency is called a builder.
      a. Most builders are water softeners and may include phosphates.
         i. Many locales have banned the use of phosphates because they promote eutrophication of lakes.
      b. Other builders include zeolites, complex aluminosilicates that tie up the hard-water ions.
   4. Almost all detergents include fluorescent dyes called optical brighteners.
      a. Optical brighteners make clothes appear brighter by absorbing ultraviolet light (invisible) and reemitting it as blue light (visible).
      b. Optical brighteners appear to have low toxicity to humans but do cause skin rashes in some people.
   5. Some detergent formulations include lipases (enzymes that work on lipids) to help remove fats, oils, and blood.
D. Dishwashing detergents.
   1. Liquid detergents for washing dishes by hand generally contain one or more surfactants; few contain builders, but they may contain enzymes to help remove greases and protein stains.
   2. Detergents for automatic dishwashers are different than those for hand dishwashing.
      a. They are often strongly alkaline (some contain sodium hydroxide) and should never be used for hand dishwashing.

b. They depend mainly on their strong alkalis, heat, and on vigorous agitation of the machine for cleaning.

Answers to Self-Assessment Questions

1. b   The hydrocarbon chain of ABS is branched and resistant to biodegradation.
2. c $CH_3(CH_2)_9CH(CH_3)C_6H_4SO_3Na$ is an LAS detergent.
3. b   Carbonate ions (CO_3^{2-}) react with water to form HCO_3^-(aq) and OH^-(aq).
4. a   Hard water ions react with carbonate ions to form products such as $CaCO_3$(s).
5. b   An ion exchange resin retains hardness ions (Ca^{2+}, Mg^{2+}, and Fe^{2+}) when it softens water.
6. b   An optical brightener converts ultraviolet light to blue light.
7. c   Amylase, which catalyzes the breakdown of starch, works on stains from foods such as potatoes, pasta, and rice.
8. a   Lipase catalyzes the breakdown of stains from fats and oils.
9. b   Protease catalyzes the breakdown of protein stains such as those from blood and eggs.
10. d   Cocamido DEA is a nonionic detergent.
11. a   Because it is so alkaline, detergent for automatic dishwashers is the most likely to irritate skin.

21.3   Laundry Auxiliaries: Softeners and Bleaches
   A. Fabric softeners.
      1. The working part of a cationic surfactant is a positive ion.
      2. Most cationic surfactants are quaternary ammonium salts; they have four alkyl groups attached to a nitrogen atom that has a positive charge.
      3. Quaternary ammonium salts with two long hydrocarbon tails (and two smaller groups on nitrogen) act as fabric softeners.
         a. They form a film on fibers, lubricating them for flexibility and softness.
   B. Laundry bleaches: whiter whites.
      1. Bleaches are oxidizing agents that remove stains from fabrics.
      2. There are two main types of laundry bleaches: chlorine bleaches and oxygen bleaches.
         a. Liquid laundry bleaches ("chlorine bleaches") are dilute solutions of sodium hypochlorite (NaOCl).
            i.   These solutions release chlorine rapidly and can damage fabrics and turn polyester fabrics yellow.
            ii. "Ultra" chlorine bleaches have a higher concentration of NaOCl.
         b. Solid bleaches release chlorine slowly in water to minimize damage to fabrics.
      3. Oxygen-releasing bleaches usually contain sodium percarbonate or sodium perborate.
         a. In hot water they release hydrogen peroxide which acts as a strong oxidizing agent.
         b. Borates are somewhat toxic.
      4. Bleaches work by acting on certain light-absorbing chemical groups, called chromophores, which cause a substance to be colored.

Answers to Self-Assessment Questions

1. d $CH_3(CH_2)_{16}CH_2N^+(CH_3)_2CH_2(CH_2)_{16}CH_3Cl^-$ could serve as a fabric softener. Note the two long alkyl chains attached to the nitrogen atom.
2. d   Quaternary ammonium compounds are the most common fabric softeners.
3. c   Bleaches are oxidizing agents.
4. c   NaOCl is the main component of household bleach, often called "chlorine bleach."
5. c $NaBO_2 \cdot H_2O_2$ is an "oxygen bleach."
6. d   Bleaches act by oxidizing chromophores.

21.4   All-Purpose and Special-Purpose Cleaning Products
  A. All-purpose cleaners.
      1. All-purpose cleaners for use in water may contain surfactants, sodium carbonate,
          ammonia, solvent-type grease cutters, disinfectants, bleaches, deodorants, and other
          ingredients.
      2. Household ammonia has many uses.
          a. It can be used undiluted to loosen baked-on grease, burned-on food, or diluted to
              clean glass.
          b. Mixed with detergent, ammonia removes wax from linoleum.
      3. Baking soda is a mild abrasive cleanser which absorbs odors from refrigerators and
          freezers.
      4. Vinegar is a good grease cutter but should not be used on marble because it reacts with
          marble causing surface pitting.
  B. Hazards of mixing cleaners.
      1. Mixing bleach with other household chemicals can be quite dangerous.
          a. Mixing hypochlorite bleach with hydrochloric acid produces poisonous chlorine gas.
              i.   Mixing bleach with toilet bowl cleaners that contain HCl is especially dangerous
                   because bathrooms are seldom well-ventilated.
          b. Mixing bleach with ammonia is extremely hazardous because two of the gases
              produced are chloramine (NH_2Cl) and hydrazine (NH_2NH_2), both of which are toxic.
  C. Special-purpose cleaners.
      1. Toilet bowl cleaners are acids that dissolve the "lime" build-up that forms in toilet bowls.
          a. Solid crystalline cleaners usually contain sodium bisulfate ($NaHSO_4$) and the liquid
              cleaners include hydrochloric acid, citric acid, or some other acidic material.
      2. Most scouring powder cleansers contain an abrasive such as silica (SiO_2) that scrapes soil
          from hard surfaces and a surfactant to dissolve grease.
          a. Some scouring powders include bleach.
          b. Scouring powders can scratch surfaces.
      3. Glass cleaners are volatile liquids that evaporate without leaving a residue.
          a. A common glass cleaner is isopropyl alcohol (rubbing alcohol) diluted with water.
          b. Most commercial glass cleaners contain ammonia or vinegar.
      4. Drain cleaners often contain sodium hydroxide, either in solid form or as a concentrated
          liquid.
          a. Sodium hydroxide reacts with water to generate heat which melts the grease that was
              clogging the pipes.
          b. Some products also contain bits of aluminum metal that react with the sodium
              hydroxide solution to form hydrogen gas which bubbles out of the clogged area,
              creating a stirring action.
          c. Many liquid drain cleaners contain bleach (NaOCl), as well as concentrated sodium
              hydroxide.
      5. The active ingredient in most oven cleaners is sodium hydroxide.
          a. Sodium hydroxide converts greasy deposits to soap.
      6. Hand sanitizers contain a high concentration of alcohol which kills bacteria and
          evaporates rapidly during use, leaving hands clean and dry.
          a. A surfactant provides additional germicidal properties, and a thickening agent makes
              the sanitizer easier to apply.
      7. Home mechanics use waterless hand cleaners with lanolin, pumice, an oil with a
          fragrance, and a surfactant.
      8. Green cleaners generally have more ingredients derived from plants.
          a. While more of the ingredients in these products come from plants, the lack of
              regulations makes green cleaners difficult to evaluate.

D. Practicing green chemistry at home.
   1. Buy and use only what you need.
   2. Choose safer products.
   3. Choose products that minimize depletion of resources.
   4. Select reusable, recyclable, or readily degradable materials when possible.
   5. Keep informed about new developments and product safety regulations.
   6. Prevent accidents by reading product labels, using proper protective gear, maximizing ventilation, and choosing the safest products.

Answers to Self-Assessment Questions

1. a Household ammonia cannot be safely used for cleaning aluminum because it erodes the surface.
2. c Vinegar cannot be safely used for polishing marble surfaces because it causes pitting.
3. d Baking soda (sodium bicarbonate) cannot be used safely for neutralizing bleach.
4. c Mixing vinegar and ammonia together forms ammonium acetate, a salt.
5. d Mixing hypochlorite bleach and an acid forms toxic Cl_2 gas.
6. d Mixing hypochlorite bleach and ammonia forms chloramine and hydrazine, which are both toxic gases.
7. a Lime ($CaCO_3$) deposits in toilet bowls are best removed by treatment with HCl.
8. a The most effective way to keep drains open is to keep grease and hair from going down them.

21.5 Solvents, Paints, and Waxes
   A. Solvents.
      1. Solvents are used to remove paint, varnish, adhesives, waxes, and other materials.
         a. Most organic solvents are volatile and flammable, and many have toxic fumes.
         b. Long-term sniffing of the fumes can cause permanent damage to vital organs, especially the lungs, as well as irreversible brain damage and heart failure.
   B. Paints.
      1. Paint is a broad term used to cover lacquers, enamels, varnishes, oil-base coatings, and a number of different water-base finishes.
      2. A paint contains three basic ingredients: a pigment, a binder, and a solvent.
         a. Titanium oxide, a brilliant white nontoxic pigment is used as the foundational pigment to which small amounts of colored pigments or dyes are added to achieve the desired color.
         b. The binder, or film former, is a substance that binds the pigment particles together and holds them on the painted surface.
            i. In oil paints the binder is usually tung oil or linseed oil (oil-based paints)
            ii. In water-based paints the binder is a latex-based polymer such as polyvinyl acetate.
         c. The solvents keep the paint fluid until it is applied to a surface and is usually alcohol, a hydrocarbon, an ester, or water.
         d. Paint may also contain additives: a drier (or activator) to make the paint dry faster, a fungicide to act as a preservative, a thickener to increase the paint's viscosity, an antiskinning agent to keep the paint from forming a skin inside the can, and a surfactant to stabilize the mixture and keep the pigment particles separated.
   C. Waxes
      1. A wax is an ester of long-chain, organic (fatty) acid and a long-chain alcohol.
         a. Waxes are produced by plants and animals mainly as protective coatings.
         b. Beeswax, carnauba wax, spermaceti wax, and lanolin are some examples.

Answers to Self-Assessment Questions

1. a   Organic solvents in household and commercial products are flammable.
2. c   The three basic components of a paint are a pigment, a solvent, and a binder.
3. d $CH_3(CH_2)_{14}COOCH_2(CH_2)_{28}CH_3$, an ester of a long-chain organic acid and a long-chain alcohol, is a wax.

21.6   Cosmetics: Personal Care Chemicals
   A. Cosmetics are defined by the U.S. Food, Drug, and Cosmetic Act of 1938 as "articles intended to be rubbed, poured, sprinkled, or sprayed on, introduced into, or otherwise applied to the human body or any part thereof, for cleansing, beautifying, promoting attractiveness, or altering the appearance."
       1. Soap, antiperspirants, and antidandruff shampoos are excluded from this definition.
       2. The main difference between drugs and cosmetics is that drugs must be proven safe and effective before they are marketed while cosmetics generally do not have to be tested before being marketed.
   B. Skin creams and lotions.
       1. Skin is the body's largest organ, with an area of about 18 ft².
       2. The outer layer of skin is the epidermis, divided into two layers: dead cells and the corneal layer.
           a. The corneal layer of the epidermis is mainly keratin, a tough, fibrous protein with a moisture content of about 10%.
           b. Below 10% moisture, skin is dry and flaky.
           c. Above 10% moisture, microorganisms flourish.
           d. Sebum (skin oils) protects the skin from loss of moisture.
       3. Lotions and creams are applied to the dead cells of the corneal layer.
           a. Lotions are emulsions of oil in water that help hold moisture in.
               i. Typical oils include mineral oil, petroleum jelly, and natural fats and oils.
           b. Creams are emulsions of water in oil that help hold moisture in.
           c. Creams and lotions protect the skin by coating and softening it.
               i. Emollients are skin softeners which provide a protective coating on the skin to prevent loss of moisture.
           d. Moisturizers that hold moisture in skin usually contain lanolin or collagen.
           e. Some cosmetics contain humectants which hold water by hydrogen bonding.
           f. Some cosmetics contain exfoliants which cause dead cells to fall off more rapidly than without them.
       4. Sunscreen lotions offer physical or chemical protection from ultraviolet radiation. The first common ingredient was *para*-aminobenzoic acid but it is seldom used today.
           a. Skin protection factors (SPF) indicate how many times longer a person can remain in the sun without burning.
   C. Lipsticks and lip balms.
       1. Lipsticks and lip balms are similar to skin creams in composition and function.
           a. They are made of an oil and a wax, with a higher proportion of wax than in creams to make them firmer than creams.
   D. Eye makeup.
       1. Various chemicals are used to decorate the eyes.
       2. Some people have allergic reactions to ingredients in eye makeup or get eye infections caused by bacterial contamination.
           a. It is recommended that eye makeup be discarded after 3 months.
   E. Nanoparticles in cosmetics.

1. The new technology promises new advantages and possible risks that will need to be evaluated.
F. Deodorants and antiperspirants.
   1. Deodorants contain perfume to mask body odor and a germicide to kill odor-causing bacteria.
   2. Antiperspirants retard perspiration.
      a. Nearly all antiperspirants have aluminum or zirconium chlorohydrate as the only active ingredient.
      b. Aluminum or zirconium chlorohydrate is an astringent; it constricts the openings of sweat glands.
G. Toothpaste: soap with grit and flavor.
   1. Toothpastes have two essential ingredients: a detergent and an abrasive.
      a. Sodium lauryl sulfate is a typical detergent used in toothpastes, but any pharmaceutical-grade soap or detergent is satisfactory.
      b. Other ingredients include flavors, colors, aromas, and sweeteners.
   2. Tooth decay is caused by bacteria that convert sugars to plaque, a biofilm composed of thousands of bacteria, small particles, proteins, and mucus deposited on teeth when they are not well cleaned.
   3. Fluorides harden tooth enamel, reducing the incidence of decay.
      a. Fluorides convert hydroxyapatite to fluorapatite, a harder material that is more resistant to decay.
   4. Hydrogen peroxide and baking soda are used to prevent gum disease, which is the major cause of adult tooth loss.
H. Perfumes, colognes, and aftershaves.
   1. Perfumes are among the most ancient and widely used cosmetics.
      a. A good perfume may have one hundred or more constituents.
      b. The components are divided into three categories, called notes, based on differences in volatility.
         i. The most volatile fraction is called the top note and is made up of relatively small molecules responsible for the odor when the perfume is first applied.
         ii. The middle not (or heart note) is intermediate in volatility and responsible for the lingering aroma after most of the top-note compounds have vaporized.
         iii. The end note (or base note) is the low-volatility fraction and is made up of compounds with large molecules, often with musky odors.
   2. A perfume usually consists of 10–25% fragrant compounds and fixatives dissolved in ethyl alcohol.
   3. Colognes are perfumes diluted with ethyl alcohol or an alcohol-water mixture.
      a. Colognes are only about one-tenth as strong as perfumes, usually containing only 1–2% perfume essence.
   4. Aftershave lotions are similar to colognes.
      a. Most are 50–70% ethanol, the remainder being water, perfume, and food coloring.
      b. Some contain menthol for a cooling effect on the skin; others contain an emollient to soothe chapped skin.
I. Some hairy chemistry.
   1. Hair is composed of the fibrous protein keratin.
   2. Protein molecules in hair are strongly held together by four types of forces.
      a. Hydrogen bonds—disrupted by water.
      b. Salt bridges—destroyed by changes in pH.
      c. Disulfide linkages—broken and destroyed by permanent wave and hair straightening treatments.
      d. Dispersion forces.

J. Shampoo.
  1. When hair is washed, the keratin absorbs water. The water disrupts hydrogen bonds and some salt bridges.
     a. The hair is softened and made more stretchable.
     b. Acids and bases are particularly disruptive to salt bridges, making pH control important.
        i. The number of salt bridges is maximized at a pH of 4.1.
  2. Hair shafts are dead; only the root is alive. The hair is lubricated by sebum.
     a. Dirt adheres to sebum.
     b. Washing hair removes the oil and dirt.
  3. Modern shampoos use a synthetic detergent as a cleansing agent.
     a. Shampoo for adults usually has an anionic surfactant, such as sodium dodecyl sulfate, as the principal active ingredient.
     b. Baby shampoos have an amphoteric surfactant with both a negatively-charged oxygen and a positively-charged nitrogen.
  4. Most components other than a detergent are in a shampoo only as the basis for advertising claims.
  5. Hair is protein with both acidic and basic groups.
     a. Most shampoos have a pH between 5 and 8, which does not damage hair or scalp.
     b. Protein shampoos condition hair by coating the hair shaft with protein (glue).
     c. Shampoos for dry or oily hair differ only in the relative amounts of detergent.
K. Hair coloring.
  1. The color of hair and skin is determined by the relative amounts of two pigments: melanin and phaeomelanin.
     a. Melanin is responsible for brown and black colors.
     b. Phaeomelanin is the pigment in red hair.
     c. Blondes have little of either pigment; brunettes can become blondes by oxidizing the pigments with hydrogen peroxide.
  2. Permanent hair dyes often are derivatives of p-phenylenediamine. These compounds penetrate the hair shaft and are oxidized to colored products (presumably quinones).
     a. P-phenylenediamine produces a black color.
     b. P-aminodiphenylamine sulfonic acid is used for blondes.
     c. Intermediate colors use other derivatives.
     d. Several of the hair-coloring diamines have been shown to be carcinogenic or mutagenic.
  3. Hair treatments that restore color gradually use lead acetate solutions.
     a. The lead ions penetrate the hair and react with sulfur to form black, insoluble lead sulfide.
L. Permanent waving: chemistry to curl your hair.
  1. Adjacent protein molecules in hair are cross-linked by disulfide groups. To put curl in hair:
     a. A reducing agent such as thioglycolic acid is used to rupture the disulfide linkages.
     b. The hair is set on curlers; the protein chains slide in relation to one another.
     c. Disulfide linkages are formed in new positions.
     d. The same chemical process can be used to straighten hair.
M. Hair sprays.
  1. Hair can be held in place by resins (often polyvinylpyrrolidone, PVP, or its copolymers).
     a. The resin can be dissolved in a solvent and applied as a spray.
  2. Holding resins can also be formulated as mousses (foams or froths).
N. Hair removers (depilatories).

1. These are strongly basic sulfur compounds such as sodium sulfide or calcium thioglycolate formulated into a lotion that destroys peptide bonds.
2. Hair removers can damage skin.
O. Hair restorers.
1. Minoxidil (Rogaine®) dilates blood vessels and produces growth of fine hair on skin containing hair follicles.
a. To be effective, it must be used continuously.
P. The well-informed consumer.
1. Most cosmetics are formulated from inexpensive ingredients.
2. You don't have to pay a lot for extra ingredients that contribute little to the performance of the product.

Answers to Self-Assessment Questions

1. a A manufacturer does not have to prove it safe and effective for its intended use to market a new cosmetic.
2. b Ultraviolet-B rays in sunlight cause the skin to darken by triggering the production of melanin.
3. c Lipsticks are usually made with a colored pigment, an oil, and a wax.
4. a The basic ingredients of any toothpaste are a detergent (or soap) and an abrasive.
5. a Sugar contributes to tooth decay by being converted by bacteria into acid that corrodes tooth enamel.
6. d The top note of a perfume is made up of the smallest molecules.
7. a Ethanol is the main ingredient in most aftershave lotions.
8. c Perfumes are responsible for many allergic reactions, so a cosmetic advertised as being hypoallergenic will likely not contain any perfume.
9. a When hair is wetted, hydrogen bonds are disrupted.
10. c A detergent is the essential ingredient in a shampoo.
11. b Disulfide linkages are broken by reducing agents applied during a home permanent, so the hair can be wound around a curler and the disulfide linkages reformed.

LEARNING OBJECTIVES

You should be able to...

1. Describe the structure of soap, and explain how it is made and how it works to remove greasy dirt. (21.1)

2. Explain the reasons for the advantages and disadvantages of soap. (21.1)

3. List the advantages and disadvantages of synthetic detergents. (21.2)

4. Classify surfactants as amphoteric, anionic, cationic, and nonionic, and describe how they are used in various detergent formulations. (21.2)

5. Identify a fabric softener from its structure, and describe its action. (21.3)

6. Name two types of laundry bleaches, and describe how they work. (21.3)

7. List the major ingredient(s) (and their purposes) of some all-purpose cleaning products and some special-purpose cleaning products. (21.4)

8. Identify compounds used in solvents and paints, and explain their purposes. (21.5)

9. Identify waxes by their structure. (21.5)

10. Identify the principal ingredients in various cosmetic products. (21.6)

11. Describe the chemical nature of skin, hair, and teeth. (21.6)

12. Use green chemistry principles to help select greener household products.

DISCUSSION

In this chapter we apply some of the principles learned earlier to a study of some of the chemicals used in and around the home. Our main focus is on chemicals used in cleaning, for these are among the most common—and often the most dangerous—of the household chemicals. Others are discussed elsewhere. Pesticides, fertilizers, and other "farm" chemicals (discussed in Chapter 20) are also used on lawns, on gardens, and on household plants.

In this chapter we also apply our knowledge of chemistry to the substances we put on our skin and hair to make us look or smell better. Some of the properties are desirable; often some are not. The properties are independent of our wishes. Often they fall far short of extravagant advertising claims. With this introduction to cosmetics you will be better equipped to judge for yourself the validity of some of the assertions of advertisers.

ANSWERS TO ODD-NUMBERED REVIEW QUESTIONS AND SOLUTIONS FOR ODD-NUMBERED END OF CHAPTER PROBLEMS

Review Questions

1. Soaps are excellent cleansers in soft water, relatively nontoxic, derived from renewable sources, and are biodegradable. Their biggest disadvantage is their solubility in hard or acidic water. Because soaps are the anions of weak acids, they lose their charge when exposed to acidic water and precipitate out of solution. Also, the cations associated with hard water, Ca^{2+} and Mg^{2+}, form insoluble compounds with soaps, causing them to precipitate from solution where they are ineffective as cleansers.

3. (1) CH_3COOH, acetic acid, is an ingredient in vinegar (answer a).
    (2) $Na_2Al_2Si_2O_8$, an aluminosilicate, is a zeolite (answer f).
    (3) $NaHCO_3$, sodium bicarbonate, is a mild abrasive cleaner (answer b).
    (4) $NaOCl$, sodium hypochlorite, is used as bleach (answer c).
    (5) $NaOH$ is used to make soap (answer d).
    (6) Na_3PO_4, trisodium phosphate, is a water softener (answer e).

5.   Diluted ammonia solutions loosen baked-on grease and burned-on food, and clean mirrors, windows, and other surfaces. Because ammonia vapors are highly irritating, these solutions should not be mixed with chlorine bleaches or used in a closed room.

7.   Baking soda is a mild abrasive and it absorbs odors.

Problems

9.   Potassium soaps are softer and produce a finer lather than sodium soaps.

11.   Most scouring soaps contain an abrasive such as silica or pumice.

13.   Sodium palmitate, the salt of palmitic acid, and glycerol are produced when tripalmitin reacts with lye (sodium hydroxide).

15.   The reaction products are: $3\ CH_3(CH_2)_{10}COO^- Na^+ + HOCH_2\text{-}CH(OH)\text{-}CH_2OH$ (glycerol)

17.   Trisodium phosphate softens water by precipitating calcium and magnesium ions as insoluble calcium phosphate and magnesium phosphate, and making the water more alkaline.

19.   a.   The reaction of phosphate ions with water to produce a basic solution is:
$$PO_4^{3-} + H_2O \rightarrow HPO_4^{2-} + OH^-.$$
       b.   The reaction of carbonate ions with water to produce a basic solution is:
$$CO_3^{2-} + H_2O \rightarrow HCO_3^- + OH^-.$$

21.   A detergent builder is any substance added to a substrate to increase its detergency.

23.   Zeolites exchange calcium and magnesium ions for sodium ions, which allow the detergents to be more effective.

25.   An amphoteric surfactant is a molecule that carries both a positive and a negative charge at different parts of its structure.

27.   Cationic surfactants have a positive charge on the active part of the molecule. While they are not particularly good detergents, they do have germicidal properties, which is the reason they are used in the food industry.

29.   With no branching, all three structures, I, II, and III, are biodegradable.

31.   Structure II, $CH_3(CH_2)_{11}OSO_3^- Na^+$ is an alkyl sulfate.

33.   A quaternary salt with two long carbon chains and two smaller groups in the nitrogen, such as hexadecyltrimethylammonium chloride, acts as a fabric softener.

35.   Cyanurate-type bleaches are available in solid form and release chlorine very slowly to minimize damage to fabrics.

37.   Organic solvents are used to remove paint, varnish, adhesives, and the like.

39.   The hazards of petroleum distillates include inhaling toxic fumes, which are narcotics at high concentrations, and their flammability..

41. Emollients are creams and lotions that protect the skin by coating and softening it.

43. OMC, octyl methoxycinnamate, is not soluble in water and will not wash off as easily as PABA does when an individual sweats or is swimming.

45. Lipsticks have a higher proportion of wax than do skin creams, which makes them firmer. They also contain pigments which skin creams do not contain.

47. Tooth decay is caused primarily by bacteria that convert sugars to plaque, a biofilm that is deposited on the teeth when they are not cleaned adequately. These bacteria convert sugars to acids such as lactic acid, and the acids dissolve tooth enamel.

49. Fluorides strengthen tooth enamel by converting hydroxyapatite to fluorapatite, which is harder and more resistant to decay.

51. A perfume is a complex mixture of compounds used to make the wearer smell pleasant. A cologne is a perfume that has been diluted with ethyl alcohol.

53. Menthol is added to aftershave lotions because it creates a cooling effect on the skin.

55. Temporary dyes are water soluble and can be washed out. Permanent dyes penetrate the hair and remain there until the hair is cut or falls out. Because permanent dyes affect only the dead outer portion of the hair shaft, new hair will grow out in the original shade.

57. A reducing agent is used to break the disulphide linkages in hair. An oxidation-reduction reaction occurs.

59. Oxidation occurs when colored pigments in hair are converted to colorless compounds.

61. Structure II, $CH_3(CH_2)_{10}COO^-$, is the anion of a fatty acid and is a soap.

63. Structure I, $CH_3(CH_2)_{15}N^+H_2CH_2COO^-$, is an amphoteric surfactant of the type used in baby shampoos.

65. The structure of isopropyl palmitate is $CH_3(CH_2)_{14}COOCH(CH_3)_2$.

67. The chemical equation for the reaction forming SnF_2 from SnO is:
$$SnO + 2HF \rightarrow SnF_2 + H_2O$$
mass of SnF_2 = (10.0 g SnO)(1 mol SnO/134.71 g SnO)(1 mol SnF_2/1 mol SnO)
(156.71 g SnF_2/mol SnF_2) = 11.6 g SnF_2

69. Quats refers to quaternary ammonium salts used as surfactants.

71. No, the energy from ultraviolet is transferred into blue light.

73. a. The acid is $CH_3(CH_2)_{24}COOH$.
     b. The alcohol is $CH_3(CH_2)_{28}CH_2OH$.

75. The answer is c. Water is neither volatile nor an organic compound. The other three substances are both organic compounds and volatile.

77.
a. NaOCl, sodium hypochlorite, is a bleaching agent (answer 3).

b. $CH_3(CH_2)_{14}COO^-Na^+$, sodium palmitate, is the salt of a fatty acid, which can be used as a soap (answer 1).

c. $Na_5P_3O_{10}$, sodium tripolyphosphate, is a detergent builder (answer 4).

d. $CH_3(CH_2)_{14}COOCH_2(CH_2)_{28}CH_3$ is the ester of a long-chain fatty acid and a long-chain alcohol, which is a wax (answer 2).

CHAPTER

22

Poisons

Toxicology: What Makes a Poison?

CHAPTER SUMMARY

22.1. Natural Poisons
  A. A toxin is a poison that is naturally produced by a plant or animal.
    1. Many insects and lots of microorganisms also produce poisons.
  B. Poisonous plants in the garden and home.
    1. Because many natural poisons are alkaloids that occur in plants, it is not surprising that poisons are found in gardens and on farms or ranches.

Answers to Self-Assessment Questions

1. d The study of poisons is called toxicology.
2. c A poison is best defined by dose.
3. a Many natural poisons are heterocyclic amines called alkaloids.
4. b The active ingredient in the poison given to Socrates was an alkaloid.

22.2 Poisons and How They Act
  A. Strong acids and bases as poisons.
    1. Both acids and bases can hydrolyze proteins, destroying their function.
    2. Acids break down lung tissue.
  B. Oxidizing agents as poisons.
    1. Ozone and other oxidizing agents deactivate enzymes by oxidizing sulfur-containing groups.
    2. The amino acid tryptophan undergoes a ring-opening oxidation with ozone.
    3. Oxidizing agents can break bonds in many other chemical substances in a cell.
  C. Metabolic poisons.
    1. Carbon monoxide bonds tightly to the iron atom in hemoglobin and hinders the transport of oxygen in the bloodstream or by interfering with oxidative processes in the cells.
    2. Nitrates are reduced to nitrites by bacteria in the digestive tract.
      a. Nitrites oxidize the iron in hemoglobin from Fe^{2+} to Fe^{3+}. The resulting methemoglobin cannot transport oxygen.
        i. In infants, this condition is called "blue baby syndrome."
      b. Cyanides, compounds that contain a $C\equiv N$ group, are among the most well-known poisons.

   i. Cyanide, as HCN or its salts, is lethal in amounts of 50 to 60 mg.

   ii. Cyanides act by blocking the oxidation of glucose inside cells; cyanide ions form a stable complex with iron(III) ions in oxidative enzymes called cytochrome oxidases.

   iii. Antidotes for cyanide poisoning can be in the form of providing 100% oxygen to support respiration, giving sodium nitrite intravenously to oxidize the iron atoms in enzymes back to the active 3+ form followed by treatment with sodium thiosulfate ($Na_2S_2O_3$) which transfers sulfur atoms to the cyanide ions, converting them to thiocyanate ions.

D. Make your own poison: fluoroacetic acid.

 1. Our cells use acetic acid to produce citric acid, which is then used as an energy source.

 2. When fluoroacetic acid is ingested, it is incorporated into fluorocitric acid.

  a. Fluorocitric acid blocks the energy-producing citric acid cycle by tying up the enzyme that acts on citric acid. Energy production ceases, and the cell dies.

 3. Sodium fluoroacetate (Compound 1080) was used both to poison rats and to poison predators such as coyotes.

  a. Its use is banned on federal land because of the devastating effect it had on the eagle population.

  b. Sodium fluoroacetate is found in the South African *gifblaar* plant and is used by the natives to poison arrow tips.

E. Heavy metal poisons.

 1. Metals with densities at least five times that of water are called heavy metals.

 2. Most metals and their compounds show some toxicity when ingested in large amounts.

  a. Even essential mineral nutrients can be toxic when taken in excessive amounts.

  b. In many cases, too little of a metal ion (a deficiency) can be as dangerous as too much (toxicity).

 3. Iron (as Fe^{2+} ions) is an essential nutrient.

  a. Too little iron leads to deficiency (anemia).

  b. Too much iron can be fatal, especially to a small child.

 4. Some heavy metals, including mercury, inactivate enzymes by reacting with sulfhydryl (SH) groups on enzymes.

  a. Mercury metal is a liquid at room temperature; its vapor is especially hazardous.

  b. Mercury is a cumulative poison with a half-life in the body of 70 days.

  c. British Anti-Lewisite (BAL) is an antidote for mercury poisoning.

   i. It acts by chelating (tying up) mercury ions, thus preventing them from attacking enzymes.

   ii. BAL antidote is effective only when used right away.

 5. Lead and its compounds are quite toxic.

  a. Metallic lead is generally converted to Pb^{2+} in the body.

  b. Lead, a soft, dense metal that is corrosion resistant, has many uses.

  c. We get lead in foods, drinking water, and the air.

  d. Large amounts of Pb^{2+} in a child's blood can cause mental retardation, behavior problems, anemia, hearing loss, developmental delays, and other physical and mental problems.

  e. Adults can excrete about 2 mg of lead per day.

  f. Lead poisoning in children causes mental retardation and neurological damage.

  g. Lead poisoning is treated with BAL and ethylenediaminetetraacetic acid (EDTA).

   i. The calcium salt of EDTA replaces the lead ions with calcium ions and the lead-EDTA complex is then excreted.

  h. Damage to the nervous system is largely irreversible.

 6. Cadmium is used in alloys, electronics, and rechargeable batteries.

a. In cadmium poisoning, cadmium ions substitute for calcium ions; this leads to a loss of calcium from bones, leaving them brittle and easily broken.
7. Cadmium poisoning from drinking water contamination in Japan led to a strange, painful malady known as itai-itai, the "ouch-ouch" disease.

Answers to Self-Assessment Questions

1. a Of the compounds listed, HCN is the only one that is not corrosive.
2. d Carbon monoxide and cyanides are metabolic poisons.
3. d Nitrites poison by oxidizing the Fe^{2+} of hemoglobin.
4. a Cyanides poison by blocking the actions of cytochrome oxidase.
5. d The most important toxic heavy metals are lead, mercury, and cadmium.
6. c The main source of mercury in the environment is the burning of coal.
7. a One reason for the dramatic decrease in lead found in the environment is the banning of leaded gasoline.
8. a Lead poisoning can be treated by EDTA, a chelating agent.
9. c Cadmium compounds cause painful "ouch-ouch" disease.

22.3 More Chemistry of the Nervous System
A. Acetylcholine (ACh) is a neurotransmitter; it carries messages across the synapse between cells.
   1. After carrying its message, acetylcholine is broken down by the enzyme cholinesterase to acetic acid and choline.
   2. Acetylase then converts acetic acid and choline back to acetylcholine, completing a cycle.
B. Nerve poisons and the acetylcholine cycle.
   1. Various chemical substances affect the acetylcholine cycle at different points.
      a. Botulin blocks the synthesis of acetylcholine.
         i. No messenger is formed: no message is sent.
      b. Curare, atropine, and some local anesthetics block the receptor sites.
         i. The message is sent but not received.
      c. Anticholinesterase poisons block the action of cholinesterase. This blocks the breakdown of acetylcholine; the nerves fire wildly and repeatedly, causing convulsions and death.
C. Organophosphorus compounds as insecticides and weapons of war.
   1. Organic phosphorus insecticides are well-known nerve poisons.
   2. Chemical warfare agents are Tabun (Agent GA), Sarin (Agent GB), and Soman (Agent GD); these are among the most toxic synthetic chemicals known (but not as toxic as botulin).
      a. Nerve gases kill when inhaled or absorbed through the skin.
      b. The antidote for nerve gas is an atropine injection.
   3. The insecticides malathion and parathion are closely related to the warfare agents but are far less toxic.
   4. Nerve poisons have helped us gain a better understanding of the nervous system.

Answers to Self-Assessment Questions

1. a Receptor sites for the neurotransmitter acetylcholine (ACh) are blocked by atropine.
2. a Botulin acts on the acetylcholine (ACh) cycle by blocking the synthesis of ACh.
3. c Most people are likely to encounter nerve poisons when handling insecticides.
4. a Because it is an insecticide and the other listed compounds are nerve agents, malathion is much less toxic than the other compounds.
5. d The most hazardous nerve poisons are organophosphorus compounds.

257

22.4   The Lethal Dose
        A. LD_{50}: a measure of toxicity.
            1. The LD_{50} is the dose that kills 50% of a population of test animals.
            2. The larger the LD_{50} value, the less toxic the substance.
        B. The botox enigma.
            1. Botulin is the most toxic substance known, with a median lethal dose of only 0.2 ng/kg of body weight.
            2. Botulin, in a commercial formulation called Botox®, is used medically to treat intractable muscle spasms and is widely used in cosmetic surgery to remove wrinkles.
                a. Botox is also used to treat afflictions such as uncontrollable blinking, crossed eyes, and Parkinson's disease.
                b. Botox curbs migraine headache pain in some people and is also used to treat excessive sweating.

Answers to Self-Assessment Questions

1.   a LD_{50} is the dose that kills half a tested population.
2.   c   Of the substances listed, ketamine is the most toxic because it has the smallest LD_{50} value.

22.5   The Liver As a Detox Facility
        A. The liver is able to detoxify some poisons by oxidation or reduction or by coupling them with amino acids or other normal body chemicals.
            1. The most common route of detoxification is oxidation.
                a. Ethanol is oxidized to acetaldehyde, then to acetic acid, and finally to carbon dioxide and water.
                b. Nicotine is oxidized to less toxic cotinine.
            2. The P-450 enzyme system in the liver can oxidize fat-soluble substances into water-soluble ones that can be excreted.
                a. They can also conjugate compounds with amino acids.
                    i. Toluene is oxidized to benzoic acid, which is conjugated with glycine to form hippuric acid, which is excreted.
            3. Oxidation, reduction, and conjugation don't always detoxify.
                a. Methanol is oxidized to more toxic formaldehyde.
                b. Liver enzymes, built up through years of heavy ethanol use, deactivate the male hormone testosterone, leading to alcoholic impotence.
                c. Benzene is oxidized to an epoxide that attacks key proteins.
                d. Carbon tetrachloride is converted to trichloromethyl free radical, which can trigger cancer.

Answers to Self-Assessment Questions

1.   a   It is not true that benzene is inert and thus nontoxic.
2.   a   Nicotine is oxidized to cotinine in the liver.

22.6   Carcinogens and Teratogens
        A. Carcinogens cause the growth of tumors (abnormal growth of new tissue).
            1. Benign tumors are characterized by slow growth; they do not invade new tissue.
            2. Malignant tumors (cancers) generally grow irreversibly and invade and destroy other tissues.
        B. What causes cancer?
            1. Most cancers are caused by lifestyle factors.

2. Nearly two-thirds of all cancer deaths in the United States are linked to tobacco, diet, or a lack of exercise with resulting obesity.
C. There are many natural carcinogens (for example, sunlight, radon, aflatoxins, and safrole).
D. How cancers develop.
1. Some carcinogens modify the DNA, scrambling the code for replication and protein synthesis.
2. Carcinogens, radiation, and some viruses activate oncogenes, which regulate cell growth and division. In addition, suppressor genes must be inactivated before a cancer can develop.
E. Chemical carcinogens.
1. Best known are polycyclic aromatic hydrocarbons (PAHs), such as 3,4-benzopyrene.
   a. Found in grilled meat, coffee, and cigarette smoke.
2. Aromatic amines (ß-naphthylamine, benzidine) make up another class of carcinogens and are often compounds used in the dye industry.
F. Anticarcinogens.
1. Antioxidant vitamins (vitamins C, E, and beta-carotene, a precursor to vitamin A) are believed to protect against some forms of cancer, and the food additive butylated hydroxytoluene (BHT) may protect against stomach cancer.
G. Three ways to test for carcinogens.
1. The Ames test is used to test chemicals to see if they cause mutations in bacteria. Mutagens are often carcinogens.
2. Animal tests employ large doses of the suspected substance on small numbers of laboratory animals such as rats.
   a. Such tests have limited relevance; humans are exposed to lower doses for longer periods, and human metabolism can differ from that of the experimental animals.
   b. However, good correlation exists between known human carcinogens and cancer in laboratory animals.
3. Epidemiological studies correlate the incidence of various cancers in human populations with various occupations, dietary practices, and exposures to chemicals.
H. Birth defects: teratogens.
1. A teratogen is a substance that causes birth defects.
   a. The most notorious is the tranquilizer thalidomide.
   b. The drug was used in Germany and Great Britain but Frances Kelsey of the FDA saw evidence to doubt the drug's safety and it was never introduced in the U.S.
2. Other chemicals that act as teratogens include isotretinoin (Accutane®), a prescription medication approved for treating severe acne.
3. By far the most hazardous teratogen, in terms of the number of babies born with birth defects, is ethyl alcohol, which causes fetal alcohol syndrome.

Answers to Self-Assessment Questions

1. b One type of gene when switched on that is involved in cancer development is oncogene.
2. d Suppressor genes are involved in preventing cancer and when they are switched off, cancers can develop.
3. c Benzidine is not a naturally occurring carcinogen.
4. b A source of polycyclic aromatic hydrocarbons (PAHs) is automobile exhausts.
5. d Vinyl chloride is a prominent aliphatic carcinogen.
6. c Butylated hydroxytoluene is an anticarcinogen.
7. a The fastest way to determine whether a substance is likely to be a carcinogen is by performing an Ames test.
8. d The Ames test is a test for mutagenicity used as a screen for potential carcinogens.
9. a A teratogen is a substance that causes birth defects.

10. a Ethanol is the teratogen that causes damage to the greatest number of fetuses.

22.7 Hazardous Wastes
   A. Hazardous wastes are those that can cause or contribute to death or illness or that threaten human health or the environment when improperly managed.
      1. There are four types of hazardous wastes:
         a. Reactive wastes react spontaneously or vigorously with air or water.
            i. They explode when exposed to shock or heat.
            ii. Examples of reactive wastes are sodium metal, TNT, and nitroglycerin.
         b. Flammable wastes are those that burn readily upon ignition, presenting a fire hazard.
            i. Hexane is an example of a flammable waste.
         c. Toxic wastes contain or release toxic substances in quantities that pose a hazard to human health or the environment.
            i. Examples of toxic wastes include polychlorinated biphenyls (PCBs).
         d. Corrosive wastes corrode their containers.
            i. Examples of corrosive wastes include strong acids and bases.
   B. What price poisons?
      1. We have to decide whether the benefits we gain from hazardous substances are worth the risks we assume by using them.

Fishing for a Greener World
   A. The burden for proof for chemical safety seldom lies with the chemical manufacturer.
      1. More commonly, it is the responsibility of the federal government, which requires expertly generated experimental data from tests on animals that respond much like human beings.

Answers to Self-Assessment Questions

1. c Reactive wastes tend to react vigorously with water.
2. a Common strong acids and bases are corrosive wastes.
3. d Discarded unused pesticides are toxic wastes.
4. c Sodium metal is a reactive waste.
5. d The best way to handle hazardous wastes is to minimize or eliminate their use.

LEARNING OBJECTIVES

You should be able to...

1. Name some natural poisons and their sources. (22.1)

2. Distinguish among corrosive poisons, metabolic poisons, and heavy metal poisons, and explain how each type acts. (22.2)

3. Identify antidotes for some common metabolic poisons and heavy metal poisons. (22.2)

4. Define *neurotransmitter*, and describe how various substances interfere with the action of neurotransmitters. (22.3)

5. Explain the concept of an LD_{50} value, and list some of its limitations as a measure of toxicity. (22.4)

6. Calculate lethal doses from LD_{50} values and body weights.   (22.4)

7. Describe how the liver is able to detoxify some substances.   (22.5)

8. Describe how cancers develop.   (22.6)

9. List some chemical carcinogens and anticarcinogens.   (22.6)

10. Name and describe three ways to test for carcinogens.   (22.6)

11. Define *hazardous waste*, and list and give an example of the four types of such wastes.   (22.7)

12. Identify new approaches for testing the toxicity of synthetic chemicals.

13. Discuss the importance of toxicity screening in the manufacture of safe chemicals.

DISCUSSION

"All things are poison." That isn't far from the truth, but some things are much more toxic than others. Also, some present an immediate hazard (acute poisons), whereas others exhibit their harmful effect only over a much longer period of time (chronic poisons). The public often gets contradictory, misleading and misinformation about toxic chemicals. A few chemical principles will help you to gain a better understanding of what toxic substances are, how they act, and what can be done about toxic wastes.

ANSWERS TO ODD-NUMBERED REVIEW QUESTIONS AND SOLUTIONS FOR ODD-NUMBERED END OF CHAPTER PROBLEMS

Review Questions

1. Taken in small amounts, table sugar (sucrose) is not poisonous. Larger amounts can cause problems for diabetics, and taken in abnormally large amounts, the same substance can be poisonous for anyone.

3. Examples of the toxicity depending upon the route of administration are the toxicity of water when it is inhaled, and the fact that nicotine is 50 times more toxic when taken intravenously than when taken orally. The route of administration affects the speed of the poison's action and the rate at which it can be detoxified.

5. Some sources of mercury are broken thermometers, dental fillings, fish consumption, and agricultural uses. Some sources of lead are the lead that leaches from lead pipes and lead solders, the lead in paint, and the lead in the glazes on some food containers.

7. Sunlight, radon, and safrole in sassafras are examples of natural carcinogens. In addition, plants produce compounds to protect themselves from fungi, insects, and higher animals, some of which are carcinogenic. For example, natural carcinogens are found in mushrooms, basil, celery, figs, mustard, pepper, fennel, parsnips, and citrus oils.

Problems

9.   Nitric acid (b) and potassium hydroxide (d) are corrosive poisons.

11.   The hydrolysis of amides is the reaction involved when an acid breaks down protein molecules. The acid catalyzes the disruption of the peptide linkages.

13.   Metabolic poisons prevent cellular oxidation of metabolites by blocking the transport of oxygen in the bloodstream or by interfering with the oxidative processes in the cells. Carbon monoxide and nitrates are examples of metabolic poisons.

15.   Cyanides act by blocking the oxidation of glucose inside cells; cyanide ions form a stable complex with iron(II) ions in oxidative enzymes called cytochrome oxidases.

17.   Lead (a) is a heavy metal.

19.   Mercury ions (Hg^{2+}) deactivate enzymes by reacting with the sulfhydryl groups attached to the amino acids that are component parts of the enzyme.

21.   EDTA ties up, or forms chelates with, lead ions into complexes which can be excreted.

23.   Three nerve gases that were developed for use in warfare are tabun, sarin, and soman.

25.   Anticholinesterase poisons are nerve poisons. They inhibit the enzyme cholinesterase.

27.   The liver detoxifies ethanol through a series of oxidations, first to acetaldehyde (ethanal), which is then oxidized to acetic acid (ethanoic acid), and, finally, to carbon dioxide and water.

29.   No, P-450 enzymes do not always detoxify foreign substances. The enzymes just catalyze oxidation. Some substances become more toxic.

31.   Cotinine is less toxic than nicotine, and the added oxygen atom makes it more water soluble, and thus, more readily excreted in the urine, than nicotine.

33.   Lethal dose = (125 lb)(0.454 kg/lb)(140 mg/kg) = 7950 mg or 7.95 g of methyl isocyanate

35.   Oncogenes are genes that trigger or sustain the processes that convert normal cells to cancerous cells.

37.   Polycyclic hydrocarbons are formed during the incomplete burning of nearly any organic material. For example, they have been found in charcoal-grilled meats, cigarette smoke, and automobile exhausts.

39.   Animal tests involving low dosages and millions of rats would cost too much, so tests are usually done by using large doses and a few dozen rats, with an equal number of rats serving as controls. The tests are not conclusive because humans are not usually exposed to comparable doses and there may be a threshold below which a compound is not carcinogenic. Further, human metabolism is somewhat different from that of the test animals, so a carcinogen might be active in rats but not in humans (or vice versa). There is only a 70% correlation between the carcinogenesis of a chemical in rats and that in mice, and the correlation between carcinogenesis in either rodent and that in humans is probably less.

41. A mutagen is a substance that alters one or more genes in some way. Teratogens are compounds that cause birth defects.

43. A flammable waste is one that burns readily on ignition. Hexane and other organic solvents are examples of flammable wastes.

45. number of molecules in lethal dose = (66 kg)(200 pg botulin/kg)(1 x 10^{-12} g/pg)
(1 mol botulin/1.50 x 10^5 g)(6.02 x 10^{23} molecules botulin/mol botulin)
= 5.3 x 10^{10} molecules

47. a. The molecular formula of thujone is $C_{10}H_{16}O$.
b. Lethal dose = (55 kg)(87.5 mg thujone/kg) = 4800 mg or 4.8 g.
c. Mass of thujone = (10 mg/L)(0.50 L) = 5 mg.

49. a. % smokers in study = (1350 smokers/1357 studied)(100%) = 99.48%
% smokers in control group = (1296 smokers/1357 studied)(100%) = 95.50%
The control group contained a few percent fewer smokers. The proportion of smokers in both groups was roughly equivalent.
b. The odds of smoking for cancer sufferers were 0.9948:1. The odds of smoking for the control group were 0.9550:1.
c. The odds ratio is 0.9550/0.9948 = 0.96:1 which indicates that the control group was a good representation of the cancer sufferer group.

51. The data in Table 22.1 indicate that one would have to ingest relatively large masses of some compounds (for example sucrose) before the dose reached the LD_{50} level, but only extremely small amounts of other substances (ricin and botulin toxin, for example) to surpass the LD_{50} level.

53. lethal dose = (55 kg female)(200 μg/kg)(1 mg/1 x 10^3 μg) = 11 mg
a. A 1.5-mg dose is less than 11 mg, so it is not lethal.
b. A 20-mg dose is greater than 11 mg, so it is lethal.

55. Benzene is generally inert in the body. If it is ingested, it does not react until it reaches the liver where it is slowly oxidized to an epoxide. The epoxide is a highly reactive molecule that can attack certain key proteins, sometimes resulting in leukemia, a form of cancer.

57. a. Volume, mL = (395 g rat)(1 kg/1000 g)(10.3 g ethanol/kg rat)(1 mL vodka/0.92 g vodka)
(100 mL vodka/50 mL ethanol) = 8.8 mL vodka
b. Mass of water in rat = (395 g rat)(0.67 g water/1.0 g rat) = 265 g water in rat
The density of water is 1.0 g/mL so 265 g H_2O = 265 mL H_2O.
Blood alcohol level, mg/mL = (8.8 mL vodka)(0.46 g alcohol/1.0 mL vodka)
(1000 mg/g)(1/265 mL water in rat) = 15.3 mg/mL

59. The answer is b.

61. Saving millions of dollars, improved consumer safety, and reducing the load of poisons in the environment.